W9-BXQ-189

ETHICS AND LAW FOR SCHOOL PSYCHOLOGISTS

ETHICS AND LAW FOR SCHOOL PSYCHOLOGISTS

Third Edition

Susan Jacob-Timm

Timothy S. Hartshorne

John Wiley & Sons, Inc.

New York • Chichester • Weinheim • Brisbane • Singapore • Toronto

This book is printed on acid-free paper. ∞

Published simultaneously in Canada.

Library of Congress Cataloging-in-Publication Data:

Jacob-Timm, Susan, 1949–
Ethics and law for school psychologists / by Susan Jacob-Timm, Timothy S. Hartshorne, — 3rd ed.
p. cm.
Includes bibliographical references (p. 308) and index.
ISBN 0-471-19261-9 (cloth : alk. paper)
1. School psychologists—Professional ethics—United States.
2. School psychologists—Legal status, laws, etc.—United States.
I. Hartshorne, Timothy S. II. Title.
LB3013.6.J33 1998
174′.93717′130683—dc21 97-37891

Printed in the United States of America.

10 9 8 7 6 5 4

This book is dedicated to the memory of
Michael David Salem Hartshorne (1984–1992) and
Katherine Swift Hartshorne (1991–1992).
The brevity of their lives reminds us
just how precious are all children.

Preface

There are a number of excellent texts, journal articles, and book chapters on ethics in psychology, legal issues in school psychology, and special education law. However, our experience as school psychology trainers suggested a need for a single sourcebook on ethics and law specifically written to meet the unique needs of the psychologist in the school setting. Consequently, *Ethics and Law for School Psychologists* was written to provide up-to-date information on ethics, professional standards, and law pertinent to the delivery of school psychological services. Our goals for this third edition of the book remain unchanged. We hope that the book will continue to be useful as a basic textbook or supplementary text for school psychology students in training and as a resource for practitioners.

As noted in the preface to the first edition, one goal in writing the book was to bring together various ethical and legal guidelines pertinent to the delivery of school psychological services. We also introduce an ethical-legal decision-making model. We concur with the suggestion that the educated practitioner is the best safeguard against ethical-legal problems (Diener & Crandall, 1978; Keith-Spiegel & Koocher, 1985). School psychologists with a broad knowledge base of ethics and law are likely to anticipate and prevent problems. Use of a decision-making model allows the practitioner to make informed, well-reasoned choices in resolving problems when they do occur (Eberlein, 1987; Tymchuk, 1986).

WHAT'S IN THE BOOK

Chapter 1 provides an introduction to ethical codes and professional standards, an ethical-legal decision-making model, and the four broad ethical principles of respect for the dignity of persons (welfare of the client), responsible caring (professional competence and responsibility), integrity in professional relationships, and responsibility to community and society. Chapter 2 provides an introduction to education law that protects the rights of students and their parents in the school setting. Chapter 2 also addresses certification and licensure of school psychologists, mechanisms that help to ensure psychologists meet specified qualifications before they are granted a legal sanction to practice. In Chapter 3, we discuss privacy, informed consent, confidentiality, and record keeping—ethical-legal concerns that cut across all of the school psychologist's many roles. Chapters 4 through 9 focus on ethical-legal issues associated with specific roles: psychoeducational assessment (Chapter 4), delivery of services to pupils with disabilities (Chapters 5 and 6), counseling and therapeutic interventions (Chapter 7), consultation (Chapter 8), and research (Chapter 9). Special consultation topics are discussed in Chapter 10, including ethical-legal issues associated with current special education reforms (inclusionary models of special education service delivery, the delivery of services without labels, problem-solving assistance teams), school testing programs, school entry and grade retention decisions, discipline (corporal punishment, expulsion, and suspension), and schooling for pupils with other special needs (limited English proficiency, gifted and talented students, and students with communicable diseases). In Chapter 11, we describe ethics committees, and ethical and legal sanctions for professional misconduct.

WHAT'S NOT IN THE BOOK

We have chosen to focus on ethical-legal issues of interest to current and future school practitioners. Consistent with this focus, we did not include a discussion of issues associated with private practice. Interested readers are encouraged to consult Bersoff (1995) and Rosenberg (1995). The text does not address ethical-legal issues associated with the supervision of school psychology students and interns. Readers are referred to Conoley and Bahns (1995); Harrar, VandeCreek, and Knapp (1990); and Sherry (1991) for information on this topic. We also did not address the legal rights of psychologists as employees in the public schools.

THIRD EDITION REVISIONS

There have been a number of changes in ethical guidelines and law pertinent to the practice of school psychology since we completed work on the second edition of the text early in the spring of 1994. The National Association of School Psychologists revised its "Principles for Professional Ethics" and "Standards for the Delivery of School Psychological Services" in 1997. President Clinton signed into law *Goals 2000: Educate America Act* (Pub. L. No. 103-227), the *Improving America's Schools Act* (Pub. L. No. 103-382), and the *School-to-Work Opportunity Act* (Pub. L. No. 103-239) in 1994. *Goals 2000* has provided a framework for national education reform. All three laws have impacted school policies and practices. On June 4, 1997, the *Individuals with Disabilities Education Act Amendments* (Pub. L. No. 105-17) became law. The discussion of special education law in this edition incorporates the 1997 amendments to *IDEA* as well as recent developments in case law.

Other changes to the book include the addition of study questions at the end of each chapter to focus on key concepts. We also included discussion topics and/or vignettes to stimulate interesting classroom debate.

We welcome your suggestions for improving future editions of *Ethics and Law for School Psychologists.* Please contact: Susan Jacob-Timm, Professor of Psychology, 206 Sloan Hall, Central Michigan University, Mt. Pleasant, MI 48859. E-mail: Susan.Jacob_Timm@cmich.edu.

TWO DISCLAIMERS

This text provides an overview and summary of constitutional, statutory, and case law pertinent to the practice of psychology in the schools. It does not provide a comprehensive or detailed legal analysis of litigation in education or psychology. The material included in the book, particularly the portions on law, is based on our review of the available literature. We are not attorneys. We often consulted the writings of attorneys and legal scholars for guidance in the interpretation of law rather than attempting to interpret it ourselves. However, original sources also were consulted when feasible, and citations have been provided so that interested readers can do the same.

Nothing in this text should be construed as legal advice. School psychology practitioners are encouraged to consult their school attorney through appropriate administrative channels when legal questions arise. Our interpretations of ethical codes and standards should not be viewed as reflecting the official opinion of any specific professional association.

THE CAST OF CHARACTERS

Throughout the text we have included a number of case incidents to illustrate specific principles. Some of the incidents are from case law; others are fictitious. To make it easier for the reader to follow who's who in the vignettes, we have used the same five school psychologists throughout the book. Our cast of characters includes (in order of appearance):

SAM FOSTER: Worked as a school psychologist for several years and then returned to school to pursue his Psy.D. degree. He is currently a doctoral intern in a suburban school district.

CARRIE JOHNSON: Provides school psychological services in a rural area. She faces the special challenges of coping with professional isolation and works in a community where resources are limited.

HANNAH COOK: Serves as a member of a school psychological services team in a medium-sized city. She is particularly interested in school-based consultative services.

CHARLIE MAXWELL: As a school psychologist for a middle and senior high school in a large metropolitan district, he is a strong advocate of school efforts to prevent mental health problems.

WANDA ROSE: Provides services at the preschool and elementary level in a small town. Children, babies, parents, and teachers love Wanda Rose. She has been a school psychology practitioner for many years. Wanda needs an occasional push from her colleagues to keep current with changing practices, however.

SUSAN JACOB-TIMM
TIMOTHY S. HARTSHORNE

Central Michigan University
Mt. Pleasant, Michigan

Acknowledgments

We would like to acknowledge the research assistance provided by the following Central Michigan University students: Jim Corr, Shawn Kent, and Trisha Powell. Karen Bellingar provided secretarial assistance in preparing the manuscript.

We also wish to thank Kelly A. Franklin, executive editor and associate publisher at Wiley, for her assistance and support, and Nancy M. Land, copyeditor, for her patient and careful work.

A special thank you also is due to family members for their support during the completion of this and previous editions of the book: Andy Neal; Abby, Laura, and Larry Timm; Nancy, Seth, Jacob, Joshua, and Nathan Hartshorne.

Contents

Chapter 1

ETHICS IN SCHOOL PSYCHOLOGY: AN INTRODUCTION

In the late 1970s, the American Association for the Advancement of Science (AAAS) conducted a study of the ethical concerns of its affiliated societies (Chalk, Frankel, & Chafer, 1980). Haas, Malouf, and Mayerson (1986) summarized the AAAS findings as follows:

> Recent years have been marked by a rise in professional consciousness about ethical and legal responsibilities and by a concurrent rise in public consciousness about legal rights. The result, in part, is a level of concern (and confusion) about proper professional behavior that is unprecedented in all professions and is particularly evident in psychology. (p. 316)

Because the decisions made by school psychologists have an impact on human lives, and thereby on society, the practice of school psychology rests on the public's trust. School psychologists—both practitioners and trainers—have shared in the rising concerns about proper professional conduct.

QUALITY CONTROL IN SCHOOL PSYCHOLOGY

There are a number of sources of "quality control" in the provision of school psychological services. Ethical codes and professional standards for the delivery of psychological services are discussed in this chapter. Chapter 2 provides an introduction to law that protects the rights of students and their parents in the school setting. Education law provides a second source of quality assurance. Chapter 2 also addresses the credentialing of school psychologists, a third mechanism of quality control. Credentialing helps to ensure psychologists meet specified qualifications before they are granted a legal sanction to practice (Fagan & Wise, 1994). Training program accreditation is an additional mechanism of quality control. Program accreditation helps to ensure adequate preparation of school psychologists during their graduate coursework and field experiences. (For a discussion of training program accreditation, see Fagan & Wise, 1994.)

The present chapter focuses on the what and why of professional ethics, ethics training and competencies, and the ethical codes and professional standards of the National Association of School Psychologists (NASP) and the American Psychological Association (APA). Four broad ethical principles are introduced, along with an ethical-legal decision-making model.

WHAT AND WHY OF PROFESSIONAL ETHICS

The term *ethics* generally refers to a system of principles of conduct that guide the behavior of an individual. Ethics derives from the Greek word *ethos,* meaning character or custom, and the phrase *ta ethika,* which Plato and Aristotle used to describe their studies of Greek values and ideals (Solomon, 1984). Accordingly, ethics is first

> of all a concern for individual character, including what we blandly call "being a good person," but it is also a concern for the overall character of an entire society, which is still appropriately called its "ethos." Ethics is participation in, and an understanding of, an ethos, the effort to understand the social rules which govern and limit our behavior. . . . (p. 5)

A system of ethics develops within the context of a particular society or culture and is closely connected to social customs. Ethics is composed of a range of acceptable (or unacceptable) social and personal behaviors, from rules of etiquette to more basic rules of society.

The terms *ethics* and *morality* are often used interchangeably. However, according to philosophers, the term *morality* refers to a subset of ethical rules of special importance. Solomon suggests moral principles are "the most basic and inviolable rules of a society." Moral rules are thought to differ from other aspects of ethics in that they are more important, fundamental, universal, rational, and objective (pp. 6–7). W. D. Ross (1930), a 20th-century English philosopher, identified a number of moral duties of the ethical person: nonmaleficence, fidelity, beneficence, justice, and autonomy. These moral principles have provided a foundation for the ethical codes of psychologists and other professionals (Bersoff & Koeppl, 1993).

Our focus here is on *applied professional ethics.* Applied professional ethics is the application of broad ethical principles and specific rules to the problems that arise in professional practice (Beauchamp & Childress, 1983). Applied ethics in school psychology is thus a combination of ethical principles and rules, ranging from more basic rules to rules of professional etiquette, that guide the conduct of the practitioner in his or her professional interactions with others.

Professionalism and Ethics

Professionalization has been described as "the process by which an occupation, usually on the basis of a claim to special competence and a concern for the quality of its work and benefits to society, obtains the exclusive right to perform a particular kind of work, to control training criteria and access to the profession, and to determine and evaluate the way the work is to be performed" (Chalk et al., 1980, p. 3). Professional associations or societies function to promote the profession by publicizing the services offered, safeguarding the rights of professionals, attaining benefits for its members, facilitating the exchange of and development of knowledge, and promoting standards to enhance the quality of professional work by its members (Chalk et al., 1980).

Codes of ethics appear to develop out of the self-interests of the profession and a genuine commitment to protect the interests of persons served. Most professional associations have recognized the need to balance self-interests against concern for the welfare of the consumer. Ethical codes are one mechanism to help ensure that members of a profession will deal justly with the public (Bersoff & Koeppl, 1993; Keith-Spiegel & Koocher, 1985).

However, the development of a code of ethics also serves to foster the profession's self-interests. A code of ethics is an indicator of the profession's willingness to accept responsibility for defining appropriate conduct, and a commitment to self-regulation of members by the profession (Chalk et al., 1980). The adoption of a code of ethics has often been viewed as the hallmark of a profession's maturity. Ethical codes may thus serve to enhance the prestige of a profession and reduce the perceived need for external regulation and control.

The field of psychology has shown a long-standing commitment to activities that support and encourage appropriate professional conduct. As will be seen in this chapter, both the National Association of School Psychologists and the American Psychological Association have developed and adopted codes of ethics. These codes are based on the consensus of association members about what constitutes appropriate professional conduct. They serve to protect the public by sensitizing professionals to the ethical aspects of service delivery, educating practitioners about the parameters of appropriate conduct, and helping professionals to monitor their own behavior. They also provide guidelines for adjudicating complaints (Keith-Spiegel & Koocher,

1985). By encouraging appropriate professional conduct, associations such as NASP and APA strive to ensure that each person served will receive the highest quality of professional service, and therefore build and maintain public trust in psychologists and psychology.

Ethical Codes v. Ethical Conduct

Codes of ethics serve to protect the public. However, ethical conduct is not synonymous with simple conformity to a set of rules outlined in professional codes and standards (Hughes, 1986). As Kitchener (1986) and others (Bersoff, 1994; Hughes, 1986; Keith-Spiegel & Koocher, 1985) have noted, codes of ethics are imperfect guides to behavior for several reasons. First, ethical codes in psychology are composed of broad, abstract principles along with a number of more specific statements about appropriate professional conduct. They are at times vague and ambiguous (Bersoff, 1994; Hughes, 1986).

Second, there are often competing ethical principles that apply in a particular situation (Bersoff & Koeppl, 1993; Haas & Malouf, 1989), and specific ethical guidelines may conflict with federal or state law (Keith-Spiegel & Koocher, 1985; Kitchener, 1986). In some situations, a primary or overriding consideration can be identified in choosing a course of action (Haas & Malouf, 1989).

In other situations, however, no one principle involved clearly outweighs the other (Haas & Malouf, 1989). For example, the decision to allow a minor child the freedom to choose (or refuse) to participate in psychological services often involves a consideration of law, ethical principles (client autonomy and self-determination versus welfare of the client), and the likely practical consequences of affording choices (e.g., enhanced treatment outcomes versus refusal of treatment).

A third reason ethical codes are imperfect is because they tend to be reactive. They frequently fail to address new and emerging ethical issues (Bersoff & Koeppl, 1993; Eberlein, 1987). Committees within professional associations are often formed to study the ways in which existing codes relate to emerging issues, and codes may be revised in response to new ethical concerns. Concern about the ethics of behavior modification techniques was a focus of the 1970s; in the 1980s, psychologists scrutinized the ethics of computerized psychodiagnostic assessment. Recent changes in the ethical codes of psychologists reflect concerns about sexual harassment and fair treatment of individuals, regardless of their sexual orientation.

Ethical codes thus provide guidance for the professional in his or her decision making. Ethical conduct, however, involves careful choices based on knowledge of codes and standards, ethical reasoning, and personal values. In many situations, more than one course of action is acceptable. In some situations, no course of action is completely satisfactory. In all situations, the responsibility for ethical conduct rests with the individual practitioner (Eberlein, 1987; Haas et al., 1986; Keith-Spiegel & Koocher, 1985).

ETHICS TRAINING AND COMPETENCIES

Prior to the late 1970s, many applied psychology graduate programs (clinical, school) required little formal coursework in professional ethics. Ethics was often taught in the context of supervised practica and internship experiences, a practice Handelsman labeled "ethics training by 'osmosis'" (1986a, p. 371). Handelsman (1986a, 1986b) and others have argued persuasively that there are a number of problems with this unsystematic approach to ethics training. Student learning is limited by the supervisor's awareness and knowledge of ethical issues (Dalton, 1984) and the range of issues that arise by chance in the course of supervision (Handelsman, 1986b). Results of a survey of practicing psychotherapists found that respondents gave only moderate ratings to their internship experience as a source of ethics education (Haas et al., 1986).

It is now generally recognized that ethical thinking and problem solving are skills that need to be explicitly taught as a part of graduate coursework (Haas et al., 1986; Handelsman, 1986a, 1986b; Tymchuk, 1985; Tymchuk et al., 1982). Both the National Association of School Psychologists and the American Psychological Association currently require formal coursework in ethics as a component of graduate training.

In the 1980s, psychology trainers began to ask, "What should be the goals of ethics education in psychology?" (Haas et al., 1986; Kitchener, 1986), "What are the desired cognitive, affective, and behavioral 'ethics competencies' for school psychologists?", and "How should ethics be taught?"

A number of goals for ethics training have been suggested in the literature. An emerging picture of desired competencies includes:

1. Competent practitioners are sensitive to "the ethical components of their work" and are aware that their actions "have real ethical consequences that can potentially harm as well as help others" (Kitchener, 1986, p. 307; also Rest, 1984; Welfel & Kitchener, 1992).
2. Competent psychologists have a sound working knowledge of the content of ethical codes, professional standards, and law pertinent to the delivery of services (Fine & Ulrich, 1988; Welfel & Lipsitz, 1984).

3. Competent practitioners are committed to a proactive rather than a reactive stance in ethical thinking and conduct (Tymchuk, 1986). They use their broad knowledge of ethical codes, professional standards, and law along with ethical reasoning skills to anticipate and prevent problems from arising.
4. Skilled practitioners are able to analyze the ethical dimensions of a situation and demonstrate a well-developed "ability to reason about ethical issues" (Kitchener, 1986, p. 307). They have mastered and make use of a problem-solving model (Tymchuk, 1981, 1986).
5. Competent practitioners are aware of their personal feelings and values and the role of their feelings and values in ethical decision making (Corey, Corey, & Callanan, 1993; Kitchener, 1986).
6. Competent practitioners appreciate the complexity of ethical decisions and are tolerant of ambiguity and uncertainty. They acknowledge and accept that there may be more than one appropriate course of action (Kitchener, 1986).
7. Competent practitioners have the personal strength to act on decisions made and accept responsibility for their actions (Kitchener, 1986).

How should ethics be taught? There is a growing consensus that ethics education needs to be taught as part of a planned, multilevel approach that includes formal coursework along with supervised discussion of ethical issues in practica and internship settings (Fine & Ulrich, 1988; Meara, Schmidt, & Day, 1996). Formal coursework provides opportunities to introduce the student to broad ethical principles, professional codes, and a decision-making model in a systematic manner (Eberlein, 1987; Fine & Ulrich, 1988; Handelsman, 1986b; Tymchuk, 1986).

Methods of ethics training include instruction in ethical problem solving, analysis of case incidents, and role playing difficult situations (Bersoff, 1995; Gawthrop & Uhlemann, 1992; Kitchener, 1986; Plante, 1995). These methods provide a means to enhance sensitivity to ethical issues and encourage development of ethical reasoning skills.

Only a few empirical investigations of the effectiveness of formal ethics training have appeared in the literature (Welfel, 1992). Baldick (1980) found that psychology interns who received formal ethics training were better able to identify ethical issues than interns without prior coursework in ethics. Gawthrop and Uhlemann (1992) found that students who received specific instruction in ethical problem solving demonstrated higher quality decision making in response to a case vignette than students who did not receive the training. Several studies, however, have reported a gap between knowledge of the appropriate course of action and willingness to carry out that action (Bernard & Jara, 1986; Smith, McGuire, Abbott, & Blau, 1991). Even when practitioners can identify what ought to be done, many would choose to do less than they believe they should (Bernard & Jara, 1986). Thus, at this time, additional research is needed to identify the types of ethics training that are most effective in developing ethical sensitivity and reasoning and in encouraging appropriate professional conduct (Nagle, 1987; Tymchuk, 1985; Welfel, 1992).

ETHICAL CODES AND PROFESSIONAL STANDARDS

APA and NASP Codes of Ethics

Brown (1979) suggests that school psychology emerged as an identifiable profession in the 1950s. Two professional associations, namely the American Psychological Association and the National Association of School Psychologists, have shaped the development of the profession. Exhibit 1–1 provides a brief overview of these two organizations. Each organization has

Exhibit 1–1. A Brief Look at the American Psychological Association (APA) and the National Association of School Psychologists (NASP)

The American Psychological Association

The American Psychological Association was established in 1892 (Engin, 1983). When APA reorganized in 1944, the reorganization included Division 16, The Division of School Psychology (Tindall, 1979). APA leadership has stressed the view that school psychology is psychology practiced in the school setting (Brown, 1979; Tindall, 1979), and that only those highly trained in psychology (i.e., those who hold doctoral degrees) are competent to function without supervision as psychologists in the schools. Although a doctorate is not required for full membership in Division 16, its membership is largely composed of those who hold doctorates.

The National Association of School Psychologists

APA was seen by many as representing the scientific and academic interests of school psychology, rather than the practitioner. The National Association of School Psychologists was formed in 1969 to better represent the school psychology practitioner (Brown, 1979; Engin, 1983). NASP has traditionally viewed school psychology as a blend of education and psychology—and as a unique discipline distinct from clinical psychology. NASP has set the specialist level (or sixth year) with three years of successful supervised experience as the appropriate entry level for unsupervised practice.

developed its own ethical code, professional standards for the delivery of services, and standards for training programs.

In joining APA or NASP, members agree to abide by the association's ethical principles and professional standards. Additionally, psychologists who are members of the National School Psychologist Certification System and those who are members of state associations affiliated with NASP are bound to abide by NASP's code of ethics. School psychology practitioners should be thoroughly familiar with NASP's "Principles for Professional Ethics" and "Standards for the Provision of School Psychological Services" (NASP, 1997), APA's "Ethical Principles of Psychologists and Code of Conduct" (APA, 1992), and the *Standards for Educational and Psychological Testing* (American Educational Research Association, American Psychological Association, and National Council on Measurement in Education, 1985) whether or not they are members of a professional association.

Throughout this text, we focus primarily on the ethical codes and standards of APA and NASP. Occasionally other codes were consulted and found helpful, including "A Canadian Code of Ethics for Psychologists" (Canadian Psychological Association or CPA, 1991).

NASP's "Principles for Professional Ethics"

"Principles for Professional Ethics" (NASP-PPE) was first adopted by the National Association of School Psychologists in 1974 and revised in 1984, 1992, and 1997 (NASP, 1984, 1992, 1997). (See Appendix A.) NASP's ethical principles were developed to provide guidelines specifically for school psychologists employed in the schools or working in private practice. NASP's code focuses on protecting the well-being of the student/client; it also prescribes conduct to protect the rights and welfare of the parents, teachers, and other consumers of school psychological services.

NASP's "Principles for Professional Ethics" provides guidelines in the following areas: professional competence and maintaining competence; professional relationships and responsibilities to students, parents, the school, the community, related professions, and other school psychologists; advocacy of the rights and welfare of the student/client; professional responsibilities in assessment and intervention; use of materials and technology; research, publication, and presentation; reporting data and sharing results; and professional responsibilities in private practice settings.

APA's "Ethical Principles of Psychologists and Code of Conduct"

The "Ethical Standards of Psychologists" was first adopted by the American Psychological Association in 1953. Eight revisions of APA's code of ethics were published between 1958 and 1990. The current version, "Ethical

Principles of Psychologists and Code of Conduct" (EP), was adopted in 1992. (See Appendix B.) APA's *EP* differs from NASP's "Principles for Professional Ethics" in that it was developed for psychologists with training in diverse specialty areas (e.g., clinical, industrial-organizational, school) who work in a number of different settings (private practice, industry, hospitals and clinics, public schools, university teaching, and research). As Keith-Spiegel and Koocher (1985) observed, APA's code attempts to prescribe guidelines to protect "a variety of publics including psychotherapy clients, students, supervisors and employees, employers and employing agencies, human and animal research participants, and society in general" (p. 2).

The "Ethical Principles of Psychologists and Code of Conduct" consists of an Introduction, a Preamble, General Principles, and Ethical Standards. As noted in the Introduction to *EP,* the Preamble and General Principles are "*aspirational* goals to guide psychologists toward the highest ideals of psychology" and should be considered in ethical decision making. The Ethical Standards are "*enforceable* rules for conduct as psychologists." The Ethical Standards are organized under the following headings: General Standards; Evaluation, Assessment, or Intervention; Advertising and Other Public Statements; Therapy; Privacy and Confidentiality; Teaching, Training Supervision, Research, and Publishing; Forensic Activities; and Resolving Ethical Issues.

In addition, APA prepares and publishes *Ethical Principles in the Conduct of Research with Human Participants* (1982). This brief text provides extensive discussion of ethical issues in research with human participants (see Chapter 9). APA members agree to abide by these guidelines in conducting research; NASP (1997) also makes reference to this document in its "Standards for the Provision of School Psychological Services."

Professional Standards for Practice

Both organizations have developed a set of standards for the delivery of school psychological services. NASP's "Standards for the Provision of School Psychological Services" was developed in 1978 and revised in 1984, 1992, and 1997. (See Appendix C.) APA's "Specialty Guidelines for the Delivery of Services by School Psychologists" was adopted in 1981.

Professional standards for the delivery of school psychological services differ from ethical codes in both scope and intent. The standards represent a consensus of trainers and practitioners about roles and duties of school psychologists, desirable conditions for the effective delivery of services, and the nature of competent professional practice. For example, NASP's "Standards for the Provision of School Psychological Services" includes guidelines for federal and state administrative agencies involved in developing regulations that have an impact on school psychologists and service delivery, guidelines for employing agencies (organization of service delivery, supervision of school psychologists, accountability and evaluation of services, conditions for effective service delivery), and guidelines for the practitioner in the delivery of services. NASP and APA seek to ensure that members abide by their respective ethical codes and investigate and adjudicate code violations. In contrast, professional standards provide guidelines for the delivery of quality services, but they are not adjudicated.

In joining either APA or NASP, school psychologists also agree to be familiar with and consider the *Standards for Educational and Psychological Testing (Standards)* developed by a committee of members from the American Educational Research Association, American Psychological Association, and the National Council on Measurement in Education (1985). As will be seen in Chapter 4, these *Standards* provide guidelines for psychologists and educators to use in evaluating whether their tests and assessment procedures meet acceptable technical standards. A joint committee with members representing each of the three sponsoring organizations drafted a revision of the *Standards* and plans to submit it for approval in the spring of 1998 (Goh, 1997).

FOUR BROAD ETHICAL PRINCIPLES

This portion of the chapter provides an introduction to some of the ethical issues associated with the delivery of school psychological services. As noted earlier, codes of ethics are composed of broad principles along with more specific rule statements. Ethical principles are more general and fundamental than rule statements (Beauchamp & Childress, 1983).

A number of writers have identified general principles that provide the foundation for ethical choices in psychology (e.g., Bersoff & Koeppl, 1993; Fine & Ulrich, 1988; Kitchener, 1986; Prilleltensky, 1997). Our thinking about ethical principles was influenced by the content and organization of "A Canadian Code of Ethics for Psychologists" (CPA, 1991; Eberlein, 1987). We have organized our introduction to ethical issues in terms of the following themes or broad principles: (a) Respect for the Dignity of Persons, (b) Responsible Caring (Professional Competence and Responsibility), (c) Integrity in Professional Relationships, and (d) Responsibility to Community and Society. An overriding principle underlying all ethical choices is a commitment to promoting the welfare of individuals and the welfare of society (CPA, 1991).

Respect for the Dignity of Persons

Case 1–1

Sam Foster obtained permission from the school board to gather the data for his Psy.D. research project in the school district where he is an intern school psychologist. His study explores young children's feelings toward family members (mother, father, siblings) in the first year following divorce. Sam has located just enough families willing to participate in his study to ensure an adequate sample size. On the last day of data collection, he asks a 7-year-old study participant to express her feelings toward family members by giving messages to dolls that represent members of her family. She begins the task, but soon becomes visibly upset and asks to return to her classroom. Sam is uncertain whether to coax her to continue the data collection.

Psychologists "accept as fundamental the principle of respect for the dignity of persons" (CPA, 1991, p. 9; *EP* Principle D). They apply their professional skills "in ways that protect the dignity and rights of those involved" (NASP-PPE, III, A, #1). According to NASP's ethical code, school psychologists "consider the student or clients to be their primary responsibility" (NASP-PPE, IV, A, #1). Concern for protecting the rights and welfare of students is "the top priority in determining services" (NASP-PPE, IV, A, #2). However, practitioners also strive to protect the rights of parents, teachers, and other recipients of services (NASP-PPE, IV, A, #1).

The general principle of respect for the dignity of persons encompasses respect for the client's right to *self-determination and autonomy, privacy and confidentiality,* and *fairness and nondiscrimination.*

Self-Determination and Autonomy

In providing services, practitioners respect the client's right to self-determination and autonomy. To the maximum extent feasible, school psychologists respect the client's right of choice to enter, or to participate, in services voluntarily (NASP-PPE, III, B, #3). Decisions to participate in services are based on informed consent about the nature of services offered (*EP* 4.02; NASP-PPE, III, A, #4, B, #2).

Respect for the client's right to self-determination and autonomy poses special problems when working with children. As will be seen in Chapter 3, school psychologists must seek the informed consent of parents to provide services to children who are minors. But what of the child's right to self-determination and autonomy, that is, to make choices about whether to participate in the services offered?

"A Canadian Code of Ethics for Psychologists" (CPA, 1991) specifically addresses the issue of *developmentally appropriate* rights to self-determination and autonomy. This code attempts to balance the rights of self-determination and autonomy against concerns for the welfare of the child and advises the psychologist to, "Seek willing and adequately informed participation from any person of diminished capacity to give informed consent, and proceed without this assent only if the service or research activity is considered to be of direct benefit to that person" (1991, p. 12).

Sam Foster (Case 1–1) is ethically obligated to discontinue his data collection because participation in the research promises no direct benefit to the child. As will be seen in Chapter 9, he is further obligated to ensure there are no harmful after-effects to the child from her brief but upsetting experience as a study participant.

Privacy and Confidentiality

Psychologists respect the *privacy* of pupil/clients and others; every effort is made to avoid undue invasion of privacy (*EP* 5.03; NASP-PPE, III, B, #1). School psychology practitioners do not seek or store personal information that is not needed in the provision of services to the client (*EP* 5.03).

Practitioners also use appropriate safeguards to protect the *confidentiality* of client disclosures. They inform clients about the limits of confidentiality at the onset of offering services. In situations in which confidentiality is promised or implied, school psychologists ensure that the release of information is based on consent of the client. Only in unusual circumstances, such as when disclosure is necessary to protect the client or others from harm, is confidential information released without client consent (*EP* 5.05; also NASP-PPE, III, A, #9, #10, #11). (See Chapter 3 for in-depth discussion of these issues.)

Fairness and Nondiscrimination

Respect for the dignity of persons also encompasses the obligation of professionals to ensure fairness and nondiscrimination in the provision of services. School psychologists strive to respect and treat all persons impartially regardless of "physical, mental, emotional, political, economic, social, cultural, ethnic and racial characteristics, gender and sexual orientation, and religion" (NASP-PPE, III, A, #2, E, #3; also see APA, 1993a).

Responsible Caring (Professional Competence and Responsibility)

> **Case 1–2**
>
> *Carrie Johnson, a school psychologist in a rural district, received a referral to evaluate Melissa Gardner, a 4-year-old. Melissa receives special education and related services because she is hearing impaired; now her parents and teachers have begun to suspect she has learning and emotional problems as well. Carrie has no formal training or supervised experience working with hearing-impaired preschoolers and she is uncertain how to proceed with the referral.*

A shared theme in ethical codes of the helping professions is that of *beneficence.* Beneficence, or *responsible caring,* means that psychologists engage in actions that are likely to benefit others, or at least do no harm (CPA, 1991; Kitchener, 1986; Welfel & Kitchener, 1992; also NASP-PPE I). To do this, psychologists must practice *within the boundaries of their competence* and *accept responsibility* for their actions.

Competence

"School psychologists recognize the strengths and limitations of their training and experience, engaging only in practices for which they are qualified" (NASP-PPE, II, A, #1; also *EP* Principle A, NASP-PPE, I). They perform only those services for which they have acquired "an acknowledged level of experience, training, and competency" (NASP-PPE, I).

School psychology practitioners are "aware of their limitations and enlist the assistance of other specialists in supervisory, consultative or referral roles as appropriate in providing services" (NASP-PPE, II, A, #4). Carrie Johnson (Case 1–2) needs to seek assistance in evaluating Melissa to ensure a fair and valid assessment. Psychologists who step beyond their competence in assessing children place the pupil at risk for misdiagnosis, misclassification, miseducation, and possible psychological harm (see Chapter 4).

School psychologists are obligated to renew and update their skills to maintain an acceptable level of professional competence. They recognize the need for continued learning and pursue opportunities to engage in continuing professional development (NASP-PPE, II, A, #1). They "remain current regarding developments in research, training, and professional practices that benefit children, families, and schools" (NASP-PPE, II, A, #5; also *EP* Principle A).

Practitioners "refrain from any activity in which their personal problems or conflicts may interfere with professional effectiveness. Competent assistance is sought to alleviate conflicts in professional relationships" (NASP-PPE, II, A, #6; *EP* Principle B, 1.13).

Responsibility

Psychologists accept responsibility for their actions and the consequences of their actions (*EP* Principle C; NASP-PPE, III, A, #1). In all areas of service delivery, they strive to maximize benefit and avoid doing harm, and they work to offset any harmful consequences of decisions made.

Integrity in Professional Relationships

Case 1–3

Madeleine Fine, a new first-grade teacher, asks Hannah Cook, the school psychologist, for some ideas in handling Kevin, a child who has become a behavior problem in the classroom. After observing in the classroom, it is evident to Hannah that Madeleine needs some help working with Kevin and developing effective classroom management strategies. Hannah offers to meet with Madeleine once a week over a six-week period to work on classroom management skills, and Madeleine agrees. Shortly after their third consultation session, the building principal asks Hannah for her assessment of Madeleine's teaching competence. The principal indicates she plans to terminate Madeleine during her probationary period if there are problems with her teaching effectiveness. Hannah is not sure how to respond to the principal's request.

School psychology practitioners are obligated to inform students/clients of all relevant aspects of the potential professional relationship prior to beginning psychological services of any type (NASP-PPE, III, A, #3, B, #2, C, #1, D, #3). They strive to be honest, accurate, and straightforward about the nature and scope of their services. When the practitioner's commitments, objectives, or personal loyalties may influence a professional relationship, the school psychologist informs all concerned persons of relevant issues in advance (NASP-PPE, III, A, #3).

Case 1–3 illustrates the importance of openly defining the parameters of the services to be offered in the school setting. Madeleine has become Hannah's consultee in this consultant–consultee relationship. Hannah is bound by the obligation and expectation that what is shared and learned in their professional interaction is confidential; she may not share information about her consultee with the principal without Madeleine's explicit consent to do so.

In defining their job role to the school community, school psychologists are obligated to identify the services they provide and those that are outside the scope of their job role (NASP-PPE, III, D, #3; *EP* Principle B). It is the job role of the building principal, not the school psychologist, to gather information on teacher effectiveness. If Hannah violates the confidentiality of the consultative relationship and shares information about Madeleine's teaching with the school administration, her actions would most likely undermine teacher trust in school psychologists and diminish her ability to work with other teachers in need of consultative services. The ethical issues associated with the consultation role are discussed further in Chapter 8.

The general principle of integrity in professional relationships also suggests that psychologists must be honest and straightforward about their competencies. Competence levels, education, training, and experience are accurately represented to clients and others in a professional manner (NASP-PPE, II, A, #2, III, F, #3; *EP* Principle B). School psychology interns and practicum students identify themselves as such prior to the initiation of services (NASP-PPE, III, C, #1).

Carrie Johnson (Case 1–2) is obligated to let her supervisor know that she has little expertise in the assessment of hearing-impaired preschoolers so that a course of action (referral or consultation) can be pursued that is in the best interests of the child.

Practitioners also respect and understand the areas of competence of other professionals in their work setting and community and they work in full cooperation with other professional disciplines to meet the needs of students (NASP-PPE, III, F, #1, #2, #4; *EP* Principle C). They "encourage and support the use of all resources to best serve the interests of students and clients" (NASP-PPE, III, F, #2).

The general principle of integrity in professional relationships further suggests that school psychologists must avoid conflicts of interest. When such situations arise, they "attempt to resolve situations in which there are divided or conflicting interests in a manner which is mutually beneficial and protects the rights of all parties involved" (NASP-PPE, III, A, #5; also *EP* Principle B, E). As noted in NASP's code, "Personal and business relations with students/clients or their parents may cloud one's judgment. School psychologists are aware of these situations and avoid them whenever possible" (NASP-PPE, III, A, #7).

School psychologists "do not exploit clients through professional relationships nor condone these actions in their colleagues" (NASP-PPE, III, A, #6). Furthermore, they do not expose any individuals, including students, clients, employees, colleagues, and research participants to deliberate comments, gestures, or physical contacts of a sexual nature. School psychologists "do not engage in sexual relationships with their students, supervisees, trainees, or past or present clients" (NASP-PPE, III, A, #6; also *EP* 1.11, 1.19).

Psychologists also do not take credit for work that is not their own (NASP-PPE, IV, C, #4; *EP* 6.22, 6.23).

Responsibility to Community and Society

Case 1–4

Charlie Maxwell, a school psychologist, is concerned about the frequent use of corporal punishment to discipline children in the district where he works. He assumes a highly visible leadership role in advocating a ban on corporal punishment at the local and state level despite objections to his activities by two school board members.

"Psychology functions as a discipline within the context of human society. Psychologists, both in their work and as private citizens, have responsibilities to the societies in which they live and work, such as the neighborhood or city, and to the welfare of all human beings in those societies" (CPA, 1991, p. 19; also *EP* Principle F). As Prilleltensky has suggested, "school psychologists have a moral responsibility to promote not only the well-being of their clients but also of the environments where their clients function and develop" (1991, p. 200).

Charlie's conduct (Case 1–4) is highly ethical. There is ample research evidence to suggest that the use of corporal punishment in the schools is not in the best interests of children (see Chapter 10). Charlie's advocacy of a ban on corporal punishment suggests a commitment to promoting the welfare of all children in the schools (NASP-PPE, III, D, #5).

School psychologists know and respect federal and state law and school policies (NASP-PPE, III, D, #2). They abide by these laws and policies unless there is a conflict with ethical guidelines, in which case they "seek to resolve such conflict through positive, respected and legal channels" (NASP-PPE, III, E, #5; *EP* 1.02).

Consistent with the principle of responsibility to community and society, school psychology practitioners accept responsibility for self-monitoring and peer monitoring to safeguard the welfare of others and maintain the public trust in psychology. If they become aware of unethical conduct by another school psychologist, they "attempt to resolve suspected detrimental or unethical practices on an informal level" (NASP-PPE, III, A, #8). Practitioners "make every effort to discuss the ethical principles with other professionals who may be in violation" (NASP-PPE, III, A, #8). However, if not resolved on an informal level, practitioners are obligated to file an ethics complaint with an appropriate professional organization (*EP* 8.04, 8.05; NASP-PPE, III, A, #8).

Psychologists also accept the obligation to contribute to the knowledge base of psychology and education in order to further improve services to children, families, and others and, in a more general sense, promote human welfare (*EP* Preamble, Principle F).

Summary

In this section, four broad ethical principles were introduced. The first was respect for the dignity of persons. Consistent with this principle, we value client autonomy and safeguard the client's right to self-determination, respect client privacy and the confidentiality of disclosures, and are committed to fairness and nondiscrimination in interactions with the client and others. The second broad principle was responsible caring. We engage in actions that are likely to benefit others. To do so, we work within the boundaries of our professional competence and accept responsibility for our actions. The third principle was integrity in professional relationships. We are candid and honest about the nature and scope of the services we offer and work in cooperation with other professionals to meet the needs of children in the schools. The fourth principle was responsibility to community and society. We recognize that our profession exists within the context of society and work to ensure the science of psychology is used to promote human welfare.

ETHICAL-LEGAL DECISION MAKING

Ethics involves "making decisions of a moral nature about people and their interactions in society" (Kitchener, 1986, p. 306). Individuals may make choices of a moral nature primarily on an *intuitive* level, or a *critical-evaluative level* (Hare, 1981; Kitchener, 1986). Choices made on the intuitive level are based on "people's immediate feeling responses to situations," along with personal beliefs about what they should or should not do (Kitchener, 1986, p. 309).

Psychologists, however, have special obligations when making ethical choices in the context of a professional relationship (Haas & Malouf, 1989). In the provision of psychological services, decision making on a critical-evaluative level is consistent with sound professional practice.

The critical-evaluative level of ethical decision making involves following a systematic procedure. This procedure may involve exploration of feelings and beliefs, but also includes consideration of general ethical principles, a review of codes of ethics and guidelines, and possibly consultation with colleagues. Psychologists need to be aware of their own feelings and values and how they may influence their decisions (Newman, 1993). However, reliance on feelings and intuition alone in professional decision making may result in poor decisions or confusion (Corey et al., 1993; Kitchener, 1986).

How do we evaluate whether a course of action is ethical or unethical? Haas and Malouf (1989) suggest an act or decision is likely to be viewed as ethical if it has the following characteristics: (a) The decision is *principled,* based on generally accepted ethical principles; (b) the action is a *reasoned* outcome of a consideration of the principles; and (c) the decision is *universalizable,* that is, the psychologist would recommend the same course of action to others in a similar situation (pp. 2–3). The consequences of the course of action chosen must also be considered, namely, will the action chosen result in more good than harm? Evaluation of whether a course of action is ethical involves consideration of characteristics of the decision itself (i.e., based on accepted principles, universality), the process of decision making (i.e., reasoned), and the consequences of the decision.

Eight-Step Problem-Solving Model

Eberlein (1987) and others (Haas & Malouf, 1989; Kitchener, 1986; Tymchuk, 1986) suggest that mastery of an explicit decision-making model or procedure may help the practitioner make informed, well-reasoned, ethical choices in professional practice. Tymchuk (1986) has also noted that, in difficult situations, the course of action chosen may be challenged. Use of a systematic problem-solving strategy will allow the practitioner to describe *how* a decision was made. This may afford some protection when difficult decisions come under the scrutiny of others.

The following eight-step problem-solving model is adapted from Keith-Spiegel and Koocher (1985, pp. 19–20):

1. Describe the parameters of the situation.
2. Define the potential ethical-legal issues involved.
3. Consult ethical-legal guidelines, if any, already available that might apply to the resolution of each issue. Consider the broad ethical principles as well as specific mandates involved (Kitchener, 1986).
4. Evaluate the rights, responsibilities, and welfare of all affected parties (e.g., pupil, teachers, classmates, other school staff, parents, siblings).
5. Generate a list of alternative decisions possible for each issue.
6. Enumerate the consequences of making each decision. Evaluate the short-term, ongoing, and long-term consequences of each possible decision (Tymchuk, 1986). Consider the possible psychological, social, and economic costs to affected parties. Eberlein (1987) advises consideration of how each possible course of action would "affect the dignity of and the responsible caring for all of the people involved" (p. 353). Consultation with colleagues may be helpful.
7. Present any evidence that the various consequences or benefits resulting from each decision will actually occur (i.e., a risk-benefit analysis).
8. Make the decision. Consistent with codes of ethics (APA, NASP), school psychologists accept responsibility for the decision made and monitor the consequences of the course of action chosen.

Crisis Decision Making

In the course of their career, practitioners may encounter situations in which there is little time to consider and weigh alternative action plans. Keith-Spiegel and Koocher (1985) offer a number of suggestions to prepare for crisis decision making. We have adapted them for the school setting:

1. Know the resources available in your school and community. Identify the professionals in your school who are experienced in handling crisis situations. Keep an up-to-date listing of colleagues you can contact in an emergency situation. If your district does not have a crisis management team, consider working to develop one with other pupil personnel specialists, building administrators, and teachers. Know the special areas of expertise of various team members and develop plans for handling potential crisis situations.
2. Keep abreast of state law and local school board policies. Consult with the school administration and/or school attorney if aspects of

law or policy are not clear to you. For example, know the procedures for reporting suspected child abuse.

3. Take advantage of opportunities to learn about crisis management (e.g., formal coursework, workshops, and seminars). Discuss "what if" situations with a professional support group. Keep abreast of the crisis management literature and maintain an up-to-date file of written materials that may be helpful in handling crisis situations.
4. Recognize the boundaries of your competence. Do not attempt to handle situations beyond the scope of your training and competence. Medical emergencies (e.g., drug overdose) require medical care.

Professional literature suggests a growing awareness of the need to prepare for crisis situations in the schools (for example, see Poland, Pitcher, & Lazarus, 1995). In Chapter 7, the ethical and legal responsibilities of the practitioner in a number of crisis situations will be explored.

CONCLUDING COMMENTS

Students and practitioners often complain that codes of ethics are bothersome to read, a confusing and boring list of "shoulds" and "should-nots." Wonderly (1989) suggests, however, that codes of ethics in psychology are not so overwhelming if we remember their primary purpose, namely, to protect the public. Professionals do not have *rights* under a code of ethics, only *obligations.* We will be exploring those obligations in more detail in the chapters ahead.

STUDY AND DISCUSSION

Questions for Chapter 1

1. What are the sources of "quality control" in the provision of school psychological services?
2. What does the term *ethics* mean?
3. What does the term *applied professional ethics* mean?
4. Why do professional groups, such as school psychologists, develop a code of ethics?
5. Summarize the desired ethics competencies of school psychology practitioners.

(Continued)

6. Why are codes of ethics imperfect guides to behavior?
7. Summarize the broad ethical principles discussed in Chapter 1.
8. How do you evaluate whether a course of action is ethical?

Discussion

1. According to Corey et al. (1993), ethics involves what is right and correct in professional practice. Values have to do with what we view as desirable. Is it possible for school psychologists to provide value-free or value-neutral services? Is it desirable? See Chapter 3 of Corey et al. (1993) for a discussion of values and the helping relationship. Also see Bergin (1991), Newman (1993), and Prilleltensky (1997).

2. Meara et al. (1996) suggest that ethics training include instruction in virtue ethics along with principle-based ethics. Virtue ethics focuses on ideals, rather than principles, and the character of the professional, rather than the action itself. Do you believe virtue ethics should be adopted as a guiding construct? Read Meara et al. (1996) along with Bersoff's (1996) critique of the construct.

VIGNETTES

Eberlein and others have suggested that mastery of an explicit, decision-making model or procedure may help the practitioner make informed, well-reasoned, ethical choices when difficult situations arise in professional practice. In Chapter 1, we introduced an eight-step problem-solving model adapted from Keith-Spiegel and Koocher (1985).

The incidents below are included to provide an opportunity to practice the problem-solving model. Assume the role of the school psychologist involved and then follow a decision-making model to determine the course of action most appropriate. Compare your decisions with those of colleagues or fellow students.

1. A few months after Carrie Johnson was hired as the school psychologist in a rural school district, the district superintendent of schools asked to meet with her. During this meeting, he said, "You'll be working closely with the principal at Pine Lake. Rumor has it he drinks a lot on the job. He's been caught twice and fined for driving while intoxicated. I think he's nuts and we've got to get rid of him. Keep notes on what he says and does. I want a report later." How should Carrie handle this situation? (Vignette source unknown.)

2. After a series of devastating floods destroyed homes and schools in a nearby community, many Native American families moved into Carrie Johnson's school district. Carrie began receiving referrals from a number of teachers because the Native American children were having difficulty coping with the loss of their homes and adjusting to their new school and community. Carrie had no experience working with Native American children and their families, or with those who had suffered such losses. How should Carrie handle the referrals for assessment and counseling of the Native American pupils now attending her school?

3. As part of her effort to build a strong working relationship with school staff and community members, Hannah Cook joined the PTA (Parent-Teacher Association), and regularly attends their meetings. During a public meeting of the PTA, a parent openly complains about the treatment her daughter is receiving in world history class at a school where Hannah is the psychologist. The parent contends that the history teacher lacks mental stability, and is consequently causing her child much anguish. How should Hannah handle this situation? (Adapted from Bailey, 1980).

4. Mrs. French, a middle-school English teacher, stops by to see the school psychologist, Charlie Maxwell. Mrs. French is upset about a love note she intercepted between two students in one of her classes. The note was written by a 14-year-old boy named Derek to another boy in the class. Derek knows that Mrs. French has read and kept the note, but she has not spoken with him about the matter. Mrs. French wants Charlie to confront Derek with the note and talk with Derek's parents so that he will "get help to cure him of this sick stuff before it's too late." How should Charlie respond to this situation? (Adapted from Eversole, 1993; also see Lasser & Tharinger, 1997).

5. Michelle Phillips was born with Sanfilippo syndrome, a genetic disorder that results in progressive neurological deterioration and limited life expectancy. There is no effective treatment for the disorder. Wanda Rose, a school psychologist, has worked with the Phillips family since Michelle was diagnosed six years ago, and she has formed a warm working relationship with them. Michelle is now in the third and final phase of the disorder. She is severely mentally impaired, unable to communicate, and unable to sit or walk without support. She has difficulty swallowing and chokes frequently.

Mr. and Mrs. Phillips have made an appointment with Wanda. They believe Michelle is experiencing much pain and suffering. While they want all comfort care to continue for their daughter, they do not want medical interventions that would prolong her life. They have brought along DNR orders (do not resuscitate, do not institute basic choking rescue) from Michelle's physician and they would like Wanda's help in ensuring that the orders will be honored at school. How should Wanda respond to this situation? (See Rushton, Will, & Murray, 1994).

ACTIVITIES

To learn more about APA and NASP, visit their websites: http://www.apa.org and Http://www.naspweb.org.

Chapter 2

LAW AND SCHOOL PSYCHOLOGY: AN INTRODUCTION

This chapter provides a brief introduction to the American legal system and law pertinent to the delivery of school psychological services. The three basic sources of public school law within the American legal system will be briefly explored: the U.S. Constitution, statutes and regulations, and case law. This chapter closes with an overview of the credentialing of school psychologists.

THE U.S. CONSTITUTION

The U.S. Constitution is the supreme law of the land. All statutes enacted by the U.S. Congress, state and local governments, and even boards of education are subject to the provisions of the Constitution (Reutter, 1994).

The original Constitution outlined the duties and powers of the federal government. Concern that the Constitution provided the foundation for a federal government that was too powerful led to the passage of 10 amendments to the Constitution in 1791, the Bill of Rights. The Bill of Rights was created to provide a more distinct balance of power between the federal government and the states, and to safeguard the rights of individual citizens. The remaining amendments, 11th through 26th, were adopted between 1795 and 1971.

There is no fundamental right to an education guaranteed citizens under the Constitution (see *San Antonio Independent School District v. Rodriguez,* 1973). Nevertheless, the Constitution has been the foundation for many decisions affecting public school education, including the right to equal educational opportunity, student rights in the school setting, and church–state–school relationships. Portions of the Constitution most pertinent to education law are shown in Exhibit 2–1. The 10th, 14th, First, and Fourth Amendments are discussed in the following paragraphs.

Exhibit 2–1. The U.S. Constitution: Selected Amendments

Amendment 1
Freedom of Religion, Speech, and the Press; Rights of Assembly and Petition

Congress shall make no law respecting an establishment of religion, or prohibiting the free exercise thereof; or abridging the freedom of speech, or of the press; or the right of the people peaceably to assemble, and to petition the government for a redress of grievances.

Amendment 4
Search and Arrest Warrants

The right of the people to be secure in their persons, houses, papers, and effects, against unreasonable searches and seizures, shall not be violated, and no warrants shall issue, but upon probable cause, supported by oath or affirmation, and particularly describing the place to be searched, and the persons or things to be seized.

Amendment 9
Powers Retained by the People

The enumeration in the Constitution, of certain rights, shall not be construed to deny or disparage others retained by the people.

Amendment 10
Powers Retained by the States and the People

The powers not delegated to the United States by the Constitution, nor prohibited by it to the states, are reserved to the States respectively, or to the people.

Amendment 14
Civil Rights

No state shall make or enforce any law which shall abridge the privileges or immunities of citizens of the United States; nor shall any state deprive any person of life, liberty or property, without due process of law; nor deny to any person within its jurisdiction the equal protection of the law.

The 10th Amendment

The Constitution does not specifically refer to education as a duty of the federal government. Under the 10th Amendment, the "powers not delegated to the United States by the Constitution, nor prohibited by it to the States, are reserved to the States, respectively, or to the people." Thus, under the 10th Amendment, state governments have assumed the duty to educate, the power to tax citizens of the state to finance education, and the power to compel school attendance.

Both federal and state governments have an interest in an "educated citizenry," as educated citizens are more capable of self-government and of making a positive contribution to community life (Hubsch, 1989). As noted above, the duty to educate children and the power to do so have been left to the states. Most states delegate much of the authority for the management of public schools to local school boards. Public schools are consequently considered to be an "arm of the government" (Turnbull, 1990). When school boards, principals, teachers, and school psychologists make decisions in their official roles, their actions are seen as actions by the state.

A public education is considered to be an *entitlement* given by the state to its citizens under state constitutional or statutory law. On the basis of state law, all children within a state have a legitimate claim of entitlement to a public education. This right to a public education given by state law is considered to be a *property right.*

The 14th Amendment

As previously noted, the Bill of Rights was passed to ensure a clearer balance of power between the federal government and the states, and to safeguard the rights of individual citizens. The 14th Amendment was created to prevent state governments from trespassing on the rights of individual citizens: "No state shall make or enforce any law which shall abridge the privileges or immunities of citizens of the United States . . . without due process of law . . . ."

As education is a duty left to the states, the courts have long held the position that "judicial interposition in the operation of the public school system requires care and restraint" (*Epperson v. State of Arkansas,* 1968). As the Supreme Court stated in *Epperson,*[1] "By and large, public education in our Nation is committed to the control of state and local authorities. Courts do not and cannot intervene in the resolution of conflicts which arise in the daily operation of school systems and which do not directly and sharply implicate basic constitutional values" (p. 104).

The 1950s, 1960s, and 1970s were decades of increasing federal court involvement in school-related issues, however, because of school actions that violated the constitutional rights of students and their parents. Two aspects of the 14th Amendment have been extremely important in decisions regarding schools: the *equal protection clause* and the requirement for *procedural due process.*

[1] This case concerned an Arkansas state law that prohibited the teaching of the Darwinian theory of evolution in the schools. The Court held the law to be an unconstitutional violation of First Amendment safeguards of freedom of speech and inquiry and belief.

Equal Protection Clause

The *equal protection clause* provides that no state shall "deny any person within its jurisdiction the equal protection of the laws." Beginning in the years of the Warren Court (1953–1969), this clause has been interpreted to mean that a state may not make a free public education available to some children but not to others within the state, and that the state must provide equal educational opportunity to all citizens within its jurisdiction.

In the 1954 landmark Supreme Court ruling, *Brown v. Board of Education,* the Court made it clear that each state must provide equal educational opportunity to all children within its jurisdiction regardless of race. The Court ruled that the assignment of African American children to separate and inferior public schools is a denial of equal protection under the 14th Amendment of the Constitution. In two important subsequent cases, *Pennsylvania Association for Retarded Children v. Commonwealth of Pennsylvania* (1971, 1972) and *Mills v. Board of Education* (1972), the courts ruled that exclusion of children with handicaps from public school education is a denial of equal protection.

During the years since *Brown,* the courts have sent an unwavering message to the states that they have a duty to provide equal educational opportunities to all children regardless of race, color, national origin, native language, sex, and handicapping condition under the 14th Amendment (see Chapter 6). The 14th Amendment equal protection clause has also protected school access rights of pregnant and married students.

Due Process

The 14th Amendment also provides that no state shall "deprive any person of life, liberty, or property, without due process of law." Courts have identified two aspects of due process: substantive and procedural. *Substantive due process* applies to the content of a law. A state may not pass a law that deprives citizens of life, liberty, or property if the law is not related to a legitimate governmental purpose; arbitrary and capricious laws that impact on citizen rights will be ruled unconstitutional. In the public schools, substantive due process has been interpreted to mean that school rules restricting student rights must be reasonably related to the purpose of schooling. (See discussion of *Tinker v. Des Moines Independent Community School District* [1969].)

Procedural due process means that a state may not take away life, a liberty interest, or a property right without some sort of procedural fairness to safeguard citizens from unfair or wrongful infringement of rights by the government (Bersoff & Hofer, 1990). The requirement for procedural due process applies only to the infringement or deprivation of a liberty or property interest protected by the 14th Amendment; citizens are guaranteed procedural due process only if a substantive liberty or property interest is affected. The specific liberty and property interests protected under the umbrella of the 14th Amendment have been identified in court interpretations of the scope of substantive rights. In *Goss v. Lopez* (1975), the Supreme Court held that education is a property right protected by the 14th Amendment.

Procedural due process "is a flexible concept whose precise contours change relative to the nature and gravity of the interest infringed" (Bersoff & Prasse, 1978, p. 402). Notice (being told what action the state proposes to take and the reason for that action) and the opportunity to be heard are basic components of due process when state action may deprive a citizen of a liberty or property interest (Bersoff & Prasse, 1978).

Under the due process clause of the 14th Amendment, schools may not suspend or expel children from school (and therefore deprive them of their property interest) without some sort of fair, impartial due process procedures. The due process procedures required for school suspension or expulsion generally do not have to be complex or elaborate, but must include notice and the opportunity to be heard (*Goss v. Lopez,* 1975). (The suspension or expulsion of students with disabilities for more than 10 days requires more formal procedures because of the protections afforded students with disabilities under statutory law. See Chapter 10.)

The due process clause of the 14th Amendment also protects individuals from arbitrary or unwarranted stigmatization by the state that may interfere with the ability to acquire property. More specifically, the courts have ruled that a school may not classify a child as "mentally retarded" without due process; that is, without some sort of fair decision-making procedure that includes parent notice of the proposed classification and the right to an impartial hearing to protest the classification (Bersoff & Ysseldyke, 1977) (see Chapter 5).

As noted above, the 14th Amendment also protects the basic personal freedoms of citizens outlined in the Bill of Rights from arbitrary infringement by the state. The First and Fourth Amendments are an important source of fundamental rights.

The First and Fourth Amendments

In 1969, the Supreme Court decided an important case concerning student rights in the public schools, *Tinker v. Des Moines Independent Community School District* (1969). This case involved three students who were suspended from school for violating a school policy prohibiting pupils from wearing black armbands in protest of the war in Vietnam. In *Tinker,* the Court recognized the need to balance the school's interest in maintaining discipline in order to foster learning, and fundamental personal freedoms guaranteed citizens in the Bill of Rights. In the Court's view, the school's policy of banning armbands was seen as an unreasonable violation of the students' constitutional right to freedom of expression because there was no evidence that the silent wearing of armbands interfered with or disrupted the functioning of the school.

Thus, although children in the school setting are not afforded the full range of personal freedoms guaranteed citizens by the Bill of Rights, they do maintain certain fundamental rights in the school setting. In *Tinker,* the Court stated that "students in school as well as out of school are 'persons' under our Constitution . . . possessed of fundamental rights which the State must respect" (p. 511).

Freedom of Speech and Assembly

The First Amendment prohibits the government from interfering with the rights of free speech and assembly and freedom of religious choice. In *Tinker* and subsequent cases, the courts have generally acknowledged the right of students to free speech and assembly, as long as the exercise of those rights does not significantly interfere with or disrupt the functioning of the school. Freedom of speech and assembly can be restricted when their exercise "materially and substantially" interferes with schooling. The right to free speech does not protect the use of "obscene" language, gestures, or materials (see Fischer & Sorenson, 1996).

Privacy Rights

There is no "right to privacy" expressly mentioned in the Constitution. A number of different privacy rights have been carved out of the First Amendment concept of "liberty," Fifth Amendment protections against self-incrimination, Ninth Amendment reservation of rights to the people, and the Fourth Amendment prohibition against unreasonable search and seizure (Hummel, Talbutt, & Alexander, 1985).

In a case that received considerable attention from legal scholars, a federal district court ruled that parents of school children have a right to be free from invasion of family privacy by the school (*Merriken v. Cressman,* 1973; see Chapter 9). This right to privacy was recognized only for the parents or family unit; the courts have generally not recognized an independent student right to privacy in the schools. However, federal education law (e.g., the Protection of Pupil Rights Amendment discussed below) now provides some guidance regarding protection of the privacy rights of pupils and their parents.

Under the Constitution, the courts have generally held that students have a Fourth Amendment right to be free from unreasonable search and seizure in the schools. The courts have ruled that students have a legitimate expectation of privacy rights with regard to their person and possessions, but they have allowed a more lenient standard of "reasonable suspicion" as opposed to "probable cause" for conducting searches in school. (Privacy is discussed further in Chapter 3.)

Freedom of Religion

The First Amendment also assures the basic right to free exercise of religious choice, and, under the 14th Amendment, both Congress and the states are prohibited from passing laws "respecting an establishment of religion." As Reutter (1994) notes, the First Amendment is the source of two types of church–school–state cases: those involving use of public funds for parochial schools and those involving school policies or classroom procedures objected to on religious grounds.

In general, court interpretations of the First Amendment suggest that the state is not allowed to provide funds or equipment directly to parochial schools. However, under the "child benefit theory," the state may provide some educational services for pupils attending parochial schools as long as those services directly aid the pupil and are not used for the purpose of religious instruction, and there is no impermissible entanglement of church and state.

In *Wolman v. Walter* (1977), the Supreme Court was asked to rule on the constitutionality of an Ohio statute that provided public school aid to children attending church-related schools. The Court upheld those portions of the law allowing the use of public school funds for secular textbooks (those approved for use in the public schools); standardized testing services; and speech, hearing, and psychological diagnostic services provided by public school personnel on the premises of the nonpublic school. The Court also upheld the provision of therapeutic services (guidance services and remedial instruction) but only if performed by public school personnel in public schools or centers located off the premises of the nonpublic school. The Court reasoned that teaching or counseling services posed a risk of fostering ideological views, an impermissible church–state entanglement, whereas diagnostic services did not.

Similarly, in *Aguilar v. Felton* (1985), the Supreme Court was asked to rule on the constitutionality of the City of New York's program of providing remedial instruction and guidance services to pupils in parochial schools. The program was funded by Title I of the Elementary and Secondary Education Act of 1965 and carried out by public school teachers, guidance counselors, psychologists, and social workers on the premises of the nonpublic schools. The City of New York monitored the religious content of the Title I instruction, and teachers and other professionals were directed to avoid involvement with religious activities conducted by the private schools. The Supreme Court held that New York City's program of providing Title I instruction and services on the premises of parochial schools violated the Establishment Clause of the First Amendment.

On June 23rd, 1997, however, the Supreme Court overturned its *Aguilar v. Felton* ruling. In writing the majority opinion in *Agostini v. Felton* (1997), Justice O'Connor stated that case law decisions since 1985 dictate that *Aguilar v. Felton* is no longer good law. The Court held that the City of New York public schools may now provide Title I instruction and services on the premises of parochial schools. Thus, Court interpretation of the First Amendment regarding the types of educational services the state may provide at the site of parochial schools has changed. The provision of remedial instruction on the premises of a parochial school is no longer viewed as an impermissible church-state entanglement.

STATUTES AND REGULATIONS

A second source of law within the American legal system is statutory law. American government is composed of three parallel systems of government at the federal, state, and local levels, a form of government known as "federalism" (Turnbull, 1990). At the federal level, the Constitution is the basic law of the land. Congress is empowered to enact federal laws as long as they do not violate the U.S. Constitution. Similarly, each state has its own constitution and legislative body for enacting laws at the state level. State laws may not violate either the state or federal constitutions.

Many countries have a nationalized school system operated by the central government (Hubsch, 1989). Under the 10th Amendment of the Constitution, our Congress is forbidden from creating a nationalized school system. However, the U.S. Congress has the power to shape educational policy and practices by offering monies to states contingent on compliance with federal mandates. Congress has passed two types of legislation that have had a dramatic impact on the public schools, *antidiscrimination legislation* and *federal education legislation* (Martin, 1979). Key federal statutes affecting the schools are highlighted in the paragraphs that follow.

Federal Education Legislation

Some federal education legislation is grant legislation; that is, funds are provided to states on the condition that schools comply with certain educational policies and practices. The Improving America's Schools Act and the Individuals with Disabilities Education Act are important examples of this type of legislation. Other federal education legislation stipulates that no federal funds will be made available to schools unless they adhere to specific educational policies and practices outlined in the law; the Family Educational Rights and Privacy Act of 1974 (FERPA) is an example of this type of legislation.

Elementary and Secondary Education Act of 1965

As noted previously, education has generally been regarded as a responsibility of state and local governments. The Elementary and Secondary Education Act of 1965 (ESEA) (Pub. L. No. 89-750), was one of the first major federal programs to aid education. With the passage of ESEA, Congress accepted the proposition that although "education is primarily a state function . . . the Federal Government has a secondary obligation to see that there is a basic floor under those essential services for all adults and children in the United States" (Taft, 1965, p. 1450). ESEA was initially a permissive law that gave the schools much latitude in how funds would be spent. A major thrust of early amendments of the law was to target funds more specifically for economically disadvantaged school children.

The Improving America's Schools Act of 1994 (IASA) (Pub. L. No. 103-382) includes the most recent amendments to ESEA. IASA provides financial assistance for schools with high concentrations of children from low-income families. Monies are provided to meet the educational needs of children with limited English proficiency; children of migrant workers; Indian children; children who are neglected, delinquent, or at risk of dropping out; and young children and their parents who are in need of family-literacy services.

Goals 2000: Educate America Act

The Goals 2000: Educate America Act (Pub. L. No. 103-227) also was passed in 1994. This legislation is designed to improve learning and teaching by providing a national framework for education reform. Funds available under this Act promote school improvements consistent with eight national goals. These goals address pupil readiness to learn at school entry; high school completion rates; student achievement and citizenship; teacher education and professional development; mathematics and science achievement;

adult literacy and lifelong learning; safe, disciplined and drug-free schools; and parental participation. (For a discussion of *Goals 2000* and psychology's role, see APA, 1995.)

School-to-Work Opportunity Act

The School-to-Work Opportunity Act of 1994 (Pub. L. No. 103-239) was designed to encourage states to develop a statewide system to better prepare students for employment or postsecondary education. The purpose of the Act is to encourage states to prepare students for high-wage jobs by integrating academic and occupational learning, and increasing opportunities for postsecondary education. The Act encourages the formation of partnerships between schools and local employers, and funds may be used to advance a variety of school-to-work activities, such as cooperative education and youth apprenticeships. (See Ysseldyke & Geenen, 1996, for additional information.)

Individuals with Disabilities Education Act

Prior to 1990, the Education of the Handicapped Act (EHA),[2] referred to a series of federal statutes concerning the education of children with handicapping conditions (e.g., Pub. L. No. 94-142). In 1990, President Bush signed into law the Education of the Handicapped Act Amendments of 1990 (Pub. L. No. 101-476) which changed the name of EHA to the Individuals with Disabilities Education Act (IDEA). On June 4, 1997, President Clinton signed into law the Individuals with Disabilities Education Act Amendments of 1997 (Pub. L. No. 105-117). This Act reauthorized IDEA and introduced a number of changes to improve the law.

IDEA-Part B allocates funds to states that provide a free and appropriate education to all children with disabilities as defined by the law. In order to receive funds, each state must have developed a plan to assure that every child with disabilities receives special education and related services in conformance with an individualized education program. Children must be assessed on the basis of nondiscriminatory testing and evaluation procedures, and provided an individualized education program in the least restrictive (most normal) setting feasible. Individualized education planning decisions are made by a multidisciplinary team that includes the pupils' parents, and a number of safeguards are required in the law to ensure parent participation in decision making (see Chapters 4 and 5).

---

[2] Also EAHCA.

IDEA-Part C provides funds to states that offer early intervention programs for infants and toddlers with known or suspected disabilities in conformance with an individualized family service plan (see Chapter 5).

Family Educational Rights and Privacy Act of 1974

This law (a part of Pub. L. No. 93-380) is commonly called FERPA or the Buckley Amendment. FERPA is a 1974 amendment to the Elementary and Secondary Education Act of 1965. Under FERPA, no federal funds will be made available to schools unless they adhere to the pupil record-keeping procedures outlined in the law. FERPA record-keeping guidelines are designed to ensure confidentiality of records and parent access to school records concerning their children. In accordance with FERPA, parents have access to all official school records of their children, the right to challenge the accuracy of those records, and the right to a hearing regarding the accuracy of them. Pupil records are to be available only to those in the school setting with a legitimate educational interest, and parent consent must be obtained before records are released to agencies outside of the school (see Chapter 3).

The Protection of Pupil Rights Amendment

The Protection of Pupil Rights or "Hatch Amendment" was a 1978 amendment to the Elementary and Secondary Education Act of 1965. It was revised in 1994 by Goals 2000. This amendment was introduced to protect student and family privacy in programs that receive funding from the U.S. Department of Education. It requires schools to obtain written parental consent before a pupil can be required to submit to a survey, analysis, or evaluation that reveals certain types of personal information (e. g., political affiliation, potentially embarrassing psychological problems, sexual or criminal behavior, family income). (See Chapter 3.)

Federal Antidiscrimination Legislation

Congress also has passed antidiscrimination or civil rights legislation that has had an impact on public school policies and practices. These statutes prohibit state and school authorities from discriminating against individuals on the basis of race, color, or national origin;[3] sex;[4] or handicapping condition in any program or activity receiving any federal funding. A state department of education may choose not to pursue monies available under

[3] Title VI of the Civil Rights Act of 1964.

[4] Title IX of the Education Amendments of 1972.

federal grant statutes (e.g., funds for infants and toddlers with disabilities). School districts must comply with antidiscrimination legislation if they receive *any* federal funds for any purpose, however.

The Rehabilitation Act of 1973

Section 504 of The Rehabilitation Act of 1973 (Pub. L. No. 93-112) specifically prohibits discrimination against any otherwise qualified individual solely on the basis of a handicapping condition in any program or activity receiving federal financial assistance. Section 504 is discussed in Chapter 6.

Americans with Disabilities Act of 1990

The Americans with Disabilities Act of 1990 (ADA) (Pub. L. No. 101-336) is considered to be the most significant federal law assuring the civil rights of all individuals with disabilities. ADA guarantees equal opportunity to individuals with disabilities in employment, public accommodation, transportation, state and local government services, and telecommunications. Title II, Subtitle A, is the portion of the law most pertinent to public schools (see Chapter 6).

Civil Rights Act of 1871

School personnel should also be familiar with Section 1983 of the Civil Rights Act of 1871. This statute was passed following the Civil War as a reaction to the mistreatment of African Americans, and it was originally known as the Ku Klux Klan Act. Under Section 1983, any person whose constitutional rights (or rights under federal law) have been violated by a government official may sue for damages in federal court, and the official may be held liable for damages. State laws may protect school employees from lawsuits under state law. Under Section 1983, however, a pupil whose civil rights have been violated may sue the school board, principal, teacher, and/or school psychologist responsible in federal court. Section 1983 has been the legal foundation for a number of student lawsuits concerning school actions that violated constitutional rights (see Chapters 10 and 11).

Rules and Regulations

When federal legislation is enacted, an executive agency is charged with the responsibility of developing rules and regulations implementing the law. For example, rules and regulations implementing IDEA and FERPA are issued by the Department of Education. For all intents and purposes, rules and regulations have the same impact as actual legislation. School psychologists need to be familiar with both the statute itself and the rules and regulations implementing the law.

Federal statutes are compiled and published in the *United States Code* (USC). Rules and regulations implementing a law first appear in a daily publication called the *Federal Register* and are subsequently published in the *Code of Federal Regulations* (C.F.R.), which is updated each year. These government publications can typically be found in state or university libraries. Citations for important federal statutes are provided in the Table of Federal Legislation at the back of this book.

State Education Laws

As Hubsch (1989) notes, the majority of public school *statutory* law is enacted at the state level. School psychologists must become familiar with the laws pertinent to the delivery of school psychological services in the state where they are employed, in addition to federal statutes and regulations. Copies of relevant state laws and rules and regulations can typically be obtained by contacting the state government's lead agency for education (e.g., a state Department of Education).

CASE LAW

A third source of law is case law. Case law, or common law, is law that emerges from court decisions (Reutter, 1994). The common-law system can be traced back to medieval England. At that time, it was widely accepted that there were "laws of nature" to guide solutions to problems if those laws could be discovered. Legal scholars studied past court decisions for the purpose of discovering these "natural laws." The rules and principles that judges customarily followed in making decisions were identified and, at times, articulated in case decisions, and judges tended to base new decisions on these earlier "legal precedents." Common law is thus discovered law rather than enacted law (Reutter, 1994, p. 1).

Many aspects of public school law today are based on common law rather than enacted law (Reutter, 1994). For example, the courts have generally upheld a teacher's right to use corporal punishment to discipline students where there are no state laws or school board policies prohibiting its use. The court's acceptance of the use of corporal punishment in the schools has a long history in case law (see Chapter 10).

There are 51 court systems in the United States; the federal court system and a court system within each state (Fischer & Sorenson, 1996). The federal court system has three tiers or layers; most state court systems also have three tiers or layers. As Turnbull has observed, "It is a matter of great complexity why a case may be tried in one court, appealed or reviewed by another, and finally disposed of by yet another" (1990, p. 6). A brief discussion of the state and federal court systems may serve our purpose here.

State court systems vary in organization and complexity. Cases filed in the lowest court may be appealed to an intermediate-level court, if a state has them. Decisions may then be appealed to the supreme court of the state, the "court of last resort" (Reutter, 1994). The U.S. Supreme Court may review cases from a state court if a question of federal law is involved.

Within the federal system, at the lowest level are the trial courts, called district courts. There are nearly 100 federal district courts. At the intermediate level there are 11 numbered federal circuits or geographical areas and the District of Columbia. Each court at this level is called a Circuit Court of Appeals. The highest court in the federal system is the U.S. Supreme Court. A person who loses a case in a federal court of appeals or the highest state court may submit a written petition requesting the Supreme Court to review the case. The Court agrees to review a case by granting a *writ of certiorari* (an order calling up a case from a lower court for review). However, the Supreme Court selects only those cases it considers most important to review, and consequently only a small percentage of the requests for review are granted.

The federal court system decides both civil and criminal cases. Federal courts rule only on cases that involve federal constitutional or statutory law, or cases that involve parties from two different states. The U.S. Supreme Court has the final authority in interpreting the U.S. Constitution and federal statutes. State courts also decide both civil and criminal cases. State courts rule on cases involving state constitutional and statutory law, but also may rule on cases involving the federal constitution and statutory laws.

The role of the courts is to resolve disputes involving citizens, organizations, and the government. Courts also decide the guilt or innocence of those accused of crimes. In education, most disputes are decided in civil court.

Courts decide conflicts by applying law to a given set of facts and interpreting the meaning of the law in that context (Turnbull, 1990). It is the function of courts to say what the Constitution or statute means in a given case, set forth the findings of fact that the interpretation is based on, and enter an order commanding the parties in the case to take certain action (or, if the case is on appeal, the judge may enter an order for another court to take action) (Turnbull, 1990). If there is no *codified* law (no Constitutional or statutory provision) found controlling in a case, then the court is likely to rely on common law (legal precedents) in rendering a decision (Hubsch, 1989).

In reading about court rulings, it is important to remember that decisions of the U.S. Supreme Court are binding throughout the country. The decisions of the lower federal courts are binding only within their jurisdictions, and the decisions of state courts are binding only within the state (Fischer & Sorenson, 1996).

SUMMARY

We have explored the three basic sources of public school law within the American legal system, namely the Constitution, statutes and regulations, and case law. It is evident from the material presented that the federal courts and legislature have had a powerful impact on public schools, particularly since *Brown,* in 1954. But, as Hubsch (1989) points out, there are limits to the role the federal government can play in fostering quality public education in our nation's schools. Court decisions spanning more than 40 years have sent a clear message that our schools must provide equal educational opportunities for all children. Equal educational opportunity for all children is not the same as a quality education for all, however (Hubsch, 1989). By providing grants and resources, the federal government can encourage quality educational programs, but the bulk of the responsibility for ensuring a quality education for all children must be carried at the state and local levels. Individual teachers, principals, and school psychologists must accept and share in this responsibility.

CREDENTIALING OF SCHOOL PSYCHOLOGISTS

As part of the obligation to protect the health and welfare of their citizens, state governments enact laws to regulate the provision of psychological services. State credentialing of professionals, such as school psychologists, protects the consumer by requiring individuals to hold specified qualifications before they are granted a legal sanction to practice within the state. There are generally two types of legislation that regulate school psychologists. Title acts limit who may use the title *school psychologist.* These laws, or regulations, are typically referred to as *certification* acts (Pryzwansky, 1993). In contrast, a *licensing* act "restricts service or practice activity to a group of professionals holding a certain title, or protects professionals in regard to the legitimacy of their offering particular services" (Pryzwansky, 1993, p. 221).

Credentialing for School-Based Practice

Certification laws typically regulate public school professionals. In most states, the state department of education (SDE) certifies school psychologists for practice in the school setting. An SDE certificate is the credential most commonly held by school psychology practitioners (Fagan & Wise, 1994).

The credentialing of school psychologists for school-based practice is a state matter. Although there are commonalities in credentialing standards across states, equivalence of requirements between states is the exception rather than the rule. Furthermore, different states may use differing titles or designations (e.g., school psychologist, school diagnostician), and some states have more than one level of certification, depending on level of graduate preparation and years of experience.

Brown (1979) identified four models of certification: course-based, area-based, competency-based, and program approval. *Course- and area-based certification* require the reading of transcripts by officials at the state certifying agency to determine whether the applicant has taken the required set of courses or had training in the required areas. *Competency-based certification* requires the applicant to demonstrate or give evidence of competence on tasks described by the state certification standards. The *program approval* process means that applicants who have the recommendation from an approved state training program will be certified by the state agency. The procedure used may be different for applicants from in-state training programs and those from out-of-state.

Because certification and licensure are controlled at the state level, students and practitioners need to contact the state in which they wish to practice for up-to-date information about credentialing. The *Handbook of Certification and Licensure Requirements for School Psychologists* may be a helpful resource (Curtis, Hunley, & Prus, 1995). Also, see Prus, Draper, Curtis, and Hunley (1995) for a summary of credentialing requirements.

Credentialing for Private Practice

Licensure acts typically regulate the private practice of psychology. Licenses are usually issued by a state board of psychology or psychological examiners (Prus, White, & Pendleton, 1987). In some states, there is only one board that issues a generic license to practice psychology. In other states, the board that licenses school psychologists is different from that licensing other psychologists. School psychology licensure also may be handled by a subdivision of a more general licensing board. Currently about 11 states license school psychologists for private practice at the subdoctoral level. (See Prus & Mittelmeier [1995] for a summary of licensure requirements.)

Nonpractice Credentials

In addition to state credentials to practice, there also are nonpractice credentials that recognize quality of professional preparation or practice (Fagan & Wise, 1994). The National School Psychology Certification System allows school psychologists who complete training consistent with NASP standards, achieve a passing score on the National School Psychology Examination, and meet continuing education requirements, to be identified as a Nationally Certified School Psychologist or NCSP. It is important to recognize that the NCSP title alone does not authorize a school psychologist to render services (Fagan & Wise, 1994); practitioners must hold a valid certificate or license in the state where they wish to practice. However, 7 states have adopted the NCSP or its equivalent for certification, 11 states require the National School Psychology Examination as part of their certification process, and at least 1 state recognizes the NCSP credential for the independent practice of school psychology (Pryzwansky, 1993).[5]

CONCLUDING COMMENTS

This chapter has provided a brief overview of the sources of public school law and the credentialing of school psychologists. Legal aspects of the delivery of psychological services in the schools will be dealt with in more detail in the chapters ahead. School psychologists are obligated to be familiar with law pertinent to the delivery of psychological services in the schools and to keep abreast of changes in law affecting school psychology practices.

---

[5] Additional information about the National Certified School Psychologist system can be obtained from NASP, 4340 East West Highway, Suite 402, Bethesda, MD 20814.

STUDY AND DISCUSSION

Questions for Chapter 2

1. What are the three sources of public school law within the American legal system?
2. Why was the Bill of Rights passed? What is the significance of the 10th amendment with regard to public education? Do citizens have a right to a public education under the U.S. Constitution?
3. Identify the two aspects of the 14th amendment that have been extremely important in court decisions regarding public schools.
4. What was the significance of the Supreme Court decision in *Tinker v. Des Moines Independent School District?*
5. If public education is a duty of the states, how does the U.S. Congress have the power to shape educational policy and practices? Cite two examples of federal education legislation and two examples of federal antidiscrimination legislation.
6. What is case law and why is it important?

ACTIVITIES

1. The majority of public school statutory law is enacted at the state level. School psychologists must become familiar with the laws pertinent to the delivery of school psychological services in the state where they are employed. Obtain a copy of the rules governing special education and school psychological services in the state where you live. State special education rules can typically be obtained by contacting the state government's lead agency for education.

2. Visit a nearby law library or law collection. Can you locate your state school code? IDEA? The *Federal Register?* Supreme Court decisions?

3. What are the school psychologist certification requirements in the state where you plan to work?

Chapter 3

PRIVACY, INFORMED CONSENT, CONFIDENTIALITY, AND RECORD KEEPING

This chapter explores four important ethical-legal concepts in the delivery of psychological services in the schools: privacy, informed consent, confidentiality, and privileged communication. School record keeping is also discussed. The chapter closes with a discussion of parent access to test protocols and the use of computers in record keeping.

PRIVACY

The term *privacy* meshes complicated concepts from case law, statutory law, and professional ethics. We will first briefly explore privacy as a legal concept and then discuss respect for privacy as an ethical mandate.

Privacy and Law

Case Law

As noted in Chapter 2, "right to privacy" is not expressly mentioned in the Constitution (Bersoff & Hofer, 1990). However, a number of privacy rights have been carved out of the First Amendment concept of liberty, the Fifth Amendment protections against self-incrimination, Ninth Amendment reservation of rights to the people, and Fourth Amendment prohibition against unreasonable search and seizure (Hummel, Talbutt, & Alexander, 1985).

Court decisions regarding the rights of students have recognized the need to balance the interest of the state (school) in fulfilling its duty to maintain order, ensure pupil safety, and educate children, and the personal freedoms and rights generally afforded citizens. Thus, in the school setting, students do not have the full range of privacy rights afforded adult citizens. Two court cases that addressed the issue of the privacy rights of students are *Merriken v. Cressman* (1973) and *New Jersey v. T.L.O.* (1985).

In *Merriken v. Cressman* (1973), a case decided in federal district court, the court ruled that parents of schoolchildren have a right to be free from invasion of family privacy by the school. However, this right to privacy was recognized for the parents only; the court did not recognize an independent student right to privacy in the schools. (This case is discussed further in Chapter 9.)

In *New Jersey v. T.L.O.* (1985), the Supreme Court held that students have the Fourth Amendment right to be free from unreasonable search and seizure in the schools. The case concerned whether school officials had the right to search a student's purse. The Court ruled that the actions of school officials are actions by the state, and school officials cannot claim immunity from Fourth Amendment provisions regarding search and seizure under the doctrine *in loco parentis* (in the place of the parent) (Zirkel & Reichner, 1986).

While holding that students have a legitimate expectation of privacy rights with regard to their person and possessions in school, the Court upheld the standard of "reasonable suspicion" as opposed to "probable cause" for conducting searches, thus giving more latitude in the case of students than provided adults by the Fourth Amendment. The Court also noted that search must not be "excessively intrusive in light of the age and gender of the pupil and the nature of the infraction" (*T.L.O.*, 1985, p. 342). The more personal the search (i.e., the closer the search comes to the body), the more serious the reasons the school must have for conducting the search. Interested readers may wish to consult Sanchez (1992) for a review of recent court cases addressing the meaning of "reasonable suspicion" and the scope of constitutionally valid school searches.

Statutory Law

The Protection of Pupil Rights (PPRA) or "Hatch Amendment" (part of P. L. 95-561) and the Family Educational Rights and Privacy Act of 1974 or FERPA (P. L. 93-380) now provide some statutory protection for the privacy rights of pupils and their parents. The rules and regulations implementing PPRA and FERPA are found in 34 *Code of Federal Regulations* (C.F.R.) Subtitle A, Sections 98 and 99, respectively. The requirements of FERPA are discussed in the portion of this chapter devoted to record keeping.

The Protection of Pupil Rights (PPRA) Amendment was enacted in 1978 to provide protection from school actions that intrude on pupil or family privacy. PPRA was amended in 1994 by the Goals 2000: Educate America Act. The privacy protections of PPRA apply only to programs receiving funding from the U.S. Department of Education (DOE). However, the law is seen as reflecting current legal opinion of appropriate school conduct in safeguarding pupil and family privacy. In accordance with PPRA, no student may be required to submit without prior consent to a survey, analysis, or evaluation funded by DOE that reveals information concerning one or more of the following: (1) political affiliations; (2) mental and psychological problems potentially embarrassing to the student or his or her family; (3) sex behavior and attitudes; (4) illegal, antisocial, self-incriminating and demeaning behavior; (5) critical appraisal of other individuals with whom the student has close family relationships; (6) legally recognized privileged and analogous relationships; or (7) income, other than required by law to determine eligibility for participation in a program or for receiving financial assistance under a program. The pre-1994 regulations specifically required parent consent for psychological examination, testing, or treatment that reveals personal information. *Prior consent* was defined as the prior consent of the student, if the student is an adult or emancipated minor; or prior written consent of the parent or guardian, if the student is an unemancipated minor (34 C.F.R. § 98.4). Readers should consult the *Federal Register* for new PPRA regulations (expected late 1997).

If an adult or emancipated student, or the parent of a minor child, feels they have been affected by a violation of PPRP, they may file a complaint in writing with the U.S. Department of Education (DOE). DOE investigates complaints and may terminate federal funds if a school refuses to comply with the Act within a specified time period (34 C.F.R. § 98.5).

Privacy as an Ethical Issue

Privacy is also an ethical issue. Siegel has defined privacy as "the freedom of individuals to choose for themselves the time and the circumstances under which and the extent to which their beliefs, behaviors, and opinions are to be shared or withheld from others" (1979, p. 251).

Consistent with the general principle of respect for the dignity of persons and the valuing of autonomy, *psychologists respect the client's right to self-determine the circumstances under which they disclose private information.* Furthermore, every effort is made to minimize intrusions on privacy (*EP* Principle D, 5.03; also NASP-PPR, III, B, #1). Psychologists do not seek or store personal information about pupils, parents, teachers, or others that is not needed in the provision of services.

INFORMED CONSENT FOR PSYCHOLOGICAL SERVICES

Privacy and Informed Consent

Ethical codes and law are consistent in respecting the individual's right to self-determine whether to share private thoughts, behaviors, and beliefs with others. In ethics and law, the requirement for informed consent grew out of deep-rooted notions of the importance of individual privacy. As Bersoff notes, "It is now universally agreed, though not always honored in practice, *that human beings must give their informed consent prior to any significant intrusion of their person or privacy*" (italics added, 1983, p. 150).

In the school setting, the Hatch Amendment (PPRA) suggests parent consent (or the consent of an adult student) is needed for school actions that may result in a significant intrusion on personal or family privacy beyond what might be expected in the course of ordinary classroom and school activities (Corrao & Melton, 1988; also see Bersoff, 1983; DeMers & Bersoff, 1985). *Ethical codes, professional standards, and law show growing agreement that informed consent should be obtained prior to the provision of school psychological services.*

The Meaning of Informed Consent

Knowing, Competent, Voluntary

Case law and statutory regulations concur that the three key elements of informed consent are that it must be *knowing, competent,* and *voluntary* (Bersoff & Hofer, 1990; Weithorn, 1983). *Knowing* means that the individual giving consent must have a clear understanding of what it is they are consenting to. The person seeking consent must make a good faith effort to disclose enough information to the person from whom consent is sought that they can make an *informed choice* (Bersoff & Hofer, 1990).

In seeking consent for the provision of psychological services, the practitioner is obligated to provide information about the nature and scope of services offered, assessment-treatment goals and procedures, the expected duration of services, any foreseeable risks or discomforts for the student/client (including any risks of psychological or physical harm), the cost of the services to the parent or student (if any), the benefits that can reasonably be expected, the possible consequences/risks of not receiving treatment/services, and information about alternative treatments/services that may be beneficial. This information must be provided in language (or other mode of communication) understandable to the person giving consent

(Weithorn, 1983). It also is appropriate to discuss the extent to which confidentiality of information will be maintained as part of the informed consent procedures.

The individual giving consent must also be *legally competent* to give consent. As Bersoff and Hofer (1990) have observed, the law presumes that every adult is competent to consent, unless they have been judged incompetent following a full hearing conducted by an impartial factfinder. However, in the legal system, children are generally presumed to be incompetent and not capable of making legally binding decisions (Bersoff, 1983). Consequently, in the school setting, informed consent typically is sought from the parent or guardian of a minor child, or from the student if an adult.

The third element of informed consent is that it must be voluntary. Consent must be "obtained in the absence of coercion, duress, misrepresentation, or undue inducement. In short, the person giving consent must do so freely" (Bersoff & Hofer, 1990, p. 951).

Specific ethical and legal requirements for informed consent vary across different situations within the school setting. Informed consent for release of school records is discussed in this chapter, and special consent issues are addressed in Chapter 4 on psychoeducational assessment, Chapter 7 on counseling and therapeutic intervention, and Chapter 9 on participation in research.

The Consent of Minors for Psychological Services

Consent of Minors as a Legal Issue

As noted above, legally, in the school setting, informed consent or permission for psychological services rests with the parent of a minor child. Legislators and the courts have generally presumed that minors are not developmentally competent to consent to (or refuse) psychological assessment or treatment on their own. The courts have viewed parents as typically acting in their children's best interests and have reasoned that allowing minors a right to consent to (or refuse) services/treatment independent of parental wishes might be disruptive to the parent–child relationship, and interfere with effective treatment programs (*Parham v. J.R.*, 1979).

Parham (1979) was an important case regarding the competence of minors to participate in decisions affecting their own welfare. In *Parham,* the Supreme Court upheld a Georgia statute allowing parents to commit a minor child to a mental institution for treatment (with the approval of a physician) in the absence of a formal or quasi-formal hearing to safeguard the child from arbitrary commitment. Although the Court recognized that children have an interest in being free from misdiagnosis and unnecessary confinement, the Court viewed minors as incompetent to make decisions concerning their own need for treatment. (See Walding, 1990, for additional discussion.)

It should be noted, however, that minors are granted access to psychological or medical treatment without parental consent in emergency situations, and most states allow minors access to treatment independent of parent notice or consent for certain health-related conditions (e.g., venereal disease, alcohol, or drug abuse).

Consent of Minors as an Ethical Issue

Although minors are not generally seen as legally competent to consent autonomously to (or refuse) psychological services in the schools, practitioners are ethically obligated to respect the dignity, autonomy, and self-determination of their student/clients.

We find the notion of developmentally appropriate rights to self-determination and autonomy suggested in "A Canadian Code of Ethics" (CPA, 1991) more satisfactory than an absolute stance that children always (or never) be afforded the choice to accept or refuse psychological services. In the delivery of psychological services to children, it is at times necessary to balance the child's rights to privacy and self-determination against concerns for the welfare of the child (CPA, 1991). As suggested in the Canadian code, in some situations it may be ethical to proceed without the child's explicit consent if the service is considered to be of direct benefit to the child. We concur with Corrao and Melton (1988) that it is disrespectful to solicit consent from the child if refusal will not be honored.

Minors and Capacity to Consent: A Research Perspective

Findings from cognitive-developmental research suggest that many children have a greater competence to consent and participate effectively in treatment/intervention decisions than suggested in law. The research literature on children's competence to consent in treatment situations is summarized next.

However, first, we will consider current tests or standards of competency that have been identified in law and professional practice. The following tests of competency to consent have been applied to psychological treatment situations:

1. The simple expression of a preference relative to alternative treatment choices;
2. The choice is seen as one a "reasonable" person might make;

3. A logical or rational decision-making process was followed; and
4. The person giving consent demonstrates understanding (factual or abstract) of the situation, choice made, and probable consequences (adapted from Weithorn, 1983, pp. 244–245).

Evidence of a preference is probably the most lenient standard; evidence of understanding, the most stringent (Weithorn, 1983).

Current research evidence suggests that a pupil's capacity to consent and effectively participate in treatment/intervention decisions depends on a number of factors including cognitive and personal-social development and functioning, motivation to participate, prior experiences with decision making, and the complexity of the situation and choices under consideration (Melton, Koocher, & Saks, 1983).

Preschoolers have limited language and reasoning abilities. However, they may be able to express preferences when choices are presented in concrete, here-and-now terms (Ferguson, 1978). Although children in middle childhood (ages 6–11) have not attained adult reasoning capabilities, research suggests they are typically able to make sensible treatment choices (Weithorn, 1983), and parents and professionals have judged the participation of children this age in treatment decisions to be effective (Taylor, Adelman, & Kaser-Boyd, 1985).

The years between ages 11 and 14 are seen as transitional ones with much individual variation in cognitive development and the ability to make truly voluntary choices. Pupils in this age range, like younger children, may defer to authority in decisions, or they may make choices based on anti-authority feelings. Minors age 14 and older typically have reasoning capabilities similar to adults, and many are capable of participating in treatment decisions as effectively as adults (Grisso & Vierling, 1978). Cooper (1984) proposes the use of a written therapist-child agreement as a strategy for involving minors ages 9 and older in treatment decisions.

Research findings not only suggest that minors have greater capacity to consent and participate in treatment decisions than generally recognized in law, but that a child's participation in intervention decisions may lead to enhanced motivation for treatment, an increased sense of personal responsibility for self-care, greater treatment compliance, and reduced rates of early treatment termination (Holmes & Urie, 1975; Kaser-Boyd, Adelman, & Taylor, 1985; Weithorn, 1983). Thus, Weithorn (1983) suggests practitioners permit and encourage student/client involvement in decision making within the parameters of the law and the child's capacity to participate. However, psychologists must guard against overwhelming children with choices they do not wish to make for themselves.

In sum, the decision to allow a minor child the opportunity to choose (or refuse) psychological services and participate in treatment decisions involves a consideration of law, ethical issues (e.g., self-determination versus welfare of the client), the child's competence to make choices, and the likely consequences of affording choices (e.g., enhanced treatment outcomes versus choice to refuse treatment).

It also is important to distinguish between the right to consent to (or refuse) services, and *the right to be informed about the services offered* (E. Fleming & D. Fleming, 1987). Practitioners have an ethical obligation to inform student/clients of the scope and nature of psychological services whether or not children are given a choice about participating (NASP-PPE, III, B, #2).

Informed Consent v. Notice

Case 3–1

Wanda Rose was concerned about the children in her elementary school experiencing adjustment difficulties related to parent separation and divorce. She decided to form counseling groups for children experiencing parent separation and those from single-parent homes. She asked teachers to identify pupils who might benefit from the group counseling, and then sent letters home with the children, notifying parents their child would be seen for group counseling sessions. She asked parents to contact her if further information about the counseling was desired.

Informed consent differs from *notice.* The term notice means that the school supplies information about impending actions. *Consent* requires "*affirmative permission* before actions can be taken" (Bersoff & Hofer, 1990, p. 950). Wanda's letter to parents is not sufficient; it does not meet the requirement of informed consent for services. If parents do not receive the letter, they have no opportunity to deny consent (J. H. Correll in Canter, 1989). Wanda also has failed to fulfill her ethical obligation to seek direct parent contact prior to the provision of nonemergency counseling services (NASP-PPE, III, C, #2; also see Chapter 7).

In seeking informed consent from the parents, Wanda is obligated to describe the nature, scope, and goals of the counseling sessions, their expected duration, any foreseeable risks or discomforts for the student/client (e.g., loss of pupil and family privacy), any cost to parent or student (e.g., loss of classroom instructional time), any benefits that can reasonably be expected (e.g., the possibility of enhanced adjustment to parent separation), alternative services available, and the likely consequences of not receiving services. After consideration of the ethical issues involved and the possible consequences of her decision, Wanda also must decide whether to offer each child the opportunity to make an informed choice about participating (or not participating) in the counseling groups.

Blanket Consent Practitioners also should be aware that blanket consent procedures (i.e., the psychologist requests parental consent to provide services "as needed") do not meet the requirements for informed consent. Blanket consent is not permissible because parents are not fully informed of the specific nature of the services to be provided (J. H. Correll in Canter, 1989).

CONFIDENTIALITY

Confidentiality is primarily a matter of professional ethics. Confidentiality has been described as "an ethical decision not to reveal what is learned in the professional relationship" (Hummel et al., 1985, p. 54). Siegel describes confidentiality as "an explicit promise or contract to reveal nothing about an individual except under conditions agreed to by the source or subject" (1979, p. 251). Although primarily a matter of professional ethics, in some states psychologists can be held civilly liable under state law for impermissible breach of client confidentiality (Swoboda, Elwork, Sales, & Levine, 1978).

APA's ethical code states, "Psychologists have a primary obligation and take reasonable precautions to respect the confidentiality rights of those with whom they work or consult, recognizing that confidentiality may be established by law, institutional rules, or professional or scientific relationships" (*EP* 5.02; also NASP-PPE, III, A, #9, #10, #11). In situations where confidentiality is promised or implied, psychologists ensure that the release of confidential information is based on the informed consent of the client. However, it is ethically permissible to disclose confidential information in unusual situations involving danger to the client or others.

The interpretation of the principle of confidentiality as it relates to the delivery of psychological services in the school setting is a complicated matter. However, one clear guideline emerges from the literature on confidentiality in the school setting. School psychologists must define the parameters of confidentiality at the onset of offering services (Davis & Sandoval, 1982; Gallessich, 1982; also *EP,* 5.01; NASP-PPE, III, A, #11). The parameters of the promise of confidentiality will vary depending on the nature of the services offered. In the paragraphs that follow, we discuss confidentiality and its limits in providing direct services to the student, services that involve collaboration with the teacher or parent, and consultative services to the teacher.

Confidentiality and Direct Service to the Student

For our purposes, the provision of "direct services to the student" means that the practitioner works with the student directly (e.g., individual counseling) and there is little or no collaboration with others. The provision of direct services to the student is similar to the therapist–client relationship in nonschool settings.

Consistent with the principle of integrity in professional relationships, the psychologist explains important aspects of their professional relationship in a manner that is understood by the student at the onset of offering services (NASP-PPE, III, B, #2; also *EP* 5.01). The "initial interview with any client . . . should include a direct and candid discussion of the limits that may exist with respect to any confidences communicated in the relationship" (Keith-Spiegel & Koocher, 1985, pp. 57–58; also *EP* 5.01; NASP-PPE, III, A, #11).[1]

Much has been written about the importance of confidentiality for building and maintaining the trust essential to a helping relationship (Siegel, 1979; Watson & Levine, 1989). However, as Taylor and Adelman (1989) have observed, the promise of confidentiality can also limit the psychologist's ability to help when the client is a minor child. Consequently, school psychologists must weigh a number of factors in deciding the boundaries of a promise of confidentiality (e.g., age and maturity of the student/client, self-referral or referral by others, reason for referral). Whatever the parameters, the circumstances under which the psychologist might share confidences with others must be clear.

Taylor and Adelman (1989) provide suggestions as to how to discuss confidentiality with minors in developmentally appropriate language. Findings from a study by Muehleman, Pickens, and Robinson (1985) suggest that discussion of the limits of confidentiality with clients does not limit self-disclosure if self-disclosure is verbally encouraged. However, as Taube and

[1] It is generally not necessary to discuss confidentiality with preschool-age student/clients. Preschool children lack cognitive awareness that their own thoughts and feelings differ from those of the people around them, and consequently discussions of confidentiality have little meaning for this age group.

Elwork (1990) point out, the impact of discussions of confidentiality on client disclosure is likely to depend on client characteristics and circumstances.

In the provision of direct services to the student, there are three situations in which the school psychologist is obligated to share confidential student/client disclosures with others (Hummel et al., 1985). First, when the student requests it. Second, as noted previously, confidential information may be disclosed when there is a situation involving danger to the student or others. Situations involving danger are discussed later under "duty to protect." Third, it may be necessary for the psychologist to disclose confidential information when there is a legal obligation to testify in a court of law. This is discussed under "privileged communication."

If it becomes apparent in working with a student/client that confidentiality must be broken, the decision to divulge information should be discussed with the student. Taylor and Adelman (1989) suggest three steps:

1. Explaining to the pupil the reason for disclosure,
2. Exploring with the pupil the likely repercussions in and outside the student–psychologist relationship, and
3. Discussing with the pupil how to proceed in a manner that will minimize negative consequences and maximize potential benefits.

Duty to Protect

Case 3–2

Prosenjit Poddar, a foreign student from India attending Berkeley, was in psychotherapy with a psychologist at the university's health center. The psychologist recognized that Poddar was quite dangerous, based in part on his pathological attachment to Tatiana Tarasoff, his ex-girlfriend, toward whom he made some threats. After consultation with his supervisor, the psychologist notified the campus police that Poddar was dangerous and should be committed. The police visited Poddar, who denied he had any intentions of harming Tarasoff. Poddar subsequently refused to return for therapy and two months later killed Tarasoff. Tarasoff's parents brought suit against the Regents, the student health center staff members involved, and the campus police. Ultimately the California Supreme Court ruled twice on the case.

Case 3–2 *(Continued)*

*The 1974 ruling held that the therapists had a duty to warn Tarasoff. The court held that "public policy favoring protection of the confidential character of patient–psychotherapist relationships must yield in instances in which disclosure is essential to avert danger to others; the protective privilege ends where the public peril begins" (*Tarasoff v. Regents of California, *1974, p. 566).*

*The second ruling, in 1976, held that a therapist has a "duty to exercise reasonable care to protect the foreseeable victim" from harm (*Tarasoff v. Regents of California, *1976, p. 345).*

The *Tarasoff I* court decision triggered a lengthy debate between APA psychologists who asserted that confidentiality is absolute and can be broken under no circumstances, and those who insisted that limits to confidentiality be built into APA's ethical code. The 1981 revision of APA's *Ethical Principles of Psychologists* included the statement that psychologists reveal confidential information to others "only with the consent of the person or the person's legal representative, *except in those unusual circumstances where not to do so would result in clear danger to the person or others*" [italics added]. The current code states that "Psychologists disclose confidential information without the consent of the individual only as mandated by law, or where permitted by law for a valid purpose, such as . . . to protect the patient or client or others from harm . . ." (*EP* 5.05; also NASP-PPE, III, A, #9). Psychologists refer to this obligation to breach confidentiality to ensure the safety of the client or others as the *duty to warn* (Tarasoff I) or, more generally, a *duty to protect* (Tarasoff II).

Following the Tarasoff decisions, a number of states enacted laws requiring psychologists to make reasonable efforts to warn potential victims of violent clients, and in some states, appropriate law enforcement agencies must be notified as well. There also have been a number of additional court rulings related to Tarasoff and the duty to protect (Waldo & Malley, 1992).

Although direct service to the student is in many ways analogous to the therapist–client relationship in nonschool settings, there are some important differences. Schools have a strong obligation to protect and safeguard the welfare of students under their supervision. Furthermore, most students are minors. Consequently, in the school setting, student confidences may need to be disclosed to others in situations involving dangerous students, potential student suicide or other self-injurious behavior, student substance abuse, and suspected child abuse. The ethical-legal responsibilities of the school psychologist in situations involving a duty to protect are discussed in Chapter 7.

Collaboration and Confidentiality

As noted earlier, school psychologists may provide direct services to the student/client. However, they typically work in collaboration with teachers, parents, and others to assist the student/client, a situation that complicates the translation of the principle of confidentiality into appropriate action. In collaboration, the individuals involved carry joint responsibility for assisting the student (Hansen, Himes, & Meier, 1990). Thus, if the psychologist is working in collaboration with the teacher and/or parent in assisting the student, information will most likely be shared by those involved in the collaborative effort.

At the onset of offering services, the psychologist needs a clear prior agreement about confidentiality and its limits among those involved in the collaborative effort. The student is informed of those who will receive information regarding the services and the type of information they will receive (NASP-PPE, III, A, #4, #11, B, #2).

In interactions with the parent, practitioners discuss confidentiality and its limits (NASP-PPE, III, A, #9), and parent and student rights regarding "creation, modification, storage, and disposal of confidential materials that will result from the provision of school psychological services" (NASP-PPE, III, C, #6). Teachers and other staff involved in the collaborative effort also need a clear understanding of the parameters of confidentiality.

If information received in a confidential situation is subsequently disclosed in order to assist the teacher or parent in meeting the needs of a student, it is recommended that *only generalizations,* not specific confidences are shared (Davis & Sandoval, 1982; also NASP-PPE, III, A, #10). Furthermore, generalizations are shared with others involved in the collaborative effort *only* if those generalizations "are essential to the understanding and resolution" of the student's difficulties (Davis & Sandoval, 1982, p. 548). Similarly, Zingaro (1983) suggests that the psychologist share insights about pupils with others in terms of what they can do to help the child.

In sum, information obtained in a professional relationship and subsequently shared with others is discussed only for professional purposes, and only with persons clearly concerned with the situation (*EP* 5.03). This is often called the "need-to-know" principle.

Case 3–3

Carrie Johnson is exhausted. She just completed another parent conference with Mrs. Farwell. Mrs. Farwell's daughter, Amy, age 3, was diagnosed as having a rare genetic disorder characterized by mild-to-moderate mental retardation. After the diagnosis was made over a year ago, Mr. Farwell soon focused his attention on how to best help his daughter, but Mrs. Farwell has not yet been able to accept her daughter's diagnosis. She has spent hundreds of dollars over the past year shopping for a different diagnosis and seeking miracle cures. She continues to refuse Carrie's referrals for family counseling and involvement with a support group for parents of children with disabilities. Although she finally acquiesced to Amy's special education placement, she continues to insist that Amy will "grow out of it" and doesn't seem to hear Carrie's careful explanations of Amy's abilities, limitations, and needs. Today Carrie learned that Mr. and Mrs. Farwell have separated, and that Amy's older siblings are showing many adjustment problems at home and in school. She enters the teacher's lounge for a cup of coffee and is greeted by Amy's teacher who asks, "How's it going with the Farwells?" What, if anything, should Carrie disclose?

In Case 3–3, Carrie may wish to discuss the parent conference with Amy's teacher in a private setting, but she must take care not to disclose specific information conveyed during her conference with Mrs. Farwell. For example, Amy's teacher, in working with Mrs. Farwell, may need to know about her difficulty in accepting Amy's disabilities. She does not need to know about Mrs. Farwell's specific disclosures (e.g., the details of her search for a miracle cure).

As Davis and Sandoval (1982) note, sometimes there are social pressures to "gossip," particularly in the teacher's lounge or lunchroom, in order to be accepted as part of the school staff. Resisting the temptation to "join in" when teachers and other staff share their frustrations about pupils, parents, and school life may be particularly difficult for Carrie because of her professional isolation in a rural area. However, in order to safeguard confidential disclosures and maintain teacher trust in her as a professional, Carrie must avoid discussing her knowledge of pupils, parents, or school staff in casual conversations with others.

Confidentiality and Consultation

Maintaining confidentiality can be particularly problematic for practitioners when the teacher is the primary recipient of services. In consultation with the teacher, the parameters of confidentiality should be discussed at the onset of the delivery of services, and, consistent with the notion of integrity in professional relationships, the psychologist should have a clear prior agreement about those parameters with others in the school setting (e.g., principal).

In general, in consultation with the teacher, the guarantees of client confidentiality apply to the consultant–consultee relationship. All that is said between the psychologist and teacher must be kept confidential by the psychologist, particularly when the psychologist is confronted by requests for information about the teacher from administrators (Davis & Sandoval, 1982). As noted in Chapter 1, violation of confidentiality in consultation with teachers is likely to result in a loss of trust in the psychologist, and impair his or her ability to work with the consultee and other staff.

PRIVILEGED COMMUNICATION

School psychologists must be familiar with the term *privileged communication.* Privileged communication is a legal term that refers to "the right of a person in a 'special relationship' to prevent the disclosure in legal proceedings of information given in confidence in the special relationship" (Fischer & Sorenson, 1996, p. 18).

Under English law, the courts first began to recognize a duty for witnesses to testify in judicial proceedings over 400 years ago. The rule that witnesses can be compelled to testify is based on the principle that the administration of justice benefits all members of society, and the determination of justice requires full access to relevant information (Shah, 1969). It is now well established that courts should have broad access to evidence to ensure fair and just decisions (Knapp & VandeCreek, 1985).

However, the need for information in the determination of justice at times conflicts with the need to safeguard the trust and privacy essential to special relationships, such as the relationship between attorney and client, and husband and wife. Historically, privileged communication applied only to the attorney–client relationship (Swoboda et al., 1978). Most jurisdictions now also recognize the communications between marital partners and clergy–penitent as having privileged communication status (Knapp & VandeCreek, 1985).

Many states have enacted legislation to expand privilege to include other special relationships such as between physician and patient, and psychologist and client. In a 1985 survey, Herlihy and Sheeley (1987) found 42 states granted privileged communication status to psychologists. Thus, privilege status for psychologists, where it exists, "is granted by statutes, protects the client from having his/her communications revealed in a judicial setting without explicit permission, and is vested in the client by legislative authority" (Siegel, 1979, p. 251).

Privileged communication refers to the right of the *client* (the parent or guardian of a minor child) to prevent disclosure of confidential information in a legal proceeding. The client may voluntarily waive privilege, and then the psychologist must provide the relevant testimony. As Knapp and VandeCreek (1985) note, the waiver belongs to the client, and the psychologist has no independent right to invoke privilege against the client's wishes.

Practitioners need to consult state laws to determine whether their state grants privileged communication to school psychologists. There are several key questions to ask:

1. Does the state in which you are employed have a specific law granting privileged communication to school psychologists?
2. Does the law grant privilege in civil cases, criminal cases, or both?
3. Does the law list exceptions such as child abuse matters?
4. Does the law state that the court may waive the privilege when it deems the professional's testimony necessary for fairness and justice? (adapted from Hummel et al., 1985, p. 57).

In the absence of state legislation specifically granting privilege to psychologists, practitioners probably can be required to testify in court (Hummel et al., 1985). Refusal to testify may result in the psychologist being held in contempt of court.

In a recent Supreme Court decision, *Jaffee v. Redmond* (1996), the Court held that communications between a licensed psychotherapist (a master's level social worker) and her client are privileged and do not have to be disclosed in federal court cases. Most lawsuits are tried in state courts. However, the *Jaffee* decision may give impetus to the passage of strengthened state privileged communication statutes for mental health professionals (Remley, Herlihy, & Herlihy, 1997).

Even in states that grant privileged communication status to school psychologists, the court may not view all disclosures to the psychologist as privileged, and, as noted above, many states allow the judge to waive privilege during a court proceeding to ensure justice. Psychologist–client privilege is typically waived in legal proceedings involving child abuse, danger to the client or others, court-ordered psychological examination of a client, and malpractice suits filed by a client against the psychologist.

In states where school psychologists are not specifically granted privileged communication status, the practitioner may ask that privilege be extended to them during a legal procedure. As Herlihy and Sheeley (1987) note, judges are reluctant to extend privilege to relationships not covered by existing law. However, school psychologists are most likely to be successful in being granted privilege status if they can demonstrate that their relationship with the client meets the following four requirements identified by Wigmore (1961):

1. The communication must have originated in the confidence that it would not be disclosed.
2. Confidentiality must be essential to full and satisfactory maintenance of the psychologist–client relationship.
3. The relationship must be one which, in the opinion of the community, should be sedulously fostered.
4. The injury to that relationship, caused by disclosure, would be greater than the benefit gained to the process of litigation.

Additional strategies for coping with subpoenas or compelled testimony regarding client records are outlined in Herlihy and Sheeley (1987) and the APA's Committee on Legal Issues (1996).

The issue of whether communication between the school psychologist and client has privileged communication status can raise difficult legal questions. School psychologists are urged to consult their school attorney when questions arise.

RECORD KEEPING IN THE SCHOOLS

In 1925, the National Education Association (NEA) recommended that schools maintain health, guidance, and psychological records on each student so that information would be available about the "whole child" along with the academic record (Schimmel & Fischer, 1977). Although these records were to be made available to governmental agents, employers, and other nonschool personnel, they were to be closed to parents and students.

In 1969, the Russell Sage Foundation convened a conference on the ethical and legal aspects of school record keeping, and many abuses of school records began to be identified:

1. Public elementary and secondary school officials released student records to law enforcement agencies, creditors, prospective employers, and so on, without obtaining permission from parents or students.
2. Parents and students typically had little knowledge or information concerning the contents of student records, or how those records were used. Parent and student access to records was usually limited to attendance and achievement records.
3. The secrecy with which the records were maintained made it difficult for parents or students to ascertain the accuracy of information contained in them. Because procedures for challenging the veracity of the information did not exist, an unverified allegation of misconduct could become part of a student's permanent record and passed on, unbeknownst to the student or parents, to potential employers, law enforcement agencies, and other educational institutions.
4. Few provisions existed for protecting school records from examination by unauthorized persons.
5. Formal procedures for regulating access to records by nonschool personnel did not exist in most schools (Russell Sage Foundation, 1970).

Family Educational Rights and Privacy Act

In 1974, the Family Educational Rights and Privacy Act (FERPA) was passed, sponsored by Senator James Buckley (sometimes referred to as the Buckley Amendment). This legislation specifically addresses the privacy of student records and access to those records. The Individuals with Disabilities Education Act outlines similar requirements for parent access to records.

Although FERPA was passed over 20 years ago, it still generates considerable confusion among teachers, school officials, and school psychologists. In the text that follows, FERPA is discussed under the following headings: (a) Educational Records Defined, (b) Right to Inspect and Review Records, (c) Right to Confidentiality of Records, (d) Right to Request Amendment of Records, and (e) Complaints. Practitioners also need to be familiar with their state's laws regarding confidentiality and disclosure of student records.

Educational Records Defined

Under FERPA, *educational records* are defined as any records maintained by the schools (or their agent) that are directly related to the student (34 C.F.R. § 99.3). There are a number of different types of records maintained by schools that are explicitly excluded from the definition under FERPA, for example, records maintained by a school-based law enforcement unit for the purpose of law enforcement; records of employees are excluded (records of a student who is employed as a result of student status are educational records and not exempt, however). In the case of an eligible student (one who is 18 or attending a post-secondary institution), education record does not apply to the records of a physician, psychiatrist, psychologist, or related professional, working in a treatment capacity with the student, unless that treatment is in the form of remedial education or is a part of the instructional program.

The Act also defines another category of record, called *directory information.* This includes information such as name, address, telephone, activities and sports participation, and degrees and awards received. As long as the school informs parents or eligible students about what kind of directory information they maintain and gives them an opportunity to object to the release of this information, the school may freely release such information (34 C.F.R. § 99.3).

The definition of education record under FERPA does not include:

> Records of instructional, supervisory, and administrative personnel and educational personnel ancillary to those persons that are kept in the sole possession of the maker of the records, and are not accessible or revealed to any other person except a temporary substitute for the maker of the record. . . . (34 C.F.R. § 99.3)

In a law review article on the genesis of FERPA, the authors identify several reasons for the exclusion of "private notes" from the definition of education records ("Federal Genesis of," 1975). First, they suggest that private notes were excluded from the definition of education records to "protect the privacy of individual teachers, counselors, and other institutional personnel" (p. 85). Second, they suggest that lawmakers did not intend to inhibit teachers or administrators from making useful observations and memoranda for their own use. And third, they point out that "notes and records of this type, even before enactment of FERPA, did not present the serious problems associated with normal education records" (p. 85).

A number of attorneys and psychologists have interpreted FERPA to suggest it is permissible for school psychologists to keep private or personal notes about their contacts with pupils (Martin, 1979; Slenkovich, 1988, March-a). One court ruling (discussed below) suggests raw test data and test protocols cannot be considered private notes.

School psychologists who keep private notes need to be aware of two cautions. First, any information about the child that is shared with other persons (except for a school psychologist's substitute) is no longer private and becomes part of the student's education record whether or not it is kept separately from the student's cumulative folder (1979, p. 122; also see *Parents Against Abuse in Schools v. Williamsport Area School District,* 1991). Second, a psychologist's personal notes can be subpoenaed (Slenkovich, 1988, March-a). In a court of law, the problem reverts to one of privilege.

Right to Inspect and Review Records

FERPA was developed to ensure appropriate access to school records by parents or eligible students. *Parent* is defined as a parent of a student and includes "a natural parent, a guardian, or an individual acting as a parent in the absence of a parent or guardian" (34 C.F.R. § 99.3). Parental separation, divorce, and custody do not affect the right to inspect records, unless there is a court order or legally binding document specifically revoking parental right to access records (34 C.F.R. § 99.4). In the absence of notification to the contrary, school personnel may assume that a noncustodial parent has access to the records of his or her child (see *Fay v. South Colonie Central School District,* 1986).

An *eligible student* is a student who is 18 years of age or older, or enrolled in a post-secondary school. When a student reaches the age of 18, the rights of the parent transfer to the student (34 C.F.R. § 99.5). However, parents maintain the right to inspect and review the files of a student age 18 or older as long as the student is a dependent as defined by federal tax law (34 C.F.R. § 99.32).

Under FERPA, schools must provide annual notice to parents and eligible students of their right to inspect, review, and request amendments of the student's education records (34 C.F.R. § 99.7). On request, the school must provide parents with a written copy of its procedures and policies for review and amendment of records, and a list of the types and the location of all education records (34 C.F.R. § 99.6).

When parents or eligible students make a request to inspect records, the school must comply with the request for access to records "within a reasonable period of time, but in no case more than 45 days after it has received the request." The school must respond to "reasonable requests for explanations and interpretations of the records." The school also must "give the parent or eligible student a copy of the records if failure to do so would effectively prevent the parent or student from exercising the right to inspect and review the records." The school may charge a fee for copies unless the fee effectively prevents parents or eligible students from exercising their right to inspect records. An eligible student also has the right to have his or her physician/psychologist treatment records reviewed on his or her behalf by an appropriate professional. The school may not destroy any records if there is an outstanding request to review them (34 C.F.R. § 99.10-99.11).

School psychologists occasionally receive reports from physicians or psychologists outside the school setting that include sensitive information about a student or the student's family (e.g., comments about a marital problem, parent drug or alcohol abuse). This may pose a dilemma for the practitioner who feels the report should not become part of the student's education record, yet it also includes some information about the student that is helpful in meeting educational needs. A strategy for handling this dilemma is to return the report to the sender with a request that the sender delete any private information not needed in the school setting.

Right to Confidentiality of Records

FERPA was designed in part to protect the privacy of students and their parents. The school may not disclose personally identifiable information from student education records without informed consent of the parent or eligible student, except for disclosures specifically authorized by the Act. When records are disclosed to specific persons or agencies at the request of the parent or an eligible student, the school must obtain the signed written consent of the parent or eligible student. The written consent must specify the records to be disclosed, state the purpose of the disclosure, and identify the party to whom the disclosure may be made (34 C.F.R. § 99.30).

Certain disclosures of education records are specifically authorized by FERPA and do not require the special permission of the parent or eligible student. The Act specifies that school personnel who have "legitimate educational interests" may have access to pupil records. Additionally, access is granted to officials of other schools upon notification by parents of a transfer of schools.

Certain governmental representatives also may have access for audit or regulation enforcement purposes, and other officials in health or safety emergencies, or when required by state laws. Also, organizations conducting appropriate research studies on behalf of the school may have access, as long as personally identifiable information concerning students or their families is destroyed when no longer needed. Schools may be required to release education records in compliance with a valid subpoena or judicial order. However, under FERPA, the school must notify parents before records are released in response to a subpoena or judicial order because the parents may be entitled to a hearing regarding the release (Johnson, 1993).

The school must maintain a record of disclosures, that is, a listing of the persons other than school officials who have been granted access to the student's records.

Right to Request Amendment of Records

There are essentially three bases for a parent or eligible student to request an amendment to records:

1. If the information is inaccurate,
2. If the information is misleading, or
3. If the information violates the privacy or other rights of the student.

The school may then agree and so amend the record, or disagree, and so advise the parent or student, and inform the parent or student of their right to a hearing on the matter.

The hearing is to be conducted by an individual who has no direct interest in the outcome, but it may be an official of the school. The parent or student may present any evidence they choose to, and be represented by any individual they choose. The school then makes a decision about whether to amend the record and must present written findings related to its decision. If it agrees with the parent or student, the record is then amended. If it disagrees, the parent or student may then place in the file a statement commenting on the record (34 C.F.R. § 99.20).

Complaints

Persons may file complaints about violations of FERPA with the U.S. Department of Education (DOE). Complaints are investigated by an office within DOE, and DOE may terminate federal funds to schools that do not comply with FERPA within a specified time period. Some federal courts have allowed parents to pursue Section 1983 lawsuits against school districts because of alleged FERPA violations (*Fay v. South Colonie Central School District,* 1986).

Summary

Schools must have a written policy consistent with FERPA regarding parent access to education records and confidentiality of records, and provide annual notice to parents and eligible students of their right to inspect records. School psychologists should be familiar with and abide by district policies and procedures.

Parental Access to Test Protocols

Another concern in the area of record keeping is that of parent access to test protocols. Psychological test protocols or answer sheets that contain personally identifiable information are part of the child's education records. Policy letters (FERPA Office dated December 2, 1986; Hehir dated October 25, 1993; Irvin dated January 9, 1979), legal opinion (Bersoff & Hofer, 1990; Martin, 1979), and at least one court ruling (*John K. and Mary K. v. Board of Education for School District #65, Cook County,* 1987) clearly suggest that test protocols cannot be considered as private notes.

In *John K. and Mary K.* (1987), parents sought access to their daughter's verbatim responses to the Rorschach test. The court found that raw test data fall within the definition of education records under FERPA, and that such materials are subject to disclosure to parents. The judge also noted that the school must provide access to raw test data to a second professional when the parent seeks an independent evaluation of the school's results and recommendations.

Thus, under FERPA, parents and eligible students have the right to inspect and review all education records that contain personally identifiable information, including test protocols, and the school is required to make copies of education records if failure to do so would prevent the parent or student from exercising their right to inspect the records. The parent access requirements of FERPA consequently appear to conflict with the school psychologist's obligation to maintain test security and observe copyright laws that protect test protocols.

APA's Standard 2.10 states, "Psychologists make reasonable efforts to maintain the integrity and security of tests and other assessment techniques consistent with law, contractual obligations, and in a manner that permits compliance with the requirements of the Ethics Code." When school psychologists must balance the obligation to protect test security against the parent's legal right to inspect test protocols, the parent's right to inspect records is of paramount importance (also see Canter, Bennett, Jones, & Nagy, 1994). However, practitioners may be able to avoid parent requests to inspect test protocols by establishing a good collaborative relationship early in the assessment process, by explaining the conflict between their professional obligation to maintain test security and the parents' right to review records, and by communicating assessment findings in a manner that satisfies the parents' need for information about their child. Providing handouts for parents that describe what a test measures with fictitious sample items may be helpful (see, for example, Sattler, 1988, p. 120).

If, nevertheless, parents do request to see their child's test protocols, FERPA requirements are met if the school allows the parent to examine and discuss the protocols under school supervision (Irvin dated January 9, 1979). APA's Division 16 Ethics Committee recommends this inspection might include "a discussion of sample test items and responses to them."

This should be done under the supervision of the school psychologist or other appropriately trained person, and the parent should not be allowed to copy down questions and answers (Martin, 1985, reprinted in Sattler, 1988, p. 772). Psychologists have no obligation under FERPA to disclose "nonidentifying information" to parents. Thus, it is appropriate to deny parent requests to inspect test materials (e.g., manuals and stimulus materials) that are not part of the child's individual performance record (Hehir, October 25, 1993).

Many states have adopted freedom of information laws to ensure that citizens have access to information regarding the activities of government, and to safeguard against abuse of power by officials. Parents and others occasionally request access to test questions and answers under such laws. Tests used in academic settings typically are exempt from disclosure under freedom of information acts unless a court determines that public interest in disclosure outweighs public interest in nondisclosure. Practitioners need to consult their state laws on this matter, however.

As noted by Canter et al. (1994), *copies* of test protocols should not be released unless required by law. The Bureau for the Education of the Handicapped (BEH) suggested that if the school provides an opportunity for the parent to inspect protocols under school supervision, the school is not legally required to provide copies of protocols except under the following unusual circumstances:

> An agency must give test protocols to parents if (a) the parent cannot come to school during a 45-day period after a request has been made to review the records if the reasons for not coming during this period are serious illness, extended travel, or related reasons, and if parents request copies of their child's protocol, or (b) if the parents or agency request a due process hearing in which the test questions will be introduced by either party as evidence at the hearing. (BEH policy letter by Irvin, dated January 9, 1979, also reprinted in Sattler, 1988, p. 771)

Storage and Disposal of Psychological Records

Practitioners need to consult their school district policies and state education laws regarding what types of information to maintain in school psychological records and how long such records must be retained before disposal. When obsolete confidential information is purged from files, psychologists are obligated to ensure it is shredded or otherwise destroyed (NASP-PPE, III, A, #9, #10). See NASP's *Standards for the Provision of School Psychological Services* (1997; section 3.6) and APA's "Record Keeping Guidelines" (1993b) for additional guidance.

Technology and Record Keeping

Computers and other technological devices can provide school personnel with quick access to pupil information. However, computerized record keeping may result in unauthorized access to student files and violations of the confidentiality of pupil records, particularly if a networked computer-information system is used. Confidentiality of student information can be protected by requiring passwords to gain access to sensitive files or by substituting child codes for names in computerized record keeping and information storage (see *EP* 5.05; 5.07). School psychologists also need to ensure that "student/client records are not transmitted electronically without a guarantee of privacy. (For example, a receiving fax machine must be in a secure location and operated by employees cleared to work with confidential files; E-mail messages must be encrypted or else stripped of all information that identifies the student/client)" (NASP-PPE, IV, C, #8).

Computerized storage makes it possible to keep on file large amounts of information about individuals that may or may not be needed in the provision of services. As Zachary and Pope (1984) have suggested, the indiscriminate gathering and storage of nonessential personal information is an unnecessary invasion of privacy (also *EP* 5.03).

CONCLUDING COMMENTS

In light of the ethical and legal issues of privacy, confidentiality, and school record keeping, Eades' (1986) recommendation is helpful: School psychologists need to ensure that the statements they make orally or in writing are necessary, permitted, and required as a part of their employment and their responsibility as a professional to their client.

STUDY AND DISCUSSION

Questions for Chapter 3

1. What is "privacy?"
2. Do school children have a legal right to privacy in the public schools?
3. The chapter states that "Codes of ethics, professional standards, and law show growing agreement that informed consent should

(Continued)

be obtained prior to the provision of school psychological services." What does *informed consent* mean?

4. Under what circumstances is it ethically permissible to provide psychological services to a child without his or her explicit assent for services?
5. Research suggests that involving children in treatment decisions may result in better treatment outcomes. What factors affect a child's capacity to participate effectively in treatment decisions?
6. What does *confidentiality* mean? Identify three situations in which the school psychologist is obligated to share student disclosures with others.
7. What is the *need-to-know* principle?
8. What is *privileged communication?* Who has the right to waive privilege in a legal proceeding?
9. Briefly discuss school responsibilities under FERPA with regard to (a) ensuring parent access to pupils records, (b) safeguarding the privacy of pupil's records, and (c) affording parents opportunities to ensure the accuracy of records.

VIGNETTES

1. Todd, a student with a history of behavior problems, made an appointment with Sam Foster. Now that he has turned 18, he would like to see all of the psychological reports that have been written about him over the years. He also would like to restrict his parent's right of access to his school records. How should Sam respond? What are the ethical-legal issues involved? (Adapted from Davis & Mickelson, 1994).

2. Sam Foster opens his door to a man who states he is the father of Jeff Blume, a child Sam recently evaluated. The man asks politely to see the test results, including protocols, Sam obtained. He also wants to know what comments, if any, Jeff may have made about his parents, as they are divorced, and Mr. Blume plans to go to court seeking custody of Jeff. What, if anything, should Sam share with this man?

3. As a result of Hannah Cook's assessment and other information gathered by the school's multidisciplinary team, the school recommended John

Malamo be classified as educable mentally impaired in the team meeting with his parents. Mr. Malamo is furious with Hannah and the school. He has made an appointment with Hannah to review the results of the psychological evaluation in more detail. When he appears for his appointment, Mr. Malamo demands copies of all information in John's psychological file, including the WISC-III test protocol, so that he can seek an independent opinion about John's needs from a psychologist in private practice. How should Hannah handle this situation?

4. John Smith is a first-grader in Wanda Rose's school district. He was referred to Wanda for evaluation because of suspected learning and emotional problems. John lives with his aunt and uncle, Mr. and Mrs. Martin. In a meeting with Mrs. Martin, Wanda learns that John's parents died in "an accident." John has a history of emotional difficulties, and has been seen by a psychotherapist in private practice. Mrs. Martin makes arrangements to have a report forwarded to Wanda from John's therapist because she feels it will be helpful in meeting John's needs at school. When the report arrives, Wanda finds that the therapist made a number of excellent recommendations about John's emotional and educational needs. In reading the report, she also learns that John's father murdered his mother and then committed suicide. How should Wanda handle the report and the information it contains? (Adapted from Keith-Spiegel & Koocher, 1985.)

Chapter 4

ETHICAL AND LEGAL ISSUES IN PSYCHOEDUCATIONAL ASSESSMENT

> Psychological testing and assessment techniques, in common with most tools, can be used for a diversity of purposes, some destructive and some constructive, and their use cannot be separated from the training, competence, and ethical values of the clinician-user. (Matarazzo, 1986, p. 18)

Surveys of school psychologists have consistently found that practitioners spend the greatest proportion of their professional time in assessment activities. Based on a sample selected from the membership roster of the National Association of School Psychologists, Reschly and Wilson (1995) found that practitioners devote an average of 22 hours per week to assessment. This chapter focuses on ethical and legal issues associated with the school psychological assessment of individual pupils. School testing programs are discussed in Chapter 10.

TESTING VERSUS ASSESSMENT

In their work with teachers, parents, and children (and in their own thinking), it is important for school psychologists to distinguish between *testing* and *assessment.* Testing and assessment are not synonymous, interchangeable terms (Matarazzo, 1986, p. 18). A test is a tool that may be used to gather information as part of the assessment process.

Assessment is a broader term. Mowder has defined the assessment process as "the planning, collection, and evaluation of information pertinent to a psychoeducational concern" (1983, p. 145). Psychoeducational assessment is conducted by a psychologist trained to gather a variety of different types of information (review of school history and health records, observations, interviews, test results) from a number of different sources (pupil, teacher, parents, specialists) and to interpret or give meaning to that information in light of the unique characteristics of the pupil and his or her situation.

Practitioners also need to be familiar with the distinction between the medical and ecological models of school psychological assessment. In past years, practitioners were often trained to accept a medical model. The medical model views learning and behavior problems as a result of within-child disorders or disabilities (Ysseldyke & Christenson, 1988). In contrast, the ecological model encourages an assessment approach that takes into account the multiple factors that affect learning and behavior, including classroom variables, teacher and instructional variables, characteristics of the referred student, and support available from the home for school achievement. The ecological perspective has gained acceptance in recent years because it is viewed as potentially more beneficial and less harmful to the child. In order to reverse a student's pattern of poor progress, systematic assessment of factors in the child's learning environment is needed (Ysseldyke & Christenson, 1988). Messick (1984) has suggested that a child should not be exposed to the risk of misdiagnosis unless deficiencies in instruction have first been ruled out.

The psychologist has certain pre-assessment responsibilities to parent and pupil. After discussing these, ethical-legal concerns associated with assessment planning, selection of technically adequate tests and evaluation procedures, data collection and interpretation, report writing, and sharing findings are addressed. Two somewhat controversial topics—nonbiased assessment and projective personality assessment—are then discussed. The final portions of the chapter focus on the professional issues of competence and autonomy in conducting psychoeducational evaluations and the use of computers in assessment.

There are a number of ethical codes, professional standards, and legal documents that provide guidelines for psychological assessment in the schools. NASP's *Principles for Professional Ethics* (NASP-PPE) (1997) and APA's *Ethical Principles of Psychologists and Code of Conduct* (EP) (1992) each include ethical principles for psychological assessment. NASP's *Standards for the Provision of School Psychological Services* (NASP-SPSPS) (1997) outlines professional standards for the delivery of psychoeducational assessment services and nonbiased assessment.

The *Standards for Educational and Psychological Testing* or *Standards* (American Educational Research Association, American Psychological Association, and National Council on Measurement in Education, 1985) provides guidelines for psychologists and educators to use in evaluating whether their tests and assessment procedures meet acceptable technical standards. The *Standards* have no official legal status. However, the *Standards* have been referred to in federal regulations concerning acceptable testing practices, and they have been cited in Supreme Court cases as an authoritative source on issues concerning the technical adequacy of testing practices (Adler, 1993). A draft of a new revision of the *Standards* has been completed and will be submitted to the sponsoring organizations for approval in the spring of 1998 (Goh, 1997).

The Individuals with Disabilities Education Act (IDEA) and Section 504 of The Rehabilitation Act of 1973 each outline legal requirements for evaluation procedures used in the identification of children with disabilities. The regulations implementing IDEA-Part B that pertain to tests and evaluation procedures are shown in Exhibit 4–1. Note that these regulations predate the most recent set of amendments of IDEA (Pub. L. No. 105-17). Consequently, the reader is encouraged to consult the new regulations when they are available.

PRE-ASSESSMENT RESPONSIBILITIES

Parental Involvement and Consent

Codes of ethics and special education law contain provisions to ensure parental involvement when a pupil is referred for psychoeducational evaluation (NASP-PPE, III, C, #2; IDEA). Practitioners are ethically obligated to ensure there is direct parent contact before beginning pupil assessment procedures (NASP-PPE, III, C, #2). This initial contact with the parents hopefully sets the stage for effective home–school collaboration.

Standards for professional practice require the informed consent of the parent (or student if of the age of majority) prior to initiating an individual psychological testing or assessment procedure (NASP-SPSPS 3.5.4.1; *Standards,* p. 85; also Protection of Pupil Rights Amendment). Under IDEA, written consent of the parent is needed for the initial pre-special education placement evaluation. Parent consent also is required for subsequent reevaluations, unless the school can demonstrate that it has taken reasonable measures to obtain consent and the child's parent failed to respond (Pub. L. No. 105-17, § 614, 111 Stat. 81 [1997]). Bersoff (1983) includes diagnostic pupil observations and interviews as part of the assessment procedure requiring prior informed parental approval when a child is suspected to have an educational disability under IDEA.

Professional standards and regulations implementing IDEA are highly similar with regard to the necessary components of the informed consent agreement for psychoeducational assessment. According to the *Standards* (p. 85) and consistent with the regulations implementing IDEA, the parent granting permission for the diagnostic evaluation should be made aware of the reasons for the assessment, the type of tests and evaluation procedures

Exhibit 4–1. Excerpt from the Regulations Implementing the *Individuals with Disabilities Education Act*

Protection in Evaluation Procedures

§ 300.530 General.

(a) . . . .

(b) Testing and evaluation materials and procedures used for the purposes of evaluation and placement of children with disabilities must be selected and administered so as not to be racially or culturally discriminatory.

§ 300.531 Preplacement evaluation.

Before any action is taken with respect to the initial placement of a child with a disability in a program providing special education and related services, a full and individual evaluation of the child's educational needs must be conducted in accordance with the requirements of § 300.532.

§ 300.532 Evaluation procedures.

State educational agencies and LEAs shall ensure, at a minimum, that:

(a) Tests and other evaluation materials

(1) Are provided and administered in the child's native language or other mode of communication, unless it is clearly not feasible to do so;

(2) Have been validated for the specific purpose for which they are used; and

(3) Are administered by trained personnel in conformance with the instructions provided by their producer.

(b) Tests and other evaluation materials include those tailored to assess specific areas of educational need and not merely those that are designed to provide a single general intelligence quotient.

(c) Tests are selected and administered so as best to ensure that when a test is administered to a child with impaired sensory, manual, or speaking skills, the test results accurately reflect the child's aptitude or achievement level or whatever other factors the test purports to measure rather than reflecting the child's impaired sensory, manual, or speaking skills (except where those skills are the factors that the test purports to measure).

(d) No single procedure is used as the sole criterion for determining an appropriate educational program for a child.

(e) The evaluation is made by a multidisciplinary team or groups of persons, including at least one teacher or other specialist with knowledge in the area of suspected disability.

(f) The child is assessed in all areas related to the suspected disability, including, if appropriate, health, vision, hearing, social and emotional status, general intelligence, academic performance, communicative status, and motor abilities.

Note: Children who have speech or language impairment as their primary disability may not need a complete battery of assessment (e.g., psychological, physical, or adaptive behavior). However, a qualified speech-language pathologist would: (1) Evaluate each child with a speech or language impairment using procedures that are appropriate for the diagnosis and appraisal of speech and language impairments, and (2) if necessary, make referrals for additional assessments needed to make an appropriate placement decision.

Source: 34 C.F.R. § 300.531–300.532.

to be used, what the assessment results will be used for, and who will have access to the results. This information must be presented to the parent in his or her native language, or other mode of communication. Many pupil services teams have developed materials for parents describing the evaluation procedures and assessment instruments used by multidisciplinary team members. Bersoff (1983) notes that a simple listing of the test names does not meet the intent of the law; an explanation of the nature and purpose of assessment instruments should be provided.

Psychologists also may wish to explain their professional commitment to maintaining test security during a preassessment meeting with parents. This will allow parents to know in advance that the psychologist has an ethical obligation to limit disclosure of test items in reporting findings.

Most parents cooperate with school attempts to secure approval for psychoeducational assessment. However, a school has several means of overcoming parent refusal to consent (Bersoff, 1983). Under IDEA, the school may use mediation and other due process procedures (e.g., a hearing by an impartial hearing officer) to pursue evaluation of a child without parental consent (Pub. L. No. 105-17, § 614, 111 Stat. 81 [1997]). In unusual circumstances, state child neglect laws may provide another means to override parental refusal (Bersoff, 1983).

School psychologists should be aware that this requirement for parental approval prior to initiating an individual psychoeducational assessment does not extend to testing that is done as part of regular school activities (*Standards,* p. 85). Whether the school seeks parental consent for educational testing that is part of normal school activities (e.g., schoolwide testing programs) is left to the discretion of the school administration. However, as noted in the *Standards,* providing parental notice of testing is recommended and may help to ensure good school–parent relationships. Parental permission for testing done as part of school-based research is discussed in Chapter 9.

Responsibilities to the Pupil

In addition to prior parental consent to initiate a psychoeducational evaluation, school psychologists also have a number of obligations to the student/client. Consistent with good testing practices, practitioners need to make full use of their professional skills to gain the active cooperation of the pupil. It is ethically permissible to assess a minor child without his or her explicit assent if the assessment promises to benefit his or her welfare (e.g., the planning of an individualized instructional program to enhance student learning). As mentioned earlier, we concur with Corrao and Melton (1988) that it is disrespectful to solicit the assent of the child if refusal will not be honored.

As noted in Chapter 3, children are not seen as *legally* competent to make autonomous decisions about whether to participate in a psychological assessment; minors have no *legal* right "to consent, assent, or object to proposed psychoeducational evaluations" (Bersoff, 1983, p. 153). Children who refuse to cooperate during individual testing are often nevertheless evaluated using alternative measures, such as observations or teacher and parent ratings.

Every student/client has the right to be fully informed about the scope and nature of the assessment process whether they are given a choice to consent to (or refuse) services. Practitioners are ethically obligated to explain the assessment process to the pupil in a manner that is understood by the student. This explanation includes the uses to be made of assessment information, who will receive information, and possible implications of results (NASP-PPE, III, B, #2). Even preschoolers and mentally impaired youngsters should receive an explanation in a language they can understand as to why they are being seen by the school psychologist (*Standards,* p. 85).

ASSESSMENT PLANNING

Each phase of the assessment process—assessment planning, information gathering, and interpretation of findings—requires professional judgment and decision making. School psychologists are obligated to make decisions that promote the welfare of the student in each phase of the assessment process, and accept responsibility for decisions made (NASP-PPE, I; III, A, #1). The following case description illustrates how psychological test results can have a powerful impact on the lives of children:

Case 4–1

Joseph McNulty was the unwanted child of a woman who was raped. He was placed in Willowbrook State Hospital in 1966 at the age of 4, after being diagnosed as "an imbecile" on the basis of an IQ score of 32. Subsequent re-evaluations suggested Joseph had some hearing problems, but those findings were "initially ignored or simply not seen." Joseph grew up among severely retarded children and adults,

Case 4–1 *(Continued)*

and during his stay at Willowbrook he was given high doses of drugs including Valium, Thorazine, and Haldol. In 1976, at the age of 14, an audiologist observed that Joseph showed a greater interest in learning than other severely retarded youth, and confirmed that Joseph was hearing impaired. After years of intensive therapy, Joseph's IQ tested in the normal range in 1980. In his late 20s, Joseph was not yet able to live independently, and he continued to need therapy and training. In 1988, he won a $1.5 million damage suit against the State of New York for medical malpractice (adapted from Bauder, 1989, p. B–1).

Five Ethical-Legal Concerns

Psychologists have long recognized that the use of an IQ score in isolation is not sound practice in the diagnosis of mental retardation. However, prior to the passage of Pub. L. No. 94-142 in 1975 (now IDEA), IQ test scores were frequently the sole basis for labeling children as mentally retarded (Matarazzo, 1986). The 1960s and 1970s were years of increasing court and federal government involvement in the regulation of psychological testing as a result of this type of misuse of tests.

Five broad ethical-legal concerns emerge from an analysis of our codes of ethics, professional standards, and federal laws that address psychological assessment: Psychologists must strive to ensure that psychoeducational evaluations are *multifaceted, comprehensive, fair, valid,* and *useful.* Each of these concerns will be briefly addressed, then the selection of technically adequate assessment instruments will be discussed.

Multifaceted

Psychoeducational assessment of a child with suspected disabilities must be based on a variety of different types of information from different sources. No decisions should be made on the basis of a single test score (IDEA; *Standards,* p. 54).

Comprehensive

Children with suspected disabilities "must be assessed in all areas related to the suspected disability, including, if appropriate, health, vision, hearing, social and emotional status, general intelligence, academic performance, communicative status, and motor abilities" (34 C.F.R. § 300.532). As was apparent in Case 4–1, failure to have a child evaluated for possible sensory impairments can result in misdiagnosis with tragic consequences for the child.

Fair

In the selection of assessment tools, the psychologist strives to choose the most appropriate instruments and procedures in light of the child's age, gender, native language, disabilities, and socioeconomic and ethnic background (NASP-PPE, IV, B, #1). Regulations implementing IDEA-Part B outline requirements for the assessment of children with limited English proficiency, pupils with disabilities, and those from culturally different backgrounds.

Limited English Proficiency Regulations implementing IDEA-Part B require that tests and other evaluation materials used in the evaluation of children with suspected disabilities "are provided and administered in the child's native language or other mode of communication, unless it is clearly not feasible to do so" (34 C.F.R. § 300.352). *Native language* is defined as "the language normally used by the child" and includes other modes of communication, such as sign language and braille (Note at 34 C.F.R. § 300.12).

Psychoeducational assessment of the "linguistically different" child is a challenging task. For children who come from homes where English is not the primary language, it is important to assess native and English language proficiency. This assessment should include evaluation of spoken and written language skills in each language, using both formal and informal measures, in order to obtain a full picture of functional language usage. Language proficiency information is needed to guide selection and interpretation of measures of aptitude, achievement, and adaptive behavior, and in planning instruction and interventions (see Jitendra & Rohena-Diaz, 1996). Valid assessment of the cognitive abilities of pupils with limited English proficiency is particularly problematic (see Lopez, 1995, 1997).

Children with Disabilities IDEA-Part B also mandates careful selection of assessment procedures for children with sensory, motor, or speech impairments. Regulations implementing the law require that "Tests are selected and administered so as best to ensure that when a test is administered to a child with impaired sensory, manual, or speaking skills, the test results accurately reflect that child's aptitude or achievement level, or whatever other factors the test purports to measure, rather than reflecting the child's impaired sensory, manual, or speaking skills (except where those are the factors which the test purports to measure)" (34 C.F.R. § 300.532). In other words, evaluation procedures should be selected so that a child with disabilities is not penalized on measures of cognitive ability, achievement, and adaptive behavior because of failures due to his or her disability.

Ethnic Minority Children Codes of ethics, professional standards, and special education law also mandate *nonbiased* assessment of children from minority cultural, ethnic, and racial backgrounds. As the issue of bias is complex, it is discussed separately later in the chapter.

Valid

School psychologists are obligated to select tests and other evaluation procedures that meet high professional standards and are valid for the purpose for which they are used (NASP-PPE, IV, B, #2; also *Standards* pp. 9–18; IDEA).

Useful

Tests and other evaluation procedures must be selected to provide a profile of the child's strengths and difficulties to aid in instructional planning. Regulations implementing IDEA state that "Tests and other evaluation materials include those tailored to assess specific areas of educational need and not merely those that are designed to provide a single general intelligence quotient" (34 C.F.R. § 300.532). The assessment is planned to ensure the information gathered will result in maximum feasible assistance to the child (NASP-PPE, IV, B, #2).

Selecting Technically Adequate Instruments

School psychology practitioners "maintain the highest standard for educational and psychological assessment" (NASP-PPE, IV, B, #1), and they select assessment techniques that are consistent with responsible, research-based practice (NASP-PPE, IV, B, #4). As previously mentioned, the *Standards* were developed to provide criteria to assure that relevant issues are addressed in evaluating tests and assessment procedures (p. 2). They were developed for use in selecting instruments for a variety of different measurement applications (psychodiagnosis, applicant selection for jobs and colleges, program evaluation, research) in diverse settings. Consequently, absolute psychometric standards of technical adequacy based on specific statistical procedures are not prescribed. Evaluating the adequacy of assessment practices "ultimately rests with the test user and involves professional judgment based on sound knowledge of psychological measurement principles, behavior science, the particular use of the instrument, and knowledge of alternatives" (p. 2).

When assessment results play an important role in decision making for the individual pupil, the school psychologist is obligated to choose the best available assessment procedures. However, the appropriateness of a specific test use "cannot be evaluated in the abstract but only in the context of the larger assessment process" (*Standards,* p. 41). There is considerable agreement in the school psychology literature that a variety of different types of information are appropriate within the framework of a *successive-levels model* of psychoeducational assessment. Consistent with this model, primary emphasis is given to scores and information from the most reliable and valid sources (e.g., composite scores on technically adequate measures) in interpretation and decision making. However, findings from less reliable and valid sources (scores on various subtest groups, individual subtest scores, performance on individual items, observations and impressions) may also play a role in generating hypotheses about the student's profile of abilities, skills, and needs. These hypotheses may then be confirmed or abandoned by collecting additional information that verifies (i.e., cross-validates) or disconfirms the hypothesis (Kaufman, 1994).

According to the *Standards,* evaluating the technical adequacy of assessment instruments and procedures involves careful consideration of the evidence for test *reliability, validity,* and the *adequacy of the standardization norms.* Each of these areas is addressed next.

Test Reliability

Test reliability refers to the degree to which test scores are "relatively free from random, or unsystematic, errors of measurement" (Aiken, 1987, p. 42; also *Standards,* p. 19). Two types of reliability information should be reported in the manuals for tests to be used in psychoeducational decision making: test stability and internal consistency reliability. Test stability or test-retest reliability studies provide information about the consistency of scores from one testing session to another. This information is typically obtained by administering the same test to the same group of examinees on two occasions and correlating the resultant test scores (Sattler, 1988).

Internal consistency reliability is based on scores obtained during one administration of the test. The reliability coefficient obtained in this manner provides information about the extent to which items on the test are intercorrelated. According to the *Standards,* coefficients of internal consistency should not be substituted for estimates of stability unless evidence supports that interpretation in a particular context (p. 21).

How reliable must a test be? There is no simple answer to this question. Shorter, less time-consuming, and less reliable measures may be adequate when tests are selected to provide information about groups rather than individuals (as in program evaluation and research), or when the results are used for decisions that are tentative and reversible (as when teacher-made tests are used to group children for reading instruction).

A review of the current literature suggests that there is growing consensus in the field of school psychology about desirable levels of reliability for tests used in the schools. Reliability coefficients of .60 to .65 are seen as adequate for measures of group performance, coefficients of .80 to .85 are acceptable for screening instruments, while correlations of .90 or above are desirable for instruments that play a key role in making educational decisions about individual pupils (Hammill, Brown, & Bryant, 1989; Salvia & Ysseldyke, 1988).

Test producers have primary responsibility to obtain and report reliability information (*Standards,* p. 19). Unlike some types of validity information (e.g., predictive validity) that require a longitudinal design, reliability data can be gathered during test development and standardization, and should be included in the supporting manuals when the test is marketed. The *Standards* recommend that reliability estimates be provided for each total score, subscore, or combination of scores that the test reports (p. 20). Both internal consistency and test stability estimates should be reported for each age or grade level and population for which the test is intended, along with a description of the research procedures and sample used in the reliability studies (pp. 20–23). The test user is responsible for evaluating this information to ensure the test selected is reliable for its intended use.

Validity

Validity is the single most important consideration in evaluating tests and assessment procedures (*Standards,* p. 9). Validity refers to the degree to which a test or assessment procedure measures what it purports to measure. However, "no test is valid in general or in the abstract"; tests are valid (or not valid) for a specific purpose (Sattler, 1988, p. 30). IDEA and the *Standards* require that assessment instruments used in the identification of children with suspected disabilities "Have been validated for the specific purpose for which they are used" (34 C.F.R. § 300.532).

There are a number of different ways test producers gather and report validity information. A distinction is often made among content-related, construct-related, and criterion-related validity, although validity information typically does not fall neatly or exclusively into one of these three categories.

Content-related validity refers to "the degree to which the sample of items, tasks, or questions on a test are representative of some defined universe or domain of content" (*Standards,* p. 10). Test authors are obligated to "specify adequately the universe of content that a test is intended to represent" (*Standards,* p. 10) and provide evidence that the test content agrees with specifications of what the test should measure (p. 11).

Criterion-related validity refers to evidence "that test scores are systematically related to one or more outcome criteria" (*Standards,* p. 11).

Criterion-related validity is typically reported as a correlation between scores on the test and scores on some type of outcome of interest, called the "criterion" measure. As suggested in the *Standards,* the key issue is "How accurately can criterion performance be predicted from scores on the test?" (p. 11).

Two types of criterion-related evidence may be provided. Concurrent validity studies involve obtaining information from the predictor and criterion measures at the same point in time. Predictive validity studies involve administering the criterion measure after a specified time interval in order to evaluate how well a test correlates with future performance.

What levels of criterion-related validity are acceptable for tests used in psychoeducational assessment? Again, there is no simple answer; estimates of criterion-related validity are affected by a number of factors. The extent to which the predictor and criterion tests measure the same traits and abilities affects validity estimates; the greater the similarity in what is measured, the higher the likelihood of strong correlations. Test reliability of the predictor and criterion measures affects validity; theoretically, the highest correlation that can be obtained between a predictor and criterion measure is equal to the square root of the product of their respective reliabilities (Mehrens & Lehmann, 1978). The heterogeneity or spread of scores on either measure also affects validity estimates; a restricted range of scores on the predictor or criterion results in lower correlations. The time interval between administration of the two measures affects validity estimates. The longer the interval, the higher the likelihood of change in the trait or ability being measured due to learning and/or development.

According to the *Standards,* criterion-related validity studies should be described by the test producer in enough detail to evaluate the adequacy of the research design and findings. This description should include the types of test-takers, research procedures including the time interval between tests, and statistical analysis including any correction for attenuation of range of scores (p. 16). The psychometric characteristics of the criterion measure also should be described in detail (pp. 16–17).

Construct-related validity is a type of validity that focuses on the test score as a measure of a psychological characteristic or trait such as intelligence, scholastic ability, reading comprehension, anxiety, or sociability. These characteristics or traits are referred to as "constructs" because they are "theoretical constructions about the nature of human behavior" (*Standards,* p. 9). Psychological constructs are embedded in a theory or conceptual framework. Construct validity of a test or other measure is "an index of the extent to which the test scores are related to measures of behavior in situations where the psychological construct supposedly being assessed by the test is an important variable" (Aiken, 1987, p. 48).

No single study can establish the construct validity of a test or other measure (Messick, 1995). Evidence for construct validity may be based on studies of test content (item analysis, factor analysis) and an accumulation of evidence based on a multitrait–multimethod construct validation paradigm. This model of construct validation suggests that evidence should be provided showing that the test correlates well with other measures of the same construct (convergent evidence), but does not correlate highly with measures of theoretically unrelated constructs (discriminant evidence) (Campbell & Fiske, 1959; see also *Standards,* p. 15).

How do you decide if a test instrument is valid? Both the quality and quantity of the supporting evidence are important in evaluating the validity of a test for the child being evaluated (*Standards,* p. 9). Although the test manual and supportive materials are the starting points for test review, practitioners are ethically obligated to keep abreast of the recent research related to the validity of tests used in psychoeducational diagnosis.

Adequacy of Test Norms

Norm-referenced tests allow us to interpret a child's test performance in comparison with a reference group of children of the same age, in the same grade, or perhaps with the same type of disability. In selecting norm-referenced instruments, the school psychologist has a responsibility to evaluate the adequacy and appropriateness of the test norms for the intended use of the test. Test norms must be (a) based on a sample representative of the intended target population for the test, (b) recent, and (c) appropriate for the child being evaluated.

Test producers have a responsibility to identify the intended target population for a test and to describe fully the extent to which the norm group is characteristic of that specific population. Norming studies should be described in the test manual or supportive materials in sufficient detail for the user to evaluate their adequacy and appropriateness for intended test use (*Standards,* p. 33).

INFORMATION GATHERING

Invasion of Privacy

The school psychologist seeks to gather the information needed to develop a picture of the pupil that is comprehensive enough to be useful in decision making and in planning appropriate interventions. However, in responsible psychological assessment, the practitioner also remains sensitive to pupil and family privacy (Matarazzo, 1986). School psychologists are ethically obligated to respect the privacy of others (*EP* Principle D). They do not seek or store personal information about the student/client, parents, teachers, or others that is not needed in the provision of services (*EP* 5.03).

Assessment Conditions

School psychologists also must ensure that the assessment conditions are in the best interests of the pupil being evaluated. The testing environment should be "of reasonable comfort and with minimal distractions" (*Standards,* p. 83), otherwise findings may not be accurate and valid. Testing done by computers should be monitored to ensure results are not adversely affected by a lack of computer test-taking skills or by problems with the equipment (*Standards,* p. 83).

Modifications of standard test administration procedures are made "only on the basis of carefully considered professional judgment" (*Standards,* p. 83), and "any modification of standard test administration procedures or scoring should be described in the testing reports with appropriate cautions regarding the possible effects of such modifications on validity" (p. 84).

In accordance with professional standards and law, tests and other assessment procedures must be "administered by trained personnel in conformance with the instructions provided by their producer" (34 C.F.R. § 300.353). Psychological and educational tests should only be administered by individuals qualified to do so (*EP* 2.06). School psychologists "do not condone the use of psychological or educational assessment techniques . . . by unqualified persons in any way" (NASP-PPE, IV, B, #5).

Test Security

The development of valid assessment instruments requires extensive research and considerable expense. Disclosure of the underlying principles or specific content of a test is likely to decrease its validity for future examinees. Disclosure of test content also may infringe on the intellectual property/copyright interests of the test producer (APA, 1996c). Psychologists are obligated to "make reasonable efforts to maintain the integrity and security of tests and other assessment techniques consistent with law, contractual obligations, and in a manner that permits compliance with the Ethics Code" (*EP* 2.10; also NASP-PPE, IV, C, 1, 2).

ASSESSMENT INTERPRETATION

School psychologists combine observations, background information, multidisciplinary results, and other pertinent data in order to reach comprehensive conclusions and present the most valid picture possible of the student (NASP-PPE, IV, B, #3). In reporting assessment results, psychologists indicate any reservations that exist concerning validity or reliability due to assessment circumstances or norm appropriateness (*EP* 2.05; NASP-PPE, IV, E, #3).

Psychologists also are obligated to ensure that assessment results are useful. Assessment findings should be linked to appropriate intervention strategies. Criterion-referenced testing and curriculum-based assessment are assessment strategies that have gained popularity because they facilitate the linking of data gathered to appropriate instructional interventions (see Shinn, 1995).

Psychological assessment often results in the assignment of a formal diagnostic label. Legally and ethically, practitioners are obligated to ensure that when labels are assigned they are based on valid assessment procedures and sound professional judgment. As noted in Chapter 2, students have a legal right to be free from unwarranted stigmatization by the state. Furthermore, when labels are used, "The least stigmatizing labels, consistent with accurate reporting, should always be assigned" (*Standards,* p. 86). (See Chapter 10 for a discussion of the use of labels in special education.)

Report Writing and Sharing Findings

The goal of assessment is to provide maximal assistance to the student; consequently, practitioners must ensure that "information is adequately interpreted so that the recipient can better help the student or client" (NASP-PPE, IV, E, #1). The school psychologist shares his or her findings through the written report and in conferences with the parent, student, and teacher, and takes responsibility to ensure there is follow-up on decisions made.

Report Writing

The written psychological report documents the assessment process and outcomes and outlines recommendations to assist the child. It potentially serves a number of different purposes. A report may be used in making special education decisions and identifying instructional needs and pupil progress goals. It may serve as a history of psychological performance for subsequent evaluations of pupil progress or deterioration. It also may be used as a communication tool in referrals to professionals outside the school setting (neurologist, clinical psychologist), and as documentation in a legal proceeding such as hearings and court procedures (Sattler, 1988).

Along with these potential multiple purposes, the writer of a psychological report must take into account the fact that it may be read by professionals and nonprofessionals (Harvey, 1997). In accordance with NASP's code of ethics, school psychologists take responsibility for preparing information that is written in terms that are "readily understood by the intended recipient" (IV, E, #2). Furthermore, as noted above, reports should emphasize recommendations and interpretations rather than a simple passing along of test scores (NASP-PPE, IV, E, #3). Unedited computer-generated reports and preprinted check-off or fill-in-the-blank reports are seldom useful (NASP-PPE, IV, E, #3).

School psychologists also are obligated to ensure the accuracy of their reports by reviewing them and signing them only when correct (NASP-PPE, IV, E, #4). Reports prepared by interns and practicum students should be co-signed by the supervising school psychologist (NASP-PPE, IV, E, #4). Alterations of reports previously released should be done only by the original author of the report (NASP-PPE, IV, E, #3).

Practitioners ensure the confidentiality of assessment findings as outlined in Chapter 3, and they ensure that assessment findings are not misused by unqualified persons (NASP-PPE, III, B, #5).

Sharing Findings with the Parent and Pupil

School psychologists "secure continuing parental involvement by a frank and prompt reporting to the parent of findings and progress" (NASP-PPE, III, C, #2; also *EP* 2.09, *Standards,* p. 85). School psychologists are obligated to confer with parents in language understandable to the parent and "strive to propose a set of options which takes into account the values and capabilities of each parent" (NASP-PPE, III, C, #1). Discussion includes recommendations for assisting the student and alternatives associated with each set of plans. School practitioners "encourage and promote parental participation in designing services provided to their children. When appropriate, this includes linking interventions between the school and the home, tailoring parental involvement to the skills of the family, and helping parents to gain the skills needed to help their children" (NASP-PPE, III, C, #3). The parents are advised of the sources of help available at school and in the community (NASP-PPE, III, C, #5).

School psychologists also discuss the outcomes of the assessment with the student/client. Recommendations for program changes or additional services are discussed with the student/client, along with any alternatives which may be available (NASP-PPE, III, B, #4). Ethical codes and professional standards clearly indicate that the student should be afforded opportunities to share in decision making.

NONBIASED ASSESSMENT

Nonbiased assessment is both an ethical and a legal mandate. Under IDEA, "Testing and evaluation materials and procedures used for the purposes of evaluation and placement of children with disabilities must be selected and administered so as not to be racially or culturally discriminatory" (34 C.F.R. § 300.530; also NASP-PPE, IV, B, #1).

Many different definitions of test bias have been suggested in the literature (Flaugher, 1978). Messick (1965, 1980) observed that it is important to distinguish test bias *as a question of psychometric adequacy of the test itself* from the appropriateness or fairness of its use. For the purposes of the following discussion, bias in assessment will be discussed in terms of *test bias, bias in clinical application,* and *fairness of consequences.* Test bias here refers to the psychometric adequacy of the instrument, that is, evidence that a test or procedure is not equally valid when used with children from differing ethnic or racial backgrounds (Coles, 1981; Reynolds & Kaiser, 1990). Bias in clinical application refers to fairness in administration, interpretation, and decision making. The use of biased tests may lead to unfair decisions. However, poor decisions can be made on the basis of fair tests. School psychologists are obligated to select nonbiased test instruments and procedures, and administer and interpret them in a way that is not racially or culturally discriminatory.

An additional source of concern is fairness of the consequences of test use. This involves an appraisal of the outcomes or consequences of test use (Messick, 1980).

Test Bias

As Reynolds and Kaiser (1990) have suggested, the issue of test bias is, simply, a special question of test validity for children from a particular ethnic minority group. Thus, in selecting tests for minority group children, the practitioner needs to ask, "Is this test a valid measure of what it purports to measure for examinees from this ethnic group?"

Test bias may be defined and evaluated in terms of *content validity, criterion-related validity,* and *construct validity.* "An item or subscale of a test is considered to be *biased* in content when it is demonstrated to be relatively more difficult for members of one group than another when the general ability level of the groups being compared is held constant and no reasonable theoretical rationale exists to explain group differences on the item (or subscale) in question" (Reynolds & Kaiser, 1990, p. 498). The question of content bias is resolved by research that shows equal (or unequal) item difficulties for various groups (Flaugher, 1978).

Test bias may also be defined in terms of differential concurrent or predictive (criterion-related) validity. "A test is considered biased with respect to predictive validity when the inference drawn from the test score is not made with the smallest feasible random error or if there is constant error in an inference or prediction as a function of membership in a particular group" (Reynolds & Kaiser, 1990, p. 511). A test may be shown to be nonbiased in criterion-related validity if it predicts the criterion-measure performance equally well for children from different ethnic backgrounds.

Test bias may also be defined in terms of construct validity. "*Bias* exists in regard to construct validity when a test is shown to measure different hypothetical traits (psychological constructs) for one group than another or to measure the same trait but with differing degrees of accuracy" (Reynolds & Kaiser, 1990, p. 504). Studies that show a test has the same factor structure for children from different ethnic backgrounds provide evidence that the test is measuring the same construct for different groups, that it is nonbiased with respect to construct validity.

Reynolds and Kaiser reviewed the available research for a number of popular ability and achievement measures in 1990 and found little evidence of test bias when content, criterion-related, and construct validity for various ethnic groups was evaluated. Less is known about bias in adaptive behavior and personality assessment instruments. The *Standards* recommend test developers research and report results of differential concurrent and predictive validity studies for various groups, particularly if test results may be used in making classification decisions (pp. 12, 17). The practitioner is obligated to evaluate the research on test bias when selecting instruments for ethnic minority children and to choose the fairest and most appropriate instruments available.

Bias in Clinical Application

Practitioners also are obligated to consider the potential problem of bias in clinical application. Technically adequate tests can be used to make poor decisions because of atmosphere bias and bias in interpretation and/or decision making. *Atmosphere bias* refers to factors in the testing situation that may inhibit performance of children from ethnic minority backgrounds (Flaugher, 1978). Such factors include limited test-taking skills (e.g., lack of responsiveness to speed pressures), wariness of the examiner (e.g., race of the examiner effects, reluctance to verbalize), and differences in cognitive style and test achievement motivation that hinder optimal performance.

Sattler (1988) suggests that atmosphere bias can be minimized by a competent, well-trained examiner who is sensitive to the child's personal and cultural background. Skilled practitioners use a variety of formal and less formal assessment strategies (testing-the-limits, test-teach-test) and interpret findings in light of the child's background to ensure a valid and useful picture of abilities and educational needs (see Sattler, 1988).

In order to minimize bias in interpretation, psychologists must be keenly sensitive to culture and ethnicity as factors that impact on behavior. APA's "Guidelines for Providers of Psychological Services to Ethnic, Linguistic, and Culturally Diverse Populations" (1993a) identifies needed knowledge and skills for assessment and intervention with students/clients from ethnic minority backgrounds, and provides a list of relevant references (also see Dana, 1994).

Fairness in Consequences

A third area of concern is that the use of tests may in some way result in unfair consequences or outcomes for a particular group. If testing and assessment practices result in children from a particular ethnic group being placed in inferior educational programs, then the outcomes or consequences of testing are biased and unfair, no matter how adequate the tests and decision-making procedures (Reschly, 1997).

PROJECTIVE PERSONALITY ASSESSMENT

Three ethical-legal concerns associated with the use of personality tests in the schools, in particular projective techniques, have been identified in the literature. First, there has been a long-standing concern among psychologists that the use of personality tests may result in unwarranted invasion of privacy (Messick, 1965). Personality tests have been a special focus of concern because, unlike achievement or ability tests, questions on personality tests are often indirect, and the test-taker may unknowingly reveal aspects of the self, including emotional problems, that he or she is not prepared to unveil (Messick, 1965).

Two strategies to safeguard privacy in the use of personality tests have been suggested. First, consistent with ethical codes and legal requirements (e.g., IDEA), explicit informed consent should be obtained before administering such tests, and second, the psychologist must consider carefully whether the use of such tests is justified in assisting the pupil, that is, weigh the risk of intrusion on pupil and family privacy against the likelihood such techniques will result in information helpful in promoting pupil welfare.

A second ethical-legal issue specifically regarding the use of projective personality tests in the schools focuses on whether such tests meet professional and legal standards for demonstrated test validity. A number of writers have argued that evidence for the technical adequacy of many projective techniques is lacking or does not support their use with children, and that projective test results appear to lack educational relevance (Batsche & Peterson, 1983; but also see Knoff, 1983).

There can be no absolute answer about whether or not to use projectives with school children. Concerns about the validity and usefulness of personality tests, like other assessment tools, are appropriately addressed by considering test properties in relation to the purposes of the assessment (Messick, 1965; *Standards,* 1985). Practitioners must strive to select tests that have demonstrated validity for the purpose used, and ensure that findings are cross-validated within the framework of a multimethod model.

A third concern about the use of projectives is that school psychologists may not be adequately trained in their use. Consistent with the broad ethical principle of responsible caring, school psychologists must evaluate their own competence to use particular assessment strategies. Practitioners who use personality tests need to have knowledge of the test's conceptual model of personality development and deviation, skills in the administration and interpretation of the particular assessment tool, and competent judgment about when to use that test or strategy. Projective tests should only be used by psychologists with verifiable training in their use.

PROFESSIONAL COMPETENCE AND AUTONOMY

Competence

Case 4–2

Hannah Cook accepted a position as a school psychologist with an Intermediate School District in Michigan after working for several years as a school psychologist in another state. Her graduate coursework and prior work experiences focused only on school-aged children; she had no formal training in preschool child development and assessment. In her new job in Michigan, she began receiving referrals for the evaluation of infants with suspected developmental delays. She read the Bayley Scales manual and began conducting assessments of the referred babies (adapted from Keith-Spiegel & Koocher, 1985).

School psychologists are ethically obligated to recognize and define the boundaries of their competence and to offer assessment services only within those boundaries (*EP* Principle A; NASP-PPE, II, A, #1). As noted in Chapter 1, psychologists who step beyond their competence in assessing children place the student/client at risk for misdiagnosis, misclassification, miseducation, and possible psychological harm. This question of competence is likely to arise when practitioners are asked to assess children whose characteristics (e.g., age, native language, or cultural background) or suspected problems are outside the scope of their training or supervised experience (*Standards,* p. 43). In such situations, practitioners need to "enlist the assistance of other specialists in a supervisory, consultative or referral role as appropriate in providing services competently" (NASP-PPE, II, A, #4). Practitioners are well-advised to develop a directory of colleagues with expertise in evaluating children from special backgrounds or with low-incidence disabilities.

Seeking assistance through supervision, consultation, and referral are appropriate strategies for psychologists faced with a difficult or unusual case. However, practitioners who plan to shift or expand their services to a new age group or special pupil population are obligated to seek appropriate and verifiable training or professional supervision before offering such services (APA, 1981, p. 674). Hannah was obligated to clarify the scope of her expertise before accepting the position in Michigan and make arrangements for training (coursework and/or supervised experience) before accepting referrals for infant assessments.

Professional Autonomy

Case 4–3

A Director of Special Education felt clearer guidelines were needed to determine whether or not children qualified as learning disabled under IDEA-Part B. *He developed a district policy that required all children with suspected learning disabilities to be evaluated using the Woodcock-Johnson Psycho-Educational Battery—Revised (Woodcock & Johnson, 1989) and that comparisons of scores on the Cognitive Ability and Achievement Subtests be used to identify children with aptitude-achievement discrepancies suggestive of a learning disability.*

IDEA-Part B requires the consideration of certain types of pupil information in the evaluation of children with suspected disabilities. For example, intellectual ability, achievement, adaptive behavior, and developmental history all must be considered in evaluation of children who may qualify for services as mentally impaired. State education laws and local district policy may specify additional *types* of information to be considered in evaluation of children with suspected disabilities. School psychologists need to be knowledgeable of these requirements. However, in order to serve the best interests of the student/client, school psychologists must insist on professional autonomy in the selection of specific assessment instruments and procedures. District-mandated assessment batteries, that is, when the school administration dictates the specific tests the school psychologist must use, are inconsistent with professional standards for the provision of school psychological services and may result in unsound assessment choices for the pupil being evaluated (NASP-SPSPS, 3.5.1.2; 4.4). Such policies clearly violate the intent of special education laws that require tests be selected in light of the unique characteristics of the individual child.

COMPUTERS IN PSYCHOEDUCATIONAL ASSESSMENT

Case 4–4

The school board of a suburban high school was concerned about an increase in drug abuse and suicide attempts among high school students. They decided to ask a member of their school psychological services team to become involved in the identification of troubled adolescents and set up a counseling program in cooperation with the local mental health clinic. Sam Foster, the school psychologist assigned to this new job role, felt inadequately trained in the diagnosis of adolescent emotional problems. He decided to purchase a computer-administered suicide risk and depression personality scale he saw advertised in a professional newsletter. Computer administration of the scale required only 20 minutes. Results were computer-scored and printed out in narrative form. Sam had a number of high school students take the computer-administered test. He then included paragraphs from the narrative printout in his reports (adapted from Jacob & Brantley, 1989).

Software programs are now available for the administration, scoring, and interpretation of a variety of psychological tests. In addition, computerized classification programs have been marketed that integrate information from a battery of tests and recommend special education classification under IDEA-Part B. A special challenge of this new assessment technology has been to interpret our ethical codes, professional standards, and special education laws as they relate to computer-assisted assessment (Jacob & Brantley, 1987a). APA's *Guidelines for Computer-Based Tests and Interpretations* (GCBTI) (1986) were formulated to interpret the APA's *EP* and the *Standards* as they relate to computer-based testing and test interpretation. Jacob and Brantley (1987b) also developed a list of informal suggestions for best practices for computer use in school psychology.

Case 4–4 illustrates a number of important ethical-legal considerations associated with computer-assisted assessment. First, and perhaps most important, it is the psychologist's responsibility to ensure that all assessment procedures, including those that are computer-assisted, yield valid results prior to using the results in decision making (GCBTI, p. 8; NASP-PPE, IV, B, #2, C, #6; *Standards,* pp. 41–42). Many software programs have not been developed according to accepted standards for psychodiagnostic assessment tools and lack adequate documentation of their validity. Selection of psychodiagnostic software should be limited to those programs that have been reviewed by experts in the field and found to meet high standards for professional practice (NASP-PPE, IV, C, #5).

It also is important to note that Sam is not personally qualified to evaluate the validity of the computer-generated results for the individual students tested because of his lack of training in diagnosis of adolescent emotional problems. He is attempting to use a computer program to extend his competence beyond its current boundaries. This blind acceptance of computer-generated findings places the students at high risk for misdiagnosis and possible psychological harm. Computer-generated test interpretations should be considered as a tool to be used in conjunction with the clinical judgment of well-trained professionals (NASP-PPE, IV, C, #5).

Finally, some view verbatim copying of paragraphs from a computer-generated summary as unethical. In copying paragraphs from the computer-generated report, Sam is taking credit for work that is not his own (see NASP-PPE, III, C, #5).

CONCLUDING COMMENTS

Many school psychologists desire a decrease in assessment responsibilities so that more time can be devoted to consultation and intervention activities. However, even if a shift away from assessment responsibilities is realized, the school psychologist will continue to be one of the members of the pupil services team most knowledgeable in assessment. School psychologists must continue to accept the responsibility to ensure that tests and assessment procedures are used only in ways that protect the rights and promote the well-being of students.

STUDY AND DISCUSSION

Questions for Chapter 4

1. What is the difference between *testing* and *assessment?*
2. Identify the school psychologist's ethical-legal obligations to the parent prior to beginning an assessment and during interpretation of findings.
3. Describe five ethical-legal concerns a psychologist should consider in planning and conducting psychoeducational assessments.
4. What is *test bias, bias in clinical application,* and *fairness of consequences?*
5. Identify the ethical-legal problems associated with district-mandated assessment batteries.
6. Identify the ethical concerns associated with the use of projective personality tests with school children.
7. Identify the ethical-legal issues associated with the selection and use of computer-assisted test interpretation programs.

Discussion

1. Research has shown that children who enjoy good peer relationships in early childhood are less likely to experience academic difficulties in school. As part of their efforts to prevent school failure, school psychologists may wish to use sociometric testing to identify children who are not well accepted by their peers and who may benefit from social skills training. Sociometric *nomination* involves asking children to name peers who fit a certain criterion such as "Name a child who shares." Sociometric *ratings* involve asking children to rate their peers on items such as "How much do you like this child?" What are the ethical issues involved in using sociometric measures in a classroom? What can be done to minimize the risk of psychological and social harm to children when using such procedures? See Bell-Dolan and Wessler (1994) for an excellent discussion of this topic.

2. How will you determine whether you are competent to assess a child from a culturally different background?

VIGNETTES

1. Wanda Rose's school district has a backlog of referrals for children suspected of qualifying for special education services. In order to increase the number of evaluations she could complete, Wanda carefully trained a teacher's aide in the administration of the WISC-III and several achievement tests. She used the results of the tests administered by the teacher's aide to determine whether or not the referred pupils qualified for special education services. What are the ethical-legal issues involved in this vignette?

2. Hannah Cook, school psychologist, and Bob Smoke, the reading consultant at the junior high school, were interested in decreasing the amount of time needed to complete individual assessment of reading achievement so that more time could be devoted to consultation activities. They contacted the high school computer sciences teacher and worked together to create a computer-administered version of a popular, well-standardized paper and pencil test of reading comprehension. Students referred for assessment of reading achievement were then routinely given the computer-administered version of the test in a testing carrel in the school library. The computer program computed raw scores, and the raw scores were then transformed to standard scores by the reading consultant using tables from the test manual. The test scores were used by the psychologist and reading consultant for both placement and program planning purposes. What are the ethical-legal issues involved in this vignette? (Adapted from Jacob & Brantley, 1989.)

3. Mary, a recently arrived Mexican adolescent, has been failing in school. The building principal requested that the school psychologist assess her to determine her IQ and current academic performance levels. The building principal wondered if she were eligible for special class placement. What are some of the issues involved in conducting an assessment of a child like Mary? Briefly outline a plan (the steps you will take) in assessing Mary.

4. A director of special education decided to hire a school psychologist on a per case basis to administer the WISC-III to children referred for evaluation. In discussing the job offer with Sam Foster, the director made it clear that Sam would be paid only to administer the IQ test and report the scores. The director would then give the IQ scores to her secretary, who would use the scores to print out a computer-generated psychological report. This report would be interpreted to the parents by a teacher consultant and used by the school in making placement recommendations. (Adapted from Sainker, 1984.) How should Sam respond to this situation and job offer?

ACTIVITIES

A 7-year-old child has been referred for psychoeducational assessment because of her slow academic progress. Her teacher suspects that she may qualify for special education services as educable mentally impaired. Role play your initial meeting with the child's parents during which you seek informed consent for assessment. Role play your meeting with the child during which you describe the scope and nature of the assessment process.

SUPPLEMENTARY MATERIAL

The book *Responsible Test Use: Case Studies for Assessing Human Behavior* (Eyde et al., 1993) provides examples of the misuse and appropriate use of psychological test data. Cases 4, 20, 25, and 26 are of particular interest to school psychologists.

Chapter 5

ETHICAL-LEGAL ISSUES IN THE EDUCATION OF PUPILS WITH DISABILITIES UNDER IDEA

> Education law is one thing; educational action is quite another. Between the two events, the passing of a law and the behavior of the school, must occur a chain of intermediate events: The interpretation of the law in terms of practice; the study of the feasibility of the interpretation; the successive adjustments, reorganizations, retrainings, and redesign of administrative procedures; the self-monitoring and reporting—the reality testing. (Page, 1980, p. 423)

This chapter provides a summary of law pertinent to providing services to children with disabilities. It focuses on the Individuals with Disabilities Education Act (IDEA). Special education services for children with disabilities ages 3 through 21 are discussed first in some detail (IDEA-Part B). This is followed by a summary of the federal legislation that provides funds for early intervention services for infants and toddlers with disabilities (IDEA-Part C).

EDUCATION OF CHILDREN WITH DISABILITIES: A HISTORICAL PERSPECTIVE

It is important for school psychology practitioners to have some knowledge of the history of IDEA in order to appreciate fully the meaning of current law. In the text that follows, we have summarized case law and early legislation that foreshadowed the most important special education law, the Education of All Handicapped Children Act of 1975 (Pub. L. No. 94-142), renamed the Individuals with Disabilities Education Act (IDEA) in 1990.

Pre-IDEA Case Law

Right-to-Education

As discussed in Chapter 2, there is no fundamental right to an education mentioned in the U.S. Constitution. Public education is an entitlement granted to citizens of a state under state law. However on the basis of state laws, all children within a state have a legitimate claim to an education at public expense. In legal terms, education is a property right, and property rights are protected by the 14th Amendment of the Constitution, which provides that no state shall "deny any person within its jurisdiction the equal protection of the laws."

For many years, children with disabilities, particularly those with severe or multiple impairments, were routinely excluded from a public education. School districts typically had policies that required a child to meet certain admissions standards (e.g., toilet trained, ambulatory, mental age of at least 5 years) before they were allowed to enter school. One of the responsibilities of many school psychologists prior to 1975 was to assess pupils to certify they were not eligible or unable to profit from public school education and therefore excused from school attendance. Children who were behavior problems in the classroom or simply too difficult to teach were often expelled from school.

There were few options for the parents of children who did not qualify to attend public school. Institutionalization was the recommended treatment for children with impairments prior to the 1960s. Well-to-do families often placed their children in private schools. Others kept their children at home.

In the 1960s, following successful court challenges to racial discrimination in the public schools (e.g., *Brown v. Board of Education* [1954]), parents of children with disabilities began to file lawsuits against public school districts, alleging that the equal protection clause of the 14th Amendment prohibits states from denying school access to children because of their disabilities. Two landmark court cases, *Pennsylvania Association for Retarded Children v. Commonwealth of Pennsylvania (P.A.R.C.)* (1971, 1972) and *Mills v. Board of Education of District of Columbia (Mills)* (1972), marked a turning point in the education of children with disabilities and gave impetus to the development of federal legislation assuring a free and appropriate education for all children with disabilities.

P.A.R.C. In *P.A.R.C.*, parents of retarded children brought suit against the state of Pennsylvania in federal court because their children were denied access to public education. In a consent decree (where parties involved in a lawsuit consent to a court-approved agreement), parents won access to public school programs for retarded children, and the court ordered comprehensive changes in policy and practices regarding education of retarded children in the state. The consent decree in *P.A.R.C.* marked the beginning of a redefinition of education in this country, broadened beyond the "three Rs" to include training of children with disabilities toward self-sufficiency (Martin, 1979). The consent decree in *P.A.R.C.* stated:

> Expert testimony in this action indicates that all mentally retarded persons are capable of benefiting from a program of education and training; that the greatest number of retarded persons, given such education and training, are capable of achieving self-sufficiency, and the remaining few, with such education and training, are capable of achieving some degree of self-care; that the earlier such education and training begins, the more thoroughly and the more efficiently a mentally retarded person can benefit at any point in his life and development from a program of education and training. (p. 1259)

P.A.R.C. is a particularly important case as it foreshadowed and shaped subsequent federal laws regarding schools' responsibilities in educating children with disabilities. The state of Pennsylvania was required to locate and identify all school-age persons excluded from the public schools, to place all children in a "free program of education and training appropriate to the child's capacity," to provide home-bound instruction if appropriate, and to allow tuition grants for children who needed alternative school placements. *P.A.R.C.* also required parent notice before children were assigned to special education classes and an opportunity for an impartial hearing if parents were unsatisfied with the placement recommendation for their child.

Mills *Mills* was a lawsuit filed on behalf of seven children with behavioral, emotional, and learning impairments in the District of Columbia.[1] The court order in *Mills* reiterated many of the requirements of *P.A.R.C.*, and a number of additional school responsibilities in educating children with disabilities were identified. The decision required the schools to "provide each handicapped child of school age a free and suitable publicly supported education regardless of the degree of the child's mental, physical or emotional disability or impairment" (p. 878). The decision also required the schools to prepare a proposal outlining a suitable educational program for each child with a disability, and the court set limits on the use of disciplinary suspensions and expulsions with children with disabilities.

Following the successful resolution of *P.A.R.C.* and *Mills*, 36 right-to-education cases were soon filed in 27 jurisdictions (Martin, 1979). These

---

[1] The suit was initially resolved by a consent decree in 1972. However, the District of Columbia Board of Education failed to comply with the consent decree, and the suit ultimately resulted in a contempt of court judgment against the school board.

cases signaled to Congress that there was a need for federal laws to ensure educational opportunities for all children with disabilities.

Early Legislation

Congress's attempts to address the needs of pupils with disabilities took two routes: the passage of antidiscrimination legislation and the amendment of federal education laws (Martin, 1979). One of the first bills that attempted to ensure equal educational opportunity for children with handicaps in the public schools was an amendment to Title VI of the Civil Rights Act of 1964. The bill later became Section 504 of The Rehabilitation Act of 1973, civil rights legislation that prohibits discrimination against pupils with handicaps in school systems receiving federal financial assistance. School responsibilities under 504 to pupils with handicaps are discussed in Chapter 6.

In addition to antidiscrimination legislation, Congress attempted to meet the needs of pupils with handicaps by amending federal education laws. In 1966, Congress amended the Elementary and Secondary Education Act of 1965 (Pub. L. No. 89-750) to provide grants to states to assist them in developing and improving programs to educate children with handicaps. In 1970, Congress repealed the 1966 law but established a similar grant program to encourage states to develop special education resources and personnel (Pub. L. No. 91-230) (Turnbull, 1990). Four years later, Congress passed the Education Amendments of 1974 (Pub. L. No. 93-380), which increased aid to states for special education and served to put the schools on notice that federal financial assistance for special education would be contingent on the development of state plans with "a goal of . . . full educational opportunities to all handicapped children." Congress intended that this interim legislation would encourage states to begin a period of comprehensive planning and program development to meet the needs of pupils with handicaps. The Education Amendments of 1974 is primarily of historical interest now, except for Section 513, The Family Rights and Privacy Act, discussed in Chapter 3 (Martin, 1979).

INDIVIDUALS WITH DISABILITIES EDUCATION ACT

The most important federal statute concerning the education of children with handicapping conditions is The Education of All Handicapped Children Act of 1975 (Pub. L. No. 94-142). This legislation was originally introduced as a Senate bill in 1972. A Senate subcommittee on the handicapped held extensive hearings on the proposed legislation. The witnesses (numbering over 100) included teachers, parents, education associations, parent organizations, and legislators, among others (Martin, 1979). Their testimony made it increasingly evident that more clear-cut federal incentives were needed to assure educational opportunities for children with handicapping conditions. As of 1975, it was estimated that there were more than eight million handicapped children in the United States. More than half were not receiving an appropriate education, and one million were excluded from public education entirely (Pub. L. No. 94-142, § 601 [b]).

In 1975, Congress passed the Education of All Handicapped Children Act (EHA) (Pub. L. No. 94-142), and President Ford signed it into law. The purpose of the law is

> to assure that all handicapped children have available to them . . . a free appropriate education which emphasizes special education and related services designed to meet their unique needs, to assure that the rights of handicapped children and their parents or guardians are protected, to assist States and localities to provide for the education of all handicapped children, and to assess and assure the effectiveness of efforts to educate handicapped children. (Pub. L. No. 94-142, § 601 [c])

In 1990, President Bush signed into law the Education of the Handicapped Act Amendments of 1990 (Pub. L. No. 101-476), which changed the name of the Education of All Handicapped Children Act to Individuals with Disabilities Education Act (IDEA).[2] Throughout the law, the term *handicap* was replaced by *disability.* On June 4, 1997, President Clinton signed into law the Individuals with Disabilities Education Act Amendments of 1997 (Pub. L. No. 105-17), which reauthorized IDEA and introduced changes to improve the law.

IDEA provides funds to state (SEA) and local (LEA) educational agencies that provide a free and appropriate education to children with disabilities in conformance with the requirements of the law. The 1997 amendments restructured the law into four parts: Part A, General Provisions; Part B, Assistance for Education of All Children with Disabilities; Part C, Infants and Toddlers with Disabilities, and Part D, National Activities to Improve Education of Children with Disabilities. IDEA-Part B refers to special education legislation that provides funds for services to children with disabilities ages 3 through 21. IDEA-Part C provides funds for early intervention services for infants and toddlers. IDEA-Part C is discussed later in this chapter.

[2] Pub. L. No. 94-142 was amended in 1978 (Pub. L. No. 98-773), 1983 (Pub. L. No. 98-199), twice in 1986 (Pub. L. No. 99-457 and Pub. L. No. 99-372), 1988 (Pub. L. No. 100–630), 1990 (Pub. L. No. 101-476), and 1991 (Pub. L. No. 102-119).

Rules and regulations implementing IDEA are developed by the U.S. Department of Education (DOE). The Part B regulations cited in this chapter pre-date the recent amendments of IDEA. Regulations implementing the 1997 amendments are to be issued by June 1998 (Pub. L. No. 105-17, § 612, 111 Stat. 69 [1997]). Readers should consult the *Federal Register* for the new regulations.

The major provisions of IDEA-Part B are discussed under the following headings: (a) State Plans and Single Agency Responsibility, (b) The Zero Reject Principle, (c) Children Eligible for Services, (d) Pupil Evaluation Procedures, (e) Individualized Education Program, (f) Least Restrictive Environment, (g) The Meaning of Appropriate Education, (h) The Scope of Required Related Services, (i) Procedural Safeguards, and (j) Right of Private Action.

State Plans and Single Agency Responsibility

State Plans

In order to receive funds, IDEA-Part B requires each state educational agency (SEA) (usually the state department of education) to have submitted to the U.S. Secretary of Education a state plan with the goal of providing "full educational opportunity" to all children ages birth through 21. The plan must describe state policies and procedures to assure a free appropriate public education for all children with disabilities residing within the state between the ages of 3 and 21, inclusive. The SEA is not required to provide special education and related services to children in the 3- to 5- and 18- to 21-year age groups if the provision thereof is in conflict with state law or practice. The 1997 amendments specify that assurances for a free appropriate public education must extend to children with disabilities who have been suspended for more than 10 days or expelled from school. However, states are not required to provide special education and related services to youth ages 18 through 21 who are incarcerated in adult correctional facilities if they were not identified as disabled or did not have an individualized education program (IEP) prior to their incarceration (Pub. L. No. 105-17, § 612, 111 Stat. 60-61 [1997]).

Federal funds are provided to each state that develops an acceptable state plan. DOE may require revisions in state plans following changes in law or findings of compliance problems (Pub. L. No. 105-17, § 612, 111 Stat. 71 [1997]). To ensure responsiveness to the needs of children with disabilities and their parents, the SEA must provide opportunities for public comment prior to a revision of its plan. Each state also must maintain an advisory panel for the purpose of providing policy guidance with respect to special education and related services for children within the state (Pub. L. No. 105-17, § 612, 111 Stat. 69 [1997]).

The Office of Special Education Programs (OSEP) within DOE monitors compliance with IDEA at the level of the state and only indirectly (e.g., through the review of the state plan). OSEP responds to written inquiries regarding interpretation of IDEA, but it does not attempt to enforce compliance at the level of the individual school district (Zirkel & Kincaid, 1993).

Single Agency Responsibility

In legislating IDEA-Part B, Congress sought to assure there was a single state agency responsible for carrying out the requirements of the law (Turnbull, 1990). The single agency responsibility aspect of the law has several implications.

First, under IDEA-Part B, the SEA is the agency responsible for monitoring all educational programs for children with disabilities ages 3 through 21 within the state and ensuring they meet appropriate education standards. IDEA-Part B allows the SEA to delegate the responsibility to provide special education and related services to intermediate school districts (or other regional units) and local educational agencies (LEAs). An LEA is usually the board of education of a public school district or the educational administrative unit of a public institution (e.g., school for the deaf, blind). The SEA must ensure that policies and programs administered by intermediate and local education agencies (LEAs) are in conformance with IDEA-Part B requirements. If an LEA is unable or unwilling to provide appropriate services under IDEA-Part B, the SEA must ensure special education and related services are provided to students with disabilities residing in those areas (Turnbull, 1990). In accordance with the 1997 amendments, LEAs are required to serve children with disabilities who attend charter schools and provide funds to charter schools in the same manner funds are provided to other schools (Pub. L. No. 105-17, § 612, 111 Stat. 74 [1997]).

Second, consistent with the idea of single agency responsibility, the SEA also must ensure IDEA-Part B rights and protections to children with disabilities who are enrolled in programs administered by other state agencies. As illustrated by the Joseph McNulty case (Case 4–1), many state residential facilities provided custodial care but little training or education for children with disabilities prior to 1975. Under IDEA-Part B, the SEA is responsible for assuring an appropriate education for all children with disabilities in the state, including those residing in mental health facilities, homes for the developmentally disabled, and hospitals. The 1997 amendments, however, allow an SEA to delegate its responsibility for providing special education to youth in adult prisons to another agency (e.g., the prison system) (Pub. L. No. 105-17, § 612, 111 Stat. 64 [1997]).

Third, the SEA must assure that special education and related services are available to children with disabilities enrolled in private schools or facilities. Congress identified two types of private school placements:

1. A child with a disability may be placed in a private school or facility by the SEA or LEA as a means of providing special education and related services.
2. Children may attend private schools or facilities by parent choice.

Private School Placement by the IEP Team

Some children with disabilities are placed in a private school or facility as a means of providing the child appropriate special education and related services. Children placed in a private school or facility by the SEA or LEA must be provided special education and related services in conformance with an individualized education program (IEP) developed by an IEP team as described in the law. A representative of the private school or facility must attend (or in some way participate in) an annual meeting to develop an individualized education program (34 C.F.R. § 300.348). Publically placed private school students are entitled to the same benefits and services as those attending public schools. The child must retain all IDEA rights in the private school setting, and the SEA or LEA must monitor the services provided to ensure compliance with IDEA requirements (Pub. L. No. 105-17, § 612, 111 Stat. 63 [1997]). When the placement is made by the SEA or LEA, the placement must be at no cost to the parents, including the program, nonmedical care, and room and board if placement is in a residential facility (34 C.F.R. 300.302, 300.401-402).

Unilateral Placement by Parents

If the SEA or LEA makes available a free appropriate public education for a child with a disability, but the parents choose to place their child in a private school, the SEA or LEA is not required to pay for the cost of the child's private school education. However, the SEA or LEA must provide opportunities for a child enrolled in a private school to participate in special education and related services in conformance with an IEP.

In the past several years, the courts have issued differing interpretations regarding the extent of an LEA's obligation to provide special education and related services to parentally placed private school students. Publically placed private school students are entitled to benefits and services comparable to those provided to children attending public schools. In contrast, parentally placed private school students are only entitled to a genuine opportunity to participate in public special education services. The 1997 amendments to IDEA clarify the LEA's obligations to children with disabilities who attend private schools by parent choice. Pub. L. No. 105-17 states that consistent with the number and location of parentally enrolled children with disabilities attending private schools, provision is made for the participation of those children by providing special education and related services as follows: Amounts expended for the provision of services by an LEA must be equal to a proportionate amount of available federal funds. These services may be provided on the premises of private schools, including parochial schools, to the extent consistent with law (Pub. L. No. 105-17, § 612, 111 Stat. 62 [1997]). (See also *Agostini v. Felton,* 1997.)

Parents have, at times, recovered private school tuition costs from the SEA or LEA through administrative hearings or lawsuits in which they demonstrated that the SEA or LEA failed to offer their child an appropriate education program in the public schools, leaving them no option but to place him or her at their own expense (see *School Committee of the Town of Burlington, Massachusetts v. Department of Education of Massachusetts,* 1985). The 1997 amendments of IDEA specifically address this issue. If the parents of a child with a disability who previously received special education under the authority of a public agency enroll the child in a private school without the consent or referral of the agency, a court or hearing officer may require the agency to reimburse the parents for the cost of enrollment if it is found that the agency failed to make a free appropriate public education available to the child in a timely manner prior to that enrollment (Pub. L. No. 105-17, § 612, 111 Stat. 63 [1997]).

However, Pub. L. No. 105-17 also states that the cost of reimbursement may be reduced or denied if:

1. At the most recent IEP the parents attended prior to removal of the child from the public school, the parents did not inform the IEP team that they were rejecting the placement proposed by the public agency, including stating their concerns and their intent to enroll their child in a private school at public expense;
2. The parents did not give written notice of their concerns and their intent to enroll their child in a private school at public expense to the public agency at least 10 business days prior to the removal of the child from the public school;

3. If the public agency notified the parents of its intent to evaluate the child (and the reasons for the evaluation) prior to the parents' removal of the child from the public school but the parents did not make the child available for such evaluation; or
4. Upon judicial finding that the actions taken by the parents were unreasonable.

The cost of reimbursement may not be reduced or denied for failure of the parent to provide notice of his or her intent if (a) the parent is illiterate and cannot write in English; (b) compliance would likely result in physical or serious emotional harm to the child; (c) the school prevented the parent from providing notice; or (d) the parents had not been informed of the notice requirement (Pub. L. No. 105-17, § 612, 111 Stat. 63-64 [1997]).

Many children with disabilities attend parochial schools by parent choice. There have been a number of court rulings that address the issue of how the LEA might provide opportunities for these children to participate in special education services without violating First Amendment constitutional requirements for separation of church and state. As noted in Chapter 2, the Supreme Court decisions in *Wolman v. Walter* (1977) and *Aguilar v. Felton* (1985) suggested that while diagnostic services might be provided at the site of a church-related school, special education instruction and counseling services must be provided to parochial school students at a "neutral" site. In June 1997, however, the Supreme Court overturned its previous *Aguilar v. Felton* ruling. In *Agostini v. Felton* (1997), the Court held that changes in Establishment Clause law now allow the provision of remedial instruction and services on the premises of parochial schools.

The Zero Reject Principle

Child Find

Consistent with the court decisions in *P.A.R.C.* and *Mills,* Congress recognized that in order to assure services to all children with disabilities (i.e., the zero reject principle), it was necessary for the SEA to actively seek to locate all children with disabilities within the state. This aspect of the law is called the *child find* requirement. IDEA requires the SEA to implement policies and procedures to assure that all children with disabilities (including those who attend private schools) are identified, located, and evaluated (Pub. L. No. 105-17, § 612, 111 Stat. 61-62 [1997]). The SEA also must ensure that accurate child counts are made to Washington each year (Pub. L. No. 105-17, § 618, 111 Stat. 101 [1997]).

Severity of the Disability

The zero reject principle also encompasses the notion that the SEA must provide full educational opportunity to all children with disabilities, regardless of the severity of their disability. A 1989 court case raised the question of whether some children are so severely impaired that they do not qualify for services under IDEA. *Timothy W. v. Rochester, New Hampshire School District* concerned a child who was profoundly retarded, deaf, blind, spastic, and subject to convulsions. The school alleged that Timothy was so impaired he was "not 'capable of benefitting' from an education, and therefore was not entitled to one" (1989, p. 956). In a surprise ruling, the district court agreed with the school. On appeal, however, this decision was reversed. In a lengthy opinion the court stated, "The language of the Act [IDEA] in its entirety makes clear that a 'zero-reject' policy is at the core of the Act . . ." (p. 960). As the court noted in *Timothy W.,* there is no requirement under IDEA that a child be able to demonstrate he or she will benefit from special education in order to be eligible for services.

Children Eligible for Services

The funds available under IDEA-Part B are earmarked to provide special education and related services only for children with disabilities as defined by the law. Under IDEA-Part B, a *child with a disability* means a child evaluated in accordance with the procedures in the law as having

> mental retardation, hearing impairments (including deafness), speech or language impairments, visual impairments (including blindness), serious emotional disturbance (hereafter referred to as "emotional disturbance"), orthopedic impairments, autism, traumatic brain injury, other health impairments, or specific learning disabilities; and . . . who, by reason thereof, needs special education and related services. (Pub. L. No. 105-17, § 602, 111 Stat. 43 [1997])

It is important to note that eligible children under IDEA-Part B must have a disability as outlined in one of the 13 disability categories (see Exhibit 5–1), and they must need special education and related services because of that disability. A child is not eligible for special education and related services if "the determinant factor for such determination is lack of instruction in reading or math or limited English proficiency" (Pub. L. No. 105-17, § 614, 111 Stat. 82 [1997]).

IDEA-Part B allows states to use a broader definition of disability for children ages 3 through 9. States may use the term *child with a disability*

Exhibit 5–1. Disability Categories Under IDEA-Part B

Autism

A developmental disability significantly affecting verbal and nonverbal communication and social interaction, generally evident before age 3, that adversely affects educational performance. Characteristics often associated with autism are engagement in repetitive activities and stereotyped movements, resistance to environmental change or change in daily routines, and unusual responses to sensory experiences. The term does not apply if a child's educational performance is adversely affected because the child has a serious emotional disturbance. (A note at § 300.7 states that if a child manifests characteristics of the disability category autism after age 3, that child still could be diagnosed as having autism if the criteria outlined are satisfied.)

Deaf-Blind

Concomitant hearing and visual impairments, the combination of which causes such severe communication and other developmental and educational problems that they cannot be accommodated in special education programs solely for children with deafness or children with blindness.

Deaf

A hearing impairment that is so severe that the child is impaired in processing linguistic information through hearing, with or without amplification, that adversely affects a child's educational performance.

Hearing Impairment

An impairment in hearing, whether permanent or fluctuating, that adversely affects a child's educational performance, but that is not included under the definition of deafness in this section.

Mental Retardation

(see text)

Multiple Disabilities

Concomitant impairments (e.g., mental retardation-blindness, mental retardation-orthopedic impairment), the combination of which causes such severe educational problems that they cannot be accommodated in special education programs solely for one of the impairments. The term does not include deaf-blindness.

Orthopedic Impairment

A severe orthopedic impairment that adversely affects a child's educational performance. The term includes impairments caused by congenital anomaly (e.g., clubfoot, absence of some member), impairments caused by disease (e.g., poliomyelitis, bone tuberculosis), and impairments from other causes (e.g., cerebral palsy, amputations, and fractures or burns that cause contractures).

Other Health Impairment

(see text)

Exhibit 5–1. *(Continued)*

Serious Emotional Disturbance

(see text)

Specific Learning Disability

(see text)

Speech or Language Impairment

A communication disorder such as stuttering, impaired articulation, a language impairment, or a voice impairment that adversely affects a child's educational performance.

Traumatic Brain Injury

An acquired injury to the brain caused by an external physical force, resulting in total or partial functional disability or psychosocial impairment, or both, that adversely affects a child's educational performance. The term applies to open or closed head injuries resulting in impairments in one or more areas, such as cognition; language; memory; attention; reasoning; abstract thinking; judgment; problem solving; sensory, perceptual and motor abilities; psychosocial behavior; physical functions; information processing; and speech. The term does not apply to brain injuries that are congenital or degenerative or brain injuries induced by birth trauma.

Visual Impairment including Blindness

An impairment in vision that, even with correction, adversely affects a child's educational performance. The term includes both partial sight and blindness.

Source: 34 C.F.R. § 300.7.

for a 3- to 9-year-old who is experiencing developmental delay (as defined by the state) in one or more of the following areas: physical, cognitive, communication, social or emotional, or adaptive development; and who, for that reason, needs special education and related services (Pub. L. No. 105-17, § 602, 111 Stat. 43 [1997]).

IDEA-Part B definitions that concern sensory, motor, and speech impairments typically pose few problems. The definitions of *mental retardation, specific learning disability, serious emotional disturbance,* and *other health impairment* have frequently been a source of confusion and disagreement, and they are discussed in the text that follows.

The present discussion focuses on the federal definitions of disability categories under IDEA-Part B. School psychologists must also be knowledgeable of the broader definition of handicapped under Section 504 of The Rehabilitation Act of 1973 (Chapter 6), and their state code eligibility requirements. IDEA does not require states to label pupils, and some states have adopted a noncategorical system for the delivery of special education services (Pub. L.

No. 105-17, § 612, 111 Stat. 61 [1997]). However, states must provide data to DOE each year regarding the number of children with disabilities by disability category (§ 618, 111 Stat. 101), and federal funds are available only for those children who are eligible under the IDEA-Part B definition of a disability.

Mental Retardation

> "Mental retardation" means significantly subaverage general intellectual functioning existing concurrently with deficits in adaptive behavior and manifested during the developmental period that adversely affects a child's educational performance. (34 C.F.R. § 300.7)

Prior to the passage of Pub. L. No. 94-142, many children were labeled mentally retarded on the basis of a single IQ score (see Case 4–1). The use of an IQ score as the sole criterion for diagnosing mental retardation in the schools resulted in the overidentification of children as mentally retarded, particularly pupils from ethnic minority backgrounds and those with limited English proficiency. In the 1950s and 1960s, the American Association of Mental Deficiency argued persuasively for a change in the definition of mentally retarded. They recommended that a diagnosis of mental retardation be based on the finding of deficits in both intellectual functioning and adaptive behavior. This view gained wide acceptance and was incorporated into the IDEA-Part B definition of mental retardation.

Under IDEA-Part B, eligibility for special education is determined by a team of qualified professionals and the parents of the child. There are three types of assessment information the team must consider in determining whether a child has mental retardation: general intellectual functioning, adaptive behavior, and school performance. To be eligible for special education under the mental retardation category, the child must show subaverage performance on a measure of general intellectual functioning. Most states recommend the use of IQ tests for this measure. However, this evaluation can be accomplished by testing "or by means other than testing" as long as the procedures are valid and nondiscriminatory (Heumann, 1993, p. 539). Subaverage is usually further defined in state guidelines as performance at least two standard deviations below the population mean for the child's age group (i.e., a score below 70 on the Wechsler Scales, below 68 on the Stanford-Binet).

The child also must demonstrate concurrent deficits in adaptive behavior and school performance. Measures of adaptive behavior focus on the child's effectiveness in meeting age-appropriate standards of personal independence and social responsibility. They are typically based on observations of behavior and competencies provided by an informant (usually a parent or teacher) (Sattler, 1988). Deficits in school performance are most often assessed by standardized achievement tests. Michigan, for example, requires reading and arithmetic standardized test scores in the lowest six percentiles for a child to qualify as mentally impaired.

State regulations typically further classify pupils with mental retardation into one of three subgroups based on intellectual functioning and adaptive behavior. Educable mentally retarded children typically achieve IQ scores 2 to 3 standard deviations below the mean, trainable mentally retarded achieve scores 3 to 4.5 standard deviations below the mean, and severely mentally retarded achieve IQs 4.5 or more standard deviations below the mean.

The IDEA-Part B definition of mental retardation has generated debate among experts in the fields of school psychology and special education. Many believe the IDEA definition of mental retardation and assessment procedures continues to overidentify children as mentally retarded.

Specific Learning Disability

> "Specific learning disability" means a disorder in one or more of the basic psychological processes involved in understanding or in using language, spoken or written, that may manifest itself in an imperfect ability to listen, think, speak, read, write, spell, or to do mathematic calculations. The term includes such conditions as perceptual handicaps, brain injury, minimal brain dysfunction, dyslexia, and developmental aphasia. The term does not apply to children who have learning problems that are primarily the result of visual, hearing, or motor disabilities, of mental retardation, of emotional disturbance, or of environmental, cultural, or economic disadvantage. (34 C.F.R. § 300.7)

A team may determine that a child has a specific learning disability under IDEA-Part B if:

(1) The child does not achieve commensurate with his or her age and ability levels in one or more of the areas listed . . . when provided with learning experiences appropriate for the child's age and ability levels; and

(2) The team finds that the child has a severe discrepancy between achievement and intellectual ability in one or more of the following areas

   (i) Oral expression,
   (ii) Listening comprehension,
   (iii) Written expression,
   (iv) Basic reading skill,
   (v) Reading comprehension,

(vi) Mathematics calculation, or

(vii) Mathematics reasoning. (34 C.F.R. § 300.541)

The team may not identify a child as having a specific learning disability if the severe discrepancy between ability and achievement is primarily the result of a visual, hearing, or motor handicap; mental retardation; emotional disturbance; or environmental, cultural or economic disadvantage. (34 C.F.R. § 300.541)

The rules and regulations further require an observation of the child's academic performance in the regular classroom (or an age-appropriate setting if not in school) by a team member other than the child's teacher (34 C.F.R. § 300.542). The team report for a child found eligible under IDEA-Part B's specific learning disability (LD) definition must describe the basis for making that determination, relevant behavior noted during the observation of the child and the relationship of that behavior to academic functioning, and any academically relevant medical findings. The report also must include a statement as to whether there is a severe discrepancy between achievement and ability that is not correctable without special education and related services and the determination of the team concerning the effects of environmental, cultural, or economic disadvantage (34 C.F.R. § 300.543).

Probably the two most problematic aspects of the IDEA LD definition are determining whether a *severe discrepancy* exists between achievement and ability, and ruling out environmental, cultural, and economic disadvantage as the primary determinants of the discrepancy. Many approaches to establishing a severe discrepancy between achievement and ability have been suggested (Cone & Wilson, 1981). States may recommend the use of specific formulas to help determine whether one exists. However, formulas should be used for guidance only. In *Riley v. Ambach* (1982), the court enjoined the commissioner of education of New York from using a standard statewide formula for determining a learning disability. The court held that rigid quantitative approaches to the identification of learning-disabled children were too inflexible and not sufficiently individualized.

There is now some consensus among measurement specialists that guidelines for evaluating whether a severe achievement-ability discrepancy exists ought to include consideration of at least two types of information. First, the school psychologist needs to evaluate the likelihood that the observed difference in achievement and ability scores is due to measurement error. (For a discussion of methods for determining this, see Cone & Wilson, 1981.)

In addition to establishing that the achievement-aptitude discrepancy is most likely not due to measurement error, measurement specialists suggest that the evaluation team consider whether the magnitude of the discrepancy is unusual or uncommon for the child's age (Flanagan, Andrews, & Genshaft, 1997). Achievement-IQ discrepancies of 15 points or more occur with as many as 20% to 40% of the general population (McDermott & Watkins, 1985). Test developers have recognized the importance of standardizing ability and achievement measures on the same population so that the prevalence of various achievement-ability discrepancies can be calculated and reported by age group. This information has become increasingly available in test manuals. Regression analysis procedures also can be used to estimate the prevalence of achievement-ability discrepancies (WtL Publishing, 1995).

Once the existence of a significant discrepancy between achievement and ability has been established, IDEA requires the team to consider whether the discrepancy is primarily the result of environmental, cultural, or economic disadvantage. This portion of the definition also poses problems for team members. Based on her review of comments in the *Congressional Record* and Department of Education policy statements, Slenkovich concludes that the intent of this part of the definition is to ensure that services are targeted for children whose learning problems are primarily the result of a disorder within the child (1986, November). Congress did not intend IDEA-Part B funds for children whose learning problems stem from a disadvantaged homelife, poor teaching, immaturity, or a lack of motivation to learn.

Slenkovich also discusses two common misunderstandings in the area of LD eligibility. First, a spelling disability alone does not qualify a child as LD; the child must qualify in one of the seven categories indicated. Spelling could, however, be included as a component of the category of written expression (1986, November).

Second, to qualify for special education and related services under IDEA-Part B, the child must have a disability that adversely affects educational performance. High-ability children may demonstrate a significant and unusual discrepancy between ability and achievement in one or more of the seven categories. However, if they are achieving at or near grade level in that area, they do not qualify as LD under IDEA-Part B (Slenkovich, 1988, March-b).

The 1980s witnessed a steady increase in the number of children identified as LD. Chalfant (1989) believes that this increase raises serious questions about the concept of LD and identification practices. Furthermore, there is evidence to suggest that team members often fail to adhere to the eligibility criteria outlined in the law. Mentally or emotionally impaired pupils are at times qualified as learning disabled because LD is seen as a relatively stigma-free classification (Turnbull, 1990). Team members also sometimes classify children who are simply slow learners as LD to provide a child with more individualized instruction than is available in regular education. These practices are inconsistent with the federal regulations implementing IDEA-Part B.

Serious Emotional Disturbance

Serious emotional disturbance is defined as follows:

> (i) The term means a condition exhibiting one or more of the following characteristics over a long period of time and to a marked degree that adversely affects educational performance:
>
> (A) An inability to learn that cannot be explained by intellectual, sensory, or health factors;
>
> (B) An inability to build or maintain satisfactory interpersonal relationships with peers and teachers;
>
> (C) Inappropriate types of behavior or feelings under normal circumstances;
>
> (D) A general pervasive mood of unhappiness or depression; or
>
> (E) A tendency to develop physical symptoms or fears associated with personal or school problems.
>
> (ii) The term includes schizophrenia. The term does not apply to children who are socially maladjusted, unless it is determined that they have a serious emotional disturbance. (34 C.F.R. § 300.7)

The IDEA-Part B definition of serious emotional disturbance (SED) has been controversial since it was adopted in 1975. It is a modification of a definition of the emotionally disturbed schoolchild first outlined by Bower in 1957 (Bower, 1982). Bower's definition grew out of a California study in the late 1950s of children identified by school personnel as emotionally disturbed. This study found that emotionally disturbed children differed from their classmates on a number of characteristics: they were poor learners; had few, if any, satisfactory interpersonal relationships; they behaved oddly or inappropriately; were depressed or unhappy; and developed illnesses or phobias. These characteristics also were found among nondisturbed children; however, the disturbed children displayed the characteristics to a marked degree over a period of time (Bower, 1982).

Bower did not differentiate between emotionally disturbed and socially maladjusted (SM) children in his definition. He believed that emotionally disturbed and socially maladjusted children were not separate entities. Federal policy makers, however, feared that a definition of emotionally disturbed based on Bower's original description would result in a category of special education eligibility that was too broad and costly for schools. They consequently limited the definition to children who have serious emotional disturbances and added a clause excluding children who are socially maladjusted unless they also have a serious emotional disturbance.

The SED definition, particularly the exclusionary clause, has generated diagnostic disagreements and confusion. Slenkovich advocates a rather narrow, legally correct interpretation of seriously emotionally disturbed. She advises the team to consider the IDEA requirements point by point when making eligibility decisions for the serious emotional disturbance classification (1988, February).

Under IDEA-Part B, the term serious emotional disturbance means that the child suffers from an emotional "condition exhibiting one or more . . . characteristics over a long period of time and to a marked degree." Bower found that one or more of the emotionally disturbed characteristics were found among almost all nondisturbed students in the California study to some extent at different times. The crucial differentiation was based on the observation that in children with emotional disturbance, "the characteristics existed to *a marked degree over a long period of time*" (Bower, 1982, p. 57). Slenkovich suggested that, consistent with the psychiatric diagnosis of schizophrenia, 6 months might be seen as the minimum period of time (1988, February). Sporadic emotional outbursts due to occasional drug abuse do not, alone, indicate a condition or state of emotional disturbance.

Consistent with Bower's original definition, the disturbance also must be present to a marked degree; it must be overt and observable. The definition of emotionally disturbed "avoids presumptions about the child's intrapsychic condition, psychiatric nosology, or clinical designation. It does not presume to go beyond what is observable in the school setting. . . . It accepts as given that emotional disturbance is disturbing to others" (Bower, 1982, p. 57). As Slenkovich suggests, school personnel can perceive that the child is experiencing a problem (1988, February).

Also consistent with Bower's original definition, the emotional disturbance must adversely affect educational performance. If a student is performing within his or her expected range for age and ability, then he or she does not qualify as SED under IDEA-Part B (Slenkovich, 1988, February).

The child with a serious emotional disturbance under IDEA-Part B must exhibit one or more of five characteristics:

1. *An inability to learn* because of the emotional disturbance. Emotional difficulties interfere with the school performance of many children. However, in order to qualify as SED using this part of the definition,

the child must be so disturbed he or she cannot learn (Slenkovich, 1988, February).

2. *An inability to build or maintain satisfactory interpersonal relationships with peers and teachers.* Children who are simply unpopular or associate with an undesirable peer group do not manifest this characteristic. The child must be so disturbed that he or she cannot enter into or maintain relationships with peers and teachers.
3. *Inappropriate types of behavior or feelings under normal circumstances,* appears to mean odd, bizarre, unusual behavior; not simply behavior that is disturbing to the class and teacher.
4. *A general or pervasive mood of unhappiness or depression.* The mood of unhappiness or depression must be observable.
5. *A tendency to develop physical symptoms or fears associated with personal or school problems.*

Again, the fears or symptoms must be marked and occur over a long period of time (adapted from Slenkovich, 1988, February, pp. 153–164). The SED definition also expressly includes children diagnosed as schizophrenic. Children diagnosed as autistic are eligible under a separate disability category.

The last element of the SED definition excludes children who are socially maladjusted unless they also are emotionally disturbed. This portion of the definition has generated much discussion because the federal regulations do not define socially maladjusted, and differentiating between emotionally impaired and socially maladjusted children is problematic. The two categories are not mutually exclusive; some children are seriously emotionally disturbed *and* socially maladjusted (Clarizio, 1987; McConaughy & Skiba, 1993).

Bower (1982), as noted above, believed that attempts to differentiate between seriously emotionally disturbed and socially maladjusted children are artificial and that such distinctions miss the more important point that both groups of children are in need of special help (see also Short & Shapiro, 1993). Some have called for a broader interpretation of serious emotional disturbance to include socially maladjusted (Council for Children with Behavior Disorders Executive Committee, 1987); others have challenged regular education to develop better programs for socially maladjusted students who are not emotionally disturbed (Clarizio, 1987). As will be seen in Chapter 6, some pupils not eligible for special education and related services under the serious emotional disturbance category of IDEA-Part B may qualify as handicapped under Section 504.

Thus, aspects of the SED definition are vague, subjective, and controversial. Confusion also arises from the fact that nonschool mental health professionals are typically trained to use a system for classifying childhood disorders that differs from IDEA. The system of classification that is most frequently used outside the schools is the *Diagnostic and Statistical Manual of Mental Disorders (DSM-IV)* (American Psychiatric Association, 1994). As Slenkovich has observed, psychologists and psychiatrists in nonschool settings often assume (and state in reports to schools) that a child diagnosed as suffering from a serious emotional problem under *DSM-IV* automatically qualifies for special education and related services as seriously emotionally disturbed (1988, February). However, in order to qualify for special education as SED under IDEA-Part B, a child must be found eligible under the IDEA-Part B definition.

Other Health Impairment

> Other health impairment means having limited strength, vitality or alertness, due to chronic or acute health problems such as heart condition, tuberculosis, rheumatic fever, nephritis, asthma, sickle cell anemia, hemophilia, epilepsy, lead poisoning, leukemia, or diabetes that adversely affects a child's educational performance. (34 C.F.R. § 300.7)

Beginning in the 1980s, the courts and the Office of Special Education Programs (OSEP) began to address questions regarding whether students with Acquired Immune Deficiency Syndrome (AIDS), alcohol and chemical dependency, and Attention Deficit Disorder/Attention Deficit Hyperactivity Disorder (ADD/ADHD) qualify as having an other health impairment under Part B. Court rulings have determined that students with AIDS qualify under the other health impairment classification only if their physical condition is such that it adversely affects educational performance (*Doe v. Belleville,* 1987). However, as will be seen in Chapters 6 and 10, pupils with AIDS are protected by Section 504 of The Rehabilitation Act of 1973.

OSEP also has addressed the question of whether chemically dependent pupils (alcohol- or drug-addicted) qualify as having an other health impairment under IDEA. According to OSEP, chemical dependency does not, in and of itself, qualify a child for special education and related services within the other health impairment classification (quoted in Slenkovich, 1987, June). However, students with drug or alcohol dependency may be protected by Section 504 (see Chapter 6).

A third question is whether students with ADD/ADHD qualify for special education and related services under the other health impairment classification of IDEA-Part B. A 1991 U.S. Department of Education memorandum (September 16, 1991) addressed eligibility of students with ADD/ADHD for services under Part B and suggested that some pupils with ADD/ADHD may qualify within the IDEA definitions of other health impairment, specific learning disability, or serious emotional disturbance. Other children with ADD/ADHD who do not qualify under IDEA are handicapped within the meaning of Section 504 if their condition substantially limits a major life activity, such as learning (see Chapter 6).

Pupil Evaluation Procedures

The Problem of Misclassification

As noted previously, right-to-education court cases signaled to Congress that federal legislation was needed to assure educational opportunities for all children with disabilities. A second type of court case was important in shaping the nondiscriminatory testing, classification, and placement procedures required by IDEA-Part B. These cases concerned the misclassification of racial and ethnic minority group children as "mentally retarded," and their placement in special classes for the educable mentally retarded. Cases concerning misclassification of ethnic minority children as educable mentally retarded involve due process and equal protection guarantees of the 14th Amendment (Bersoff, 1979).

Due Process One of the liberty interests protected by the 14th Amendment is the right to be free from unwarranted stigmatization by the state. The courts have determined that under the protections of the 14th Amendment, the state (school) may not assign a negative label such as mentally retarded without due process; that is, some sort of fair and impartial decision-making procedures (Bersoff & Ysseldyke, 1977). Due process rights protect individuals from "arbitrary and capricious" labeling by the state. In the *P.A.R.C.* ruling, a number of procedural safeguards against misclassification were required. For example, parents were given the right to an impartial hearing if they were dissatisfied with their child's special education classification or placement.

Equal Protection With the landmark *Brown v. Board of Education* decision in 1954, the Supreme Court ruled that school segregation by race was a denial of the right to equal protection (equal educational opportunity) under the 14th Amendment. Following this decision, the courts began to scrutinize school practices that suggested within-school segregation; that is, where minority group children were segregated and treated differently within the schools. A number of suits against the public schools were filed in which minority group children were overrepresented in lower education tracks and special education classes. These lower tracks and special education classes were seen as educationally inferior and a denial of equal education opportunities. The claimants in these cases maintained that many children were misclassified and inappropriately placed based on racially and culturally discriminatory classification and placement procedures (see Exhibit 5–2).

The first three court cases summarized in Exhibit 5–2, along with *P.A.R.C.* and *Mills,* were extremely influential in shaping the IDEA-Part B requirements for nondiscriminatory testing and classification, and the procedural or due process safeguards against misclassification. *Larry P. v. Riles* and *P.A.S.E. v. Hannon* addressed the question of whether IQ tests are valid for the purpose of classifying and placing minority group children in special classes. The court in *P.A.S.E.* ruled that the use of IQ tests within the context of the assessment process outlined in IDEA-Part B was not likely to result in racially or culturally discriminatory placement decisions. As an additional safeguard against misclassification of ethnic minority children, the 1997 amendments to IDEA require each state to gather and examine data to determine if a significant disproportionality of race is occurring in the state in relation to the identification of children as disabled and the children's placement. If it is determined there is a significant disproportionality, the state must provide for the review and, if appropriate, revision of policies and practices (Pub. L. No. 105-17, § 618, 111 Stat. 102 [1997]).

Protection in Evaluation Procedures

The early court cases concerning the misclassification of pupils as mentally impaired prompted Congress to include a number of standards with regard to both the content and the process of assessment, classification, and special education placement in IDEA-Part B. IDEA-Part B requires each SEA or LEA to establish and implement procedures to assure a full and individual initial evaluation of each child's education needs before any action is taken with respect to the initial classification and placement in special education (Pub. L. No. 105-17, § 614, 111 Stat. 81 [1997]). Informed parental consent for assessment and the nondiscriminatory testing and assessment procedures required by IDEA-Part B were discussed in Chapter 4. In recent years, prereferral intervention programs have gained popularity in the public schools, and such programs are seen as an additional safeguard against inappropriate referral, unnecessary testing, and misclassification (see Chapter 10).

Exhibit 5–2. Cases Concerning Misclassification of Ethnic Minority Children

Hobson v. Hansen (1967, 1969)

The first significant legal challenge to the use of aptitude tests for assigning minority group children to low-ability classes was *Hobson v. Hansen.* In this case, African American and poor children were disproportionately assigned to the lower tracks in the Washington, DC, public schools on the basis of scores on group-administered aptitude tests. Federal Judge Wright noted that the tracking system was rigid, it segregated students by race, and that the lower tracks were educationally inferior. He further stated that because the aptitude tests were "standardized primarily on and are relevant to a white middle-class group of students, they produce inaccurate and misleading test scores when given to lower class and Negro students" (*Hobson,* 1967, p. 514). He ruled that the tracking system was a violation of equal protection laws and ordered the system abolished.

Diana v. State Board of Education (1970)

Diana was a class action suit filed in California on behalf of nine Mexican American children placed in classes for the educable mentally retarded (EMR) on the basis of Stanford-Binet (LM) or WISC IQ scores. Diana, one of the plaintiffs, came from a Spanish-speaking family and was placed in an EMR classroom based on an IQ score of 30. When she was later retested in Spanish and English by a bilingual psychologist, she scored 49 points higher on the same test and no longer qualified for special class placement (Bersoff & Ysseldyke, 1977). The consent decree in *Diana* required children be assessed in their primary language or with sections of tests that do not depend on knowledge of English (Reschly, 1979).

Guadalupe Organization, Inc. v. Tempe Elementary School District (1972)

Guadalupe was a class action suit filed on behalf of Yaqui Indian and Mexican American pupils. The consent decree in *Guadalupe* also required assessment in the child's primary language, or the use of nonverbal measures if the child's primary language was not English. *Guadalupe,* however, went further than *Diana* in requiring a multifaceted evaluation that included assessment of adaptive behavior and an interview with the parents in the child's home (Reschly, 1979). *Guadalupe* also required due process procedures, including informed consent for evaluation and placement.

Larry P. v. Riles (1984)

Larry P. was a class action suit filed on behalf of African American pupils placed in classes for the educable mentally retarded (EMR) in the San Francisco School District. The plaintiffs claimed that many African American children were misclassified as mentally retarded, and that IQ tests were the primary basis for classification as EMR. The court asked the schools to demonstrate that their methods of classification (i.e., use of IQ test scores) were "rational" or valid for the purpose of classifying African American children as mentally retarded and in need of special education. The school district was unable to convince the court that IQ tests were valid for the purpose of placing African American children in EMR classes, and in 1972 the court temporarily enjoined the schools from any further placement of African American children in EMR classes on the basis of IQ test results.

Exhibit 5–2. *(Continued)*

In the second phase of *Larry P.,* the trial on the substantive issues, the plaintiffs requested that the court consider their claims under both the 14th Amendment and the new federal statute, Pub. L. No. 94-142. Over 10,000 pages of testimony were presented during this phase. In his lengthy opinion, Judge Peckham characterized the EMR classes as "inferior" and "dead-end." Based on his analysis of the expert testimony, he found IQ tests to be racially and culturally discriminatory. He ruled that the school failed to show that IQ tests were valid for the purpose of selecting African American children for EMR classes, and, in his view, IQ scores weighed so heavily in decision making that they "contaminated" and biased the assessment process. He permanently enjoined the state from using any standardized intelligence tests to identify African American children for EMR classes without prior permission of the court (Bersoff, 1982; Reschly, 1979). In 1986, Judge Peckham banned the use of IQ tests to assign African American children to any special education program except for the state-supported gifted and talented program.

In 1988, a group of parents filed a suit claiming that the state's ban on IQ tests discriminated against African American children by denying them an opportunity to take the tests helpful in determining special education needs. In 1992, Judge Peckham issued an order allowing African American children to be given IQ tests with parent consent (*Crawford v. Honig,* 1994). The California State Department of Education continued to prohibit the use of IQ tests with African American children, however. The California Association of School Psychologists made an unsuccessful attempt to challenge the state's ban on IQ testing in 1994 (*California Association of School Psychologists v. Superintendent of Public Instruction,* 1994).

P.A.S.E. v. Hannon (1980)

This case was filed on behalf of African American children in the Chicago public schools. As Bersoff notes, "the facts, issues, claims and witnesses" were similar to *Larry P.,* but the outcome was different (1982, p. 81). Judge Grady carefully listened to the same expert witnesses who testified in San Francisco. He decided that the issue of racial and cultural bias could best be answered by examining the test questions himself. He proceeded to read aloud every question on the WISC, WISC-R, and Stanford-Binet (LM) and every acceptable response. As a result of his analysis, he found only eight items on the WISC or WISC-R to be biased and one item on the Stanford-Binet. He concluded that the use of IQ tests within the context of a multifaceted assessment process as outlined in IDEA was not likely to result in racially or culturally discriminatory classification decisions and found in favor of the school system (Bersoff, 1982).

Student Evaluations and Eligibility Determination

In conducting an evaluation, IDEA-Part B requires the LEA to (a) use a variety of assessment tools and strategies to gather relevant functional and developmental information, including information provided by the parent, that may assist in determining whether the child has a disability and the content of the child's individualized education program, including information related to enabling the child to be involved in and progress in the general curriculum or, for preschool children, to participate in appropriate activities; (b) not use any single procedure as the sole criterion for determining whether a child has a disability or determining an appropriate educational program for the child; and (c) use technically sound instruments that may assess the relative contribution of cognitive and behavioral factors, in addition to physical or developmental factors (Pub. L. No. 105-17, § 614, 111 Stat. 81-82 [1997]). In addition, assessment tools must be valid and fair, and the child must be assessed in all areas related to the suspected disability (see Chapter 4). The assessment strategies must provide relevant information that directly assists in determining the education needs of the child (Pub. L. No. 105-17).

After completion of the administration of tests and other evaluation materials, the determination of whether the child has a disability is made by a team of qualified professionals along with the parent. School personnel may develop *tentative* alternative proposals for meeting a child's educational needs, but actual eligibility and placement decisions must be made at a meeting with the parents (see *Spielberg v. Henrico County Public Schools,* [1988]). The group making the eligibility determination must include individuals with the knowledge and skills necessary to (a) interpret the evaluation data, (b) make an informed determination as to whether the child is a child with a disability, and (c) determine whether the child needs special education and related services. The composition of this team will vary depending upon the nature of the child's suspected disability. Some or all of the persons who serve on this eligibility determination team may also serve on the IEP team. The parent is given a copy of the evaluation report (Pub. L. No. 105-17, § 614, 111 Stat. 82 [1997]).

Under IDEA-Part B, parents have the right to obtain an independent educational evaluation of their child, and those findings must be considered by the school "in any decision made with respect to the provision of FAPE [a free appropriate public education] to the child."[3] The school, on request, must provide parents with information about where an independent

[3] For an interpretation of what is meant by the requirement to consider findings from an independent evaluation, see *T.S. v. Ridgefield Board of Education,* 1992.

educational evaluation may be obtained. If the parent unilaterally seeks and obtains an independent evaluation, then the evaluation is at private (parent) expense. If an independent evaluation is requested by the school or a hearing officer, then the evaluation is done at public expense (34 C.F.R. § 300.503).

When a child is seen for reevaluation, professionals qualified to make eligibility determinations and the IEP team review existing evaluation data on the child and, on the basis of that review (along with input from the parents), identify what additional data are needed to determine (a) whether the child continues to have a particular category of disability, (b) the present levels of performance and education needs of the child, (c) whether the child continues to need special education services, and (d) what services are needed for the child to meet education goals and participate, as appropriate, in the general curriculum. If, as part of a reevaluation, it is determined that no additional data are needed to determine whether a child continues to have a disability, then the school ensures that the child's parents are notified of that determination and the reasons for it, along with their right to request an assessment of the child, and the LEA is not required to conduct an assessment unless requested by the child's parents. However, an LEA is required to evaluate a child with a disability before determining that the child no longer qualifies as disabled under Part B (Pub. L. No. 105-17, § 614, 111 Stat. 82-83 [1997]).

Individualized Education Program

As previously noted, in the *P.A.R.C.* consent decree, the court required that instructional programs for each child with disabilities be "appropriate for his learning capabilities," and the *Mills* ruling required that a disabled child's education be "suited to his needs." This policy of providing an appropriate education for each child with disabilities is achieved in IDEA-Part B by the individualized education program (IEP). Congress viewed the IEP as a means of preventing functional exclusion of children with disabilities from opportunities to learn, and the yearly review of the IEP was seen as a safeguard against misclassification and as a way to encourage continued parent involvement (Turnbull, 1990).

The Meeting

The SEA or LEA is responsible for initiating and conducting a meeting for the purpose of developing the child's IEP. The IEP meeting must be held within 30 calendar days after the determination that the child may need special education and related services (34 C.F.R. § 300.343). The Office of

Civil Rights and the Office of Special Education Programs recently clarified the meaning of this portion of the regulations (see McKee, 1996). Schools are not required to complete the evaluation and hold the IEP meeting within 30 days of the *referral* for evaluation; the 30-day countdown to the IEP starts with the determination that the child needs special education.

The Team

The IEP team is a group of individuals composed of (a) the parents of a child with a disability; (b) at least one regular education teacher of the child (if the child is, or may be, participating in a regular education environment); (c) at least one special education teacher, or where appropriate, at least one special education provider of the child; (d) a representative of the LEA who is qualified to provide, or supervise the provision of, specially designed instruction to meet the needs of children with disabilities, who is knowledgeable about the general curriculum, and who is knowledgeable about the availability of resources of the LEA; (e) an individual who can interpret the instructional implications of evaluation results (who may already be a member of the team in another capacity); (f) at the discretion of the parent or the LEA, other individuals who have knowledge or special expertise regarding the child, including related services personnel as appropriate; and (g) whenever appropriate, the child (Pub. L. No. 105-17, § 614, 111 Stat. 85 [1997]).

If private school placement is under consideration, or if the child attends a parochial or private school, the LEA must ensure that a representative of the private school attends the meeting or in some way participates in the meeting (e.g., telephone conference call) (34 C.F.R. § 300.343-300.345).

If the purpose of the IEP meeting is consideration of transition services for the student (services to promote movement from school to postschool activities), the school must invite the student to attend. If the student is not able to attend, the school must take steps to ensure that the student's preferences and interests are considered. Schools also must ensure that representatives of agencies responsible for providing or paying for transition services attend the meeting or in some way participate in the planning of any transition services (34 C.F.R. § 300.344).

Prior to 1975, parents were often not included in special education placement decisions, and school policies of closed records made it difficult for parents to gain access to information about how such decisions were made. The 1997 amendments clarify that each SEA or LEA must ensure that the parents of a child with a disability are members of any group that makes decisions on the educational placement of their child (Pub. L. No.

105-17, § 614, 111 Stat. 88 [1997]). IDEA-Part B requires the following procedures to ensure parent participation and shared decision making in the development of the IEP: The school must provide adequate prior notice of the meeting, and the meeting must be scheduled at a mutually agreed upon time and place. Notice must include the purpose, time, place, and location of the meeting, and who will be in attendance. To ensure parents understand the proceedings of the meeting, the school must provide interpreters for parents who are deaf or whose native language is other than English. If neither parent can attend, the school must attempt to ensure parent participation using other means such as conference telephone calls (34 C.F.R. § 300.345).

The IEP meeting may be conducted without parent participation only if the school is unable to convince the parents to attend. The school must document its efforts to arrange a mutually agreed upon meeting. This documentation might include records of telephone calls and the results of those calls, copies of correspondence to parents and responses, or records of home visits or visits to the parent's place of employment (34 C.F.R. § 300.345).

Development of the IEP

IDEA-Part B outlines a number of factors the IEP team is obligated to consider in developing each child's IEP. The team must consider the strengths of the child and the concerns of the parents for enhancing the education of their child, and the results of the initial evaluation or most recent evaluation of the child. In addition, the team should consider the following special factors: (a) in the case of a child whose behavior impedes his or her learning or that of others, the team should consider strategies, including positive behavioral interventions, and supports to address that behavior; (b) in the case of a child with limited English proficiency, the team should consider the language needs of the child as such needs relate to his or her IEP; (c) in the case of a child who is blind or visually impaired, the team should consider providing instruction in Braille and the use of Braille, unless the IEP team determines after evaluation of reading and writing skills, needs, and media that use of Braille is not appropriate for the child; (d) in the case of the child who is deaf or hard of hearing, the team should consider the child's full range of needs, including language and communication needs, opportunities for direct communications with peers and professional personnel in the child's language and communication mode, opportunities for direct instruction in the child's language and communication mode, and academic level; and (e) whether the child requires assistive technology devices and services (Pub. L. No. 105-17, § 614, 111 Stat. 86 [1997]).

Content of the IEP

IDEA-Part B requires a written IEP for each child identified as disabled and in need of special education and related services that includes the following:

1. A statement of the child's present levels of educational performance, including how the child's disability affects the child's involvement and progress in the general curriculum; or for preschool children, as appropriate, how the disability affects the child's participation in appropriate activities;
2. A statement of measurable annual goals, including benchmarks or short-term objectives, related to meeting the child's needs that result from the child's disability to enable the child to be involved in and progress in the general curriculum, and meeting each of the child's other educational needs that result from the child's disability;
3. A statement of the special education and related services and supplementary aids and services to be provided to the child, or on behalf of the child, and a statement of the program modifications or supports for school personnel that will be provided for the child to advance appropriately toward attaining the annual goals, to be involved and progress in the general curriculum, and to participate in extracurricular and other nonacademic activities, and to be educated and participate with other children with disabilities and nondisabled children;
4. An explanation of the extent, if any, to which the child will not participate with nondisabled children in the regular class and in nonacademic activities;
5. A statement of any individual modifications in the administration of state or districtwide assessments of student achievement that are needed in order for the child to participate in such assessments and if the IEP team determines that the child will not participate in a particular state or districtwide assessment of student achievement (or part of such assessment), a statement of why that assessment is not appropriate for the child; and how the child will be assessed;
6. The projected date for the beginning of the services and modifications, and the anticipated frequency, location, and duration of those services and modifications;
7. Beginning at age 14, and updated annually, a statement of the transition service needs of the child that focuses on the child's courses of study (such as participation in a vocational education program); beginning at age 16 (or younger, if determined appropriate by the IEP team), a statement of needed transition services for the child including, when appropriate, a

statement of the interagency responsibilities or any needed linkages; beginning at least one year before the child reaches the age of majority under state law, a statement that the child has been informed of his or her rights that will transfer to the child on reaching the age of majority; and

8. A statement of how the child's progress toward the annual goals will be measured, and how the child's parents will be regularly informed (by such means as periodic report cards) at least as often as parents of nondisabled children, of their child's progress toward the annual goals, and the extent to which that progress is sufficient to enable the child to achieve the goals by the end of the year (Pub. L. No. 105-17, § 614, 111 Stat. 83-85 [1997]).

Special Education As noted, the IEP must include a statement of the specific special education and related services to be provided to the child. The term *special education* is defined as specially designed instruction, at no cost to the parents, to meet the unique needs of a child with a disability, including instruction in the classroom, in the home, in hospitals and institutions, and in other settings (Pub. L. No. 105-17, § 602, 111 Stat. 45-46 [1997]). Special education includes instruction in physical education and vocational education if designed to meet the unique needs of a child with a disability (34 C.F.R. § 300.17). Speech pathology instruction is included as special education; however, speech pathology also can be a related service.

IDEA-Part B requires schools to provide a statement of needed transition services for pupils with disabilities beginning at age 16 (or younger if appropriate) as part of the IEP. *Transition services* are defined as a coordinated set of activities for a student with a disability that (a) are designed within an outcome-oriented process, which promotes movement from school to post-school activities, including post-secondary education, vocational training, integrated employment (including supported employment), continuing and adult education, adult services, independent living or community participation; (b) are based upon the individual student's needs, taking into account the student's preferences and interests; and (c) include instruction, related services, community experiences, the development of employment and other post school adult living objectives, and, when appropriate, acquisition of daily living skills and functional vocational evaluation (Pub. L. No. 105-17, § 602, 111 Stat. 46 [1997]).

Related Services *Related services* means transportation and such developmental, corrective, and other supportive services as may be required to assist a child with a disability to benefit from special education. Related services includes speech-language pathology and audiology, psychological services, physical and occupational therapy, recreation (including therapeutic recreation services), social work services, counseling services (including rehabilitation counseling), orientation and mobility services, medical services for diagnostic or evaluation purposes, and early identification and assessment of disabilities in children (Pub. L. No. 105-17, § 602, 111 Stat. 45 [1997]). The term also includes school health services and parent counseling and training (34 C.F.R. § 300.16).

Under IDEA-Part B, a related service cannot "stand alone—it must be attached to a special education program, and it must be a necessary service for the child to benefit from special instruction" (Slenkovich, 1988, March-c, p. 168; also Note at § 300.17). If the child is not eligible for special education under IDEA-Part B, there can be no related services, and the child (lacking a disability) is not covered under the Act.

Supplementary Aids and Services *Supplemental aids and services* means aids, services, and other supports that are provided in regular education classes or other education-related settings to enable children with disabilities to be educated with children who are not disabled to the maximum extent appropriate (Pub. L. No. 105-17, § 602, 111 Stat. 46 [1997]).

Implementation of the IEP

The school is accountable for providing the special education instruction and related services outlined in the IEP. The description of services to be provided is an "enforceable promise" (Slenkovich, 1988, March-c, p. 168). Recommendations for nonspecial education services the school is not required to provide (e.g., for family therapy) should be made separate from the IEP (Slenkovich, 1987, December).

As noted, the IEP must include a statement of annual goals and benchmarks or short-term instructional objectives. Neither the school nor the teacher may be held accountable if a child does not achieve the IEP goals; they must, however, make a good faith effort toward helping the child achieve his or her goals (34 C.F.R. § 300.350; Note at § 300.350).

If the school and parents agree on the child's classification, placement, and proposed program plan, the IEP is implemented as soon as possible ("with no undue delay") following the meeting (34 C.F.R. § 300.342; Note at § 300.342). If parents and the school do not agree, either party may request mediation or a due process hearing. Unless parents and the school agree otherwise, the student remains in his or her present placement during any due process proceeding. This is the *stay put* rule (34 C.F.R. § 300.513).

It also should be noted that individual members of the IEP team may express a dissenting opinion in writing if they do not agree with the child's classification, placement, or proposed program plan.

Each child's IEP must be reviewed and revised at least annually, and each child must be seen for reevaluation at least once every 3 years, or more often if warranted. If the IEP team determines that no additional assessment data are needed as part of a reevaluation, the LEA is not required to conduct additional assessments unless requested by the child's parents. During the annual review of the IEP, the team must determine whether the annual goals for the child are being achieved and revise the IEP as appropriate to address (a) any lack of expected progress toward annual goals and progress in the general curriculum, (b) the results of any reevaluations conducted, (c) information about the child provided by the parents, or (d) the child's anticipated needs. The regular education teacher is required to participate in the IEP review as appropriate (Pub. L. No. 105-17, § 614, 111 Stat. 87 [1997]). The LEA also must convene an IEP meeting if an agency fails to provide the transition services described in a child's IEP.

Once a student has been placed in a particular program, the school may not change the placement without another IEP meeting. However, school officials may remove students with disabilities to an alternative placement for disciplinary reasons, as outlined in Pub. L. No. 105-17 (see Chapter 10). Court rulings have held that the decision to graduate a student with disabilities constitutes a change of placement requiring an IEP meeting (*Cronin v. Board of Education of East Ramapo Central School District,* 1988).

Least Restrictive Environment

As noted earlier in the chapter, prior to IDEA children with moderate or severe impairments were often routinely excluded from school. Children with mild disabilities were frequently segregated in special classes with few opportunities to interact with their nonhandicapped peers. In some cases, these classes were located in a separate corridor of the school. At times the less capable teachers were assigned to teach children with disabilities, and typically the classroom facilities and equipment were less adequate than for nondisabled children (Turnbull, 1990). Few special class children ever returned to the mainstream.

The "least restrictive alternative" doctrine evolved from court decisions during the 1960s (e.g., *Wyatt v. Stickney,* 1971). Turnbull (1990) summarizes this constitutionally based doctrine as follows: "[E]ven if the legislative purpose of a government action is appropriate . . . the purpose may not be pursued by means that broadly stifle personal liberties if it can be achieved by less oppressive restrictive means" (p. 146).

The doctrine of least restrictive alternative was at the foundation of the deinstitutionalization movement in the field of mental health in the late 1960s and early 1970s. The doctrine recognizes that it may be necessary to restrict personal freedoms when treating a mentally ill individual, but the state should deprive the patient of his or her liberties only to the extent necessary to provide treatment (Turnbull, 1990).

This principle also was applied to the education of the disabled in IDEA-Part B with the requirement that special education and related services be provided in a setting that is the least restrictive environment (LRE) appropriate for the child. Congress recognized that integration of children with disabilities into the educational mainstream was not likely to occur without a legal mandate. Many educators and nondisabled pupils and their parents held negative stereotypes and attitudes toward special education students (Martin, 1979). Consequently, IDEA-Part B requires the SEA or LEA to assure that:

> To the maximum extent appropriate, children with disabilities, including children in public or private institutions or other care facilities, are educated with children who are nondisabled, and special classes, separate schooling or other removal of children with disabilities from the regular educational environment occurs only when the nature or severity of the disability is such that education in regular classes with the use of supplementary aids and services cannot be achieved satisfactorily. (Pub. L. No. 105-17, § 612, 111 Stat. 61 [1997])

Congress intended that the SEA or LEA make available a continuum of alternative placements to meet the needs of children with disabilities, including instruction in regular classes with supplementary services, special classes, special schools, home instruction, and instruction in hospitals and institutions (34 C.F.R. § 300.551). Congress also intended that decisions about the extent to which pupils with disabilities can be educated with nondisabled children be made on the basis of the child's individual needs and capabilities.

A number of court decisions have addressed the school's responsibility to ensure that children with disabilities are educated in the least restrictive, appropriate environment (e.g., *Daniel R.R. v. Texas Board of Education, El Paso Independent School District,* 1989; *Greer v. Rome City School District,* 1991; *Sacramento City Unified School District, Board of Education v. Rachel H.,* 1994). In *Greer,* the judge noted that "Congress created a statutory preference for educating handicapped children with nonhandicapped children" (1991, p. 695). Furthermore, in *Holland* the court stated that the Act's preference for inclusion of children with disabilities in the regular educational environment "rises to the level of a rebuttable presumption" (1992, pp. 877–878). This means that placement decision making must begin with the assumption that the child can be educated in the regular classroom

> [B]efore the school district may conclude that a handicapped child should be educated outside the regular classroom, it must consider whether supplemental aids and services would permit satisfactory education in the regular classroom. The school district must consider the whole range of supplemental aids and services, including resource rooms and itinerant instruction, for which it is obligated under the Act. . . . Only when the handicapped child's education may not be achieved satisfactorily, even with one or more of these supplemental aids and services, may the school board consider placing the child outside of the regular classroom. (*Greer,* 1991, p. 696)

In *Board of Education, Sacramento City Unified School District v. Holland* (1992) and, on appeal, *Sacramento City School District v. Rachel H.* (1994), the *Holland* case, the courts established a 4-part test for determining compliance with IDEA's mainstreaming requirement. These rulings concerned Rachel, an elementary school child with moderate mental impairment (IQ 44), whose parents requested full-time placement in a regular classroom with supplemental services. The school district, however, believed that Rachel was too severely disabled to benefit from full-time regular class and recommended special education placement for all academic instruction. The Hollands appealed the school's placement decision to a state hearing officer who ordered the district to place Rachel in a regular classroom with supportive services. The school district appealed this determination to the district (1992) and circuit courts (1994), and to the Supreme Court (*certiorari denied,* 1994). The courts affirmed the hearing officer's decision that Rachel should be educated in the regular classroom.

In *Holland,* the courts considered the following factors in determining the least restrictive appropriate environment: (a) the educational benefits available in a regular classroom, supplemented with appropriate aids and services, as compared with the educational benefits of a special education classroom; (b) the nonacademic benefits of interaction with children who are not disabled; (c) the effect of the child's presence on the teacher and other children in the classroom; and (d) the cost of educating the child in a regular classroom (*Holland,* 1994, p. 1404).

In evaluating the educational benefit of inclusion in the regular classroom, the *Holland* rulings (1992, 1994) considered the learning opportunities available in alternative settings and the child's likely progress toward IEP goals if placed in the regular education classroom. In evaluating nonacademic benefits, the court considered whether the child was likely to interact with and learn from other children in the inclusive placement. As noted in an earlier case, the presumption of inclusion in the regular classroom is not rebutted unless the school shows the child's disabilities are so severe that he or she will receive little or no educational benefit from inclusion (*Devries v. Fairfax County School Board,* 1989).

With regard to the effect of the child's presence on the teacher and other children, Part B regulations state that when children "are so disruptive in a regular classroom that the education of other students is significantly impaired, the needs of the handicapped child cannot be met in that environment" (Note at 34 C.F.R. § 300.552). The court in *Holland* considered two aspects of disruptive behavior: (a) whether there was detriment because the child was disruptive, distracting or unruly, and (b) whether the child would take up so much of the teacher's time that the other students would suffer from lack of attention (1994, p. 1401). Thus, an IEP team may consider the impact of the child's behavior on the setting where services are provided in determining an appropriate placement. However, the education of the other children must be significantly impaired by the inclusion of the child with a disability to justify exclusion on this basis. The child may be excluded from the regular education environment only if "after taking all reasonable steps to reduce the burden to the teacher, the other children in the class will still be deprived of their share of the teacher's attention" (*Holland,* 1992, p. 879; see also *Daniel R.R. v. Texas Board of Education, El Paso Independent School District,* 1989).

Schools also may consider the cost of providing an inclusive education. However, the cost must be significantly more expensive than alternative placements to justify an exclusion from the regular classroom on the basis of cost (*Holland,* 1994).

Some state-level administrators and parents have misinterpreted the LRE requirement of the law to mean that children with disabilities cannot be placed in separate special schools or centers. However, as Turnbull notes, the courts have recognized that appropriate sometimes means more, rather than less, separation from normal or regular education (1990). The LRE "favors integration but allows separation" when separation is needed to achieve a satisfactory educational program for the child" (Turnbull, 1990, p. 163). In *A.W. v. Northwest R-1 School District,* the judge noted that the mainstreaming requirement is "inapplicable" where it cannot be achieved satisfactorily (1987, p. 163).

A school placement that allows a child to remain with his or her family is considered to be less restrictive than a residential placement. IDEA also indicates a preference for a neighborhood school. Part B regulations state that unless "the IEP of a child with a disability requires some other arrangement, the child is educated in the school which he or she would attend if not nondisabled" (34 C.F.R. § 300.552). However, while the law indicates a preference for neighborhood schooling, proximity of the school is only one factor the IEP team must consider in making placement decisions. The court in *Flour Bluff Independent School District v. Katherine M.* (1996) noted, "Distance remains a consideration in determining the least restrictive environment . . . The child may have to travel farther, however, to obtain better services" (p. 675).

The SEA or LEA also must assure that a child with a disability has opportunities to participate with nondisabled children in nonacademic and extracurricular activities (e.g., meals, recess, clubs, and interest groups) to the maximum extent appropriate to the needs of the child (34 C.F.R. § 300.553). However, in several cases (e.g., *Rettig v. Kent City School District,* 1986), the courts ruled that IDEA-Part B does not require schools to provide nonacademic and extracurricular activities to children with disabilities without regard for the child's ability to benefit from the experience.

IDEA court cases (e.g., *Devries, Greer, & Holland*) along with Section 504 enforcement efforts (see Chapter 6) have signaled an increased emphasis on the legal right of children with disabilities to an education in the least restrictive environment. At the same time, educational experts have called for special education reform, with new attention to serving pupils with disabilities in the regular classroom. Ethical-legal issues associated with inclusionary models of special education service delivery are discussed further in Chapter 10.

The Meaning of Appropriate Education

IDEA-Part B thus requires that children with disabilities be provided a free and appropriate education in the least restrictive environment. Since the passage of Pub. L. No. 94-142, there have been a number of court cases that provide further interpretation of appropriate education. In their decision making about what is appropriate, the courts have considered several different factors, including whether IDEA-Part B procedures were followed in developing the

IEP, and whether the IEP is consistent with the intent of the law (Turnbull, 1990).

Board of Education of the Hendrick Hudson Central School District v. Rowley (1982) was the first case to reach the Supreme Court in which the Court attempted to define appropriate education (Exhibit 5–3). The Supreme Court's interpretation of appropriate education in *Rowley* has shaped all subsequent court decisions concerning the meaning of appropriate under IDEA-Part B. *Rowley* suggests that IDEA assures only an education program reasonably designed to benefit the student, not the best possible or most perfect education. The *Rowley* decision set forth a two-prong test of appropriate, namely, "Were IDEA procedures followed?" and "Is the program reasonably designed to benefit the child?"

The courts also have ruled that when two or more appropriate placements are available, IEP team members may consider costs to the school in determining a child's education placement (e.g., *Clevenger v. Oak Ridge School Board,* 1984).

Extended School Year

In *Battle v. Commonwealth of Pennsylvania* (1980) and several similar cases, the courts determined that appropriate education for children with severe impairments may mean an extended school year (more than 180 days) so

Exhibit 5–3. ***Board of Education of the Hendrick Hudson Central School District v. Rowley* (1982)**

The case involved Amy, a deaf child with minimal residual hearing, who understood about 50% of spoken language by lipreading. During her kindergarten year, the school provided an FM hearing aid to amplify speech. Her IEP for first grade included continued use of the hearing aid, instruction from a tutor for the deaf 1 hour each day, and speech therapy 3 hours each week.

Amy's parents also requested the school provide an interpreter for the deaf in the classroom in order for her to make optimal school progress. The school and a hearing officer agreed that an interpreter was too costly and not needed because "Amy was achieving educationally, academically, and socially without such assistance" (p. 3040). A district court, however, found in favor of the parents and noted that without the interpreter Amy was not afforded the opportunity to achieve her full potential.

Based on a review of the history of IDEA, the Supreme Court concluded that Congress only intended to provide access to education that is sufficient to confer educational benefit for the handicapped child, or a "basic floor of opportunity." It was noted that there is no requirement under IDEA that the school provide services that maximize the potential of a child with disabilities; the "furnishing of every special service necessary to maximize each handicapped child's potential is, we think, further than Congress intended to go" (p. 3047). The Court found in favor of the school.

---

that benefits from special instruction are not lost over the summer months. The following standard for determining whether a child with disabilities is entitled to an extended school year (ESY) has gained acceptance in recent years.

> If a child will experience severe or substantial regression during the summer months in the absence of a summer program, the handicapped child may be entitled to year-round services. The issue is whether the benefits accrued to the child during the regular school year will be significantly jeopardized if he is not provided an educational program during the summer months. (*Alamo Heights Independent School District v. State Board of Education,* 1986, p. 261)

Until recently, many schools required evidence of significant regression during past summers, along with documentation that the child was unable to recoup lost skills within a reasonable period of time before determining that a child was entitled to ESY services. Some schools developed regression-recoupment formulas for determining whether ESY services would be provided, such as "regression in two or more skills which takes more than twelve weeks to recoup" (Martin, 1992, p. 215).

The most recent ESY cases have ruled that parents do not need empirical data demonstrating regression during summer and slow recoupment to establish that their child is entitled to ESY services (*Cordrey v. Euckert,* 1990; *Johnson v. Independent School District No. 4 of Bixby, Tulsa County, Oklahoma,* 1990). The court in *Cordrey* noted that it is unfair to require that a child demonstrate regression in the absence of summer programming in order to be entitled to such programming in subsequent summers. The ruling in *Cordrey* suggested that decisions about whether a child is entitled to ESY can be based on predictive factors (i.e., the child is likely to show significant regression and slow recoupment of skills). Furthermore, decisions about whether a child is likely to show regression and slow recoupment may be based on "expert opinion, based on professional individual assessment" where empirical data are not available (*Cordrey,* 1990, p. 1472). Thus, recent rulings suggest schools may not require definitive empirical evidence of prior regression and slow recoupment in determining whether a child is entitled to ESY. It also is important to note that relying solely on regression-recoupment formulas is not appropriate because such formulas fail to consider the individual needs of the child (Martin, 1992). Courts have held that schools may need to consider factors other than regression-recoupment in determining the need for ESY services, such as the parent's ability to provide educational structure at home (*Johnson v. Independent School District No. 4,* 1990).

Extended School Day/Shortened School Day

The Supreme Court decision in *Rowley* defined an appropriate education as a program that is sufficient to confer educational benefit or a "basic floor of opportunity." *Garland Independent School District v. Wilks* (1987) raised the question of whether a disabled child might require an extended school-day program (more than 6 hours) in order for the child's special education program to confer benefit. In *Garland,* the court awarded the mother of a disabled child reimbursement for the after-school tutor she paid to help her son because the school's regular day program for the child was seen as inadequate to confer academic benefit. The courts also have favored extended school-day programs as an alternative to placement in a residential facility (*Kerkam v. Superintendent., D.C. Public Schools,* 1991; *Roland M. v. Concord School Committee,* 1990).

In addition to recognition of extended school-day programs, the courts have acknowledged that some children may need a shortened school day in order to confer academic benefit (for example, see, *Christopher M. v. Corpus Christi Independent School District,* 1991).

Assistive Technology

IDEA requires schools to ensure that assistive technology devices and services are made available to a child with a disability if the child requires the devices and services in order to receive an appropriate public education. Assistance technology devices and services are to be made available if required as a part of the child's special education, related services, or supplementary aids and services. *Assistive technology device* means any item, piece of equipment, or product system, whether acquired commercially off the shelf, modified, or customized, that is used to increase, maintain, or improve the functional capabilities of a child with a disability. *Assistive technology service* means any service that directly assists a child with a disability in the selection, acquisition, or use of an assistive technology device. Assistive technology services include evaluation of the needs of a child with a disability; providing for the acquisition of an assistive technology device; selection, designing, fitting, customizing such devices; coordinating and using devices with other therapies or interventions; and training the child and the professionals involved in the use of the device (Pub. L. No. 105-17, § 602, 111 Stat. 42 [1997]).

Summary

Schools are required to provide an extended school year, extended school day, and assistive technology devices and services if they are necessary to provide a disabled child with an appropriate education reasonably designed to confer benefit. However, consistent with *Rowley,* there is no requirement under IDEA that the school provide such services in order to maximize the potential of a child with disabilities.

Scope of Required Related Services

As noted earlier in the chapter, a child must be found eligible for special education before he or she qualifies to receive related services, and the related service must be necessary to assist the child with disabilities to benefit from special education. The related services provision includes school health and counseling services, but medical services are provided only for diagnostic and evaluation purposes to determine a child's medically related disability (34 C.F.R. § 300.16). This is the *medical exclusion.*

Whether certain services fall within the parameters of school health or counseling services (and are thus provided under IDEA-Part B) has been the focus of a number of court cases. *Irving Independent School District v. Tatro* (1994) (Exhibit 5–4) was a key case in determining the scope of school health services required under IDEA-Part B. In this case, the Supreme Court ruled that the school must provide clean intermittent catheterization (CIC) for a disabled child as a related service needed for her to benefit from special education. In the Court's opinion, CIC is not a medical service because it can be performed by a trained layperson and requires only several minutes

Exhibit 5–4. *Irving Independent School District v. Tatro* (1984)

Amber Tatro was born with spina bifida and suffered from orthopedic and speech impairments, and a neurogenic bladder. Because she was unable to empty her bladder voluntarily, she required clean intermittent catheterization (CIC) every 3 or 4 hours. This procedure involves insertion of a catheter into the urethra to drain the bladder and can be performed in a few minutes by a trained layperson.

Amber first received special education services at age 3, and her IEP provided early child development classes, occupational therapy, and physical therapy. There was no provision for CIC as requested by Amber's parents, however. The school held that CIC was a medical service and, under IDEA, the school is required to provide medical services only for the purpose of diagnosis to determine the child's medically related disability.

Irving v. Tatro ultimately reached the Supreme Court, and the Court decided in favor of the parents. The Court reasoned that Amber could not attend class (and therefore could not benefit from special education) without CIC as a related supportive service, and held that CIC is not a medical service because it can be performed by a trained layperson or school nurse (i.e., a physician is not required). The Court also noted that the service is not overly burdensome to the school.

every 3 or 4 hours. Similarly, in *Department of Education, State of Hawaii v. Katherine Dorr* (1984), a federal court held that tracheotomy cleaning and reinsertion falls within the boundaries of school health services to be provided under IDEA-Part B. (See also *Cedar Rapids Community School District v. Garret F. by Charlene F.*, 1996.)

However, full-time nursing care is beyond the scope of services that must be provided by the schools. *Detsel v. Board of Education of the Auburn Enlarged City School District* (1987) concerned whether the school was responsible for the cost of a full-time nurse for a 7-year-old dependent on a respirator for life support. In *Detsel,* the child's life-threatening medical condition required "constant vigilance by an individual trained to monitor her health" (p. 1023). The child's physician testified that the services of a school nurse would be inadequate. The court held that the healthcare services required by the child were outside the scope of appropriate school health services and thus beyond the scope of related services that must be provided under IDEA-Part B.[4]

Turnbull (1990) suggests that the courts consider a variety of factors in determining whether a service is a school health service or medical treatment, including complexity (Can the service be provided by a trained layperson? Is the service within the range of services traditionally provided by a school nurse?), whether the service is designed to assist the child in benefiting from special education, and whether the cost is overly burdensome to the school. In addition, Turnbull suggests the courts are reluctant to require services seen as life-sustaining because of the potential problem of medical malpractice or healthcare negligence suits against the schools. (See also *Fulginiti v. Roxbury Township Public School,* 1996.)

Another question that arises under the related services provision of IDEA-Part B is, "When is the school responsible for the cost of psychotherapy as a related service?" Counseling services identified as related services in the regulations include "services provided by qualified social workers, psychologists, guidance counselors, and other qualified personnel" (34 C.R.F. § 300.16). Schools are required to provide these services at no cost to the parent when they are included in the child's IEP.

However, more difficult questions have arisen with regard to psychotherapy provided by a physician (i.e., psychiatric treatment) and that provided in a residential facility. Court rulings on these issues have been inconsistent (Turnbull, 1990). In *Darlene L. v. Illinois State Board of*

[4] In a court action against the Secretary of Medicaid (U.S. Department of Health and Human Services), the Detsels won Medicaid-covered nursing services for their daughter during the time she attends public school (*Detsel by Detsel v. Sullivan,* 1990).

Education (1983), the court ruled that "states may properly consider psychiatric services as medical services and therefore not related services which the state must provide as part of a free appropriate education" (p. 1345). The court in this case saw the cost of psychiatric treatment as overly burdensome to the schools.

In another case, however, the court ruled that psychotherapy provided by a psychiatrist does not automatically mean the service is a medical service. In *Max M. v. Thompson* (1984), the court held, "The simple fact that a service *could be* or *actually is* rendered by a physician rather than a nonphysician does not dictate its removal from the list of required services under EAHCA *[IDEA]*" (p. 1444). The court went on to say that the limit to psychiatric services is cost: "[A] school board can be held liable for no more than the cost of the service as provided by the minimum level health care personnel recognized as competent to perform the related service" (p. 1444). Thus, this ruling suggests that in states where a psychologist or social worker is recognized as competent to provide psychotherapy, the school is responsible only for the amount it would cost for a psychologist or social worker to perform the service.

Whether the school is responsible for the cost of psychotherapy when a pupil is placed in a residential facility also has been addressed by the courts. The key issue in these cases appears to be whether the psychotherapy provided in the facility is seen as necessary for educational reasons, that is, to assist the child in benefiting from special education (Weirda, 1987). In *In the Matter of the "A" Family* (1979), the court ruled that the school must pay for psychotherapy provided at a residential facility for a seriously emotionally disturbed child who was placed there as a way of meeting his education needs. In contrast, in *McKenzie v. Jefferson* (1983), a child was hospitalized in a treatment facility for serious mental illness. The court in this case held that the placement was not made in support of a special education program. The primary purpose of the placement was for "much needed *medical* treatment" (p. 411). Psychiatric treatment costs were not seen as a related service in this case.

Since 1990, the U.S. Department of Health and Human Services (HHS) has signaled greater willingness to allow Medicaid coverage for health-related services for children receiving special education (see the 1991 "HHS Policy Clarification" prepared by HHS in cooperation with OSEP and DOE). In its 1991 policy clarification statement, HHS stated that school districts can bill the Medicaid program for medically necessary health-related services provided at school, home, or in a residential facility if the child is eligible under the state's Medicaid plan. Medicaid now covers a broad range of medical services (e.g., physician's services, prescription drugs, therapeutic interventions such as occupational therapy), and states have considerable flexibility in defining Medicaid eligibility groups. Under the 1997 amendments of IDEA, the state's governor must ensure interagency agreements regarding Medicaid. Medicaid precedes the financial responsibility of the LEA and SEA, but the SEA remains the payor of last resort (Pub. L. No. 105-17, § 612, 111 Stat. 65-66 [1997]).

Procedural Safeguards

A number of Part B procedural safeguards to assure the rights of children with disabilities and their parents were foreshadowed in the *P.A.R.C.* and *Mills* decisions. Under IDEA-Part B, the SEA must assure that each LEA establishes and implements procedures to safeguard the parent's right to confidentiality of records and right to examine records; right to consent to pupil evaluation; right to written prior notice before changes are made in identification, evaluation, placement, and special services; right to present findings from an independent evaluation; right to resolution of complaints by mediation; right to resolution of complaints by an impartial hearing officer; and right to bring civil action in court. Notice and consent, transfer of parental rights at age of majority, surrogate parents, and mediation and due process hearings are discussed.

Consent and Notice

Consent Under IDEA-Part B, parental written consent (permission) must be obtained before conducting a preplacement evaluation and before the initial placement of a child in special education. If the parent refuses consent, the LEA may request mediation or a hearing to override a parent's refusal to consent. Parent consent also is required for subsequent reevaluations of a child, unless the school can demonstrate that it has taken reasonable measures to obtain consent and the child's parent failed to respond (Pub. L. No. 105-17, § 614, 111 Stat. 81, 83 [1997]).

Notice The 1997 amendments divide information sent to parents into two different types of notices: prior written notice and procedural safeguards notice.

Prior written notice information is required whenever the SEA or LEA proposes to change the identification, evaluation, education placement or program of the child, or refuses to change the identification, evaluation, placement, or program. Notice must be provided in a mode of communication understandable to the parent (unless it is clearly not feasible to do so) and must include a description of the proposed action (or refusal to act); an explanation of why the school proposes or refuses to take action; a description of any other options considered and why those were rejected; a description of each evaluation procedure, test, record, or report used as the basis for the school's action; a statement that the parents have protection under procedural safeguards and, if the notice is not an initial referral for evaluation, the means by which a copy of a description of the procedural safeguards can be obtained; and sources for parents to contact to obtain assistance in understanding these provisions (e.g., nonprofit groups that could assist the parents) (Pub. L. No. 105-17, § 615, 111 Stat. 88-89 [1997]).

A procedural safeguards notice includes information on protections available to the parents of a child with a disability. This information must be provided at the time of initial referral for evaluation, with each notification of an IEP meeting, on reevaluation of the child, and following registration of a complaint. It must include a full explanation of the procedural safeguards written in an understandable manner. The content of the notice must include information pertaining to: independent educational evaluation, prior written notice, parent consent, access to educational records, opportunity to present complaints, the child's placement during pendency of due process proceedings, procedures for students who are subject to placement in an interim alternative educational setting, requirements for unilateral placement by parents of children in private schools at public expense, mediation, due process hearings, state-level appeals, civil action, and attorney fees (Pub. L. No. 105-17, § 615, 111 Stat. 89-90 [1997]).

Transfer of Parent Rights at Age of Majority

Under the 1997 amendments of IDEA, a state may require that when an individual with a disability reaches the age of majority or a child with a disability is incarcerated in an adult correctional facility, all rights accorded to parents transfer to the individual with a disability. The school or other agency must notify the individual and parents of the transfer of rights. For youth who have reached the age of majority and who have not been determined to be incompetent, but who are determined not to have the ability to provide informed consent with respect to their education program, the state will establish procedures for the appointment of the parent of the youth (or other appropriate person if the parent is not available) to represent the educational interest of the youth as long as he or she is eligible for special education under IDEA (Pub. L. No. 105-17, § 615, 111 Stat. 98-99 [1997]).

Surrogate Parents

Under IDEA-Part B, the school must assure the rights of a child with disabilities are protected when no parent can be identified (e.g., the child is a ward of the state under state laws). The school must assign a surrogate parent for the child, and this surrogate may not be an employee of the school or the agency responsible for the care of the child (34 C.F.R. § 300.514).

Mediation and Due Process Hearings

The school and parents may attempt to resolve disputes regarding the identification, evaluation, educational placement or program of a child through a mediation process and/or due process hearings. The 1997 amendments of IDEA require parents to provide notice to the LEA of a complaint. The notice must include (a) the name and address of the child and the name of the school he or she is attending; (b) a description of the nature of the problem regarding the child's current or proposed identification, evaluation, placement or program, and the facts relating to the problem; and (c) a proposed resolution of the problem to the extent known and available to the parents at that time. The SEA must develop a model form to assist parents in filing a complaint in compliance with the requirements of the law (Pub. L. No. 105-17, § 615, 111 Stat. 89-90 [1997]).

Mediation Under the 1997 amendments, any SEA or LEA that receives IDEA funds must ensure procedures are established and implemented to allow parties to resolve disputes regarding the identification, evaluation, educational placement or program of a child through a mediation process. At minimum, this process must be available whenever a due process hearing is requested. The procedures must ensure that the mediation process (a) is voluntary on the part of the parties; (b) is not used to deny or delay a parent's right to a due process hearing, or to deny any other parental rights; and (c) is conducted by a qualified and impartial mediator who is trained in effective mediation techniques. The SEA or LEA may establish procedures to require a parent who chooses not to use the mediation process to meet, at a time and location convenient to the parent, with a disinterested party who is under contract with an appropriate alternate dispute resolution agency to explain and discuss the benefits of the mediation process. The SEA is responsible for maintaining a list of qualified mediators and bears the costs of the mediation process. An agreement reached by the parties is recorded in a written mediation agreement. Discussions that occur during mediation are confidential and may not be used as evidence in any subsequent due process hearing or civil proceeding (Pub. L. No. 105-17, § 615, 111 Stat. 90-91 [1997]).

Due Process Hearings IDEA-Part B also grants parents and the school a right to an impartial due process hearing on any matter regarding the identification, evaluation, educational placement or program of a child. Under IDEA-Part B, the due process hearing must be conducted by the SEA or other school agency responsible for the child. Each SEA or LEA must maintain a list of hearing officers and their qualifications. The hearing officer may not be an employee of the school, and no person with a personal or professional interest in the outcome may serve as the hearing officer. The school must inform the parents of any free or low-cost legal and other relevant services available (34 C.F.R. § 300.507–300.508). The school also must inform parents that they may be able to recover attorney fees if they prevail in a hearing or judicial proceeding (34 C.F.R. § 300.515).

IDEA-Part B further specifies a number of hearing rights. The hearing must be held at a time and place reasonably convenient to the parents. Each party has a right to be accompanied and advised by legal counsel and other experts, to present evidence and confront, cross-examine, and compel the attendance of witnesses (34 C.F.R. § 300.508). No evidence may be introduced by any party unless it was disclosed at least five business days before the hearing; each party must disclose to all other parties all evaluations completed by that date and the recommendations based on those evaluations if the findings from such evaluations will be used at the hearing (Pub. L. No. 105-17, § 615, 111 Stat. 91 [1997]). The parents are afforded the right to have their child present and to have the hearing open to the public (34 C.F.R. § 300.508).

The hearing must be held and a final decision reached within 45 days after the request for a hearing. Each party has a right to a written record of the hearing (or an electronic verbatim recording if the parent so chooses) and to a copy of the written findings of fact and the decision. The decision of the hearing officer is final unless a party initiates an appeal or begins a court action (Pub. L. No. 105-17, § 615, 111 Stat. 91 [1997]; 34 C.F.R. § 300.508–300.509).

If the parent or the school is not satisfied with the decision of the hearing officer, an appeal may be filed to the SEA for an impartial review of the hearing and the decision of the hearing officer (34 C.F.R. § 300.506–300.513).

Right to Private Action

IDEA grants the parent and the school the right to civil action if they are not satisfied with the SEA decision. This means that parents may initiate a court action against the school on behalf of a child with a disability if they believe the school has violated the provisions of IDEA with respect to their child. Except for very unusual circumstances, parents are required to exhaust administrative remedies (e.g., due process hearings) available to them before they pursue a court action.

Recovery of Attorney Fees

In 1986, Congress enacted the Handicapped Children's Protection Act of 1986 (Pub. L. No. 99-372), an amendment to IDEA which provides: "In any action or proceeding brought under this subsection, the court in its discretion, may award reasonable attorney fees as part of the costs to the parents or guardian of a handicapped child or youth who is the prevailing party" (20 U.S.C. 1415[a][4][B]). The 1997 amendments of IDEA prohibit recovery of attorney fees for an IEP meeting (unless the meeting is convened as a result of an administrative proceeding or judicial action) or for mediation that is conducted prior to filing a complaint. In addition, the amendments specify that attorney fees may be reduced if the attorney representing the parent did not provide required information to the school district (Pub. L. No. 105-17, § 615, 111 Stat. 92-93 [1997]).

Abrogation of State Sovereign Immunity

Under the 1990 amendments of IDEA, states and their departments of education can be sued by private citizens if they violate the law. This provision in IDEA waives the traditional immunity from private lawsuits that states enjoy under the 11th Amendment to the Constitution.

INFANTS AND TODDLERS WITH DISABILITIES

Pub. L. No. 99-457, The Education for the Handicapped Act Amendments of 1986 (now IDEA-Part C), provides grants to states to develop and implement a statewide, comprehensive system of early intervention services for infants and toddlers with disabilities and their families. The purpose of IDEA-Part C is (a) to enhance the development of infants and toddlers with disabilities and to minimize their potential for developmental delay; (b) to reduce the education costs to our society, including our nation's schools, by minimizing the need for special education and related services after infants and toddlers with disabilities reach school age; (c) to minimize the likelihood of institutionalization of individuals with disabilities and maximize the potential for their independent living in society; (d) to enhance the capacity of families to meet the special needs of their infants and toddlers with disabilities; and (e) to enhance the capacity of state and local agencies and service providers to identify, evaluate, and meet the needs of historically underrepresented populations, particularly minority, low-income, inner-city, and rural populations (Pub. L. No. 105-17; § 631, 111 Stat. 106 [1997]).

There are a number of similarities and differences between legislation providing a free and appropriate education for children with disabilities in the 3- to 21-year age group (IDEA-Part B) and the legislation providing grants for early intervention services for infants and toddlers (IDEA-Part C). Part C is described under the following sections: Statewide System, Child Find, Eligible Children, Evaluation and Assessment, Individualized Family Service Plan, Early Intervention Services, and Procedural Safeguards. The Part C regulations cited in the text pre-date the recent amendments of IDEA. Regulations implementing the 1997 amendments are to be issued by June 1998. Readers are encouraged to consult the *Federal Register* for the new regulations.

Statewide System

Prior to 1986, services for infants and toddlers with disabilities were typically provided by a number of different agencies in each state (social services, public health, education), often resulting in service gaps or unnecessary duplication (Gallagher, 1989). IDEA-Part C was designed to encourage states to develop and implement a statewide, comprehensive, coordinated, multidisciplinary, interagency program of early intervention services for infants and toddlers with disabilities and their families (Pub. L. No. 105-17; § 631, 111 Stat. 106 [1997]). The law requires each state to identify a lead agency responsible for administration, supervision, coordination, and monitoring of programs and activities in the state. Different states have chosen different lead agencies, including state departments of health, education, and social welfare (Gallagher, 1989). In order to receive funds, each state must have submitted an application to Washington that outlines state policies and procedures for the delivery of services consistent with the requirements of Part C. Part C also requires the development of an interagency coordinating council to advise and assist the lead agency, identify and coordinate financial resources, and promote interagency agreements (Pub. L. No. 105-17; § 637, 111 Stat. 112 [1997]).

Child Find

IDEA-Part C requires each state to establish a public awareness program and a comprehensive child find system to assure eligible children are identified and referred for evaluation in a timely manner. Each state also must develop a central directory of public and private early intervention services, resources, demonstration projects, and experts in the state that is accessible to parents of infants and toddlers with disabilities and the general public (Pub. L. No. 105-17; § 635, 111 Stat. 108-109 [1997]).

Eligible Children

IDEA-Part C defines *infant or toddler with a disability* to mean a child under 3 years who needs early intervention services because he or she (a) is experiencing developmental delays, as measured by appropriate diagnostic instruments and procedures, in one or more of the areas of cognitive, physical, communication, social or emotional, or adaptive development; or (b) has a diagnosed physical or mental condition that has a high probability of resulting in developmental delay. The term also may include, at a state's discretion, at-risk infants and toddlers (Pub. L. No. 105-17; § 632, 111 Stat. 108 [1997]). The term *at-risk infant or toddler* means a child under 3 years who would be at risk of experiencing a substantial delay if early intervention services were not provided (Pub. L. No. 105-17, § 632, 111 Stat. 106 [1997]). The factors that put the child at risk may be biological or environmental (Note at 34 C.F.R. § 303.16).

Evaluation and Assessment

IDEA-Part C requires a multidisciplinary assessment of the unique strengths and needs of each child and the identification of services appropriate to meet such needs (Pub. L. No. 105-17; § 636, 111 Stat. 111 [1997]). The evaluation must be based on nondiscriminatory procedures, be conducted by personnel trained to utilize appropriate methods and procedures, and include a review of records related to the child's current health status and medical history. The evaluation must include an assessment of the unique needs of the child in each of the following five developmental areas: cognitive, physical (including hearing and vision), communication, social or emotional, and adaptive (34 C.F.R. § 303.322–303.323). The evaluation includes the identification of services appropriate to meet the needs of the child in each of these areas. IDEA-Part C also requires a family-directed assessment of the resources, priorities, and concerns of the family, and the identification of the supports and services necessary to enhance the family's capacity to meet the development needs of the infant or toddler (Pub. L. No. 105-17; § 636, 111 Stat. 111 [1997]).

Individualized Family Service Plan

IDEA-Part C requires a written individualized family service plan (IFSP) rather than an IEP for each infant or toddler. The IFSP includes the following: (a) a statement of the infant's or toddler's present levels of physical, cognitive, communication, social or emotional, and adaptive development, based on objective criteria; (b) a statement of the family's resources, priorities, and concerns relating to enhancing the development of the infant or toddler; (c) a statement of the major outcomes expected to be achieved for the infant or toddler and the family, and the criteria, procedures, and timelines used to determine the degree to which progress toward achieving the outcomes is being made and whether modifications of the outcomes or services are necessary; (d) a statement of the specific early intervention services necessary to meet the unique needs of the infant or toddler and the family, including the frequency, intensity, and method of delivering services; (e) a statement of the natural environments in which early intervention services will appropriately be provided, including a justification of the extent, if any, to which services will not be provided in a natural environment; (f) the projected dates for the initiation of services and the anticipated duration of those services; (g) the identification of the service coordinator from the profession most immediately relevant to the child's or family's needs (or who is otherwise qualified to carry out all applicable responsibilities) who will be responsible for the implementation of the plan and coordination with other agencies and persons; and (h) the steps to be taken to support the transition of the toddler with a disability to preschool or other appropriate services (Pub. L. No. 105-17; § 636, 111 Stat. 111 [1997]).

The IFSP is to be developed within a reasonable time after the assessment is completed. With the consent of the parent, services may be provided prior to the completion of the assessment. The content of the IFSP must be fully explained to the parents and informed written consent from the parents must be obtained prior to the provision of the early intervention services described in the plan. If the parents do not provide consent for a particular service, then the early intervention services to which consent is obtained are provided (Pub. L. No. 105-17; § 636, 111 Stat. 111-112 [1997]).

The IFSP is evaluated once each year, and the family is provided with a review of the plan every 6 months, or more often if needed. The IFSP must include steps to provide a transition to preschool services under IDEA-Part B, if appropriate. In the case of a child who may not be eligible for preschool services under Part B, reasonable efforts must be made to convene a conference among the lead agency, family, and service providers to identify and discuss the services the child may need (Pub. L. No. 105-17; § 637, 111 Stat. 112-113 [1997]).

Early Intervention Services

Under Part C, early intervention services includes both special instruction and related services; an infant or toddler can receive a related service under

Part C without receiving special instruction. (This differs from the requirement under Part B that children with disabilities ages 3–21 only receive related services in order to benefit from special education.)

The term *early intervention services* means developmental services that are (a) provided under public supervision; (b) provided at no cost except where federal or state law provides for a system of payments by families; and (c) are designed to meet the development needs of an infant or toddler with a disability. Types of services include family training, counseling, and home visits; special instruction; speech-language pathology and audiology services; occupational therapy; physical therapy; psychological services; service coordination services; medical services only for diagnostic or evaluative purposes; early identification, screening, and assessment services; health services necessary to enable the infant or toddler to benefit from the other early intervention services; social work services; vision services; assistive technology devices and services; and transportation and related costs that are necessary to enable the infant or toddler and his or her family to receive other early intervention (Pub. L. No. 105-17; § 632, 111 Stat. 106-107 [1997]).

Procedural Safeguards

The procedural safeguards under Part C are similar to those under Part B. Parents are afforded the right to confidentiality of personally identifiable information; the right to examine records; the right to consent to or decline any early intervention service without jeopardizing the right to other services; the right to written prior notice before changes are made in identification, evaluation, placement, or provision of services; the right to use mediation; the right to timely administrative resolution of complaints; and the right to bring civil action in state or federal court (Pub. L. No. 105-17; § 639, 111 Stat. 115-116 [1997]).

CONCLUDING COMMENTS

Pub. L. No. 94-142 was enacted over 20 years ago. Court interpretations, changing rules and regulations, and policy statements have further shaped interpretation of special education law. Education law will continue to change. School psychologists must keep abreast of these changes to ensure the educational rights of pupils are safeguarded.

STUDY AND DISCUSSION

Questions for Chapter 5

1. Why did Congress require single agency responsibility for children with disabilities?
2. What is the *zero reject principle?*
3. What is the purpose of the IEP meeting? Who attends? Briefly describe the content of the IEP.
4. Briefly describe what is meant by *least restrictive appropriate environment* in special education law. Does this aspect of the law mean that all children with disabilities must be integrated into the regular classroom? What are the guiding principles for determination of a child's educational placement?
5. How is appropriate education defined in *Rowley?*
6. What is the medical exclusion?
7. What are some of the ways that Part C and Part B differ?

ACTIVITIES

1. Compare the 13 disability categories under IDEA-Part B with the categories and eligibility criteria that appear in the special education guidelines of your state.

2. Does your local school district distribute a special education handbook or pamphlet to parents outlining their rights and the school responsibilities under special education law? Obtain and review copies of informational materials given to parents and review forms used by school districts for referral for special education evaluation, parent consent for evaluation under special education law, team meeting decisions.

Chapter 6

SECTION 504 AND AMERICANS WITH DISABILITIES ACT

This chapter begins with a summary of those portions of Section 504 of The Rehabilitation Act of 1973 most pertinent to school psychological practice. Special attention is given to the similarities and differences between Section 504 and Individuals with Disabilities Education Act (IDEA) regarding school responsibilities to pupils with special needs.[1] The second portion of the chapter provides a brief overview of the Americans with Disabilities Act (1990).

SECTION 504 AND PUPILS WITH HANDICAPPING CONDITIONS

Section 504 of The Rehabilitation Act of 1973 is civil rights legislation that prohibits discrimination against pupils with handicaps in school systems receiving federal financial assistance. Although it was passed many years ago, Section 504 has often been ignored or misunderstood by the public schools (Martin, 1992). Since the late 1980s, however, Office of Civil Rights (OCR) enforcement activities, court decisions, and parent advocacy efforts have heightened awareness of Section 504, and the law has now begun to impact schools and school psychology.

Historical Framework

One way in which Congress attempted to assure a free and appropriate education for all children with disabilities was through federal grant legislation such as IDEA. A second way in which the federal government attempted to address the problem of discrimination against pupils with handicapping conditions was through antidiscrimination laws. One of the first bills that

[1] Portions of this chapter appeared previously in Jacob-Timm and Hartshorne (1994).

attempted to ensure equal educational opportunity for children with handicaps in the public schools was an amendment to Title VI of the Civil Rights Act of 1964. The bill was introduced in the House of Representatives by Congressman Vanek and in the Senate by Senator Humphrey and later became part of The Rehabilitation Act of 1973 (Pub. L. No. 93-112) (Martin, 1979). Section 504 of The Rehabilitation Act of 1973 states that "No otherwise qualified handicapped individual in the United States . . . shall, solely by reason of his handicap, be excluded from the participation in, or be denied the benefits of, or be subjected to discrimination under any program or activity receiving Federal financial assistance . . ." (29 U.S.C. § 794).

Both Vanek and Humphrey saw Section 504 as requiring all states to provide educational services to all children. However, The Rehabilitation Act of 1973 is concerned primarily with discrimination in employment settings, and many interpreted Section 504 as a prohibition against employment discrimination in the schools. The 1974 amendments to The Rehabilitation Act of 1973 (Pub. L. No. 93-516) clarified the intent of the law by specifically prohibiting discrimination against physically or mentally handicapped pupils in federally supported school systems (Martin, 1979).[2]

There was still no immediate impact on school policies regarding children with handicaps, however. Advocates for the rights of handicapped pupils staged wheelchair sit-ins to encourage the quick development of regulations implementing the law, while school officials quietly protested this legislation as too costly for the public schools (Martin, 1979). The Department of Health, Education, and Welfare (HEW), caught in the middle, was slow to develop and approve regulations implementing Section 504. As Martin (1979) noted, HEW did not require compliance with Section 504 until the 1978–1979 school year, a full 5 years after the law was passed.

Rules and regulations implementing Section 504 appear at 34 *Code of Federal Regulations* (C.F.R), Part 104. The Office of Civil Rights (OCR), an agency within the U.S. Department of Education, is charged with investigating Section 504 complaints pertaining to department programs or activities. Although an OCR investigation may be triggered by a complaint regarding possible discriminatory treatment of an individual student with handicaps, OCR may choose to expand its investigation to encompass school policies and practices regarding all students within the district who have a particular type of handicapping condition (e.g., mental retardation, attention deficit disorder).

[2] The Rehabilitation Act of 1973 was further amended by Pub. L. No. 98-221 in 1983, by Pub. L. No. 99-506 in 1986, and by Pub. L. No. 101-336 in 1990.

Following the passage of Pub. L. No. 94-142 in 1975, public school districts typically concentrated on fulfilling their obligation to provide special education and related services to pupils with disabilities in conformance with the requirements of IDEA-Part B. Many school administrators were unaware that the broad definition of handicapped under 504 includes a number of students who do not qualify as disabled under IDEA. They falsely believed that compliance with IDEA meant the school was in full compliance with Section 504 (Martin, 1992). In the late 1980s, a number of lawsuits and complaints to OCR were filed on behalf of pupils in regular education programs because schools failed to make accommodations for their handicapping conditions under 504 (e.g., *Elizabeth S. v. Thomas K. Gilhool,* 1987; Lake Washington [WA] School District No. 414, 1985; Rialto [CA] Unified School District, 1989).[3]

Advocacy efforts on the part of children with Attention Deficit Disorder (ADD) and Attention Deficit Hyperactivity Disorder (ADHD) also were an important trigger for increased attention to Section 504 requirements. When Congress considered the 1990 amendments of Part B, there was discussion of including ADD/ADHD as a separate eligibility category within the law. An invitation to public comment on special education for children with ADD/ADHD under Part B resulted in over 2,000 written comments (Hakola, 1992). Parents of children with ADD/ADHD testified to Congress that many schools were unwilling to make even simple modifications of educational programming because their children did not qualify for special education under Part B (Martin, 1992). Congress ultimately decided not to amend Part B to include children with ADD/ADHD. However on September 16, 1991, the U.S. Department of Education (DOE) issued a memorandum (jointly by the assistant secretaries of the Office of Special Education and Rehabilitative Services, Office of Civil Rights, and Office of Elementary and Secondary Education) to clarify DOE policy regarding appropriate education for children with ADD/ADHD.

The 1991 DOE memorandum addressed eligibility for services under IDEA-Part B, and suggested that some pupils with ADD/ADHD may qualify within the IDEA definitions of *other health impairment, specific learning disability,* or *serious emotional disturbance.* The memorandum also discussed school obligations under Section 504 to children with ADD/ADHD found not to require special education and related services under IDEA. The memorandum thus provided an explicit DOE interpretation of school responsibilities to children who have handicaps that impair their

[3] References to court cases are italicized; references to OCR opinions and administrative hearings are not.

functioning in school, but who do not qualify for special education and related services under IDEA.

Thus, a series of events including advocacy efforts, the 1991 DOE memorandum, OCR activities, and case law have made it increasingly clear that many schools in compliance with IDEA have not met their obligations to other special needs students under Section 504. Section 504 and IDEA are different in several important respects including purpose, funding, eligibility, and school responsibilities to students. Schools and school psychologists must now be knowledgeable of 504 as well as IDEA.

Purpose and Funding

Case 6–1

Mrs. Drew, a middle school special education teacher, teaches an English class for educable mentally impaired students who cannot keep pace in regular education English. After observing that several of Mrs. Drew's students had problems with handwriting, Hannah Cook offered to take Mrs. Drew and her students to the school's computer lab to show them how to use a simple word processing program for English writing assignments. When Hannah contacted the teacher responsible for scheduling the school's computer lab, she was told that in accordance with school policy, special education classes were not allowed to use the computer lab because the students were too likely to damage the expensive equipment.

As previously noted, Section 504 of The Rehabilitation Act of 1973 was designed to eliminate discrimination on the basis of handicap in any program or activity receiving federal financial assistance. Subpart D applies to preschool, elementary, and secondary education programs and activities, and requires schools to make special accommodations for students with handicaps to ensure they are afforded educational opportunity equal to their nonhandicapped peers.

Section 504 specifically prohibits schools from discriminating on the basis of handicap in providing any aid, benefit, or service, either directly or through contractual arrangements. Schools may not deny pupils with handicaps an opportunity to participate in or benefit from any of the services or benefits it affords others. This means that schools must provide aids, benefits, or services that are equal to and as effective as those provided to nonhandicapped pupils. Schools are not required to produce the identical result or level of achievement for handicapped and nonhandicapped pupils, but they *must afford students with handicaps equal opportunity* to obtain the same result, to gain the same benefit, or to reach the same level of achievement, in the most integrated setting appropriate to the pupil's needs. Schools may not provide different or separate aid, benefits, or services to pupils with handicaps unless such action is necessary to provide them with services that are as effective as those provided to others. When separate programs or activities exist in order to meet the needs of students with handicaps, a school may not deny a qualified handicapped student the opportunity to participate in programs or activities that are not separate or different (34 C.F.R. § 104.4).

Case 6–1 is based on a real-life incident. The school's policy of barring special education classes from the school's computer lab was clearly in violation of Section 504. The policy was changed quickly after it was challenged by the special education teacher and school psychologist.

Unlike IDEA, Section 504 does not require states to develop a written plan to meet the requirements of the law. However under 504, each school district must designate at least one person to coordinate its efforts to comply with the law and adopt grievance procedures that incorporate appropriate due process standards and provide for the prompt and equitable resolution of complaints alleging violations of 504 (34 C.F.R. § 104.7). Each school district also must take appropriate and continuing steps to notify students and their parents that it does not discriminate in its programs and activities on the basis of handicap (34 C.F.R. § 104.8).

Section 504 is antidiscrimination legislation; it is not a federal grant program. Unlike IDEA, Section 504 does not provide funds to schools. A state department of education may choose not to pursue monies available under federal grant statutes (e.g., IDEA-Part C funds for infants and toddlers with disabilities). School districts must comply with antidiscrimination legislation if they receive any federal funds for any purpose, however. OCR has the authority to remove federal funds from a district if it is not in compliance with 504.

Eligibility

With respect to public school educational services, Section 504 protections against discrimination apply to all pupils with handicaps who are of an age during which nonhandicapped pupils receive a public education, or who are eligible for educational services for handicapped pupils under state law, or eligible for special education within the state under IDEA (34 C.F.R.

§ 104.3). Like IDEA, schools are required to locate all pupils with handicapping conditions under 504 (i.e., a child find requirement).

As noted above, handicapped under Section 504 is more broadly defined than disability under IDEA. To be eligible for special education and related services under IDEA, pupils must be evaluated in accordance with procedures outlined in IDEA-Part B and found eligible under one of the 13 categories of disability, and they must need special education and related services because of that disability. The child's disability must affect his or her educational performance in order to receive special education and related services under Part B (see Chapter 5).

In contrast, under 504 a *handicapped person* is defined as any person who has a physical or mental impairment which substantially limits one or more of his or her major life activities (see Exhibit 6–1). *Physical impairment* means any physiological disorder or condition affecting one or more body systems. *Mental impairment* means any mental or psychological disorder, such as emotional or mental illness, or a specific learning disability. *Major life activities* means functions such as caring for one's self,

Exhibit 6–1. Section 504 Definition of Handicapped

(j) *Handicapped person.* (1) "Handicapped person" means any person who (i) has a physical or mental impairment which substantially limits one or more major life activities, (ii) has a record of such an impairment, or (iii) is regarded as having such an impairment.

(2) As used in paragraph (j)(1) of this section, the phrase:

(i) *Physical or mental impairment* means (A) any physiological disorder or condition, cosmetic disfigurement, or anatomical loss affecting one or more of the following body systems: neurological; musculoskeletal; special sense organs; respiratory, including speech organs; cardiovascular; reproductive, digestive, genito-urinary; hemic and lymphatic; skin; and endocrine; or (B) any mental or psychological disorder, such as mental retardation, organic brain syndrome, emotional or mental illness, and specific learning disabilities.

(ii) *Major life activities* means functions such as caring for one's self, performing manual tasks, walking, seeing, hearing, speaking, breathing, learning, and working.

(iii) *Has a record of such impairment* means has a history of, or has been misclassified as having, a mental or physical impairment that substantially limits one or more major life activities.

(iv) *Is regarded as having an impairment* means (A) has a physical or mental impairment that does not substantially limit major life activities but that is treated by a recipient as constituting such a limitation; (B) has a physical or mental impairment that substantially limits major life activities only as a result of the attitudes of others toward such impairment; or (C) has none of the impairments defined in paragraph (j)(2)(i) of this section but is treated by a recipient as having such an impairment.

Source: 34 C.F.R. § 104.3.

performing manual tasks, walking, seeing, hearing, speaking, breathing, learning, and working. *Handicapped* individual includes persons with a history of impairment and those regarded as having an impairment who may, in fact, have no actual impairment. This last portion of the definition protects individuals from discriminatory action based on the perception of a handicap. For example, if a high school senior was denied admission to college solely on the basis of school records showing a history of special education placement, Section 504 safeguards would be triggered.

In sum, any student who has a physical or mental impairment that substantially limits a major life activity is handicapped within the meaning of Section 504. Section 504 prohibits schools from discriminating on the basis of handicap in providing aids, benefits, or services. Any student who has a condition or disorder that substantially limits his or her ability to participate in school programs and activities and who needs special assistance because of his or her limitations is eligible for special school accommodations under 504 (*Elizabeth S. v. Thomas K. Gilhool,* 1987). All students who are disabled under IDEA are considered to be handicapped and are therefore afforded the protections of Section 504. Students who are not disabled under IDEA may nevertheless be handicapped under 504.

Seven categories of children who might not be eligible for special education services under IDEA, but who may qualify under Section 504 are identified in Exhibit 6–2. They include students: (a) with ADD/ADHD, (b) who are learning-disabled but who do not exhibit a severe discrepancy between aptitude and achievement, (c) who are graduates of special education, (d) who are socially maladjusted and emotionally impaired, (e) with drug and alcohol dependency, (f) with health needs, and (g) with communicable diseases (adapted from Martin, 1992).

Evaluation of Pupils to Determine Eligibility

The evaluation regulations that implement Section 504 are difficult to interpret because they are limited in scope and detail. Although they specifically address evaluation with regard to *placement* in special or regular education, procedures for determining 504 eligibility or needed special accommodations are not clearly addressed. However since 1991, education law experts (Council of Administrators of Special Education [CASE], undated; Hakola, 1992) and a series of OCR rulings have provided guidance in interpreting the evaluation regulations as they relate to the determination of whether a child is handicapped under 504, and the provision of appropriate school accommodations.

Exhibit 6–2. Pupils Who May Qualify as Handicapped under Section 504

ADD/ADHD

ADD and ADHD are impairments under Section 504 if the condition substantially limits a major life activity, such as learning.

Learning Disabled without Discrepancy

504 regulations define mental impairment as any mental or psychological disorder including a learning disability. Pupils with learning disabilities (e.g., dyslexia) who do not show a severe discrepancy between achievement and ability are handicapped within the meaning of 504 if their condition substantially limits a major life activity, such as learning.

Graduates of Special Education

Section 504 protects students who graduate from special education and continue in regular education programs as well as those who graduate from high school and enter postsecondary settings.

Socially Maladjusted and Emotionally Impaired

504 regulations define mental impairment as any mental or psychological disorder including emotional or mental illness. Children who are socially maladjusted or who suffer an emotional impairment (e.g., school phobia) may qualify as handicapped under 504 if the condition substantially limits a major life activity, such as the capacity for normal peer relations or learning.

Drug and Alcohol Dependency

Students with alcohol or drug dependency are handicapped persons under 504 if their impairment substantially limits one or more of their major life activities. Individuals who have completed a supervised drug rehabilitation program are protected; however, those actively involved in drug abuse are not afforded 504 protections.

Health Needs

A number of schoolchildren have health conditions that substantially impair major life activities, such as caring for one's self, performing manual tasks, walking, seeing, hearing, speaking, breathing, or learning. Pupils with a wide range of health conditions (e.g., diabetes, asthma, severe allergies, disability from an accident, arthritis, epilepsy, sleep disorders, obesity) may qualify for accommodations under 504. A pupil with a temporary handicapping condition (e.g., broken limbs) also may qualify for accommodations.

Communicable Diseases

Students with communicable diseases, such as AIDS, are protected by Section 504. Schools are prohibited from discriminating against any "otherwise qualified" pupil with a communicable disease. This means that schools may not remove an infected child from the regular classroom unless a significant risk of transmission of the disease would still exist in spite of reasonable efforts by the school to accommodate the infected child (see also Chapter 10).

Source: Adapted from Martin (1992).

An evaluation of a student is required under 504 if it is believed that the pupil may qualify as handicapped and may need special school services or accommodations. Any child referred for evaluation because of a suspected disability under IDEA-Part B and is not found eligible, should be considered for possible eligibility as handicapped under Section 504 (CASE, undated). Schools are required to advise students with handicaps and their parents of their rights and the school's duties under Section 504 (34 C.F.R. § 104.32). Schools must notify parents of their rights regarding the identification, evaluation, and placement of children with suspected handicaps prior to initiating a Section 504 evaluation. OCR has recommended that parents be notified of their procedural safeguard rights under 504 at the time the district requests parental permission for the evaluation (Cobb County [GA] School District, 1992). When a pupil is suspected of having a disability under IDEA, parent rights and school duties under both IDEA and 504 should be clearly identified.

The question of when an evaluation is triggered under Section 504 has been a source of confusion in many school districts. The 1991 DOE policy memorandum stated that a school must evaluate a pupil if the parents believe their child is handicapped under 504, suggesting that schools must evaluate children on parental demand. In April 1993, OCR clarified this policy by stating that a school must evaluate a student only when the school has reason to believe a child has a suspected handicapping condition (Lim, 1993). Like IDEA, schools are not required to evaluate children based only on parental suspicion of a handicap. However, when a school does not agree with a parental request for evaluation, it must still inform parents of their right to contest that decision and the procedures for a fair and timely resolution of the evaluation dispute.

Martin (1992) interprets Section 504 evaluation regulations as requiring determination of the following: (a) Is there a physical or mental impairment? (b) Does that impairment substantially limit a major life activity? and (c) What kind of accommodations would be needed so that the student will be able to enjoy the benefits of the school program? Section 504 does not require a specific categorical diagnosis, only the determination of a handicapping condition that substantially impairs one or more major life activities at school and requires special accommodation by the school.

Under Section 504, schools are required to establish standards and procedures for the evaluation of pupils who, because of handicap, are believed to need special school accommodations. The 504 regulations regarding evaluation procedures (34 C.F.R. § 104.35) are almost identical to those implementing IDEA-Part B. Test and evaluation materials must be valid for the purpose used, administered by trained personnel, and fair. The evaluation must be comprehensive enough to assess the nature and extent of the handicap and the needed accommodations and services.

Section 504 does not specifically require evaluation by a multidisciplinary team. However, in interpreting data and in making placement decisions, schools must "draw upon information from a variety of sources," "establish procedures to ensure that information obtained from all such sources is documented and carefully considered," and ensure that decisions are made by a "group of persons, including persons knowledgeable about the child, the evaluation data, and the placement options" (34 C.F.R. § 104.35).

Timelines for the completion of an evaluation and determination of a child's needs are not specified in 504 regulations. OCR has held that although "504 does not specify the time periods permitted at each stage of the process of identification, evaluation, and placement, it is implicit that the various steps in the process will be completed within a reasonable time period" (Cobb County [GA] School District, 1992, p. 29). It also has held that it is reasonable to expect schools to complete evaluations under 504 within the same time frame outlined in state guidelines for completion of IDEA evaluations (East Lansing [MI] Public Schools, 1992).

Section 504 does not require reevaluation of the student every 3 years, only periodic reevaluation and reevaluation prior to any significant change in placement (34 C.F.R. § 104.35). Courts have ruled that expulsion or long-term suspension (more than 10 days) of a student with a handicap is a change of placement requiring reevaluation.

Section 504, like IDEA, requires medical evaluation at no cost to the parents when it is necessary to determine a child's medically related handicapping condition (see Davila, 1991). A number of schools have expressed concern about the possible expense of medical evaluations of students suspected of having ADD/ADHD. According to federal policy makers, qualified personnel other than licensed physicians may conduct evaluations to determine whether a child has ADD/ADHD (Shrag, 1992). State regulations, however, may require diagnosis by a physician.

Free Appropriate Public Education

IDEA and Section 504 both require schools to provide a free appropriate public education to each student with handicaps regardless of the nature or severity of the handicap. *Appropriate education* is defined under 504 as: "the provision of regular or special education and related aids and services (i) that are designed to meet individual educational needs of handicapped persons as adequately as the needs of nonhandicapped persons are met and

(ii) are based on adherence to procedural safeguards" outlined in the law (34 C.F.R. § 104.33). Thus under 504, appropriate education is more broadly defined than under IDEA-Part B (34 C.F.R. § 300.8), and it can consist of education in regular classes, education in regular class with the use of supplementary services, or special education and related services (see also Lake Washington [WA] School District No. 414, 1985).

Section 504, like IDEA, also requires schools to "educate, or provide for the education of, each qualified handicapped person in its jurisdiction with persons who are not handicapped to the maximum extent appropriate to the needs of the handicapped person" (34 C.F.R. § 104.34). Students with handicaps must be placed in the regular educational environment unless it is demonstrated by the school that the education of the student in the regular environment with the use of supplementary aids and services cannot be achieved satisfactorily. In providing or arranging for the provision of nonacademic services (e.g., lunch, recess) and extracurricular activities, schools must ensure that handicapped students participate with nonhandicapped students to the maximum extent appropriate to their needs. Students with handicaps also must be afforded opportunities to participate in after school activities and informed that those opportunities are available (34 C.F.R. § 104.34; 34 C.F.R. § 104.37; also Kenowa Hills [MI] Public Schools, 1992).

When Section 504 pupils are referred to or placed in a program not operated by the school district, the district retains responsibility for assuring that Section 504 rights and protections are afforded to the student placed elsewhere (34 C.F.R. § 104.33). When selecting a child's placement, proximity to the child's home must be considered (34 C.F.R. § 104.34). When school districts refer or place pupils with handicaps in programs not operated by the school itself, the placement must be at no cost to the parent. Schools also must ensure adequate transportation to the placement site at no greater cost to the parent than would be incurred if the student were placed in program operated by the school (34 C.F.R. § 104.33).

Accommodation Plan

Under Section 504, schools must provide a free and appropriate education (FAPE) for children with handicaps, designed to meet the individual education needs of handicapped children as adequately as those of nonhandicapped students. One means of meeting this requirement is through the implementation of an individualized education program developed in accordance with IDEA standards (34 C.F.R. § 104.33). Another option is to develop an accommodation plan for 504-only students (see CASE, undated).

Consistent with the recommended evaluation procedures, the student accommodation plan should be developed by a group of persons, including persons knowledgeable of the child and the evaluation data. CASE (undated) has suggested that this plan includes: (a) a description of the nature of the concern, (b) a description of the basis for the determination of the handicap, (c) a description of how the handicap affects a major life activity, (d) a description of the reasonable accommodations that are necessary, (e) the date when the plan will be reviewed or reassessed, and (f) the names and titles of the participants at the accommodation plan meeting. The accommodation plan should be included in the student's cumulative file and reviewed on the predetermined date.

Nature of the Required Accommodations

Case 6–2

Leigh Michels is a bright and academically talented ninth grader. Born with a mild form of cerebral palsy, she walks with a scissor-leg gait. Over Christmas vacation, Leigh had surgery to reduce the spasticity in her legs. Although temporarily confined to a wheelchair following the surgery, she was eager to return to school. When Mrs. Michels called the high school principal, Mr. Hershey, to arrange Leigh's school transportation, she was told she would have to take time off from her job to transport Leigh to school herself. Mr. Hershey stated that Leigh could not be transported in the special education van equipped with a wheelchair lift because Leigh did not qualify for special education under IDEA. Distressed at the prospect of losing more time from work, Mrs. Michels phoned her friend. Carrie Johnson, who works as a school psychologist in a neighboring district. Mrs. Michels then phoned the principal again and asked for a meeting to determine whether Leigh is handicapped within the meaning of Section 504 and, if eligible, to develop a school accommodation plan including adaptive transportation.

Section 504 requires the provision of regular or special education and related aids and services designed to meet the individual needs of pupils with handicapping conditions. DOE memoranda, OCR rulings, and court cases regarding school responsibilities to pupils who are handicapped within the meaning of 504 provide some guidance regarding the kinds of school accommodations required by the law. This portion of the chapter first summarizes school responsibilities to students with handicaps that affect classroom performance (e.g., learning, emotional, or behavior problems), and then discusses the types of accommodations that might be required under 504 for pupils with physical impairments or health conditions. It is important to note that specific accommodations for a child must always be determined by a group of persons and based on individual student need. What is provided here is an overview of the kinds of accommodations DOE or OCR have found acceptable or required.

The DOE memorandum on pupils with ADD/ADHD and several OCR rulings provide an explicit interpretation of school responsibilities to children who have handicaps that impair classroom performance but who do not qualify for special education and related services under IDEA. In its memorandum of September 16, 1991, DOE stated "Should it be determined that the child with ADD/ADHD is handicapped for purposes of Section 504 and needs only adjustments in the regular classroom, rather than special education, those adjustments are required by Section 504." DOE went on to state that through the use of appropriate adaptations and interventions in regular classes, schools can effectively address the instructional needs of many ADD/ADHD (504-only) children.

DOE identified over 20 strategies available to meet the education needs of 504-only children with ADD/ADHD. It is important to note that the kinds of accommodations required by 504 for students with impairments that affect classroom performance are educational accommodations or strategies that a teacher, pupil assistance team, and/or school psychologist might recommend, and many of them are not overly costly. Possible adaptations in regular education programs suggested by DOE were as follows:

> providing a structured learning environment, repeating and simplifying instructions about in-class and homework assignments; supplementing verbal instructions with visual instructions; using behavioral management techniques; adjusting class schedules; modifying test delivery; using tape recorders, computer-aided instruction, and other audio-visual equipment; selecting modified textbooks or workbooks, and tailoring homework assignments. (U.S. Department of Education, 1991)

Other provisions for 504-only children suggested by DOE ranged from:

> consultation to special resources and may include reducing class size; use of one-on-one tutorials; classroom aides and note takers; involvement of a

services coordinator to oversee implementation of special programs and services; and possible modification of nonacademic time such as lunchroom, recess, and physical education. (U.S. Department of Education, 1991)

DOE also stated that in meeting the needs of ADD/ADHD students, state educational agencies and school districts "should take the necessary steps to promote coordination between special and regular education programs." A question raised by parents of children with handicaps and school administrators is whether school districts may use special education programs and services in making accommodations for 504-only students with handicaps. The court ruling in *Lyons by Alexander v. Smith* (1993), OCR complaint investigation findings (for example, see Lake Washington [WA] School District No. 414, 1985), and OCR policy statements indicate that children with handicaps may have access to all IDEA programs and services, even if they do not qualify under IDEA. As the court noted in *Lyons* (1993), a school system may have to provide special education to a 504-only student if such services are necessary to prevent discrimination, that is, to meet the individual educational needs of the handicapped student as adequately as those of nonhandicapped students. Thus, school districts may use IDEA-supported school psychologists or other specialists to provide evaluation and accommodations for 504-only children with handicaps. However, school districts do not receive IDEA funds for 504-only students with handicaps.

Several administrative hearings and OCR investigations have addressed accommodations for students with emotional or behavior problems. These cases concerned students who did not qualify under IDEA-Part B as having a serious emotional disturbance but who were deemed to have a mental impairment that substantially affects a major life activity. For example, a Connecticut hearing officer held that an academically gifted student who experienced serious difficulties in peer relations qualified as handicapped under Section 504, and found acceptable the school's accommodation plan which included having the school psychologist provide consultation to the teacher and parents, and counseling for the student (In the Matter of a Child with Disabilities, 1992; see also Fairfield-Suisun Unified School District, 1989; Rialto Unified School District, 1989).

The court settlement in *Elizabeth S. v. Gilhool* (1987) provides guidance to schools regarding their responsibilities to physically handicapped and other health-impaired students who do not qualify under IDEA. This class action suit was initiated when a district refused to train school personnel to monitor the blood sugar levels of a 6-year-old with juvenile diabetes. It also addressed school responsibilities to a 6-year-old with spina bifida who walked with the assistance of braces and crutches. The court stated that the required school accommodations and services for students with physical or health impairments might include, but are not limited to, development of a plan to address any medical emergencies, school health services including monitoring of blood sugar levels and arrangements for a child to take injections or medications, assistance with toileting, adjustment of class schedules, home instruction, use of an elevator or other accommodations to make school facilities accessible, adaptive transportation, and adaptive physical education and/or occupational therapy.

Case 6–2 is based on a real-life incident. When Mrs. Michels phoned the high school principal, Mr. Hershey, and began asking questions about school responsibilities to Leigh under Section 504, Mr. Hershey became so unnerved that he offered to personally transport Leigh to and from school during the weeks she was confined to a wheelchair . . . and he did. This incident illustrates the fact that some school districts have not yet developed and implemented procedures to ensure compliance with Section 504 requirements. Additionally, many school administrators are not familiar with DOE policy that allows IDEA- supported special education services to be used in making accommodations for 504-only pupils.

Procedural Safeguards under Section 504

Procedural safeguards in Section 504 regulations are stated in more general terms than those in IDEA-Part B. Under 504, schools are required "to make available a system of procedural safeguards that permits parents to challenge actions regarding the identification, evaluation, or educational placement of their handicapped child whom they believe needs special education or related services" (DOE, 1991; also 34 C.F.R. § 104.36). The system of procedural safeguards must include "notice, an opportunity for the parents or guardian to examine relevant records, an impartial hearing with opportunity for participation by the person's parents or guardian and representation by counsel, and a review procedure" (34 C.F.R. § 104.36). Compliance with procedural safeguards of IDEA-Part B is one means of fulfilling the Section 504 requirement. However, in an impartial due process hearing raising issues under Section 504, the impartial hearing officer must make a determination based on 504 regulations (Martin, 1992).

Parent Remedies

As noted, the Office of Civil Rights (OCR) is charged with investigating Section 504 complaints pertaining to DOE programs or activities. OCR investigates individual complaints, and a parent may trigger an investigation of school district compliance with 504 simply by filing a written complaint with OCR (Zirkel & Kincaid, 1993).

In addition, parents have the right to initiate a court action against the school on behalf of a child with handicaps if they believe the school has violated the provisions of Section 504 with respect to their child. In accordance with the Handicapped Children's Protection Act of 1986 (Pub. L. No. 99-372), if a Section 504 claim can be remedied under IDEA, parents must first attempt to remedy the problem under IDEA before filing a civil action on a Section 504 claim. Under IDEA parents are typically required to exhaust administrative remedies (e.g., due process hearings) available to them before they pursue a court action. In contrast, parents are not required to exhaust administrative remedies before initiating a civil action under 504. The courts may award reasonable attorney fees as part of the costs to parents when they are the prevailing party in a Section 504 suit.

AMERICANS WITH DISABILITIES ACT OF 1990

Congress passed over 20 laws proscribing discrimination against individuals with disabilities between 1973 and 1990 (Burgdorf, 1991). The Americans with Disabilities Act of 1990 (ADA) (Pub. L. No. 101-336) is considered to be the most significant federal law assuring the civil rights of all individuals with disabilities.

ADA was first introduced as a bill in Congress in 1988. In its statement of findings, Congress reported that "some 43,000,000 Americans have one or more physical or mental disabilities" (Pub. L. No. 101-336, § 2[a][1]). Congress found widespread discrimination against individuals with disabilities in all spheres of life, including employment, housing, public accommodations, education, transportation, communication, recreation, health services, and access to public services. Additionally, testimony to Congress documented a strong link between disability and poverty, joblessness, lack of education, and failure to participate in social and recreational opportunities (Burgdorf, 1991). President Bush signed ADA into law on July 26, 1990.

ADA guarantees equal opportunity to individuals with disabilities in employment, public services, transportation, state and local government services, and telecommunications. It differs from earlier laws in that it extends to programs and activities outside the federal sphere and includes a detailed set of standards prohibiting discrimination (Burgdorf, 1991). Title II, Subtitle A, is the portion of the law pertaining to public schools.

The protections of ADA extend only to those persons who have a disability as defined by the law. Like Section 504, a disability is defined as a physical or mental impairment that substantially limits one or more major life activities, a record of such an impairment, or being regarded as having such an impairment.

As noted in Chapter 5, IDEA-Part B requires schools to provide a statement of needed transition services for youth with disabilities beginning at age 16 (or younger if appropriate) as part of the individual education program (IEP). Transition services are a set of coordinated activities that promote movement from school to postschool activities. ADA promises to expand opportunities for youth with disabilities in their transition to postschool activities. School psychologists involved in planning transition services under IDEA need to be familiar with the protections against discrimination afforded by ADA in employment, education and training, transportation, recreation, and access to telecommunications. A detailed discussion of those portions of ADA is beyond the scope of this text. Readers are encouraged to consult Burgdorf (1991).

Title II, Subtitle A

Title II, Subtitle A, is the portion of ADA pertaining to public schools. Regulations implementing Title II appear at 28 *Code of Federal Regulations* (C.F.R) Part 35. ADA prohibitions against discrimination in public schools are essentially the same as those outlined in Section 504: "No qualified individual with a disability shall, on the basis of disability, be excluded from participation in or be denied the benefits of the services, programs, or activities of a public entity, or be subjected to discrimination by any such entity" (28 C.F.R. § 35.130). *Qualified individual with a disability* under Title II means "an individual with a disability who, with or without reasonable modifications of rules, policies, or practices, the removal of architectural, communication, or transportation barriers, or the provision of auxiliary aids and services, meets the essential eligibility requirement for the receipt of services or the participation in programs or activities provided by the public entity" (28 C.F.R. § 35.104).

ADA thus prohibits discrimination against qualified individuals on the basis of disability in public school services, programs, or activities. ADA, like 504, also requires schools to make reasonable accommodations for students with disabilities:

> A public entity shall make reasonable modifications in policies, practices, or procedures when the modifications are necessary to avoid discrimination on the basis of disability, unless the public entity can demonstrate that making the modifications would fundamentally alter the nature of the service, program, or activity. (28 C.F.R. § 35.130)

ADA also requires that services, programs, and activities be provided in "the most integrated setting appropriate to the needs of qualified individuals with disabilities" (28 C.F.R. § 35.130).

In accordance with ADA, each school district must conduct a self-evaluation of its policies and practices with regard to individuals with disabilities and correct any that are not consistent with ADA (28 C.F.R. § 35.105). Like Section 504, ADA requires public schools to provide notice regarding the provisions of ADA and the school's responsibilities under the law (28 C.F.R. § 35.106). Schools must designate at least one employee to coordinate their efforts to comply with the law (28 C.F.R. § 35.107). School districts also must adopt and publish grievance procedures, providing for prompt and equitable resolution of complaints alleging violations of ADA (28 C.F.R. § 35.107).

There is much overlap between 504 and ADA in school responsibilities to students with disabilities. ADA regulations state that, unless otherwise noted, ADA "shall not be construed to apply a lesser standard" than 504 (28 C.F.R. § 35.103). Thus, ADA generally requires full compliance with 504, but at times it requires more than 504 in school obligations to students with disabilities. ADA stresses the removal of architectural barriers as a top priority (Martin, 1992; see also 28 C.F.R. Part 35, Appendix A).

The Office of Civil Rights within the U.S. Department of Education has been designated as the agency responsible for enforcing ADA with regard to public schools. Complaints regarding ADA violations may be filed with OCR. The "remedies" of Section 504 are the remedies of Title II of ADA. OCR may remove federal funds from schools not in compliance with ADA. ADA also allows private lawsuits against public schools, and there is no requirement that administrative remedies (e.g., hearings) be exhausted prior to filing a lawsuit (28 C.F.R. § 35.172). The parents of a child with disabilities or an individual with disabilities may be awarded reasonable attorney fees if they prevail in any action filed under ADA (28 C.F.R. § 35.175).

Whistleblower's Protection

School psychologists also should be familiar with ADA's protection against retaliation or coercion for whistleblowers:

> (a) No private or public entity shall discriminate against any individual because that individual has opposed any act or practice made unlawful by this part or because that individual made a charge, testified, assisted, or participated in any manner in an investigation, proceeding or hearing under the Act or this part.

(b) No private or public entity shall coerce, intimidate, threaten, or interfere with any individual in the exercise or enjoyment of, or on account of his having exercised or enjoyed, or on account of his or her having aided or encouraged any other individual in the exercise or enjoyment of, any right granted or protected by the Act or this part. (28 C.F.R. § 35.134)

This portion of the law was designed in part to protect individuals who advocate for the rights of the disabled from retaliation by the agency involved. Thus, if a school district failed to meet its obligations to pupils with disabilities under ADA, and a school employee (e.g., school psychologist) assisted those students in obtaining their rights under the Act, the school district would be prohibited from retaliating against the employee. If the school did retaliate by firing or in some way demoting the employee, the employee would have the right to file a lawsuit against the school district under ADA's protection against retaliation.

CONCLUDING COMMENTS

Many school districts have not yet developed a 504 service delivery model. In those districts, school psychologists have an important role to play in working with administrators, teachers, support staff, and parent representatives to develop policies and procedures for 504 referral, evaluation, and decision making, and to safeguard pupil and parent rights. Development and implementation of a practical and efficient 504 response model will require much cooperation among regular and special education personnel, but will, it is hoped, result in greater school responsiveness to the needs of regular education students with handicapping conditions.

There is much overlap between 504 and ADA in public school responsibilities to students with handicapping conditions. However, ADA protections against discrimination in employment, education and training, transportation, recreation, and access to telecommunications all promise to expand opportunities for youth with disabilities in their transition to postschool activities.

ACTIVITIES

Does your local school district distribute a handbook or pamphlet to parents outlining their rights and the school responsibilities under Section 504 of The Rehabilitation Act of 1973? Obtain and review copies of informational materials given to parents.

STUDY AND DISCUSSION

Questions for Chapter 6

1. What type of legislation is Section 504 of The Rehabilitation Act of 1973? How does it differ from IDEA in purpose, scope, and funding?
2. How is pupil eligibility determined under 504? Identify Martin's categories of students who may qualify as handicapped within the meaning of 504 but who might not be eligible for special education under IDEA.
3. Must a child have a permanent handicapping condition to be eligible for accommodations under 504?
4. What is the meaning of *free appropriate public education* within 504?
5. Describe the content of an accommodation plan under 504 and how one is developed.
6. Briefly describe the scope and purpose of ADA as it relates to public school children.

Discussion

What are some of the ways in which Section 504 can have a positive impact on schools and schoolchildren? See Jacob-Timm and Hartshorne (1994).

Chapter 7

ETHICAL AND LEGAL ISSUES IN COUNSELING AND THERAPEUTIC INTERVENTIONS IN THE SCHOOLS

Based on their national survey, Reschly and Wilson (1995) found that school psychology practitioners devote about eight hours per week to direct interventions. This chapter explores the ethical-legal issues associated with counseling and therapeutic interventions in the schools. It begins with a discussion of pre-intervention responsibilities to the parent and pupil and includes a discussion of special consent issues (e.g., self-referrals for counseling). The responsibilities of the school psychologist in situations involving danger to the student or others are addressed, followed by an overview of the ethical-legal issues associated with pregnancy and birth control counseling. Ethical-legal issues associated with behavioral interventions in the schools, including the use of token economies and time-out, are then examined. We conclude with a brief discussion of issues associated with psychopharmacologic therapies in the school setting, using Ritalin as an example.

We focus this chapter on therapeutic interventions with individual students. Readers are referred to Lakin (1994) for a discussion of ethical issues in multiperson therapies; Corey, Corey, and Callanan (1993) for information on the ethical-legal aspects of counseling students in groups; and Hansen, Green, and Kutner (1989) for a discussion of ethical issues in the provision of family therapy by school psychologists.

School psychologists, as psychologists, are viewed differently in law than school counselors and must provide services consistent with their own professional standards (Fischer & Sorenson, 1996). However, in this chapter, we at times consult the American Counseling Association's (ACA) (1988) code of ethics on issues our own codes and standards do not fully address.

PRE-INTERVENTION RESPONSIBILITIES

Parent Involvement and Consent

As noted in Chapter 3, the Protection of Pupil Rights (PPRA) or Hatch Amendment was enacted in 1978 to provide protection for the privacy rights of pupils and their parents. It was revised in 1994. Although this amendment only applies to certain federally funded school programs, it is seen as reflecting current legal opinion about appropriate school conduct in safeguarding pupil and family privacy. The pre-1994 regulations implementing this law specifically stated that the consent of an emancipated student or the parent of a minor child must be obtained before a student can be required to participate in psychological treatment in the schools if the treatment may involve matters of family privacy. Psychological treatment was defined broadly as "any activity involving the planned, systematic use of methods or techniques that are not directly related to academic instruction and that is designed to affect behavioral, emotional, or attitudinal characteristics of an individual or group" (34 C.F.R. Subtitle A § 98.4). New regulations are expected late 1997.

Corrao and Melton conclude that, taken together, the Hatch Amendment and IDEA "show clear Congressional intent to require parental consent to school-based psychological services" (1988, p. 381). They suggest that it is generally advisable to obtain parental consent if an intervention that diverges from ordinary, expectable schooling is planned, particularly if it involves matters of personal or family privacy (see also Bersoff & Hofer, 1990). They also note that parental consent is implied for psychological interventions written in the child's individualized education plan (IEP) under IDEA, but the psychologist may want, at times, to secure continued parental consent, particularly if the intervention changes over the course of treatment.

The provision of direct services to a minor child (e.g., the psychologist works with a child in overcoming a phobia) clearly requires parental consent. The situation is less clear-cut when the psychologist serves as a consultant to the teacher, and the teacher serves as the behavior change agent. DeMers and Bersoff (1985) suggest that parental consent is probably needed and desired if the focus of the consultation is a specific child, rather than the classroom, and the child may be treated differently from others as a result of the consultation to the teacher.

Practitioners also have an ethical obligation to seek "direct parent contact prior to seeing the student/client on an ongoing basis" (NASP-PPE, III, C, #2). In addition, parents are "fully informed about all relevant aspects of school psychological services in advance" (NASP-PPE, III, A, #4). As noted in Chapter 3, confidentiality and its limits should be discussed with parents as part of the informed consent procedures.

Responsibilities to the Pupil

Legally, in the school setting, informed consent for psychological services rests with the parents of a minor child. However, the practitioner also is ethically obligated to respect the dignity, autonomy, and self-determination of the student/client. The decision to allow a student/client the opportunity to choose (or refuse) psychological treatment or intervention may involve consideration of a number of factors, including law, ethical issues (self-determination versus welfare of the client), the pupil's competence to make choices, and the likely consequences of affording choices (e.g., enhanced treatment outcomes versus choice to refuse treatment). We concur with Weithorn's (1983) suggestion that practitioners permit and encourage student/client involvement in treatment decision making to the maximum extent appropriate to the child and the situation.

Practitioners have an ethical obligation to inform the student/client of the scope and nature of the proposed intervention, whether they are given a choice about participating (NASP-PPE, III, B, #2). Once children reach school age, the initial interview with the pupil also should include a discussion of the parameters of confidentiality.

Special Informed Consent Issues

Special informed consent issues include self-referrals for counseling, consent to experimental methods of treatment, and supervision and consultation release.

Self-Referrals for Counseling

Young children are unlikely to seek help or initiate a counseling relationship on their own. However, at the high school level, many referrals for counseling are self-referrals. Students may wish to see a counselor on the condition that their parents not be notified. This raises the question of whether students who are minors can ever be seen by the school psychologist for counseling without parental permission. We are not aware of any case law decisions that specifically address this question.

A reasonable, common sense approach to the issue of counseling minor students without parental consent was suggested by C. Osip in Canter

(1989). Osip suggests allowing students one precounseling screening session without parental permission. This precounseling meeting could serve to ensure the child is safe and not in danger. During this meeting, the psychologist could discuss the need for parental consent for further counseling sessions, offer to contact the parent on behalf of the student, or offer to meet jointly with the student and parents to discuss consent and ensure ongoing parent support.

Practitioners should be aware that in some states, minors are given the right to access to certain types of treatment independent of parental notice or consent under state law. However, these rights to access to treatment are usually limited to conditions of a medical nature (e.g., drug abuse, venereal disease) and may not extend to the school setting. School psychologists need to consult their state laws to determine whether minors are given rights to seek treatment independent of parental notice or consent in their state, and under what conditions (Corrao & Melton, 1988).

Experimental Methods

In seeking informed consent for treatment, all experimental methods of treatment must be clearly indicated to prospective recipients (ACA, B.15). Experimental methods of treatment may be either methods that are nonstandard practice in the profession whose efficacy has not been established or those that are new to the repertoire of the individual psychologist.

Supervision and Consultation Release

School psychologists, interns, and practicum students need to inform parents (and adult students) at the onset of the provision of services if they will be discussing information about their case with a supervisor or consultant.

COUNSELING: ETHICAL AND LEGAL ISSUES

Tharinger and Stafford (1995) describe counseling in the schools as a process of ongoing, planned interactions between a student/client and a mental health professional. The school psychologist works to alleviate the student/client's distress by improving the child's psychological functioning and/or facilitating change in his or her environment, in particular the school and family systems. The goals of counseling may include "alleviating the child's emotional and cognitive distress, changing the child's behavior, assisting with self-understanding, helping the child meet current developmental tasks successfully, supporting needed environmental changes, and promoting a more positive fit between the child and the systems in which she or he resides (e.g., school and family)" (p. 896).

In the following portion of the chapter we will explore ethical-legal issues in special counseling situations such as working with students who are potentially dangerous to others or a threat to themselves. In providing counseling and therapeutic interventions in the schools, school psychologists strive to provide services consistent with the standard of care appropriate to our profession. In situations involving potential suicide, substance abuse, and students who are dangerous, the parameters of appropriate practice are often not clear. It is difficult to determine the implications of court decisions arising from private practice (usually with adult clients) for psychologists working with students in the schools. Because of their work setting and clientele, school psychologists must place a high priority on parent involvement and recognize the legal obligation of school personnel to protect the health and safety of students under school supervision.

Case 7–1

An 8-year-old girl, Celia, complained to her teacher that another child (a 13-year-old boy) was "playing games" with her. As it was apparent that the games involved inappropriate sexual contact, the teacher informed the school psychologist. The school psychologist counseled Celia without notifying her mother of the problem. The school principal was informed of the incidents and told the boy involved not to "bother" Celia anymore. The principal also failed to notify Celia's mother about the incidents. Meanwhile, the assaults on Celia continued over a 3-month period, both on school premises and en route to school. Celia became increasingly despondent and withdrawn. The sexual assaults ultimately led to rape. The victim's mother, after learning what had happened, filed a lawsuit against the school psychologist, teacher, and principal.

The California Supreme Court ruled that the school had a mandatory duty to warn *Celia's mother that her daughter was being sexually molested, a duty to report the assaults to a child protective agency, a duty to obtain written parent consent prior to psychological treatment dealing with matters of a sensitive sexual nature, and a duty to properly supervise the molesting student and ensure Celia's safety (adapted from* Phillis P. v. Claremont Unified School District, *1986).*

Threat to Others

Available data suggest student violence occurs with alarming frequency in our nation's schools. In 1990 there were more than 465,000 assaults committed inside a school or on school property (U.S. Census Bureau, 1992). Approximately 28,200 students are physically attacked in America's secondary schools each month, along with 5,200 secondary school teachers (Greenbaum & Turner, 1989).

Generally, under state statutory law and common law, school personnel have a duty to ensure the safety of pupils under their supervision (Schill, 1993).[1] In addition, school employment contracts often contain a provision whereby any act or failure to act that jeopardizes pupil health, safety, or welfare can result in suspension or termination of employment. Thus, school personnel may have a legal as well as an ethical obligation to protect the intended victim if a pupil is likely to do bodily harm to another and they are aware of this intent.

In addition to a duty to protect that may be created by the school–pupil relationship, a school psychologist also must be sensitive to the duty to protect created by a therapist–client relationship. The *Tarasoff* rulings and our code of ethics (NASP-PPE, III, A, #9) have placed psychologists in the position of having to decide when a client's statements constitute enough of a threat that confidentiality (and possibly the therapeutic relationship) must be breached in order to protect the potential victim or victims.

The assessment of whether a client is potentially dangerous is problematic (Borum, 1996). According to Knapp and VandeCreek, "every idle fantasy or impulsive threat is not evidence of imminent danger" (1982, p. 515). Threat is one factor to consider, but there are others, including whether the student is capable (physically, cognitively) of carrying out the threat, and the history of his or her behavioral acts (see Kagle & Kopels, 1994).

In court decisions, therapists have not been held liable for failure to warn "when the propensity toward violence is unknown or would be unknown by other psychotherapists using ordinary skill" (Knapp & VandeCreek, 1982, p. 515). In making a decision whether a student is potentially dangerous, the psychologist is well advised to consult with other professionals (Waldo & Malley, 1992).

---

[1] A number of lawsuits filed under Section 1983 of the Civil Rights Act of 1871 have raised the question of whether schools have a constitutionally based duty to protect schoolchildren. See Schill (1993).

Consistent with the guidelines for other situations involving danger, schools need to develop written procedures regarding when and how to notify school officials and legal authorities (e.g., police, the student's probation officer) if school staff become aware of a potentially assaultive student. These procedures should ensure that the intended victim is warned. If threats are made against a minor child, the parents of the threatened child must be notified (see *Phillis P.*). Parents of a potentially assaultive student must be informed of the situation, and practitioners should be prepared to refer the family to a community mental health agency, and be familiar with the procedures for voluntary and involuntary commitment of minors and adult students. School psychology practitioners should know and follow school policies regarding potentially dangerous students and document their actions in the management of a student who may become violent.

As is true of many mental health concerns in the school setting, efforts aimed at preventing student violence on a systemwide basis are preferable to the dilemmas of managing the assault-prone student. There appears to be a growing body of literature on this topic (see *School Psychology Review,* 1994, *23*(2); also Furlong, Morrison, Chung, Bates, & Morrison, 1997).

Threat to Self

Case 7–2

Brian, a 14-year-old, confronted his teacher during class with a .38 caliber revolver. The teacher persuaded Brian to talk with the vice principal alone in an empty classroom. Brian showed the vice principal a suicide note he had written and asked to speak with his favorite teacher; he was not allowed to do so. When they left the classroom, Brian was confronted by a police officer who told him he was "in trouble with the law." Brian (still armed with the gun) entered the boy's restroom where he shot himself. Brian died later that morning (adapted from Kelson v. The City of Springfield, *1985).*

Suicide is one of the three leading causes of death among adolescents. It is estimated that there are approximately 11.3 completed suicides per 100,000 adolescents in the 15- to 19-year-old age group, and 1.4 per

Case 7–3

"Nina," a 13-year-old middle-school student, became involved in satanism and developed an obsessive interest in death. She told several friends that she intended to kill herself. Nina's friends reported her suicidal intentions to their school counselor (at a different school), who conveyed the information to Nina's school counselor. Both counselors met with Nina and questioned her about her statements concerning suicide, but she denied making them. Neither counselor informed Nina's parents or other members of the school staff about her suicidal statements. One week after telling her friends about her suicidal intentions, Nina and another 13-year-old girl consummated a murder-suicide pact in a public park some distance from the middle school she attended (adapted from Eisel v. Board of Education, *1991).*

100,000 children in the 10- to 14-year-old age group (U.S. Census Bureau, 1992).

School Response to Suicidal Intent

In *Kelson* (Case 7–2), Brian's parents filed a negligence suit against the school and city in state court and a Section 1983 lawsuit against the school and city in federal court, alleging that the state interfered with their constitutionally protected liberty interest in the companionship of their son. When the Section 1983 lawsuit reached the U.S. Court of Appeals, the judge advised Brian's parents to file an amended claim against the school district after ruling on several legal questions raised by the case. In so doing, he raised the question of a possible relationship between school policy (namely, inadequate suicide training for its staff) and Brian's death. This case has been interpreted to suggest that schools should ensure at least some staff members are trained in suicide prevention and that a trained staff member be called in any potential suicide situation (Slenkovich, 1986, June).

In *Eisel v. Board of Education* (Case 7–3), Nina's father filed a negligence suit against the two school counselors, based on their failure to communicate information to him concerning Nina's contemplated suicide. Nina's father believed he could have prevented his daughter's death had he been told about her statements. The court held that a school has a special duty to protect a pupil from harm and that "school counselors have a duty to use reasonable means to attempt to prevent a suicide when they are on notice of a child or adolescent's suicidal intent" (*Eisel,* 1991, p. 456). The school counselors were viewed as having little discretion regarding whether to contact parents once information suggested a potential suicide. This case has been interpreted to suggest that schools should develop clear suicide prevention policies and procedures that include warning parents when there is any reason to believe a pupil has suicidal intentions (Slenkovich, 1992, May).[2]

Perhaps partly in response to court cases like these, there appears to be agreement in the professional literature on the following points: (a) Each school should develop a written planned response to suicidal students and ensure adequate staff orientation to district policy and procedures. (b) When it is suspected that a student is suicidal, the situation should be reported to a designated staff member who has verifiable training in suicide prevention. The school psychologist might serve as one of the designated staff. (c) The student's parents must be informed of the situation. (d) The school should be prepared to refer the parent to an appropriate agency. (e) School personnel should be prepared to have the student transported to an appropriate agency if the parent is unavailable or uncooperative (adapted from Davis, Sandoval, & Wilson, 1988; see also Poland, 1995).

Responsibilities of the School Psychologist

As Knapp (1980) suggests, a psychologist is not expected to be able to predict suicide attempts with perfect accuracy. However, practitioners are expected to apply "skill and care in assessing suicidal potential and . . . a reasonable degree of care and skill in preventing the suicide" (1980, p. 609). Practitioners thus need to be knowledgeable of the warning signs of suicide and how to evaluate the risk of suicide (see Berman & Jobes, 1991). Practitioners are well advised to develop consultative relationships with clinicians who have expertise in suicide assessment and management, whom they can contact for assistance in evaluating and managing a potential suicide situation (Jobes & Berman, 1993). Practitioners must know and follow written school policies regarding suicide prevention. As noted, when suicidal intent is known or suspected, the student's parents and the designated school

[2] This decision did not determine the school's liability; the decision only allowed action in another court to rule on the school's liability. The school counselors ultimately were not held liable for the $1 million in damages the father sought.

authorities must be notified. Practitioners should document their actions regarding risk assessment and management of pupils who may be suicidal. School psychologists also need to be familiar with community resources for referral, including the procedures for hospitalization of suicidal minors and adult students.

It has become increasingly important for school practitioners to obtain training to ensure their professional competence in the assessment and management of suicidal clients (Jobes & Berman, 1993). Additionally, psychologists who develop special expertise in suicide prevention can play an important role in the development of the school's planned response to suicidal students. There is also a growing body of literature on the development of suicide prevention programs in the schools (Brock & Sandoval, 1997; Poland, 1995; Sandoval & Brock, 1996).

Substance Abuse

Case 7–4

Nick Greene, a member of the school's winning football team, made an appointment with the school psychologist, Sam Foster. He confided that he had been taking "supervitamins" to build up his muscles over the past year. A fellow high school student bought the vitamins at a local health club and sold them in the locker room to football team members. Nick had seen some TV news stories about steroids, and he thinks maybe the supervitamins "have some of that in it." He was worried because he also heard that steroids "could make a guy act queer," and he wanted to know if that could happen to him.

A number of surveys suggest that substance abuse continues to be a problem in our schools. Alcohol is the substance most commonly abused by teenagers and adults. In 1992, 32.6% of 12- to 17-year-olds reported having consumed alcohol within the year. The rate was 11.7% for use of an illicit drug (National Center for Education Statistics, 1993). School psychologists (particularly those who work with middle and senior high students) need to be knowledgeable of drugs commonly used by adolescents and the symptoms of alcohol and drug abuse.

When substance abuse poses a threat to the student, it is appropriate to notify the parent of the problem and work with the parent in locating treatment resources (Forman & Randolph, 1987). Some states (e.g., Virginia) have enacted laws that require schools to report alcohol or substance abuse to parents. If the parent is uncooperative, the psychologist should explore treatment options that do not require parental consent. Every state has an agency responsible for coordinating substance abuse services that may be helpful in locating needed services (Forman & Randolph, 1987).

If knowledge of substance abuse involves other students in the school setting, the practitioner may need to discuss the situation with appropriate school authorities in order to ensure the safety of others. School psychologists must be cautious to avoid involvement in school disciplinary actions, particularly search and seizure (see Chapter 11).

Sam Foster (Case 7–4) needs to work with Nick and his parents to ensure Nick is seen by a physician to determine the nature of the substance taken, any harmful effects, and the appropriate course of treatment. He also needs to discuss his concerns about possible steroid abuse with high school officials (without disclosing Nick's identity) and explore ways to alert parents and students to the dangers of steroid use.

School psychologists can assume a leadership role in the development and implementation of school-based substance abuse programs, including educational programs for school staff and parents, prevention and intervention programs for students, and developing liaisons with community resources (see Forman & Pfeiffer, 1997; McNamera, 1995).

Child Abuse

Case 7–5

Pesce was a school psychologist providing services at the high school level. A female student (C. R.) gave him a note written to her by a male friend (J. D). The note included a statement made by J. D. expressing guilt and confusion about his sexual preference and possible hints of suicide. C. R. also informed Pesce that J. D. had visited the home of a male teacher where "something sexual" had occurred between them. Pesce urged C. R. to have J. D. get in touch with him to discuss these matters. Pesce did not notify anyone else of C. R.'s communications at that time.

Later the same day, J. D. visited Pesce in his office at school, and Pesce assured J. D. of the confidentiality of any information divulged

Case 7–5 *(Continued)*

and questioned him about issues raised by the letter. J. D. denied having any current suicidal intentions and denied that any sexual acts had occurred between the male teacher and him, but stated that the teacher had once shown him "pictures" when he visited the teacher's home. J. D. also expressed a desire to have help in addressing his confusion over sexual preference. Pesce arranged for J. D. to see a therapist.

Pesce reached a professional judgment that it was in J. D.'s best interest for Pesce to honor their confidential relationship and not inform school authorities about J. D.'s communications without his consent. After considering relevant state laws, school regulations, the guidelines of the American Psychological Association, and consulting with an attorney and a colleague, Pesce chose not to notify a child protection agency or any school officials of the rumored sexual activity or suicidal tendencies.

During the following week, J. D. kept two appointments with the therapist Pesce had recommended, but canceled a third. Pesce then met jointly with J. D. and the therapist. During that meeting, J. D. revealed that he and the male teacher had engaged in a sexual act. J. D. then agreed with Pesce that it would be best to reveal the information to school authorities. Pesce promptly did so.

After making his report to school officials, Pesce was given a 5-day disciplinary suspension for "failure promptly to report J. D.'s possible suicidal tendencies and the alleged sexual misconduct of a male teacher" (p. 790).

Pesce filed a suit against school officials alleging (among other claims) that the state's requirement for reporting suspected child abuse infringed unconstitutionally on his right of confidentiality in the professional relationship (derived from the student's right to privacy). The court noted that, as a school psychologist, Pesce may well be able to claim a right to confidentiality in his professional relationships with his clients. However, even if there is such a right to confidentiality, there is a greater compelling interest, namely to protect children from abuse. The court found that "the Illinois requirement that Pesce and others in similar positions of responsibility promptly report child abuse to a state agency does not unconstitutionally infringe on any federal right of confidentiality" (p. 798) (adapted from Pesce v. J. Sterling Morton High School District 201, Cook County, Illinois, *1987).*

The Child Abuse Prevention, Adoption, and Family Services Act of 1988 defined child maltreatment as "the physical or mental injury, sexual abuse or exploitation, negligent treatment, or maltreatment of a child by a person who is responsible for the child's welfare, under circumstances which indicate that the child's health or welfare is harmed or threatened" (Pub. L. No. 100-294, § 14). States are required to use a similar definition of abuse in their reporting laws in order to be eligible for federal child protection funds. There is some variation among states, however, with regard to the way abuse is defined (see Kalichman, 1993). All 50 states have enacted legislation requiring school professionals to report suspected cases of child abuse to child welfare or protection agencies.

There were 2,694,000 reported cases of child abuse or neglect in 1991. Most child abuse goes unreported, however. Researchers estimate that reported cases of child abuse constitute only about 40% of all cases (Kalichman, 1993). *School psychologists are legally required to report all cases of suspected child abuse.* All states provide immunity from civil or criminal action for making such a report, as long as it is made in good faith. Penalties for not reporting may include civil liability and loss of certification or license. In *State v. Gover* (1989), the court held that it is not necessary that school personnel be certain that the abuse took place, only that there is reason to suspect abuse.

In *Phillis P.* (Case 7–1), the California Supreme Court held that the school psychologist had a mandatory duty to report a student who was sexually molesting another student to the state child protection agency. In *Pesce* (Case 7–5), the court held that the duty to protect schoolchildren by reporting suspected child abuse outweighs any right to confidentiality of the psychologist–client relationship.[3]

School psychology practitioners must be familiar with the signs of abuse and neglect. They must know the procedures for reporting and familiarize themselves with the designated agency and its procedures for handling reports (see Horton, 1995). It is the responsibility of the child protection agency, not school personnel, to confirm or disconfirm the existence of abuse or neglect.

Most child abuse occurs in the context of the family, rather than the school. One concern about making a report about suspected abuse might be the loss of rapport with the student or with the family as a result of making

[3] The case of *Pesce* is a curious one for a number of reasons. First, there is no mention of parent involvement. Second, school officials also failed to notify protective services after Pesce notified them of his concerns. The reader may wish to consider alternative decisions that might be made in handling a situation like the one that confronted Pesce, and the possible consequences of various actions for the parties involved.

a report. However, based on a review of the available studies, Kalichman concludes that, "Little evidence exists to support the popular perceptions that reporting abuse has detrimental effects on the quality and efficacy of professional services. In fact, studies specifically addressing these issues in naturalistic settings find that reporting has minimal negative, and sometimes beneficial, effects on the treatment process" (1993, p. 54). He goes on to note, however, that additional research is needed in this area. Similarly, Meddin and Rosen note that, "After their initial and appropriate anger at the intervention of the agency, most parents feel a sense of relief that the problems has [sic] been identified, and they are usually very willing to work toward a solution" (1986, p. 30).

School psychologists can assume an important role in the prevention, identification, and reporting of child abuse (see Horton, 1995; Kalichman, 1993) and in the treatment of abused children (see Brassard, 1997; Horton & Cruise, 1997).

Pregnancy and Birth Control Information

Case 7–6

Tamara Jones, a high school English teacher, referred a 15-year-old student, Brenda, to the school psychologist for a precounseling screening. Mrs. Jones is concerned because Brenda's grades have declined markedly, and although she has discussed this with Brenda's parents, she sees no improvement. Charlie Maxwell, the school psychologist, meets with Brenda and explains both confidentiality and its limits at the onset of their meeting. He also explains to Brenda that if they decide to work together, he will need the consent of Brenda's parents for their counseling sessions. Brenda, visibly quite shaken, explains that she has been sexually active and thinks she might be pregnant. She is afraid to tell her parents.

Pregnancy

Recent years have witnessed an increase in adolescent pregnancies and the spread of serious sexually transmitted diseases among our nation's youth (Stoiber, 1997). In 1989, over 58,000 babies were born to girls between the ages of 15 and 19. An additional 1,400 children ages 10 to 14 gave birth

(U.S. Census Bureau, 1992). More than 3 million adolescents contract a sexually transmitted disease each year (Stoiber, 1997).

Brenda (Case 7–6) suspects she is pregnant. Charlie Maxwell needs to refer Brenda to a physician or clinic to confirm or disconfirm the pregnancy. School psychologists who work with adolescents must be knowledgeable of area physicians and family planning clinics that provide teens with sensitive and supportive care. Parent notification or consent is not needed for a minor to visit a family planning clinic (Brooks-Gunn & Furstenberg, 1989). It is important, however, to refer students to a neutral agency, not one perceived as an abortion clinic (Hummel et al., 1985).

With parental consent, the psychologist may continue to work with a minor student on pregnancy management. This phase of pregnancy counseling should prepare the student for the emotional issues associated with having to make decisions regarding pregnancy alternatives (Ross-Reynolds & Hardy, 1985; Stoiber, 1997). Psychologists involved in pregnancy counseling must be knowledgeable of their state laws regarding access to abortion for minors.

There have been numerous court cases involving minors and access to abortion; only a few will be mentioned here. In *Planned Parenthood of Central Missouri v. Danforth* (1976), the Supreme Court held that a Missouri statute requiring parental consent prior to an abortion in the case of an unmarried minor was unconstitutional. At this time, parental consent is required in some states, but parental permission may be required only if the law provides for a judicial bypass procedure, that is,

> . . . an alternative procedure whereby authorization for the abortion can be obtained. A pregnant minor is entitled to such a proceeding to show either (1) that she is mature enough and well enough informed to make her abortion decision, in consultation with her physician, independently of her parents' wishes; or (2) that even if she is not able to make this decision independently, the desired abortion would be in her best interests. (*Bellotti v. Baird,* 1979, p. 4973)

More recently, in *Planned Parenthood of Southeastern Pennsylvania v. Casey* (1992), the Supreme Court reaffirmed that a state "may require a minor seeking an abortion to obtain the consent of a parent or guardian, provided that there is an adequate judicial bypass procedure" (p. 4813).

Some states have laws requiring the physician to *notify* the parents of a girl who is a minor prior to an abortion. In *H.L. Etc., Appellant v. Scott M. Matheson* (1981), the Court upheld a Utah law requiring the physician to notify the parents in certain circumstances, namely, when the girl is dependent on her parents, she is not emancipated, and she makes no claim that she is mature enough to make the decision alone or that parental notice would adversely affect her relationship with her parents. Supreme Court decisions since 1981 have not modified the earlier holdings regarding parental notice. In *Hodgson v. Minnesota* (1989), the Supreme Court held that the two-parent notice requirement in Minnesota's abortion statute is constitutionally invalid. However, because the Minnesota statute provides for a judicial bypass procedure, under which a minor may obtain an abortion without parental notice, the statute as a whole was found to be valid. In *Ohio v. Akron Center for Reproductive Health* (1989), the Court upheld a one-parent notice law that also provides for judicial bypass.

Birth Control Information

The issue of school involvement in the provision of family planning information is highly controversial and involves deep-rooted family and community values. School policies run the gamut from those that forbid discussion of birth control with individual students, to experimental programs that allow easy student access to family planning information and contraceptives (e.g., health clinics on or adjacent to school grounds).

Practitioners who work with adolescents must be knowledgeable of state law and local school policy regarding the provision of birth control information by school staff, and be sensitive to community and family values. Providing competent advice on contraception to a minor in the school setting is probably permissible unless it conflicts with state or local policies (Fischer & Sorenson, 1996).

Prevention Efforts

School psychologists can play an important role in encouraging the development of programs to prevent teen pregnancies and reduce the incidence of sexually transmitted diseases among teenagers. Interested readers are referred to Peterson and Brofcak (1997) and Stoiber (1997).

Summary

Within the protection of a confidential relationship, students may report any number of behaviors that, although not immediately dangerous, have that potential. Such actions as failure to take prescribed medications, eating disorders, criminal activity, and engaging in unprotected sex and sexual promiscuity might all fall into this category.

There is no way to anticipate all possible circumstances in counseling that may prove to be a problem. The keys to dealing with most cases successfully are, first, a candid discussion of confidentiality and its limits at the onset of offering services; second, a good working relationship with the student; third, knowledge of state laws and regulations as well as school policies; fourth, familiarity with resources in the community and how to access them; and fifth, dealing openly and honestly with the student about your concerns and possible courses of action.

Competence and Responsibility

Case 7–7

Hannah Cook, school psychologist, has developed expertise in eating disorders and has successfully counseled a number of students on a one-to-one basis. She became interested in providing a counseling group for students with eating disorders and attended a one-day workshop on using group-counseling methods with anorexic and bulimic teens. She is now using this group counseling technique with students in her schools.

Competence

Consistent with the principle of responsible caring, school psychologists are obligated to "recognize the strengths and limitations of their training and experience, engaging only in practices for which they are qualified" (NASP-PPE, II, A, #1; also *EP* Principle A). A problem for the practitioner is to determine what constitutes an acceptable and recognized level of competency. Seeking assistance through supervision, consultation, and referral are appropriate strategies for handling a difficult case (NASP-PPE, II, A, #4). It is necessary and appropriate for Sam Foster to refer Nick Greene to a physician knowledgeable of the problems of steroid abuse (Case 7–4).

However, practitioners who plan to introduce new counseling techniques or expand the scope of their services must complete appropriate and verifiable training before offering such services (APA, 1981, p. 674). Is Hannah (Case 7–7) competent to provide group counseling to teens with eating disorders? The question of her competence relates to both the adequacy of the workshop she attended as well as her background. If she has had extensive training in group counseling, including prior supervised experience, she is able to claim more competence to attempt this new technique than if this workshop was her first exposure to the group counseling process. Group counseling techniques require a high degree of skill and prior supervised experience (Fischer & Sorenson, 1996).

Practitioners also must evaluate their competence to provide counseling services to students whose background characteristics are outside the scope of their training and supervised experience. School psychologists need to be aware of their own values and must be knowledgeable of and sensitive to the cultural values of the student/client. The ethical issues of multicultural counseling are currently receiving attention in the professional literature (see APA, 1993a; Burn, 1992; see also Ponterotto, Casas, Suzuki, & Alexander, 1995).

An issue related to the question of competence is whether the school psychologist is the most competent professional available to provide the counseling service. NASP's code of ethics states: "School psychologists recognize the competence of other professionals. They encourage and support the use of all resources to best serve the interests of students and clients" (NASP-PPE, III, F, #2). Charlie (Case 7–6) may have some knowledge of pregnancy management counseling, but he must consider whether Brenda might benefit more from counseling provided by another professional.

School psychologists also are ethically obligated "to refrain from any activity in which their personal problems or conflicts may interfere with professional effectiveness" (NASP-PPE, II, A, #6).

Responsibility

NASP's code of ethics states: "School psychologists develop interventions which are appropriate to the presenting problems and are consistent with data collected. They modify or terminate the treatment plan when the data indicate the plan is not achieving the desired goals" (NASP-PPE, IV, B, #6).

In providing counseling services, the practitioner may recognize that he or she is unable to help the client. The ACA code of ethics states: "If the member determines an inability to be of professional assistance to the client, the member must . . . terminate that relationship" (1988, B.12). The principle goes on to say that the member must suggest an appropriate alternative for the client, but that it is up to the client to choose or refuse the alternative. In either case, the counselor is no longer obligated to continue the counseling relationship.

BEHAVIORAL INTERVENTION

For the purpose of this discussion, behavioral intervention means the planned and systematic use of learning principles, particularly operant techniques and modeling theory, to change the behavior of individual students either by working with the student directly, or in collaboration or consultation with the teacher (or parent) who serves as the primary change agent. The discussion of ethical-legal issues associated with behavioral interventions focuses on issues associated with the stages of problem identification, intervention, and evaluation.

Problem Clarification

An ethical concern that arises during the problem clarification stage is whether or not the goals of intervention are in the best interests of the child. Teachers may at times seek assistance in changing pupil behaviors they find personally irritating or troublesome, but which are not significantly interfering with the child's school performance. Harris and Kapche suggest that, ethically, the psychologist and teacher must select target behaviors that "enhance the long-term well-being of the child" (1978, p. 27) and are consistent with the long-range goal of self-management. Goals also must be selected to ensure that the pupil will develop appropriate adaptive behaviors and not just suppress inappropriate ones (Van Houten et al., 1988).

It also is important to set goals that are realistic for the student and his or her situation. "Setting unrealistic goals is a disservice to students and to their parents, as well as a source of frustration to teachers and other staff" (Alberto & Troutman, 1982, p. 42).

Intervention

School psychologists are ethically obligated to select (or assist in the selection of) change procedures that have demonstrated effectiveness. Any experimental procedures should be clearly identified to those giving informed consent. Practitioners also are obligated to select the least drastic procedures and those that minimize the risk of adverse side effects that are likely to be effective. The notion of least drastic procedures grew out of the legal doctrine of least restrictive alternative discussed in Chapter 5 (see section on least restrictive environment).

There is some consensus in the literature about the procedures more acceptable and those that are least acceptable. First choice (Level I) strategies are based on differential reinforcement (e.g., reinforcing appropriate behaviors incompatible with problem behaviors). Second choice (Level II) strategies are based on extinction (withdrawing of reinforcement for undesired behavior). Third choice (Level III) strategies include removal of desirable stimuli (e.g., time-out procedures). The least acceptable (Level IV) strategies are those that involve presentation of aversive stimuli (from Alberto & Troutman, 1982, p. 206).

In the 1970s, a number of behavioral control or change procedures came under the scrutiny of the courts. These early cases concerned youth in juvenile corrections facilities (e.g., *Morales v. Turman,* 1974; *Pena v. New York State Division for Youth,* 1976) or residential mental health facilities (e.g., *New York State Association for Retarded Children v. Carey,* 1975). These cases provide some insight into the minimal standards that must be adhered to in the use of behavioral methods so as not to violate the constitutional rights of the children involved. More specifically, these cases suggest that behavioral control methods must not deprive pupils of their basic rights to food; water; shelter, including adequate heat and ventilation; sleep; and exercise periods. Several more recent court cases have looked more directly at the use of behavioral methods in the public schools (e.g., *Dickens by Dickens v. Johnson County Board of Education* 1987, and *Hayes v. Unified School District No. 377,* 1987).

Differential Reinforcement

The systematic use of differential reinforcement is considered to be a first-choice strategy. Access to privileges (use of the classroom computer to play games), special luxuries (colorful stickers), and social reinforcers (smiles and praise) are types of reinforcers that typically present no special concerns.

However, the early court rulings cited have been interpreted to suggest that not all types of reinforcers are acceptable. Some classroom teachers use token economies to manage behavior. In token economies, tokens or points may be earned for appropriate behavior, and the tokens are subsequently exchanged for rewards. The use of token economies may not result in denial of food, water, adequate shelter, or rest and exercise periods, and students should not be denied educational opportunities that are part of the child's expected program (e.g., gym, art) (Hindman, 1986).

Removal of Desirable Stimuli

Certain types of Level III interventions have come under legal scrutiny. Time-out is a popular behavior management strategy. Time-out typically involves removing the child from the classroom when inappropriate behavior occurs, and having him or her regain self-control in a separate room. Time-out also may involve secluding the child in a special isolation area within the classroom.

Two legal challenges to the use of time-out in the public schools found it to be an acceptable procedure to safeguard other students from disruptive behavior (*Dickens,* 1987; *Hayes,* 1987; see also *Honig v. Doe,* 1988).

Furthermore, in *Dickens,* the court noted that "judicious use of behavioral modification techniques such as 'time-out' should be favored over expulsion in disciplining disruptive students, particularly the handicapped" (1987, p. 158).

However, the use of time-out must meet reasonable standards safeguarding the rights and welfare of pupils. In finding the use of time-out permissible, the judge in *Dickens* also noted, "This is not to say that educators may arbitrarily cage students in a corner of the classroom for an indeterminate length of time" (1987, p. 158). The court considerations in *Dickens, Hayes,* and earlier cases suggest some general parameters for the use of time-out: School personnel must monitor a secluded student to ensure his or her well-being. The room must have adequate ventilation (*Morales,* 1974), the time-out room itself must not present a fire or safety hazard (*Hayes,* 1987), students must be permitted to leave time-out for appropriate reasons (*Dickens,* 1987), and the door to the time-out room must remain unlocked (*New York State Association for Retarded Children v. Carey,* 1975).

Students should be given prior notice about the types of behaviors that will result in being placed in time-out (*Hayes,* 1987), and school personnel must ensure that time-out, when used as punishment, is "not unduly harsh or grossly disproportionate" to the offense (*Dickens,* 1987, p. 158). Placement in time-out should not result in "a total exclusion from the educational process for more than a trivial period" (*Goss v. Lopez,* 1975, p. 575). Use of time-out combined with instruction in the time-out room, or requiring the child to do schoolwork while segregated or secluded, is recommended (*Dickens,* 1987).

Presentation of Aversive Stimuli

A highly controversial area in behavioral intervention is the use of aversive conditioning, where a discomforting stimulus is presented contingent upon the child's undesirable behavior. Some psychologists and educators believe that aversive conditioning must never be used; others believe its use may be justified in the treatment of extremely self-injurious or dangerous aggressive behaviors. It is beyond the scope of this book to explore the controversy fully; interested readers are referred to Jacob-Timm (1996), National Institutes of Health (1991) and Repp and Singh (1990).

Evaluation of Treatment Effectiveness

Consistent with our code of ethics, practitioners continually assess the impact of any behavioral treatment plan, "and modify or terminate the treatment plan when the data indicate that the plan is not achieving the desired goals" (NASP-PPE, IV, B, #6).

Competence

As Alberto and Troutman have observed, because "many applied behavior analysis procedures seem so simple, they are often misused by persons who do not adequately understand them" (1982, p. 40). The misapplication of behavioral techniques may result in potential harm to the child, and teachers and parents may conclude that "behavior modification doesn't work."

Practitioners interested in using behavioral interventions in the schools need verifiable training in applied behavior analysis that includes supervised practice. Ongoing consultation with an experienced behavior therapist is recommended until a high level of expertise is attained (Alberto & Troutman, 1982).

PSYCHOPHARMACOLOGIC INTERVENTIONS IN THE SCHOOLS

Case 7–8

In 1980, a California court approved the settlement of a lawsuit filed by 18 students and their parents against the school district. In the suit, the parents made claims against the school district and staff (including the school psychologist) stemming from the district's intrusion into the decision whether a child should take Ritalin to control what the schools alleged was hyperactive behavior. The parents contended that they had been subjected to extremely strong pressure to agree to the administration of the drug. One parent reported being called before an array of school district staff and told that she would be a "foolish parent" if she refused to give the drug to her son. Others were told that their children could not possibly succeed in school or remain in regular classes without the drug. Nothing was mentioned about the potentially dangerous side effects of the drug; and when parents asked about this, they were told that the drug was as harmless as aspirin. Only the most superficial of medical examinations of the children were done prior to prescribing or recommending the drug, and no follow-up monitoring at all was done. No efforts were made to alter any environmental factors (such as poor teaching) that might have contributed to the child's difficult behavior.

The suit was filed after two of the children experienced their first grand mal epileptic seizures while taking the drug. Other children

(Continued)

Case 7–8 *(Continued)*

complained of aches and pains, insomnia, loss of appetite, apathy, moodiness, nosebleeds, and other problems associated with the drug Ritalin. Expert witnesses for the parents testified that many of the children were perfectly normal and should never have been candidates for drug therapy, and that the school's procedures for diagnosis and prescription were woefully inadequate.

The settlement agreement ordered by the court included a lump-sum of $210,000.00, which the court allocated among the plaintiffs according to the severity of harm each child suffered. In addition, the settlement agreement set forth a number of policy clarifications that precluded the school district from diagnosing hyperactivity or recommending in any way that a child take behavior modification drugs (adapted from Benskin v. Taft City School District, *1980).*

This portion of the chapter alerts the practitioner to ethical and legal issues associated with the use of medications to treat children with school learning or behavior problems. Discussion here is limited to the use of Ritalin (methylphenidate hydrochloride) in the treatment of Attention Deficit Hyperactivity Disorder (ADHD) because it provides an excellent example of the promise and pitfalls of drug therapy.

Stimulant medication is the most widely used therapy for ADHD, and many experts consider it to be the most effective treatment (Barkley, 1989; Henker & Whalen, 1989; for a review, see Pelham, 1993). A number of school psychology practitioners and teachers have witnessed the dramatic improvements that occur for some children after they are placed on Ritalin. However, the use of Ritalin or other drugs to treat difficulties such as ADHD places the child at risk for physical or psychological harm because of the problems of potential misdiagnosis and drug side effects. There are a number of different types of hyperactivity, and stimulant medication is not appropriate for all types. Some children may be placed on Ritalin because of misdiagnosis, and use of the drug may consequently mask the child's true problems (Viadero, 1987).

Harm also may result from the side effects of Ritalin. Potential side effects include nervousness, insomnia, anorexia, nausea, dizziness, cardiac arrythmia, abdominal pain, and growth suppression. Although rare, there also have been reports of toxic psychosis, the development of Tourette's

Syndrome, abnormal liver function, and cerebral arteritis (inflammation) (*Physicians' Desk Reference,* 1997).

A number of lawsuits have been filed against the public schools and physicians by parents of children prescribed Ritalin. In many of these suits, children suffered physical (e.g., Tourette's Syndrome) and/or psychological harm (e.g., suicidal behavior) as a result of drug treatment recommended to them by school personnel (see Case 7–9). In some instances, parents report they were pressured by school officials to seek drug treatment for their son or daughter with threats of exclusion from school if they failed to comply (*Valerie J. v. Derry CO-OP School District,* 1991).

Based on our experiences in the schools, we believe that school personnel are sometimes too quick to suggest medication for children whose high activity level is a problem for the teacher. Correct diagnosis of ADHD is based on *DSM-IV* criteria (American Psychiatric Association, 1994) following a comprehensive assessment to determine that the child experiences difficulties with attention and hyperactivity relative to other children the same age and sex (Barkley, 1989). Barkley (1989) recommends the diagnosis of ADHD be based on use of multiple assessment methods across settings, incorporating the observations of several caregivers, and including the use of well standardized child behavior rating scales with scores adjusted for mental age (see also Bradley & DuPaul, 1997).

Barkley (1989) has developed a list of child, family, and situational factors to be examined when drug therapy is under consideration, and it is likely that the school psychologist can play a valuable role in collecting this information. However, decisions to prescribe drugs must be made by a physician (a point that should be clearly communicated to parents), and parents must be free to choose or refuse the use of such medication without undue pressure from the school. In *Valerie J. v. Derry CO-OP School District* (1991), the court held that a school may not require a pupil to take Ritalin as a precondition for attendance.

The court settlement in *Benskin* provides some guidance for school policies regarding drug treatment. Drug treatment requires careful physician–school–parent collaboration. The school should ensure that the use of drug therapy is based on informed parental consent that includes a description of the potential benefits (e.g., enhanced academic productivity, reduced disruptive behavior), and risks (e.g., drug side effects and adverse reactions). Through cooperative efforts with the physician, the school must ensure there is careful monitoring of the child. School psychologists can assist in the documentation of the effectiveness or noneffectiveness of drug treatments and thereby provide important feedback to the physician and parents (see Kubiszyn, Brown, & DeMers, 1997).

Research suggests drug treatment such as Ritalin is generally effective in improving the academic productivity of children with ADHD (Barkley, 1989). However, individualized instruction may be needed to translate improved productivity into enhanced academic achievement. Based on their review of the research, Henker and Whalen (1989) conclude that most ADHD children need tailored educational programs along with help in their social development, whether they are given medication. Thus, the practitioner's involvement does not end with the prescription of medication. (See Chapter 6 for a discussion of school responsibilities to children with ADHD under Section 504.)

CONCLUDING COMMENTS

> Teenaged parents. Academic failure. Substance abuse. Youth suicide. Divorce. AIDS. Childhood depression. Juvenile delinquency. Sexual abuse. The list of problems facing students in our schools today continues to grow and seemingly is endless. Yet, our time and resources remain limited. (Zins & Forman, 1988, p. 539)

In this chapter, we focused on the ethical-legal issues associated with counseling and therapeutic interventions in the schools. Partly in response to case law decisions, schools are beginning to recognize the importance of a planned response to crisis situations. Furthermore, consistent with NASP standards for professional practice (1997, 4.3.1.2), school psychologists also have recognized the need to place a greater emphasis on prevention efforts (Zins & Forman, 1988).

STUDY AND DISCUSSION

Questions for Chapter 7

1. When a school psychologist becomes aware of a potentially assaultive student, what actions are appropriate?
2. When a school psychologist becomes aware of a potentially suicidal student, what actions are appropriate?
3. When a school psychologist suspects child abuse or child neglect, what actions are appropriate?
4. Develop a list of guidelines for teachers on how to safeguard the ethical and legal rights of pupils when behavioral interventions are planned and implemented.

(Continued)

5. May a school require a child to take medication as a precondition for school attendance? Identify the ethical-legal issues associated with the use of medications to treat school children with learning and behavior problems.

Discussion

1. Is it possible for school psychologists to provide value-free or value-neutral counseling? Is it desirable? Again, see Chapter 3 of Corey, Corey and Callanan (1993) for an excellent discussion of values and the helping relationship. Are there counseling situations that would be difficult for you because of your personal values?

2. How do you distinguish substance use from abuse? How will you decide whether the use of alcohol or illegal drugs poses a threat to a student and that it is necessary to notify the parent? See Forman and Pfeiffer (1997).

3. How do you determine when a professional hunch becomes reasonable suspicion of child abuse? See Kalichman (1993) for a thorough discussion of the dilemmas associated with reporting suspected child maltreatment.

4. Do you believe school psychologists should be granted prescription privileges? Identify the pros and cons of granting such privileges. See DeMers (1994) and DeMers and Bricklin (1995).

5. Is it ever appropriate to use aversives in the treatment of severe behavior disorders? If yes, under what circumstances? What are the ethical-legal issues involved? See Jacob-Timm (1996) and Repp and Singh (1990).

ACTIVITIES

Role-play the following situations:

Situation #1. A teenager (age 14) has made an appointment for a counseling session with you, the school psychologist. Role-play the initial meeting during which the psychologist defines the parameters of confidentiality and discusses parent consent issues.

Situation #2. A parent, Mrs. Fox, has made an appointment with you to discuss her concerns about Bill, her 15-year-old son. She reports that Bill has become moody and difficult and that his grades have recently declined markedly. She would like you to meet with Bill to see if you can discover what the problems are, and report your findings back to her. Role-play this initial meeting, including a discussion of consent and confidentiality issues.

Situation #3. During a precounseling screening session, Joan Bellows, a 16-year-old, confides in you that she might be pregnant. Role-play how you might handle this situation.

VIGNETTES

Sam Foster, school psychologist, developed a good rapport with Frank Green, a tenth grader, when he counseled Frank about some problems in adjusting to a new stepfather. Later in the year, Frank makes an appointment to see Sam and reports that things seem to be going better at home. He confides that he stopped by to talk with Sam because he is worried about a girl in his woodshop class named "Heidi." Heidi is a friendly 16-year-old who is mentally retarded. Recently three boys in the woodshop class began to show a special interest in her. Frank saw the boys take Heidi into a storeroom near the woodshop on two occasions after class, and he thinks the boys are doing something bad to Heidi. How should Sam handle this situation?

Chapter 8

ETHICAL ISSUES IN CONSULTATION

Consultation has increasingly been viewed as deserving a dominant place in the delivery of school psychological services. Research has established a preference for consultative services among consumers of school psychological services, as well as the efficacy of consultative approaches (Gutkin & Curtis, 1990). As a result of their national survey, Reschly and Wilson (1995) found that practitioners devote an average of 7 hours per week to problem-solving consultation, defined as working with consultees (teachers or parents) with students as clients. In addition, practitioners devote an average of 2 hours each week to systems/organizational consultation. Survey respondents desired an increase in time for both types of consultation activity.

This chapter briefly explores the ethical issues associated with school-based consultation. Tokunaga (1984) suggests that rather than creating a set of ethical rules for consultants, psychologists consider existing professional standards for guidance. Consistent with Tokunaga's suggestion, our goal in this chapter is to interpret existing ethical codes as they relate to the provision of consultative services in the schools. Neither APA's "Ethical Principles of Psychologists and Code of Conduct" (1992) nor NASP's "Principles for Professional Ethics" (1997) contain more than brief references to consultation.

For the purposes of this chapter, we will adopt Conoley and Conoley's definition of consultation as "a voluntary, nonsupervisory relationship between professionals from differing fields established to aid one in his or her professional functioning" (1982, p. 1). Consultation differs from collaboration in that in consultation, the consultant's responsibility is only advisory; there is no direct responsibility over the consultee" (Hansen, Himes, & Meier, 1990, p. 4). The consultee "retains responsibility for the management of the case or program" (p. 5). Our focus here is limited to the provision of consultative services by the in-house practitioner. Readers interested in ethical issues associated with the role of external consultant are referred to Gallessich (1982) and Hansen et al. (1990).

A number of rules for the delivery of consultative services in the school have been identified. These rules are embedded in the definition of consultant and descriptions of the consultant role and consultative process. They are not ethical rules *per se* (although they may overlap with ethical principles); they are guidelines for the delivery of consultative services based on a growing consensus about best practices in school-based consultation. The rules for professional consultation are summarized as follows:

1. Consultation is voluntary. The consultant may not coerce the consultee into a relationship (Conoley & Conoley, 1982).
2. Consultation is nonsupervisory. The consultant and consultee share a coordinate status; the relationship is nonhierarchical. The consultee remains an autonomous professional and retains the right to accept or reject suggestions made by the consultant (Gutkin & Curtis, 1990). The consultee also retains responsibility for decisions; however, the consultant encourages alternative solutions until a resolution of problems is achieved.
3. The goals of consultation in the school setting must be work-related (Conoley & Conoley, 1982; Hansen et al., 1990).

ETHICAL PRINCIPLES AND CONSULTATIVE SERVICES

We do not introduce any new ethical principles in this chapter. Ethical principles and professional standards that receive special emphasis in consultation are discussed in the text that follows.

Integrity in Professional Relationships

In providing school-based consultative services, the school psychologist is working within a network of relationships. Consistent with the broad ethical principle of integrity in professional relationships, the practitioner strives to be honest, accurate, and straightforward about the nature and scope of the services he or she has to offer. Practitioners define the direction and nature of their personal loyalties, objectives, and competencies, and advise and inform all persons of these commitments (NASP-PPE, III, A, #3).

Curtis and Meyers (1985) suggest that the consultation role be clearly defined to the school community prior to offering consultative services (NASP-PPE, III, A, #4). Discussions of consultative services should include role definition, the process of goal setting during consultation, the responsibilities of the consultant and consultee, and the parameters of confidentiality. Although initially this may occur at the level of the school, the same entry stage issues are subsequently discussed with individual teachers at the beginning of a consultative relationship (Curtis & Meyers, 1985).

A means of ensuring a mutual understanding of the parameters of a consultative relationship is through contracting. "A contract is a verbal or written agreement between the consultant and the consultee that specifies the parameters of the relationship" (Conoley & Conoley, 1982, p. 115). The contract might include the following elements: (a) general goals of consultation and how specific goals will be selected; (b) tentative time frame; (c) consultant responsibilities (services to be provided, methods to be used, time commitment, how the success of the consultation will be evaluated); (d) the nature of consultee responsibilities; and (e) confidentiality rules (adapted from Gallessich, 1982, pp. 272–273).

Respect for the Dignity of Persons

Psychologists accept as fundamental the principle of respect for the dignity of persons, which encompasses respect for self-determination and autonomy, privacy and confidentiality, and the values of fairness and nondiscrimination.

Client Welfare, Autonomy, and Self-Determination

Student-Client School psychologists consider the pupils/clients to be their primary responsibility and act as advocates of their rights and welfare. Although in consultation the teacher is the recipient of services, pupil welfare "must be of primary importance to a school-based consultant" (Davis & Sandoval, 1982). The psychologist works with the teacher to ensure consultation goals and intervention strategies are selected that are likely to be ultimately beneficial to the student(s) (NASP-PPE, III, A, #1).

Because consultation is an indirect service, the ethical responsibility for the impact of this service on pupils raises certain practical difficulties for consultants (Newman, 1993). There are a number of strategies for safeguarding student welfare, autonomy, and self-determination when providing consultative services. These include involving the student as much as feasible in the selection of goals and change strategies, and selecting goals to promote student self-management. Consultants also must consider the ethical adequacy of particular intervention approaches (Newman, 1993).

Teacher-Consultee Although the student is seen as the primary client, psychologists also strive to safeguard the dignity and rights of other recipients of services (NASP-PPE, III, F, #1, #2). As noted in the rules for providing consultation to the teacher, the teacher-consultee remains an autonomous professional and retains the right to accept or reject suggestions made by the consultant. The psychologist discourages teacher dependence on the consultant (Fanibanda, 1976). The consultant also is careful to avoid stepping into the role of counselor-therapist to the consultee. Such dual relationships are contrary to the rules defining the consultant's role in the schools (Curtis & Meyers, 1985).

Consultants must be keenly sensitive to the ethical issues of manipulation and control of the consultee in providing consultative services to teachers (Hughes, 1986). The psychologist and teacher have differing fields of specialization and they may have differing values. It is important that, as consultants, we "sufficiently understand the values of the community, institution, consultee, and clients with whom we work so that we will not merely impose our values on them" (Davis & Sandoval, 1982, p. 545; also NASP-PPE, III, A, #2). As Fanibanda (1976) points out, our obligation to the welfare of the student may require us to advocate for certain decisions even if they conflict with the apparent value orientation of the consultee. Candid discussion of values and goals throughout consultation is a safeguard for teacher autonomy (Brown, Pryzwansky, & Schulte, 1987). "Given the fundamental link that exists between values and ethics, it is imperative that consultants understand their values and their relative importance in their own value hierarchies" (Newman, 1993).

Consistent with our codes of ethics, school psychologists work in full cooperation with teachers in a relationship based on mutual respect (NASP-PPE, III, F, #1). It is important to remember that teachers are our most important resource in helping children in the school setting.

Informed Consent

In offering consultative services to the teacher, the use of a verbal or written contract helps to ensure his or her informed consent for services (*EP* 1.20). Informed consent of the parent is needed if an intervention is planned for a student that diverges from ordinary, expectable schooling.

Confidentiality

Confidentiality in providing consultative services to the teacher can be problematic. The parameters of confidentiality must be discussed at the onset of the delivery of services, and at a minimum, teachers should clearly understand what and how information will be used, by whom, and for what purpose (Newman, 1993). Consistent with the notion of integrity in professional relationships, the psychologist should have a clear prior agreement about those parameters with others in the school setting (*EP* 5.06).

In general, in consultation to the teacher or other school staff, the guarantees of client confidentiality apply to the consultant–consultee relationship (Fanibanda, 1976). All that is said between the psychologist and consultee is kept confidential by the psychologist, unless the consultee requests information be disclosed to others (Davis & Sandoval, 1982). Violation of confidentiality in consultation with teachers or other staff is likely to result in a loss of trust in the psychologist and may impair his or her ability to work with the consultee and others.

Is there ever a duty to breach the confidentiality of the consultant–consultee relationship to safeguard the welfare of the student(s)? In providing consultative services to teachers, ethical responsibility requires that limits to the promise of confidentiality be identified (Conoley & Conoley, 1982; Hughes, 1986; Newman, 1993). Thus, for example, the practitioner may want to ensure a prior agreement that the consultant may breach confidentiality in those unusual instances when the consultee "chronically and stubbornly" persists in unethical activities (Conoley & Conoley, 1982, p. 216).

However, "Before breaching confidentiality, the consultant must have expended all resources at influencing the consultee to take collaborative action" (Hughes, 1986, p. 491). Such a breach of confidentiality should be given careful consideration and *would only be appropriate when the consultee's actions are harmful or potentially harmful to the student/client.* "The consultee's approach toward the client actually must be detrimental to the child rather than a less than optimal approach" (Hughes, 1986, p. 491). The consultant is obligated to discuss the need to disclose confidential information with the consultee prior to disclosure.

Fairness and Nondiscrimination

The broad ethical principle of respect for the dignity of persons also encompasses the values of fairness and nondiscrimination. School psychologists deal justly and impartially with each consultee regardless of his or her personal, political, cultural, racial, or religious characteristics. In providing consultation services, as in providing direct services, the school psychologist must be aware of his or her own beliefs, values, and prejudices and be sensitive to the worldview of the consultee (NASP-PPE, III, A, #2; APA, 1993a).

Responsible Caring

Responsible caring means that the psychologist engages in actions that are likely to benefit others, or at least do no harm. In order to be able to engage in such actions, psychologists must practice within the boundaries of their competence and accept responsibility for their actions.

Professional Responsibility in Consultation

Practitioners accept responsibility for their decisions and the consequences of their actions (*EP* Principle C; NASP-PPE, III, A, #1), and they work to offset any harmful consequences of decisions made. School psychologists "modify or terminate the treatment plan when the data indicate the plan is not achieving the desired goals" (NASP-PPE, IV, B, #6).

Models of consultation typically include four stages: an entry phase and the stages of problem identification/clarification, intervention/problem solution, and evaluation. The fourth stage of the consultation process, evaluation, encourages professional responsibility on the part of both the psychologist and consultee. During this stage, the consultant and consultee assess whether the intervention was successful in meeting the agreed-on goals, and if not, the consultant and consultee "re-cycle" back to the stage of problem identification/clarification or intervention/solution.

However, in the course of the consultative process, it may become apparent to the psychologist that he or she is unable to assist the consultee. If so, the psychologist is ethically obligated to refer the consultee to another professional. This may occur when the consultee has emotional difficulties that interfere with effective functioning. The rules of consultation suggest the practitioner generally must avoid the dual roles of consultant and counselor/therapist to the teacher (Curtis & Meyers, 1985). It also may become apparent during the consultative process that another professional is better able to assist the consultee (e.g., another psychologist with different skills, or perhaps a well-respected teacher with special expertise in the problem area) (NASP-PPE, III, F, #2).

Special problems with regard to professional responsibility sometimes occur when the practitioner steps into the role of consultant-trainer and provides in-service to teachers in the school or district. Although at first it might seem that the use of informational methods such as in-service raises no special ethical concerns, problems may arise when there is no planned follow up on the ways in which the information provided is understood and used by teachers or other staff.

For example, a number of writers have noted that brief workshop methods of teaching applied behavior analysis techniques to teachers are inadequate and may result in unintended harmful consequences for pupils. As Conoley and Conoley suggest, consultant-trainers are well-advised to view in-service training as "a means, not an end" (1982, p. 134). There are a number of options for follow-up consultation that help to ensure new ideas and techniques introduced during in-service training are used appropriately in the classroom (for suggestions, see Hansen et al., 1990).

Competence

Ethically, school psychology practitioners are obligated to provide services only within areas of competency (NASP-PPE, II, A, #1; also *EP* Principle A). As Hansen et al. note (1990), consultants need to have specialized training in consultation in order to be able to provide effective services.

Brown et al. (1987) provide a detailed outline of the knowledge base, skills, and judgmental competencies that need to be developed by consultants, and they describe the necessary components of consultation training. They suggest consultants need to be knowledgeable of models of consultation, organizational theory, and change strategies, and they need skills in communication, relationship building, contracting, mediating, and group leadership. Consultants also need judgmental competencies with regard to problem identification and solution. In addition, the personal characteristics of the consultant are important in successful school-based consultation (see Conoley & Conoley, 1982).

In order to provide consultative services effectively, practitioners also must be knowledgeable of the organization, philosophy, goals, and methodology of their school (NASP-PPE, III, D, #1), and they must be familiar with the areas of competence of other professionals in their setting.

Responsibility to Community and Society

School psychologists are ethically obligated to promote the welfare of all children in the schools. Psychologists who develop expertise in consultation may engage in consultation to the school-community. At this level, the practitioner adopts more of a systems orientation to change and attempts to modify the manner in which the school functions and its effects on student well-being (Curtis & Stollar, 1996; Meyers, Parsons, & Martin, 1979). Adequate training, knowledge of organizational theory, and knowledge of the unique characteristics of a particular school setting are of critical importance at this level of consultation.

Psychologists also have responsibilities to the communities in which they live. Conoley and Conoley (1982) provide a discussion of advocacy consultation that may be of interest to readers.

Case 8–1

Following the retirement of a member of the psychological services team, Hannah Cook was asked whether she would like to maintain her current school assignment or be assigned to provide services in Kennedy Elementary School, a school nearer her home. Before accepting the new assignment, Hannah discussed her preference for consultative services with the building principal there and carefully outlined the parameters of the consultative services she would like to provide. She negotiated her job description with the principal to include consultative services, and they agreed on strategies to document accountability for the consultative services to be provided.

Entry: *Hannah accepted the position at Kennedy and made a presentation to the staff about teacher consultative services. She was careful to describe the consultative process, the responsibilities of the consultant and consultee, and the parameters of confidentiality. She also described her training and prior experience providing consultative services to teachers.*

Several weeks after her presentation, she received a referral for psychological services from Mr. Bryant, one of the two fifth grade teachers at Kennedy. Near the place on the form for the Student's Name, Mr. Bryant typed in the names of all of his 28 students. He wrote his reason for referral to be "to determine if class qualifies as emotionally impaired." The form is signed "HELP! Mr. Bryant."

Mr. Bryant had a reputation in the district as a good teacher and a firm disciplinarian, and consequently Hannah was surprised by his request for assistance. She met with Mr. Bryant, offered her services as a consultant, and discussed the parameters of the consultative relationship with him.

Problem Identification/Clarification: *Mr. Bryant reported that he has had an unusually difficult class this year; he was frustrated by spending so much time on discipline rather than instruction, and he was beginning to feel "burnt out." Hannah listened carefully, asked questions to clarify the problems further, and made arrangements to observe Mr. Bryant in class.*

Case 8–1 *(Continued)*

Hannah visited Mr. Bryant's class and found it composed of 17 (mostly high energy) boys and 11 girls. Four of the boys were particularly active, noisy, disruptive, and rude while Hannah was observing. One boy, Frank, appeared to be the leader of this group, and he encouraged the others to talk out of turn, throw paper wads, make faces and noises, and fall out of their seats. Mr. Bryant attempted to refocus their attention on the science lesson, first by involving the boys in class discussion, but later by threats of lost privileges (no recess), some teasing put-down remarks, and finally loud and angry commands for the boys to "shape up."

Hannah met with Mr. Bryant for several more sessions to discuss the classroom dynamics further and clarify the focus of the consultative efforts. They agreed that the four boys appeared to be causing most of the class management difficulties, that Frank instigated most disruptions, and rewarded the other three for their participation by attention and laughter.

Hannah and Mr. Bryant decided to focus intervention efforts initially on changing Frank's behaviors. Mr. Bryant's first attempt at goal setting focused on "dead man" behaviors (Conoley & Conoley, 1982); his goals were for Frank to "sit still and be quiet." Hannah confronted him on these goals and helped to reframe them in terms of behaviors that will benefit Frank in school (raising his hand to participate, increased completion of classroom assignments, etc.).

Hannah also confronted Mr. Bryant on his use of shouting and pointed out how shouting may work against a classroom atmosphere conducive to learning by fostering tension and anxiety among the students. Hannah was unsure about his teasing put-downs with the boys. Such put-downs contradicted her ideas about good teaching, but she didn't want to impose her values on Mr. Bryant, particularly since the students appeared to respond positively to these interactions. Perhaps this was a way he built a sense of camaraderie with the boys in his class. She decided to take a wait-and-see approach to this issue.

Intervention/Problem Solutions: *Hannah and Mr. Bryant discussed developing a behavioral contract with Frank. Mr. Bryant contacted Frank's parents and gained their cooperation and consent*

(Continued)

Case 8–1 *(Continued)*

for intervention with Frank, and he met with Frank privately to discuss the problems and goals and strategies for change. Mr. Bryant and Frank then worked together in writing the contract.

Hannah shared her concerns with Mr. Bryant about his classroom composition, that is, 17 energetic boys in one room. She pointed out that he had earned a reputation as a strong disciplinarian and was most likely perceived as a good male role model for boys. Hannah's hunch was that a disproportionate number of boys were assigned to his class because many parents with sons specifically requested him as a teacher.

Hannah wanted to discuss this problem with the building principal, but she also wanted to be sure her actions did not violate the confidentiality of the consultant–consultee relationship. She asked Mr. Bryant to meet with her and the principal to explore this issue and ways to assure that the assignment of pupils to certain teachers is more carefully monitored in future years. Mr. Bryant agreed and they met with the principal. Hannah offered to consult with the principal on developing better procedures to ensure a balanced classroom composition for each teacher.

Evaluation: *Hannah and Mr. Bryant's initial intervention strategies with Frank were not successful; they recycled through the problem clarification and solution stages several times. For example, the initial rewards selected as part of the behavioral contract were not powerful enough to change Frank's behavior in light of the reinforcement for disruptive behavior provided by his friends. Mr. Bryant, after discussions with Frank, discovered that access to* Nintendo Secrets *magazines during free-time was an effective reinforcer for Frank. Mr. Bryant then created an opportunity for Frank to work with his friends in writing a monthly feature for the school newspaper on* Nintendo Secrets *and reviews of new games. This proved to be an excellent motivator for all four boys and helped Frank use his leadership skills in positive ways. Over the course of the intervention, the classroom disruptions by the four boys were reduced to a level Mr. Bryant found workable, and he no longer attempted to control their misbehavior by shouting reprimands at them.*

Summary

Our example here is an idealized one. Mr. Bryant was interested in Hannah's assistance and had good teaching and class management skills to build on. Many real-life consultation situations involve working with teachers or others who lack basic skills to build on and/or are resistant to change. Practitioners who offer consultative services must be prepared to cope with such difficult challenges.

CONCLUDING COMMENTS

The provision of consultative services in the schools can raise complicated ethical issues. Prevention is the most desirable response to the potential ethical dilemmas of consultation, and a careful consideration of the agreements or contract is the key to prevention.

STUDY AND DISCUSSION

Questions for Chapter 8

1. A means of ensuring a mutual understanding of the parameters of a consultative relationship is through contracting. What issues should be addressed in this contract?
2. Is there ever a duty to breach the confidentiality of the consultant–consultee relationship? If so, under what circumstances?

ACTIVITIES

Role-play the following situation:

Mrs. Finch, a first-grade teacher, is known to have a punitive classroom management style. One parent recently complained to the principal after Mrs. Finch spanked her son. Mrs. Finch has asked you (probably as a result of the principal's urging) to help her develop a more positive classroom discipline style. Role-play your initial meeting with Mrs. Finch, during which you offer your consultative services, and define the parameters of the consultant-consultee relationship.

Chapter 9

RESEARCH IN THE SCHOOLS: ETHICAL AND LEGAL ISSUES

As a result of their national survey, Reschly and Wilson (1995) found that school psychology practitioners typically devote less than 1 hour per week to research and evaluation activities, but an increase in time for research was desired. Time constraints, inadequate support for the research role, and a lack of training in methodology appropriate to applied settings have been identified as barriers to research in the schools (Martens & Keller, 1987).

The years ahead will most likely witness an increase in research activity by school psychologists, however. One reason for this anticipated change is the renewed interest in the scientist-practitioner model of professional practice in school psychology, a model that views research as a necessary part of the service delivery process (Bardon, 1987). Improved training in research methods appropriate for the school setting also may encourage more research activity by practitioners, along with the increased availability of microcomputer technology that facilitates research. Societal, legal, and professional pressures for accountability in the schools also promise to further legitimize the research role for school psychologists (Martens & Keller, 1987).

CODES OF ETHICS AND LEGAL DOCUMENTS

Ethical Principles in the Conduct of Research with Human Participants (RHP) (APA, 1982) is one source of guidance in the conduct of research. A revision of RHP is currently underway (Blanck, Bellack, Rosnow, Rotheram-Borus, & Schooler, 1992). In recognition of some of the special problems posed by research with children, the Society for Research in Child Development (SRCD) also developed ethical standards specifically for research with children (SRCD, 1990, 1991).

The National Research Act of 1974 (Pub. L. No. 93-348) outlines federal policies for research with human participants. It is interesting to note that the basic elements of APA's *Ethical Principles in the Conduct of Research with Human Participants* and federal policies for research with human participants can be traced back to the Nuremberg Code, a judicial summary made at the war trials of Nazi physicians who conducted medical experiments on war prisoners and were indicted for crimes against humanity (Keith-Spiegel, 1983).

The National Research Act mandated the formation of the National Commission for the Protection of Human Subjects of Biomedical and Behavioral Science Research. One of the charges to the commission was to identify the basic ethical principles that should underlie the conduct of research involving human subjects; its second charge was to develop guidelines to assure that research involving human participants is conducted in accordance with those principles. In 1979, the commission published *The Belmont Report: Ethical Principles and Guidelines for the Protection of Human Subjects of Biomedical and Behavioral Research.* In *The Belmont Report,* three broad ethical principles relevant to research with human subjects were identified:

1. *Respect for persons*—the obligation to respect the autonomy of individuals and protect individuals with diminished autonomy;
2. *Beneficence*—the obligation to do no harm, to maximize possible benefits and minimize possible harm; and
3. *Justice*—the obligation to ensure that all persons share equally in the burdens and benefits of research.

The Belmont Report also included specific guidelines for the protection of human subjects. These guidelines were the basis for the regulations regarding the protection of human research participants issued by the Department of Health and Human Services (HHS) in 1981. Additional protections for children were added to the regulations in 1983 (45 C.F.R. Subtitle A, Part 46). Only institutions receiving federal research support are legally required to comply with the rules and regulations drafted under the National Research Act. However, as DeMers and Bersoff note, researchers should be familiar with the Act's regulations because they "reflect current legal opinion" of appropriate conduct in research activity (1985, p. 333).

COMPETENCE, RESPONSIBILITY, AND WELFARE OF PARTICIPANTS

Professional Competence and Responsibility

The broad ethical principles of professional competence and responsibility (responsible caring) and respect for the dignity and welfare of persons provide the foundation for ethical decision making in the conduct of research in the schools. In all types of information-gathering activities, whether it is decision-oriented action research or more basic research, school psychologists are ethically obligated to conduct research "as well as they know how" (RHP, p. 15; also NASP-PPE, IV, D, #1; *EP* 6.06). As Keith-Spiegel and Koocher (1985) have noted, poorly designed research is likely to result in invalid and perhaps misleading findings. Misleading findings may result in the introduction or continuation of ineffective practices and a potential disservice to children, teachers, parents, and others. Poorly designed studies also are unfair to research participants who volunteer in hopes of contributing to the knowledge base of psychology and education.

School psychologists with limited expertise in research design should consult with experienced researchers to assure a planned study is methodologically sound. Stewart (1984) suggests that practitioners may want to explore developing cooperative research relationships with psychologists in university settings. Psychologists in the schools are able to identify research questions relevant to practice and collect needed data; psychologists in academic settings can offer expertise in design and data analysis.

As mentioned in Chapter 1, responsibility for ethical conduct rests with the individual professional. In conducting research, the responsibility for the ethical treatment of study participants remains with the individual research investigator. He or she is responsible for the actions of all members of the research team (collaborators and assistants), although each team member also bears responsibility for his or her own actions (*EP* 6.07; SRCD Introduction).

Welfare of the Participant

In planning research and data collection, priority must always be given to the welfare of the participant (*EP* 1.14; RHP, p. 18; SRCD, Introduction). The researcher is ethically obligated to identify any potential risks for the research participants and collect data in ways that will avoid or minimize such risks (RHP, p. 17; also *EP* 6.11; SRCD Principle 1). The five major types of risk are physical, psychological, social, legal, and economic. Potential risks of research participation may include pain or physical injury, exposure to stressful procedures and possible emotional discomfort or harm, invasion of privacy, loss of community standing, exposure to criminal prosecution, loss of employment or potential monetary gain, denial of potentially beneficial treatment, and violations of confidentiality.

Ethical and legal standards for research are consistent in recommending that the researcher ask the advice of others regarding the acceptability of proposed research procedures (NASP-PPE, IV, D, #2; *EP* 6.06). The greater the potential risks, the greater the obligation to seek advice and observe stringent safeguards. The SRCD recommends peer review of any and all research involving children (SCRD Introduction). Consistent with guidelines originally outlined in The National Research Act, colleges and universities typically have an institutional review board (IRB) that evaluates the ethical acceptability of research proposed by faculty and students. Policies and procedures regarding review and approval of research activities in the public schools vary. School psychologists are well advised to consult with administrators, teachers, parents, and others about the acceptability of proposed studies.

This chapter explores informed consent for research and the risks of invasion of privacy, exposure to stress or harm and denial of beneficial treatment, post data-collection responsibilities, concealment and deception, confidentiality of data, and scientific misconduct.

INFORMED CONSENT

Case 9–1

School administrators, teachers, and members of the school board were alarmed by reports of high levels of drug abuse by students in the school district. They decided to hire a private consultant in hopes of developing an effective drug abuse prevention program for junior high students. The initial phase of the program involved research to identify eighth graders at risk for drug abuse. As part of the research phase, questionnaires were administered to eighth graders, their teachers and classmates. Students were asked to rate themselves on a number of personality variables, such as level of self-confidence, and they were asked about their relationship to their parents (e.g., Did one or both of your parents hug and kiss you goodnight when you were small? Do they make you feel unloved?). Teachers were asked to identify students with antisocial behavior patterns, and students were asked to identify classmates with problem behavior patterns. The private consultant planned to collect and analyze the data and prepare a list of "potential drug abusers," for the school superintendent, that could be used to identify pupils in need of drug prevention therapy. The therapy program would use peer-pressure techniques to combat potential drug abuse, and teachers would serve as the therapists. A

(Continued)

Case 9–1 *(Continued)*

letter was sent to parents informing them of the diagnostic testing and prevention program and assuring confidentiality of the results. Parent silence in response to the letter was construed as consent for their child to participate (adapted from Merriken v. Cressman, *1973; Bersoff, 1983).*

This incident is a summary of the circumstances that prompted Sylvia Merriken, the mother of an eighth grader named Michael, to file a complaint against the school system that was subsequently decided in a federal district court in Pennsylvania in 1973. Although this incident occurred over 25 years ago, it is not hard to imagine the occurrence of similar events today as school districts continue to struggle with the problem of substance abuse.

Sylvia Merriken's complaint alleged that the school's drug abuse prevention program, particularly the research phase, violated her constitutional rights and those of her son, including the right to privacy. A central issue in this case was the school's failure to seek informed consent for the collection of personal, private information about Michael and his family. As mentioned in Chapter 3, case law and government regulations concur that waiver of an individual's rights, such as the right to privacy, must be based on informed consent. The key elements of informed consent are that it must be knowing, competent, and voluntary. The court held that the school's program violated Sylvia Merriken's right to privacy, and an injunction was issued.

Consent Must Be Knowingly Given

Informed consent in research is a written agreement between the researcher and research participant that outlines the obligations and responsibilities of both the investigator and the volunteer. The investigator informs the participant of all aspects of the research that may be expected to influence willingness to participate and answers all questions about the nature of the research procedures (*EP* 6.10, 6.11; SRCD 2, 3).

Who Gives Consent?

The individual giving consent to volunteer for research must be legally competent to do so (Bersoff, 1983). In the HHS protections for children involved as research subjects, a distinction is made between *consent,* what a person

may do autonomously, and *permission,* what a person may do on behalf of another, as when a parent or guardian grants permission for a child to participate in research (46 C.R.F. § 46.401).

When research involves children (minors) as study participants, legal standards (HHS) and codes of ethics (*EP* 6.11; SRCD 2, 3) suggest the researcher seek informed consent or permission of the parent or legal guardian for the child to participate, and the child's assent to participate, if appropriate. Assent is defined as "a child's affirmative agreement to participate in research" (46 C.F.R. § 46.402). HHS regulations note that a child's ability to make informed decisions about participation in research depends on his or her age and maturity (46 C.F.R. § 46.408).

Ferguson (1978) has observed that individual level of cognitive development and the complexity of the research situation must be taken into account in determining a child's capacity to make choices regarding research participation. She suggests that informed parental permission is both necessary and sufficient for research with infants and toddlers. The preschool-age child, however, is able to understand explanations stated in here-and-now concrete terms, with a straightforward description of what participation means for the child. The researcher is consequently obligated to seek both parental permission and affirmative assent for the child of preschool age or older. Ferguson provides some helpful guidelines for explaining research to children of various ages (1978, pp. 118–120).

SRCD suggests that the informed consent of any person whose interaction with the child is the subject of the study also be obtained (Principle 4). For example, a study of the association between children's positive or negative feelings about their classroom teacher and academic achievement would require parental permission, the child's assent to participate, and the teacher's informed consent.

Freedom from Coercion

The third characteristic of informed consent is that it must be voluntary. HHS guidelines specify that each research participant (the parent or legal representative in the case of a minor child) be given "sufficient opportunity" to decide whether or not to choose to participate in the research (46 C.F.R. § 46.116). Codes of ethics state that the investigator must respect the individual's freedom to choose to participate in research or not, as well as to discontinue participation at any time (*EP* 6.11; SRCD 2, 3, 4). Consistent with the values of respect for self-determination and autonomy, researchers must attract consent and assent without "coercion, duress, pressure, or undue enticement or influence" (Keith-Spiegel & Koocher, 1985, p. 194; also *EP* 6.14). When working with children, psychologists "seek the willing and adequately informed participation of any person of diminished capacity . . . and proceed without this assent only if the service or research activity is considered to be of direct benefit to that person" (CPA, 1991, p. 12).

In the school setting, it is important to allow potential volunteers (e.g., pupils, teachers) the opportunity to decline to participate without embarrassment (*EP* 6.11; SRCD 2, 3, 4). In the *Merriken v. Cressman* decision, Judge Davis noted that the school did not afford the students an opportunity to decline to participate without being marked for "scapegoating" and unpleasant treatment by peers (1973, p. 915).

It also is important to remember that researchers may not promise benefits from research participation unless they are able to ensure the promised outcomes (SRCD 8). For example, a researcher may not guarantee that participation in an experimental counseling group for overweight teens will result in weight loss for each participant, although weight loss might be identified as a possible benefit from participation.

Minimal Risk Research

Informed consent is not always needed for research in the schools. Whether it is needed depends on a number of factors including the purpose of the study, the research design and methodology, the protections afforded research participants, and the nature of the relationship between the investigator and the school system. Legal standards suggest that minimal risk research in public school settings probably does not require informed consent as long as information is collected and reported in a way that individuals cannot be identified. Minimal risk research generally means that the study poses little likelihood of invasion of privacy, exposure to stress, or psychological or physical harm as a result of participation in the study.

HHS regulations exempt the following types of research from its informed consent requirements: "research conducted in established or commonly accepted educational settings, *involving normal educational practices*" and research involving "the use of *educational tests* (cognitive, diagnostic, aptitude, achievement)" if information taken from these sources is recorded in such a manner that subjects cannot be identified [italics added] (45 C.F.R § 46.101). Similarly, APA's standards state that: "Research participation that is incidental to systematic study of the effects of normal variations in a regular institutional program appears not to raise serious ethical concerns even when the principle of informed consent is compromised" (RHP, p. 45).

Note that research involving psychological tests is not exempt from informed consent requirements under HHS regulations (DeMers & Bersoff, 1985). The Protection of Pupil Rights (PPRA) or Hatch Amendment and

HHS regulations thus appear to be consistent in requiring informed parental consent before a pupil can be instructed to submit to psychiatric or psychological examination, testing, or treatment not directly related to the purposes of academic instruction.

As noted in Chapter 3, PPRA (Pub. L. No. 95-561) expressly prohibits schools from gathering certain types of personal information from students (e.g., political affiliation, potentially embarrassing psychological problems, sexual or criminal behavior, family income) without informed parental consent.[1]

Research involving the study of existing school records also would be viewed as minimal risk research under HHS regulations as long as information is recorded in such a manner that subjects cannot be identified directly or through identifiers linked to the subjects (45 C.R.F. § 46.101). Similarly, under the Family Educational Rights and Privacy Act of 1974 (FERPA), organizations conducting studies *on behalf of the school* do not need parental consent for access to educational records for research purposes. However under FERPA, informed parental consent is needed for the release of personally identifiable information from educational records if the research is not being conducted on behalf of the school.

As a general rule, when we put children at risk or treat them differently than one would normally expect in the schools, then the possibility of a "legally cognizable injury" is created, and informed consent must be obtained (DeMers & Bersoff, 1985, p. 332).

The Components of the Informed Consent Agreement

HHS has outlined a number of requirements for informed consent for research (46 C.F.R. § 46.116). The consent agreement is a written agreement but it may be presented orally to the research volunteer. Oral presentation should be witnessed by a third party. The informed consent information must be presented in a language understandable to the participant or guardian granting permission for the child to participate, and the researcher may not include language that implies a release from ethical and legal responsibility to the subjects of the study.

The basic components of the informed consent agreement include the following: (a) a description of the nature and purpose of the research, and the procedures and expected duration of participation; (b) a description of "any

[1] The privacy protections of PPRA apply only to programs funded by the U.S. Department of Education. However, PPRP is seen as reflecting current legal opinion of appropriate school conduct in safeguarding pupil and family privacy.

reasonably foreseeable risks or discomforts" for the participant; (c) a description of any potential benefits to the participant that can reasonably be expected; (d) a description of available alternative treatments that might be advantageous; (e) a description of the extent to which confidentiality of information will be maintained; (f) instructions concerning who may be contacted to answer questions about the research; (g) a statement that participation is voluntary and that the participant may discontinue the study at any time without penalty; and (h) for studies that involve more than minimal risk, a description of any compensation and medical treatment available if injury occurs as a result of participation. SRCD guidelines also suggest that the professional and institutional affiliation of the researcher be identified (Principle 3). The consent form should be signed by the parent or guardian of a minor child, or the research participant if age 18 or older. Grunder (1978) has recommended using reading-level determination formulas to evaluate the readability of the consent form to assure it is understandable.

EXPOSURE TO STRESS OR HARM AND DENIAL OF BENEFICIAL TREATMENT

Consistent with the principle of responsible caring, researchers take steps to protect study participants from physical and emotional discomfort, harm, and danger (RHP, p. 51; SRCD 1). We can think of no ethically permissible studies by school psychologists that involve exposing a study participant to harm and danger. Research on the use of medications in treatment of behavior or learning problems (e.g., the use of Ritalin in the treatment of hyperactivity) exposes the child to potentially dangerous medical side effects (see Chapter 7). Although data regarding the effects of medications might be gathered in the school setting, any research involving the administration of drugs must be conducted under the supervision of a physician knowledgeable of the necessary medical and legal safeguards (see RHP, 57–58).

Prior to beginning a study, the researcher is obligated to determine whether proposed research procedures are stressful and to explore ways to avoid or minimize stress by modifying the research methodology (SRCD 1). Psychological discomfort is likely to result from failure experiences; temptations to lie, cheat, or steal; or if the investigator asks the research participant to reveal personal information that is embarrassing, or perform disturbing tasks such as rating parents (RHP, pp. 58–59). The survey questions for students in the *Merriken* case, for example, were likely to be quite stressful for some eighth graders (see also Case 1–1).

In evaluating the acceptability of a study that places the participants at risk for discomfort, the researcher is obligated to seek the advice of others and carefully consider whether the potential benefits of the study outweigh the risks, often called a risk-benefit analysis (SRCD Introduction). Assessing the potential risks of research participation for children can be a difficult and complex task (Thompson, 1990). The researcher is obligated to consider developmental factors, prior experiences, and individual characteristics of the study participants in evaluating children's vulnerability to research risk.

The researcher must obtain the fully informed consent of participants for any study that exposes the subjects to potential discomfort or harm (RHP, p. 53). HHS guidelines suggest informed consent be sought for any research that exposes volunteers to risks greater than those ordinarily encountered in daily life (46 C.F.R. § 46.102).

The researcher also must be alert to the fact that the data collection procedures may result in unanticipated discomfort or harm. It is important to monitor the research procedures, particularly when research involves children (SRCD, Introduction). Children are likely to be highly sensitive to failure, and "seemingly innocuous" questions may be stressful for some children (RHP, p. 59). If a research participant appears to show a stressful reaction to the procedures, the researcher is obligated "to correct these consequences" and should consider altering the data-collection procedures (SRCD 10).

In planning research investigations on the effectiveness of new treatments or interventions, school psychologists are obligated to select an alternative treatment known to be beneficial (a contrast group), rather than using a no-treatment control group, if at all feasible. If the new or experimental intervention is found to be effective, contrast or control group participants should be given access to the new treatment (RHP, p. 68).

POST–DATA COLLECTION RESPONSIBILITIES

The investigator is obligated to end the data collection session with "a positive and appropriate debriefing" (RHP, p. 67). After the data are collected, the investigator provides the participant with information about the nature of the study and attempts to remove any misconceptions that participants may have (*EP* 6.18). The investigator also is obligated to remove or correct any undesirable consequences that result from research participation (RHP, p. 66; SRCD 10, 12). As Holmes (1976) has observed, stress is likely to occur when participants acquire an awareness of their own inadequacies and weaknesses as a result of participation in research. Researchers are obligated to introduce procedures to desensitize participants when this occurs; that is, the investigator must eliminate any distress that results from self-knowledge acquired as a result of research (Holmes, 1976).

As APA notes, there are special postexperimental responsibilities in research with children. The investigator must "ensure that the child leaves the research situation with no undesirable aftereffects of participation" (RHP, p. 66). This may mean "that certain misconceptions should not be removed or even that some new misconceptions should be induced. If children erroneously believe that they have done well on a research task, there may be more harm than good in trying to correct this misconception than in permitting it to remain" (RHP, p. 66). When children feel that they have done poorly, corrective efforts are needed. Such efforts might include introducing a special experimental procedure "to guarantee the child a final success experience" (RHP, p. 66).

Investigators also are obligated to consider any long-range after-effects from participation in research. Research that introduces the possibility of irreversible after-effects should not be conducted (RHP, p. 59).

In *Merriken,* Judge Davis admonished the school for its failure to acknowledge the risks of harm introduced by its drug prevention program. He noted that, on the basis of responses to an unvalidated survey, a student could be erroneously labeled as a "potential drug abuser," possibly resulting in stigma, peer rejection, or a self-fulfilling prophesy, and be subjected to group therapy sessions conducted by untrained and inexperienced therapists (1973, p. 920).

CONCEALMENT AND DECEPTION

Case 9–2

A school psychologist, Carrie Johnson, decided to conduct a study of differences in teacher behaviors toward regular education and mainstreamed special education pupils to fulfill the research requirements for her Psy.D. degree. She planned to observe time-samples of reading instruction in five second-grade classrooms in the district and code the number of positive and negative comments the teachers

Case 9–2 *(Continued)*

made to regular and special education pupils. She was concerned that knowledge of the purpose of the study might alter teacher behavior, so she misinformed the teachers that the purpose of the research was to study the peer interaction patterns of special education students. The findings from her study showed that all teachers observed gave special education students more negative and fewer positive comments during reading instruction when compared with their regular education classmates. Carrie placed a xeroxed form letter in the faculty mailbox of each teacher-participant and building principal, thanking them for their help and briefly summarizing her findings. Two of the teacher-participants were angry about the deception. They demanded their observation data be destroyed, and they complained to the school administration. A third teacher was dismayed and embarrassed by her biased treatment of students with disabilities and considered abandoning her career in teaching.

Concealment

The nature and purpose of a study may require a compromise of the principle of fully informed consent (RHP, p. 36; SRCD 6). The term concealment is used to refer to studies in which the investigator gathers information about individuals without their knowledge or consent; that is, the study subject may not know he or she has participated in a research study (RHP, p. 36). These studies often involve covert (hidden) or unobtrusive observation. The National Research Act regulations and APA's code of ethics (RHP, p. 39) suggest that covert or unobtrusive observational studies can be considered minimal risk research and exempt from informed consent requirements as long as data are gathered so that subjects cannot be identified directly or indirectly, the behaviors observed are "public," the research does not deal with sensitive or illegal behaviors (sexual behaviors, drug abuse), the experience of the person is not affected by the research (i.e., the research procedures are nonreactive), and the person is not put at risk in the event of a breach of confidentiality (criminal or civil liability, financial damage or loss of employment) (45 C.F.R. § 46.101; RHP, pp. 36–39). The research described in Case 9–2 appears to present minimal risk for the pupils observed in the study.

Deception

The term deception is typically used to refer to studies in which the participants are misinformed about the purpose of the study or the meaning of the participant's behavior (RHP, p. 40). Carrie Johnson's study illustrates the use of deception with the teacher-participants; she deliberately misinformed them of the purpose of the study so as to avoid altering their typical teaching behaviors.

Studies that involve deception are controversial. The investigator has a responsibility to seek peer review and carefully evaluate whether the use of deception is justified by the value of the study and to consider alternative procedures (*EP* 6.15; RHP, p. 41; SRCD 6). Fisher and Fryberg (1994) suggest researchers ask nonparticipants from the same subject pool about the acceptability of the deception before proceeding with the study. Another alternative is forewarning subjects; that is, gaining the informed consent of participants to use deception as part of the research procedure. Some researchers maintain that the intentional use of deception with children is never justified as "children may be left with the distinct impression that lying is an *appropriate* way for adults to achieve their goals" (Keith-Spiegel, 1983, p. 201).

If, after consultation with others, it is determined that the use of deception is necessary and justified by the value of the study, the researcher incurs additional obligations to the study participants. After the completion of the data collection, the researcher must fully inform each participant of the nature of the deception, detect and correct any stressful after-effects, and provide an opportunity for the participant to withdraw from the study after the deception is revealed (RHP, p. 41). In studies involving deception, the postexperimental debriefing involves explaining to participants that they were deceived as part of the research procedures (*EP* 6.15, SCRD 6) and dealing with any resultant feelings.

In the incident described, Carrie did not fulfill her postexperimental obligations to the teacher-participants. An individual or small group meeting was needed to explain the nature of the deception, introduce appropriate desensitization procedures, and assure the confidentiality of the data gathered. It would have been beneficial for the teacher-participants to know that their differential treatment of low-achieving students is "normal" teacher behavior and most likely an unconscious response to student behavior; that is, student behavior may condition teacher behavior (Brophy & Good, 1974). Offering to work with teachers to help modify these behaviors would have been appropriate and in the best interests of everyone involved.

CONFIDENTIALITY OF DATA

Codes of ethics, case law, and legal regulations are consistent in requiring a clear prior agreement between the investigator and research participant about who will have access to information gathered during research and what types of information, if any, will be shared with others. "Information obtained about the research participant during the course of an investigation is confidential unless otherwise agreed on in advance. When the possibility exists that others may obtain access to such information, this possibility, together with the plans for protecting confidentiality, is explained to the participants as part of the procedure for obtaining informed consent" (RHP, p. 70; also SRCD 11).

In his *Merriken* decision, Judge Davis noted that the school made a blanket promise to parents that survey results would be confidential. However, documents describing the program indicated that, to the contrary, it was anticipated that a "massive data bank" would be developed, and information would be shared with guidance counselors, athletic coaches, PTA officers, and school board members, among others (p. 916). The judge also noted that the list of "potential drug abusers" could be subpoenaed by law enforcement authorities. Investigators are obligated to forewarn research participants of any such risks of violation of confidentiality.[2]

APA recommends removing identifying information from research protocols immediately (RHP, p. 82). If a coding key that links the individual to his or her data is necessary because of the nature of the research, it should be kept in a secure location. The use of any permanent recordings during data collection (e.g., videotapes) increases the risk of loss of anonymity. The researcher should seek informed consent to create and maintain such records (RHP, p. 37; also *EP* 5.07; 6.13).

Codes of ethics and standards do not prohibit the sharing of research information if informed consent to do so is obtained. Information obtained in the course of research (e.g., test scores) may be helpful in educational planning for an individual child. However, it is of critical importance that researchers in the schools have a clear prior understanding with all parties involved (pupils, parents, teachers, administrators, support staff) regarding what research information will be shared and with whom and what information will not be disclosed (RHP, pp. 70–71). School administrators may believe they have a legitimate right to information gathered about

---

[2] Investigators planning research on sensitive topics such as drug abuse may apply to HHS for a confidentiality certificate to protect subject identity from disclosure in legal proceedings. (See Blanck et al., 1992; Melton & Gray, 1988.)

individual teachers, and parents are likely to believe they have a right to information about their child's performance in a research situation unless they are advised ahead of time that the research information gathered will be confidential.

Student researchers are advised against offering to share information from psychological tests with parents or teachers. The interpretation of psychological tests by students outside the supervised internship setting raises ethical-legal questions regarding the independent practice of psychology without certification or licensure (see also SRCD 13).

In unusual circumstances, a researcher may choose to disclose confidential information deliberately for the protection of the research participant or the protection of others. "The protection afforded research participants by the maintenance of confidentiality may be compromised when the investigator discovers information that serious harm threatens the research participant or others" (RHP, 1982, p. 69). The researcher may uncover information about the participant that has important implications for his or her well-being, such as emotional or physical problems. Such situations are most likely rare in school settings. If deliberate disclosure is warranted, however, the research volunteer (parent or guardian of a minor child) should be counseled about the problem identified by someone qualified to interpret and discuss the information gathered and handle any resultant distress. If disclosure of information to a third party is anticipated, this also should be discussed with the research participant (or parent or guardian) (RHP, 1982, p. 72; also SRCD 9).

School psychologists must be sensitive to potential loss of confidentiality as a result of presentation or publication of research findings. As APA notes, there are rarely problems with loss of confidentiality when data on groups are published (RHP, p. 73). However, school psychology practitioners may be interested in presenting or publishing case studies. Often the data from case studies were obtained as part of the treatment plan and follow-up, and informed consent to use the data for research was not obtained. If a psychologist plans to present or publish case information, this should be discussed with the individuals involved (pupils, parents, teachers) and informed consent should be obtained. The researcher also should make a sincere effort to disguise the identity of the research participants (*EP* 5.08; SCRD 11).

It is usually appropriate to offer research participants a brief summary of the findings from the study based on the data from all study participants. This summary should preserve the anonymity of the participants and the confidentiality of the data gathered from individual participants.

SCIENTIFIC MISCONDUCT

Scientific misconduct here refers to reporting research findings in a biased or misleading way, fabricating or falsifying data, plagiarism, or taking credit for work that is not your own. Consistent with APA and NASP codes of ethics, school psychologists strive to collect and report research information so as to make an honest contribution to knowledge and minimize the likelihood of misinterpretation and misunderstanding. In publishing reports of their research, they acknowledge the limitations of their study, the existence of disconfirming data, and identify alternate hypotheses and explanations of their findings (*EP* Preamble; 6.21; NASP-PPE, IV, D, #3).

The publication of scientific misinformation based on false or fabricated data is a serious form of misconduct that can potentially result in harm to others. In November 1988, Dr. Stephen Breuning, a psychopharmacologist, pleaded guilty to charges of fabricating research data. The charges followed an investigation of his research that reported improved functioning for mentally retarded children treated with Ritalin or Dexedrine, research that "helped shape drug treatment policy for mentally retarded" individuals in several states (Hostetler, 1988). This was the nation's first federal conviction for falsifying scientific data. Breuning was ordered to pay over $11,000.00 in restitution and was sentenced to 60 days in jail and 5 years probation (Coughlin, 1988). Breuning's case triggered much discussion of the need to protect the public from misinformation. Psychologists and others involved in investigating the case hoped that it would serve as a warning to others about the seriousness of falsifying data in scientific research (Hostetler, 1988, p. 5).

Another type of scientific misconduct is plagiarism. When publishing, school psychologists acknowledge the sources of their ideas (NASP-PPE, IV, C, #4; also *EP* 6.22). Both published and unpublished material that influenced the research or writing must be acknowledged.

Finally, psychologists take credit "only for work they have actually performed or to which they have contributed" (*EP* 6.23). "Principal authorship and other publication credits accurately reflect the relative scientific or professional contributions of the individuals involved . . . Minor contributions to the research or to the writing for publications are appropriately acknowledged, such as in footnotes or in an introductory statement" (*EP* 6.23). (See Keith-Spiegel & Koocher for a discussion of the dilemmas associated with publication credit assignments, 1985, pp. 352–356; and Fine & Kurdek, 1993 for a discussion of determining authorship credit and authorship order on faculty-student collaborative publications.)

CONCLUDING COMMENTS

As in other areas of service delivery, school psychologists can most likely avoid ethical-legal dilemmas in research by maintaining an up-to-date knowledge of relevant guidelines, careful planning of proposed research activities, and seeking consultation and advice from others when questions arise. School psychologists conducting research need to be knowledgeable of the organization and methodology of the school and to work within the organizational framework, taking care to build and maintain good public relations within and outside of the school community during all phases of a research project.

STUDY AND DISCUSSION

Questions for Chapter 9

1. Identify the key codes of ethics and legal documents that provide guidelines for research.
2. What is the single most important ethical consideration in conducting research?
3. Identify five types of potential risks for research participants.
4. What are the key elements of informed consent for research?
5. What is the difference between consent and assent for research participation?
6. We do not always seek children's assent for the provision of psychological services. Why should we seek their assent to participate in psychological research?
7. Do we always need informed parent consent for research in the schools? What is minimal risk research?

Discussion

1. Jane Jones, a second-year student in the school psychology program at State University, administered IQ tests to children in area nursery schools as part of her thesis research. Two months after she completed the data collection, the director of one of the nursery schools requested IQ test information for a pupil she feels is developmentally delayed as a first step towards requesting a full evaluation of the child's developmental status and learning potential. How should Jane Jones respond? What are the ethical-legal issues involved?

(Continued)

2. A school psychologist working on her doctoral degree was interested in studying whether children with a history of frequent school absences in the primary grades were at higher risk for school learning problems than their classmates with few school absences. She accessed the school's computer records and made printouts of individual records (school absences, illnesses, IQ scores, achievement scores, class placement, special education services), which she then used in her research. What are the ethical-legal issues involved in this situation?

3. In order to complete the requirements for her specialist degree, Marina Torres decided to conduct a study of the effectiveness of a drug education program in reducing substance abuse at the middle school level. She plans to individually interview middle school students to ask about their patterns of drug use before and after their participation in the new drug education program. What are the ethical and legal issues associated with a study of this type?

ACTIVITIES

If you are required to complete a research project as part of your program of graduate studies and the project will involve human subjects, obtain a copy of the application you must complete for review and approval of research by your college Institutional Review Board (IRB). Gather sample consent and assent forms from faculty who have conducted research projects with children.

The video *Protecting Human Subjects: Three Instructional Films* provides information about the history, purpose, and functioning of IRBs. It is available from: Videotapes, Office for Protection from Research Risks, NIH, Building 31, Room 409, 9000 Rockville Heights, Bethesda, MD 20892.

Chapter 10

SPECIAL TOPICS IN SCHOOL CONSULTATION

The first portion of this chapter explores ethical and legal issues associated with current reforms in special education, namely, the implementation of inclusionary models of special education service delivery, the provision of special instruction and services without the use of labels, and the development of school-based problem-solving teams to ensure the diverse educational needs of pupils are met within the regular classroom, if at all possible.

The second portion summarizes ethical and legal issues associated with a number of different aspects of school decision making. School psychologists are often asked to consult with principals, teachers, and parents in decisions regarding school testing and assessment programs, grade retention, grouping pupils for instructional purposes, and school discipline. The chapter closes with a brief discussion of issues associated with public schooling for three additional groups of children with special needs: children with limited English proficiency, gifted and talented pupils, and students with serious communicable diseases.

In this chapter, we go beyond discussion of professional obligations to the individual student/client to explore some ways in which practitioners might promote school policies to enhance the welfare of all pupils in the school. The National Association of School Psychologists (NASP) has adopted position statements on a number of topics, including delivery of special education services without labels; grade retention; corporal punishment; AIDS; and racism, prejudice, and discrimination; among others (NASP statements are reprinted in Thomas & Grimes, 1995). These position statements are resolutions by the Association to advocate for certain practices seen as promoting the mental health and education needs of children and youth. Interested readers are encouraged to consult them.

SPECIAL EDUCATION REFORM

Two educational reforms that have gained momentum in recent years are a greater emphasis on inclusion of pupils with disabilities in the regular classroom and the provision of special education instruction and services without the use of labels (Bradley-Johnson, Johnson, & Jacob-Timm, 1995). There are a number of reasons for these current reforms. Beginning in the 1980s, influential federal policy statements and research documents appeared, questioning the effectiveness of pull-out special education programs and recommending changes in special education service delivery with greater emphasis on interventions in the regular classroom (Reschly, 1988; see also Kavale, 1990). In addition, parent advocacy efforts, IDEA court cases, and Section 504 enforcement efforts signaled increased emphasis on the legal right of children with disabilities to an education in the least restrictive environment. At the same time, leaders in the fields of education and psychology expressed growing dissatisfaction with the amount of professional attention devoted to testing and labeling in special education service delivery (Heller, Holtzman, & Messick, 1982). Many advocated change in the professional roles of school psychologists, with more attention to planning effective instruction (Ysseldyke & Christenson, 1988). A number of educational experts have called for the ultimate merger of special and regular education into one unitary system (National Association of State Boards of Education, 1992).

Inclusion

The rigid, dual system of special and regular education is changing. In recent years, federal policy makers have signaled an interest in limiting further expansion of special education, called for improved cooperation between special and regular education, and directed regular education to be more responsive to diverse needs of a broad range of students (e.g., see U.S. Department of Education, 1991). The 1997 amendments to IDEA allow an LEA to use funds for the cost of special education and related services provided in the regular classroom to a child with a disability, even if children without disabilities benefit from the services (Pub. L. No. 105-17, § 613, 111 Stat. 74, 1997).

As noted in Chapters 5 and 6, children with disabilities now have a well-established legal right to an education in the least restrictive appropriate setting. We share in the belief that schools have a responsibility to educate disabled and nondisabled students together so that all children will be prepared to live in an integrated society. However, the trend toward inclusion raises important questions about balancing a pupil's right to an education in the least restrictive setting (LRE) with his or her right to an individualized and appropriate education (FAPE) (Turnbull, 1990). It is clear that some schools have implemented inclusionary models of special education without considering whether inclusion will be effective in enhancing the achievement and social development of individual children (for example, see Alexander's [1992] cautions regarding placement of deaf children).

School psychologists have an ethical and legal responsibility to ensure that decisions about inclusion are made based on a consideration of the needs of the individual child, and that appropriate supports are made available to the child and his or her teachers to ensure that efforts at inclusion will benefit the child both academically and socially. Unfortunately, there is little research-based information to assist psychologists in identifying children for whom inclusion is likely to be effective (Bradley-Johnson et al., 1995). Psychologists also must accept responsibility to ensure the academic and social progress of each special-needs child is monitored when inclusionary models are implemented, so that problems can be remedied quickly.

Special Services without Labels

Federal policy makers also have indicated support for experimentation with special education programs that are noncategorical, and there has been growing interest in the development of noncategorical funding models. National Association of State Boards of Education (NASBE) (1992) has identified a number of possible models for financing special education that sever the links between funding and disability labels.

Debate about the use of special education labels has a long history in psychology and special education. Critics argue that the use of labels such as "mentally retarded" may result in stigma to the student, reduced teacher expectations, negative appraisal by the peer group, and a narrowing of future educational and occupational opportunities. Furthermore, the labeling process under IDEA often promotes assessment practices that focus on a search for deficits within the child rather than focusing on how to improve instruction (Ysseldyke & Christenson, 1988).

Others have a less negative view of the use of special education labels. Research findings on the long-range effects of diagnostic labels are not clear-cut. When children experience school failure, it is difficult to separate the effects of the diagnostic label from other factors in the child's experience (Reynolds & Kaiser, 1990). Additionally, although imperfect, diagnostic labels have been necessary in advancing research on treatment and intervention for children with various types of disabilities. Also, as

Hobbs (1975) observed some time ago, diagnostic labels have served an important social and political function by bringing parents of children with similar problems together in parent support and advocacy groups.

The most important ethical-legal issue in the development and implementation of noncategorical programs is determining how to provide services without labels while at the same time safeguarding the due process rights of students with disabilities as well as their right to a free, appropriate, individualized education. As schools experiment with noncategorical models of special education service delivery, the school psychologist will have an important role to play in ensuring that the rights of children with disabilities are safeguarded.

Problem-Solving Assistance Teams

In light of the recent emphasis on inclusion of children with disabilities in the regular classroom and the required accommodations for 504-only pupils, regular education teachers are likely to have greater need for instructional and behavioral support than in the past. One service delivery model consistent with current trends is the development of school-based teams to assist teachers in problem solving. School-based problem-solving teams have been given a number of different names, including pupil, teacher, and intervention assistance teams (R. Ross, 1995). These teams involve a systematic effort on the part of teachers, administrators, and support personnel to plan interventions for pupils with learning or behavior problems. Team goals are to assist teachers in problem solving so that students may be taught more effectively and to ensure that the diverse educational needs of pupils are met within the regular education classroom, if at all possible. Use of prereferral assistance teams has been found to reduce referrals for special education evaluation (Graden, Casey, & Bonstrom, 1985).

There are a number of ways in which school-based problem-solving teams promise to improve instruction for children with special needs. The assistance team literature encourages a problem-solving approach that involves consideration of the multiple factors that affect learning and behavior, including characteristics of the teacher, instruction, classroom, and pupil (Fuchs & Fuchs, 1988). Teams also provide an incentive for continued professional growth as members learn new strategies from each other to improve educational outcomes for children.

Assistance teams are an important component of IDEA and Section 504 child find procedures in many school districts. Assistance teams can plan and implement prereferral interventions, help to determine whether a disability is suspected, initiate a referral for evaluation when appropriate, coordinate the gathering of assessment information, serve as the "group of persons" to determine eligibility under 504, develop an accommodation plan, monitor the effectiveness of the plan, and modify it as needed.

Federal policymakers have encouraged the use of assistance teams and prereferral intervention strategies as part of a district's child find procedures. Policymakers also have indicated that it is permissible to use IDEA funds to train special and regular education staff in the use of assistance teams (Shrag, 1991). However, once a child is identified as having a suspected disability under IDEA and/or 504, parents must be notified of their rights and the school's duties under the law, and an evaluation to determine eligibility must be completed in a timely manner.

SCHOOL TESTING AND ASSESSMENT PROGRAMS

The heightened emphasis on school accountability has given impetus to the development of statewide pupil assessment programs. *Goals 2000* funds are made available to states that set goals and standards consistent with national educational goals, and funds are available to assist states in establishing assessment programs to measure student progress toward those goals. Similarly, Improving America's Schools Act (IASA) funding requires school improvement plans and measurement of student outcomes. IASA requires students with disabilities to participate in assessments (with accommodations in testing), but their results can be disaggregated from the results of nondisabled students. IDEA also requires children with disabilities to participate in state and districtwide assessment programs (with appropriate accommodations in testing), but children who cannot participate in such assessments are allowed to participate in alternative assessments.

Unfortunately, statewide testing programs can encourage school practices that are not in the best interests of children. Results of statewide programs have been used to evaluate the performance of teachers, schools, and school districts, thereby creating a "high stakes" situation for school personnel. Allington and McGill-Franzen (1992) found that, in response to high-stakes testing, schools may attempt to inflate district scores by placing more children in special education, categorizing more children as limited English proficient, and retaining more students in the early grades. Psychologists must speak out against such practices.

School psychologists can play a positive role in improving school test performance by assisting districts in evaluating the consistency among their goals, curriculum, and the test demands; promoting quality research-based instructional practices; and providing consultation to improve student test-taking skills. School psychologists also can assist districts by identifying reasonable test accommodations for students with disabilities.

In addition to statewide pupil evaluation programs, many districts have their own testing programs. Such testing programs can serve a number of purposes, including screening, student evaluation for instructional planning, and program evaluation and research. In many districts, the school psychologist is the professional with the greatest expertise in measurement. Consequently, practitioners may be asked to help administrators and teachers make decisions regarding whether a testing program is needed, clarify the purposes of a testing program, help select tests and assessment tools that are technically adequate and valid for the intended purpose, develop guidelines for appropriate test interpretation and use of results, and assist in reporting data to parents and the community.

The *Standards for Educational and Psychological Testing,* or *Standards* (American Educational Research Association, American Psychological Association, & National Council on Measurement in Education, 1985), provides guidelines for school testing programs (pp. 51–54). Practitioners also may find the *Code of Fair Testing Practices* a helpful resource in working with school staff (Joint Committee on Testing Practices, 1988). This four-page publication summarizes in nontechnical language those portions of the *Standards* most pertinent to educational tests.

Minimal competency testing, performance-based assessment, and the use of screening test results in the schools pose special ethical-legal concerns.

Minimum Competency Testing

Minimum competency testing is the practice of requiring a student to achieve a certain score on a standardized test in order to be promoted or to receive a high school diploma (Medway & Rose, 1986). Minimum competency tests are usually criterion-referenced tests that evaluate whether students have mastered important skills. There have been a number of legal challenges to the policy of requiring students to pass an examination before they are awarded a high school diploma. *Debra P. v. Turlington* (1984) is probably the most important decision in this area.

In Florida, high school seniors are required to pass a state-mandated competency test to receive a high school diploma. Students unable to pass the test are typically awarded a certificate of attendance. Debra P. was a class action suit filed on behalf of African American students in the state of Florida. The plaintiffs claimed to have a property interest in receiving a diploma, and that use of the competency exam was a denial of the equal protection clause of the 14th Amendment because the test was discriminatory against African Americans.

The court ultimately upheld the right of the state to require students to pass a competency test to receive a diploma. The court identified several issues that must be addressed in evaluating whether minimal competency tests are legally permissible. The first is whether there is adequate notice, that is, an adequate phase-in period before the test is used to determine award of a diploma. Other issues are whether the test has adequate curricular validity and whether the school can document acceptable instructional validity. Curricular validity addresses the question of whether the curriculum of the school matches what is measured by the test. Instructional validity is whether the students are, in fact, taught what is outlined in the curriculum, that is, whether the curriculum is implemented (Fischer & Sorenson, 1996; also *Debra P.*, 1984, p. 1408).

Legally, pupils with disabilities also may be required to pass a competency test to receive a high school diploma. The school must ensure that tests used with disabled students are a valid measure of school achievement and that no student is penalized due to his or her disability (Fischer & Sorenson, 1996). Medway and Rose (1986) suggest special education students who might be able to pass a high school competency test have appropriate instructional goals outlined in their individualized education programs (IEP), and teachers be able to document that adequate instruction was provided.

Performance-Based Assessment

A number of educational experts have called for a reevaluation of school testing practices, with a new emphasis on performance-based assessment (e.g., National Commission on Testing and Public Policy, 1990). Performance-based assessment has been described as "a type of testing that calls for demonstration of understanding and skill in applied, procedural, or open-ended settings" (Baker, O'Neil, & Linn, 1993, p. 1210). Proponents of performance-based assessment view it as superior to traditional testing in measuring higher order thinking skills, and suggest that the development and implementation of performance-based assessments in the schools will result in improved instruction and student learning.

Performance-based assessment comprises a number of different strategies (Baker et al., 1993). One type of performance-based assessment is authentic assessment, which focuses on measures of a student's performance on meaningful, significant, authentic tasks (Elliott, 1991). Elliott further describes authentic assessment as involving

> assessment activities like those commonly used in the world outside of the classroom: Work samples, performances, exhibitions, and self-evaluation reports. With an authentic assessment the learner must produce something new, rather than simply reproduce prior knowledge. (p. 275)

There are many unanswered questions about performance-based assessment. Empirical studies are needed to explore claims that introduction of performance-based measures results in improved instruction and student learning (Baker et al., 1993). Research also is needed to investigate the reliability and validity of performance-based measures (Gresham, 1991), and whether such measures are equitable for children with disabilities and those from diverse backgrounds. Despite the limited research base, many schools are currently developing and implementing performance-based assessment programs. School psychologists, as measurement experts, have an important role to play in ensuring that schools choose performance-based measures that are valid, fair, and useful. (See Cobb, 1995, and "Mini-series on authentic assessment," 1991, "Special section on authentic assessment," 1993.)

Screening Tests

Many public school districts implemented prekindergarten developmental screening programs in the 1970s. Developmental screening tests are designed to determine quickly and tentatively whether a child's progress is age appropriate (Lichtenstein, 1981). Children classified as potential school problems on the basis of screening test results are then referred for a more comprehensive evaluation to reject or confirm the suspected problem and plan for appropriate intervention, if indicated.

Screening test scores alone do not have adequate reliability and validity for educational decision making about individual pupils and should only be used for identifying children in need of further evaluation, or for decisions that are tentative and easily reversed. Unfortunately, our experiences suggest many schools have used screening test scores to deny or delay kindergarten entry or as the sole criterion for assigning a child to a developmental classroom (e.g., developmental kindergarten). Because of the limited technical adequacy of screening tests, decisions to assign a child to a developmental classroom are best made in cooperation with the parent, based on the consideration of a combination of factors (e.g., physical, cognitive, personal-social development).

School Entry

Case 10–1

Tommy Fields was administered a developmental screening test by Wanda Rose, the school psychologist, during the district's annual spring prekindergarten screening program. On the basis of the screening test results and the fact that Tommy had a summer birthday only a few months before the kindergarten entry cutoff date, Wanda Rose informed Tommy's mother that he was "not ready" for kindergarten and suggested she keep him at home "for another year to grow." Mrs. Fields, a single parent with a full-time job, was distressed by the screening test results and recommendation, and the prospect of paying for another year of full-time day care for Tommy.

SCHOOL ENTRY AND GRADE RETENTION DECISIONS

We are aware that many public school districts persist in the practice of advising or encouraging parents to postpone school entry an extra year. Such practices often stem from a misunderstanding of compulsory school attendance laws. Compulsory school attendance laws identify the ages (e.g., 7–16 years) during which the state (school) can compel school attendance; the school may hold the parent responsible for ensuring his or her child receives schooling during those years in accordance with state requirements (Reutter, 1994).

However, once a child reaches the age of school eligibility, the child has a property interest (created by the state or local school board) in receiving a public school education. The legal reasoning of Pennsylvania Association for Retarded Citizens v. Commonwealth of Pennsylvania (P.A.R.C.) (1972) consent decree can be seen to apply in all school districts (Kirp, 1973); that is, public school districts must offer an education program for all children who are age-eligible for school entry in their district under the equal protection clause of the 14th Amendment. No child can be turned away. If a child is not ready for regular kindergarten, the school must offer an alternative educational program at public school expense (see P.A.R.C., 1972, p. 1262).

Thus, although schools may use psychological or educational test results as one criterion for placement into the regular kindergarten program, such test scores may not be used to postpone or deny school entry to children who are age-eligible for a public school program. Because Tommy is old enough for the local school kindergarten program, the school must provide some sort of program at district expense (e.g., preschool or developmental kindergarten). (See Gredler, 1997, for additional discussion of school readiness issues.)

Grade Retention

Grade retention, or nonpromotion, is the popular practice of requiring a student to repeat a grade due to poor academic achievement. A number of studies have found no lasting beneficial effect of grade retention (see Rafoth & Carey, 1995, for a review). Some research suggests that grade retention may actually be detrimental, especially in the areas of student self-concept, personal adjustment, and social adjustment. Despite the lack of clear research support for retention, the practice is viewed favorably by most school personnel and parents. In general, the courts have preferred not to interfere with school promotion or retention decisions (Overcast & Sales, 1982). However, the court considerations in *Sandlin v. Johnson* (1981) suggest that a decision to retain a child cannot be arbitrary; that is, the method for assignment to a particular grade must be reasonably related to the purpose of providing appropriate instruction and furthering education. Furthermore, any method of determining pupil retention that has a disproportionate impact on minorities may be scrutinized more closely as a possible denial of equal educational opportunities.

School psychologists have an important role to play in promoting early identification and intervention for pupils with school difficulties, and in ensuring that retention is not used inappropriately. Alternatives to retention are discussed in Rafoth and Carey (1995).

INSTRUCTIONAL GROUPING

Grouping and Minority Students

With the landmark *Brown v. Board of Education* decision in 1954, the courts ruled that school segregation by race was a denial of the right to equal protection (equal educational opportunity) under the 14th Amendment. Following this decision, the courts began to scrutinize school practices that suggested within-school segregation, that is, where minority children were segregated and treated differently within the schools. A number of court cases were filed against the public schools in which minority group children were overrepresented in the lower educational tracks (ability groups) and special education classes (see Chapter 5).

Hobson v. Hanson (1967, 1969) was the first significant challenge to the disproportionate assignment of minority group (African American) children to lower ability tracks. The judge in this case noted that the tracking system was rigid, the lower tracks offered inferior educational opportunities, and children were grouped on the basis of racially biased group ability tests. He ruled that the tracking system was a violation of the equal protection clause of the 14th Amendment and ordered the system abolished. He did not find that ability grouping was per se unconstitutional (see also *McNeal v. Tate County School District,* 1975).

Court rulings in more recent cases also found that ability grouping is not per se unconstitutional (*Georgia State Conference of Branches of NAACP v. State of Georgia,* 1985; *Simmons v. Hooks,* 1994). In these cases, the courts held ability grouping that results in within-school segregation may be permissible if the school district can demonstrate that their grouping practices will remedy the results of past segregation by providing better educational opportunities for children.

Georgia was a class action suit decided on behalf of African American students in Georgia because of their disproportionate assignment to the lower achievement groups, resulting in intraschool racial segregation. In this case, information about grouping practices showed that students were typically assigned to achievement rather than ability groups on the basis of a combination of factors including assessment of skill level in a basal series, achievement test results, and teacher recommendations. In defending their grouping practices, the schools noted that the achievement groupings were flexible (i.e., students could easily move from one group to another) and likely to benefit students as instruction was matched to skill level. They also presented achievement data to show that pupils in the lower tracks did, in fact, benefit from the instructional grouping. The schools were consequently able to show that their grouping practices resulted in enhanced educational opportunities for African American students. The court found in favor of the schools.

Simmons v. Hook (1994) involved a school district in which students were placed in whole-class ability tracks in kindergarten through third grade, with a disproportionate number of African American students placed in the low ability classes. In grades 4 through 6, students were placed in heterogeneous classes, with within-class instructional grouping for reading, math, and language arts. The district was not able to show that whole-class ability grouping resulted in better educational opportunities for pupils in grades kindergarten through 3, and the court found this practice unconstitutionally segregative. The court did not find heterogeneous class assignment with within-class grouping for reading, math, and language arts unconstitutionally segregative.

Instructional Grouping and Children's Needs

As noted in *Simmons v. Hooks* (1994), there are a number of different types of instructional grouping practices. The grouping practice that has raised the most concern is ability-grouped class assignment, in which pupils are assigned to self-contained classes based on homogeneity of ability. Research suggests that assignment to self-contained classes based on ability level does not improve school achievement and may result in lowered self-esteem and educational aspirations for students placed in the lower tracks (Ross & Harrison, 1997). School psychologists are encouraged to be knowledgeable of the literature on classroom grouping and promote alternatives that are in the best interests of all children (Dawson, 1995; Ross & Harrison, 1997).

SCHOOL DISCIPLINE

As Overcast and Sales note, "Under the general mandate to operate the public school, school officials may exercise the necessary disciplinary power to ensure that the educational purposes of the school are carried out" (1982, p. 1089). Historically, school administrators and teachers were allowed to function quite autonomously in maintaining school and classroom discipline. In recent years, however, the courts have been called on to consider the constitutionality of school rules and of school disciplinary methods.

In considering the constitutionality of school rules, the courts have generally held that school restrictions on student behavior must be reasonably related to the purpose of schooling, school rules must be clearly stated, and the consequences for conduct code violations must be reasonably explicit (Overcast & Sales, 1982). The methods of school discipline that have frequently been the focus of judicial scrutiny include corporal punishment, suspension, and expulsion.

School discipline is the job responsibility of the building principal, not the school psychologist. Consequently, practitioners should not be directly involved in school disciplinary actions. However, they need a sound working knowledge of the ethical-legal aspects of disciplinary practices because of their role as consultant to principals, teachers, and others regarding pupils with behavior problems.

Corporal Punishment

> Why is it that school children remain the last Americans that can be legally beaten? (Messina, 1988, p. 108)

Corporal punishment is generally defined as the infliction of pain on the body by the teacher or other school official as a penalty for conduct disapproved of by the punisher. Forms of corporal punishment include spanking, beating, whipping, gagging, punching, shoving, knuckle rapping, arm twisting, shaking, and ear and hair pulling, among others (Messina, 1988).

There is a growing body of social science evidence to suggest that corporal punishment in the schools is psychologically harmful to children and that alternative approaches to maintaining school discipline are preferable and more effective (Messina, 1988; Purcell, 1984). Furthermore, children throughout the country have suffered severe and sometimes permanent physical injuries as a result of corporal punishment administered in the schools, including injuries to the head, neck, spine, kidneys, and genitals; perforated eardrums and hearing loss; facial and body scars; and chipped teeth (Hyman, 1990). Unfortunately, the use of corporal punishment in the schools is based on "social norms which are seeded deep within American culture" (Purcell, 1984, p. 188) and disciplinary practices which are deep seeded within the American schools (Messina, 1988). A 1988 survey of teachers reported that 75% favored the continued use of corporal punishment in the schools (Brown & Payne, 1988).

In the text that follows, case law and statutory law regarding corporal punishment are summarized. The role of the school psychologist in promoting alternatives to corporal punishment is then discussed.

Case Law

Historically, English common law viewed teachers as having the authority to use corporal punishment under the doctrine of in loco parentis. According to this doctrine, a child's father delegated part of his parental authority to the tutor or schoolmaster. The tutor or schoolmaster then "stood in the place of the parent" and was permitted to use "restraint and correction" as needed to teach the child (Zirkel & Reichner, 1986).

In the United States, the notion that educators have the authority to use corporal punishment under the common law doctrine of in loco parentis dates back to Colonial times, but it has gradually been replaced with the view that the state (school) has the right to administer corporal punishment because of the school's legitimate interest in maintaining order for the purpose of education.

Baker v. Owen (1975) raised the question of whether the parent can "un-delegate," or take away, the school's authority to use corporal punishment. In this case, Mrs. Baker told the school principal she did not want her son, Russell, corporally punished as he was a fragile child. Following a minor school infraction, his teacher took a drawer divider and spanked him twice, causing some bruises. Mrs. Baker filed a complaint in federal court alleging that her fundamental right to the care, control, and custody of her child had been violated when the school used corporal punishment despite her prohibition.

The court in *Baker* held that the school's interest in maintaining order by the use of reasonable corporal punishment outweighs parental rights to determine the care and control of their child, including how a child shall be disciplined. Under this ruling, schools were free to use reasonable corporal punishment for disciplinary purposes, despite parental objections to the practice.

In *Ingraham v. Wright,* a 1977 Supreme Court ruling, the parents of two schoolchildren contended that corporal punishment was a violation of a child's basic constitutional rights. The Court in *Ingraham* agreed to consider whether corporal punishment in the schools is "cruel and unusual punishment" under the Eighth Amendment, the extent to which paddling is constitutionally permissible, and whether paddling requires due process protection under the 14th Amendment.

The Court found that corporal punishment to maintain discipline in the schools does not fall under the "cruel and unusual punishment" prohibition of the Eighth Amendment because the Amendment was designed to protect those accused of crimes. The Court noted that "the schoolchild has little need for the protection of the Eighth Amendment" because the openness of the schools and supervision by the community afford significant safeguards from the abuse of corporal punishment by teachers (*Ingraham,* 1977, p. 1412).

Justice Powell, who wrote the majority opinion, acknowledged that the 14th Amendment protects the right to be free from unjustified intrusions on personal security and that liberty interests are "implicated" if punishment is unreasonable. He ruled, however, that "there can be no deprivation of substantive rights as long as disciplinary corporal punishment is within the limits of common law privilege" (p. 1415) and held that due process safeguards do not apply. Thus, the Court in *Ingraham* found that corporal punishment of schoolchildren is not unconstitutional per se. However, the opinion left unanswered the question of whether corporal punishment *is ever* unconstitutional.

Several more recent court decisions at the level of the U.S. Circuit Court of Appeals suggest excessive corporal punishment is likely to be viewed as unconstitutional. In *Hall v. Tawny* (1980) and *Garcia by Garcia v. Miera* (1987), for example, the parents of schoolchildren filed Section 1983 civil rights lawsuits against school officials after their children were severely beaten as a part of disciplinary actions. The actions of the school personnel in these cases were seen as a violation of the substantive rights of the child to be free of state intrusions into realms of personal privacy and bodily security through means the court viewed as "brutal and demeaning."

Statutory Law

As of 1994, 27 states had adopted legislation or issued regulations banning the use of corporal punishment in public schools (Hyman, Barrish, & Kaplan, 1997). Most state laws that prohibit corporal punishment allow teachers and others in the school setting to use reasonable physical restraint as necessary to protect people from immediate physical danger, or to protect property. Michigan's law, for example, allows an individual to use reasonable physical force for self-defense and in defense of others, to prevent self-injury, to obtain a weapon, and to restrain or remove a disruptive student who refuses to refrain from further disruptive behaviors when told to do so (Public Act 521 as amended by Act No. 6 of the Public Acts of 1992).

Promoting Alternatives

School psychology practitioners can work to abolish corporal punishment by sensitizing teachers to the negative consequences of corporal punishment, promoting alternatives to its use through in-service and consultation, and by advocating state legislation and school board policies banning the use of corporal punishment for school disciplinary purposes (see Hyman et al., 1997).

School psychologists also may serve an important role by sensitizing school staff to the potential legal sanctions for the use of corporal punishment. The use of corporal punishment can be costly to the principal or teacher in terms of time and legal defense fees, even if they are ultimately found innocent of any wrongdoing. In districts that have banned the use of corporal punishment, its use is likely to result in disciplinary action by the local school board, possibly including suspension or loss of employment. Even in states that allow use of corporal punishment in the schools, parents who are upset by its use with their child may pursue several courses of legal action. The majority of corporal punishment cases are filed in state courts under charges of battery, assault and battery, or negligent battery. Parents also may file a complaint under state child abuse laws. In addition, a number of parents have filed actions in federal court under Section 1983 (Henderson, 1986).

Suspension and Expulsion

Schools have been given the authority to suspend or expel students to maintain order and carry out the purpose of education. Short-term suspension is typically defined as an exclusion of 10 days or less from school or from participation in classes and activities (in-school suspension). School principals typically are given the authority to suspend students. Expulsion means exclusion of the student for a period longer than 10 consecutive school days or the equivalent, with "equivalent" determined by factors such as the number and proximity of excluded days (Hindman, 1986; Lohrmann & Zirkel, 1995). Student expulsion usually requires action by the school board.

The grounds for disciplinary suspensions and expulsions vary from state to state. School codes are likely to allow suspension or expulsion of students guilty of persistent noncompliance with school rules and directives, carrying weapons, drug-related offenses, repeated use of obscene language, stealing or vandalizing property on school grounds, and using violence or encouraging the use of violence (Hindman, 1986; Reutter, 1994).

In 1975, *Goss v. Lopez* was decided by the Supreme Court. This case was filed on behalf of several high school students suspended without any sort of informal due process hearing. The Court ruled that because education is a state-created property right, the school may not suspend or expel pupils without some sort of due process procedures to protect students from arbitrary or wrongful infringement of their interests in schooling. In writing the majority opinion, Justice White outlined the minimal due process procedures required for suspensions of 10 days or less:

> Students facing temporary suspension have interest qualifying for protection of the Due Process Clause, and due process requires, in connection with a suspension of 10 days or less, that the student be given oral or written notice of the charges against him and, if he denies them, an explanation of the evidence the authorities have and an opportunity to present his side of the story. The Clause requires at least these rudimentary precautions against unfair or mistaken findings of misconduct and arbitrary exclusion from school. (*Goss v. Lopez,* 1975, p. 740)

Justice White further noted that "longer suspensions or expulsions for the remainder of the school term, or permanently, may require more formal procedures" (p. 741). He also noted that, generally, the notice and hearing should precede the removal of the pupil from the school. However, pupils "whose presence poses a continuing danger to persons or property or an ongoing threat of disrupting the academic process may be immediately removed from school. In such cases, the necessary notice and rudimentary hearing should follow as soon as practicable" (*Goss v. Lopez,* 1975, p. 740).

Students with Disabilities

Between 1975 and 1997, numerous court decisions addressed the interpretation of IDEA and Section 504 of The Rehabilitation Act of 1973 as they relate to suspension or expulsion of pupils with disabilities. Pub. L. No. 105-17 added a number of provisions specifically addressing the discipline of children with disabilities under IDEA.

Interim Alternative Educational Setting With regard to short-term suspension, school personnel may unilaterally change the placement of a child with a disability to an appropriate interim alternative education setting (IAES), another setting, or suspension for not more than 10 school days (to the extent such alternatives would be applied to children without disabilities) (Pub. L. No. 105-17, § 615, 111 Stat. 93 [1997]). Education services need not be provided to a student removed for 10 days or less in a given school year (U.S. Department of Education Memorandum released September 19, 1997).

School personnel may order a longer change of placement to an IAES to address disciplinary infractions concerning weapons or drugs. A child with a disability who carries a weapon to school or to a school function, or who knowingly possesses or uses illegal drugs, or who solicits the sale of a controlled substance while at school or a school function, may be placed in an IAES for the same amount of time that a child without a disability would be subject to discipline, but for not more than 45 days (Pub. L. No. 105-17, § 615, 111 Stat. 93 [1997]).

In addition, a hearing officer may order a change in the placement of a child with a disability to an IAES for not more than 45 days if the hearing officer determines that the public agency has demonstrated by substantial evidence that maintaining the current placement of a child with a disability is substantially likely to result in injury to the child or to others. In ordering a change of placement, the officer must consider the appropriateness of the child's current placement, whether the public agency has made reasonable efforts to minimize the risk of harm in the child's current placement (including the use of supplementary aids and services), and the appropriateness of the alternative setting for the child (Pub. L. No. 105-17, § 615, 111 Stat. 94 [1997]).

Either before or not later than 10 days after taking a disciplinary action, the LEA must convene an IEP team meeting. If the child had a behavioral intervention plan prior to the disciplinary action, the IEP team is required to review the plan and modify it as necessary to address the problem behavior. If no behavioral plan existed prior to the disciplinary action, the LEA must convene an IEP team meeting to develop an assessment plan to address the problem behavior, conduct a functional behavioral assessment, and implement a behavioral intervention plan for the child to address the behavior that resulted in the disciplinary action (Pub. L. No. 105-17, § 615, 111 Stat. 94 [1997]).

The interim alternative educational setting (IAES) must be selected so as to enable the child to continue to participate in the general curriculum (although in another setting) and to receive the services and modifications that will enable the child to meet his or her current IEP goals. The IAES also must be selected to ensure the child will receive services and modifications designed to address the problem behavior so that it does not recur (Pub. L. No. 105-17, § 615, 111 Stat. 94 [1997]).

Manifest Determination Review If a disciplinary action is contemplated as a result of weapons, drugs, or potential injury to self or others, or if a disciplinary action involving a change of placement for more than 10 days is contemplated for a child with a disability who engaged in behavior that violated any school rule or code, a manifest determination review must be conducted. This review is conducted by the IEP team and other qualified personnel immediately after the disciplinary decision is made if possible, but no later than 10 school days after the date on which the decision to take that action was made. This review examines the relationship between the child's disability and the behavior that resulted in the disciplinary action (Pub. L. No. 105-17, § 615, 111 Stat. 94–95 [1997]).

The 1997 amendments outline a number of requirements for finding that behavior is or is not a manifestation of the child's disability. The IEP team may determine that the behavior of the child was not a manifestation of the child's disability only if it first considers, in terms of the behavior that led to the disciplinary action, all relevant information (including information supplied by the parents of the child), and then determines that (a) in relationship to the behavior subject to the disciplinary action, the child's IEP and placement were appropriate and the special education services, supplementary aids and services, and behavior intervention strategies were provided consistent with the child's IEP and placement; (b) the child's disability did not impair the ability of the child to understand the impact and consequences of the behavior subject to disciplinary action; and (c) the child's disability did not impair the ability of the child to control the behavior subject to disciplinary action (Pub. L. No. 105-17, § 615, 111 Stat. 95 [1997]).

If the result of the review is a determination that the behavior of the child with a disability was not a manifestation of the child's disability, the relevant disciplinary procedures applicable to children without disabilities may be applied to the child in the same manner that they would be applied to children without disabilities (e.g., long-term suspension), except that children with disabilities under IDEA must continue to receive a free appropriate public education (Pub. L. No. 105-17, § 615, 111 Stat. 95 [1997]). Schools may discontinue educational services to 504-only students (those protected by 504 but not eligible under IDEA) as long as nonhandicapped students received identical treatment ("Discipline Under Section 504," 1996).

Parents who disagree with a determination that a child's behavior was not a manifestation of his or her disability may request an expedited hearing. The child remains in the IAES pending the decision of the hearing officer or until the expiration of the time limit, whichever comes first, unless the parent and SEA or LEA agree otherwise. If the child is placed in an IAES and the LEA proposes to change the child's placement after expiration of the IAES, the child remains in the current placement (prior to the IAES) during any proceeding to challenge the proposed change of placement. If, however, the LEA maintains that it is dangerous for the child to be in the current placement, the LEA may request an expedited hearing (Pub. L. No. 105-17, § 615, 111 Stat. 96–97 [1997]). Thus, it is no longer necessary for a school to seek a court order to suspend or expel a pupil who is dangerous pending the resolution of a dispute about his or her appropriate placement.

A child who has not been determined to be eligible for special education and who engaged in behavior that violated any school rule or code may seek IDEA protections by asserting that the school knew the child had a disability before the behavior leading to disciplinary action occurred. The LEA is deemed to have knowledge that a child has a disability if (a) the parent had expressed concern in writing that their child is in need of special education (except for parents who are illiterate or unable to comply with this clause), (b) the behavior or performance of the child demonstrates the need for such services, (c) the parent has requested an evaluation of the child, or (d) the teacher or other school personnel have expressed concern about the child to the agency director. If a request is made for evaluation of a child during the time the child is subjected to disciplinary measures, the evaluation will be conducted in an expedited manner, and if found eligible, the child will receive special education and related services (Pub. L. No. 105-17, § 615, 111 Stat. 97 [1997]).

Referral and Action by Law Enforcement Pub. L. No. 105-17 clarifies that school personnel may report a crime committed by a child with a disability to appropriate authorities, and nothing in the law prevents law enforcement and judicial authorities from exercising their duties with regard to crimes committed by a child with a disability. The LEA that reports a crime must ensure that copies of the special education and disciplinary records of the child are transmitted for consideration by the authorities.

Monitoring of Suspension and Expulsion Rates Under IDEA, states are required to collect and examine data to determine if significant discrepancies are occurring in the rate of long-term suspensions and expulsions of children with disabilities among LEAs or compared to the rates for children without disabilities. If discrepancies are occurring, the SEA must review and, if appropriate, revise policies, procedures, and practices related to the development and implementation of IEPs, the use of behavioral interventions, and procedural safeguards (Pub. L. No. 105-17, § 618, 111 Stat. 101 [1997]).

OTHER PUPILS WITH SPECIAL NEEDS

In the last portion of this chapter, we discuss the ethical-legal issues associated with public schooling for three other groups of pupils with special needs: children with limited English proficiency, gifted and talented pupils, and students with communicable diseases.

Children with Limited English Proficiency

In 1974, the Supreme Court decided a landmark case, *Lau v. Nichols,* concerning the education of children with limited English proficiency (LEP). This case was based on a class action suit filed by non-English-speaking Chinese students in the San Francisco Unified School District. At that time, more than half of the LEP Chinese pupils were taught solely in English, with no supplemental instruction in the English language. Furthermore, proficiency in English was a requirement for high school graduation. The plaintiffs in this case claimed that the school's practice was a denial of equal opportunity under the 14th Amendment.

The case was decided on statutory grounds (Civil Rights Act of 1964), rather than the equal protection clause of the 14th Amendment. The 1964 Civil Rights Act prohibits discrimination in programs receiving federal assistance. In his decision in favor of the plaintiffs, Justice Douglas wrote "there is no equality of treatment merely by providing students with the  same facilities, textbooks, teachers, and curriculum; for students who do  not understand English are effectively foreclosed from meaningful education" (*Lau v. Nichols,* 1974, p. 566).

Lau v. Nichols has been interpreted to mean that schools must provide assistance or "take affirmative steps" to ensure children with limited English proficiency have access to a meaningful education. It is *not* seen as requiring bilingual instruction for each LEP child.

Thus, there is no federal mandate requiring bilingual education for the LEP child. The federal government has, however, provided funds for bilingual education programs and to encourage the training of bilingual teachers since 1968. In 1968, the Bilingual Education Act was added as an amendment to the Elementary and Secondary Education Act of 1965 (Pub. L. No. 100-297). Title VII of IASA (the reauthorization of ESEA) includes continued funding for bilingual education. School psychologists who serve bilingual children need to maintain up-to-date knowledge of best practices in assessment and instruction of the LEP child (see Lopez, 1995; Lopez & Gopaul-McNicol, 1997).

Gifted and Talented Students

There is no federal legislation requiring schools to provide specialized education to gifted and talented students. In 1988, the Jacob K. Javits Gifted and Talented Students Education Act was passed (part of ESEA). This legislation provided funds for programs and projects designed to meet the special instructional needs of gifted and talented students. The new Jacob K. Javits Gifted and Talented Students Education Act (Title X of IASA) reaffirms the purposes of the 1988 Act, but also encourages states and colleges to assist the public schools in developing rich and challenging curricula for all students. The identification and provision of services to gifted and talented students who may not be identified and served through traditional assessment methods is a funding priority (e.g., pupils from economically disadvantaged backgrounds). The Act also requires establishment of a National Center for Research and Development in the Education of Gifted and Talented Children and Youth.

There are many disagreements about how to identify gifted and talented children and how to provide the most effective educational programs (see Boatman, Davis, & Benbow, 1995; Callahan, 1997). School psychologists involved in the identification of gifted and talented students and the development of instructional programs are obligated to keep abreast of current literature in this area.

Students with Communicable Diseases

Because of current interest and concern, the discussion that follows focuses on students with acquired immunodeficiency syndrome (AIDS)/human immunodeficiency virus (HIV), but the issues raised are pertinent to other communicable diseases (e.g., hepatitis B).

State and local school boards have the power and authority to adopt regulations to safeguard the health and safety of students. Schools may require vaccinations or immunizations prior to school attendance, and they may deny school access to children who pose a health threat to others (Reutter, 1994). The difficulty with serious long-term communicable diseases such as AIDS/HIV is in determining whether the health threat posed by the infected child is significant enough to outweigh the child's right to schooling in the least restrictive and most normal setting.

In the text that follows, we will discuss AIDS/HIV as a handicapping condition under Section 504 of the Rehabilitation Act of 1973 and IDEA, and the obligation of school personnel to safeguard the privacy of pupils with communicable diseases.

AIDS and the Rehabilitation Act of 1973

There was initially some disagreement about whether Section 504 provides protection against discriminatory treatment for an individual with a communicable disease. However, in *School Board of Nassau County, Florida v. Arline* (1987), the Supreme Court made it clear that a person with a communicable disease is eligible for protection under Section 504. *Arline* was a case concerning a teacher dismissed from her job after she suffered a relapse of tuberculosis. In *Arline,* the Supreme Court judged it necessary to conduct a two-step individualized inquiry to determine whether a person with a communicable disease is otherwise qualified under Section 504 (1987, p. 1131).

The two-step inquiry outlined in *Arline* suggests that in determining whether a pupil is otherwise qualified, it is first necessary to evaluate whether the student poses *a significant risk of transmission* of the disease to others in the school setting. This part of the inquiry must be based on medical judgment and include consideration of the nature, duration, and severity of the risk and the probabilities the disease will be transmitted and cause varying degrees of harm. The second step in evaluating whether a student with a contagious disease is "otherwise qualified" is to evaluate, in light of the medical findings, whether the school can reasonably accommodate the pupil. A pupil who poses a significant risk of communicating an infectious disease to others in school is not otherwise qualified to be placed in the regular school setting if reasonable accommodation will not eliminate that risk.

At this time, court rulings have specifically found that pupils with AIDS or AIDS-related complex are handicapped within the meaning of Section 504 (e.g., *Doe v. Belleville Public School District No. 118,* 1987; *Martinez v. The School Board of Hillsborough County, Florida,* 1987; *Thomas v. Atascadero Unified School District,* 1987). Thus, schools that receive any federal assistance may not discriminate against any otherwise qualified school child with AIDS/HIV. *If a significant risk of transmission would still exist in spite of reasonable efforts by the school to accommodate the infected child, then the pupil is not "otherwise qualified," and removal from the normal classroom setting is permissible* (*Thomas,* 1987).

Arline and other court rulings (e.g., *District 27 Community School Board v. Board of Education of the City of New York,* 1986) suggest that the decision whether a child with AIDS or similar communicable disease should be excluded from the normal school setting must be made on a case-by-case basis. There appears to be some consensus among the Centers for Disease Control (CDC), National Education Association, and APA's Task Force on Pediatric AIDS regarding the appropriate decision-making process. All recommend a team approach to decision making. CDC suggests the team be composed of the child's physician, public health personnel, and the child's parent or guardian, along with school personnel.

Current medical opinion suggests that for most school-age children with AIDS/HIV, the normal classroom setting is appropriate. A more restricted environment is recommended for infected preschool-age children and disabled children who lack control over body secretions, and those who display behaviors such as biting and drooling. Children with open, oozing lesions that cannot be covered also may need a more restrictive environment (CDC position summarized in Kirkland & Ginther, 1988). Children at high risk for transmitting the virus may need home instruction.

AIDS and IDEA

Children with AIDS/HIV do not qualify for special education and related services under the "other health impairment" classification of IDEA-Part B unless the disease adversely affects educational performance. As noted in *Belleville* (1987), "Based on the Department of Education's opinions and the tenor of the statutory language, the Court concludes that EAHCA [IDEA] would apply to AIDS victims *only* if their physical condition is such that it adversely affects their educational performance (i.e., their ability to learn and to do the required classroom work)" (p. 345) (also *District 27,* 1986).

Pupil Privacy

Schools must protect the privacy of students with AIDS or other communicable diseases. Knowledge that a student is infected should be confined to those persons with a direct need to know. School personnel also must keep abreast of state policies regarding the disclosure of information about students with communicable diseases. In Michigan, for example, the passing of information about a person with a serious communicable disease by school personnel is a felony punishable by a prison term of up to 3 years and a $5,000 fine, or both (Public Act 488, Section 5131 [10]).

The School Psychologist and Pupils with AIDS/HIV

School psychologists can potentially serve a number of important consultation roles with regard to students with AIDS/HIV or other serious communicable diseases. School psychologists can work closely with school and community health professionals in promoting AIDS education and, more generally, health education in the schools. Practitioners also may develop expertise on the psychological aspects of serious childhood disease and provide supportive counseling to enhance the psychological well-being of infected children and their families (see Haefli, Pryor, & Landau, 1995; Landau, Pryor, & Haefli, 1995; Wolters, Brouwers, & Moss, 1995).

CONCLUDING COMMENTS

As Dawson observed, "school psychologists are often in a position to influence educational policy and administrative practices" (1987, p. 349). Maintaining up-to-date knowledge of school policies and practices that have an impact on the welfare of children and sharing that expertise in consultation with school principals and other decision makers, "may enable school psychologists to effect organizational change that can have a positive impact on large numbers of children" (Dawson, 1987, p. 348).

STUDY AND DISCUSSION

Questions for Chapter 10

1. Under IDEA, must special education students participate in statewide assessment programs? May schools require special education students to pass a minimal competency test prior to the award of a high school diploma?
2. Is the use of paddling (spanking) for disciplinary purposes in the schools constitutionally permissible? Is it ever viewed as unconstitutional?
3. What strategies does a school have under Pub. L. No. 105-17 for handling a special education student who violates school rules? What is a manifest determination review? In developing behavioral plans for disruptive special education students, schools must conduct a functional behavioral assessment of the problem behavior. What is a functional behavioral assessment?
4. Are public schools required to provide bilingual instruction under federal law?
5. Do gifted children have a right to an individualized and appropriate education under federal law?
6. Do children with AIDS/HIV qualify for special education? Under what circumstances does Section 504 allow schools to remove students with AIDS from the regular classroom?

Discussion

School psychologists are ethically obligated to act as advocates for the rights and welfare of pupils. What are some of the ways in which practitioners can promote school policies and practices to enhance the welfare of all pupils in the schools? What roles can school psychologists play in school reform efforts?

The following resources are available from the American Psychological Association Center for Psychology in the Schools and Education, 750 First Street, NE, Washington, DC 20002-4242:

American Psychological Association. (1995). *Reforming America's schools: Psychology's role.* Washington, DC: Author.

Video: *Reforming America's Schools: Psychology's Role—The Kentucky Example.*

Chapter 11

ETHICAL SANCTIONS AND LEGAL LIABILITY

This chapter begins with a discussion of unethical conduct by school psychologists. Ethics committees and the adjudication of complaints, peer monitoring, and reasons for unethical conduct also are discussed. The second portion of the chapter addresses legal liability. We review the meaning of negligence and malpractice, malpractice trends, risk management, and professional liability insurance. The chapter closes with a discussion of educational malpractice.

UNETHICAL CONDUCT

As noted in Chapter 1, one of the functions of professional associations is to develop and promote standards to enhance the quality of work by its members (Chalk et al., 1980). By encouraging appropriate professional conduct, associations such as APA and NASP strive to ensure that each person served will receive the highest quality of service and thus build and maintain public trust in psychology and psychologists. Failure to do so is likely to result in increased external regulation of the profession.

Appropriate professional conduct is defined through the development and frequent revision of codes of ethics and professional standards. "But the presence of a set of ethical principles or rules of conduct is only part, albeit an important one, of the machinery needed to effect self-regulation. The impact of a profession's ethical principles or rules on its members' behavior may be negligible . . . without appropriate support activities to encourage proper professional conduct, or the means to detect and investigate possible violations, and to impose sanctions on violators" (Chalk et al., 1980, p. 2).

APA and NASP support a range of activities designed to educate and sensitize practitioners to the parameters of appropriate professional conduct. Both include ethics coursework as a required component in their standards for graduate training, and each organization disseminates information on professional conduct through publications and the support of symposia.

APA and NASP also each support a standing ethics committee. Ethics committees are made up of volunteer members of the professional association. Ethics committees respond to informal inquiries about ethical issues. Ethics committees also investigate complaints about possible code of ethics violations by association members and impose sanctions on violators. NASP's Ethical and Professional Standards Committee is charged with investigating and making recommendations to NASP's Executive Board when a complaint is filed concerning an NASP member or any psychologist who holds a National Certificate in School Psychology (NCSP) (NASP, 1997).

Ethics Committees and Sanctions

APA has developed an extensive set of "Rules and Procedures" for investigation and adjudication of ethical complaints against Association members (APA, 1996b). According to APA's "Rules and Procedures," the primary objectives of the Ethics Committee are "to maintain ethical conduct by psychologists at the highest professional level, to educate psychologists concerning ethical standards, [and] to endeavor to protect the public against harmful conduct by psychologists . . ." (1996b, p. 532).

APA's "Rules and Procedures" lists a number of possible sanctions for ethics violations including issue of an educative letter, reprimand or censure, expulsion, and stipulated resignation. APA terminated the membership of 199 psychologists between 1985 and 1995 (APA, 1996a).

In accordance with NASP's "Procedural Guidelines for the Adjudication of Ethical Complaints" (1997), NASP's Ethics and Professional Standards Committee addresses issues of ethical misconduct "in an investigatory, advisory, educative and/or remedial role" (II). The Committee is committed to resolving cases informally, if possible. It works to "bring about an adjustment through mediative efforts in the interest of correcting a general situation or settling the particular issues between the parties involved" (IV.C.). Nevertheless, NASP procedures allow for requesting that the respondent take corrective measures, censure or reprimand, requiring restitution or apology, imposition of a period of probation, and expulsion (V). Following a formal investigation and hearing, any actions taken by NASP's Executive Board concerning a psychologist who holds an NCSP certificate are reported to the national certification board (IX).

The legality of ethical complaint adjudication was tested in court in the case of *Marshall v. American Psychological Association* (1987). The plaintiff in this case claimed that APA had no legal right to expel him or to publicize his expulsion from the association following an investigation of ethical misconduct. The court upheld the authority of APA to expel the plaintiff, noting that he agreed to be bound by APA's ethical principles when he joined the association, that the principles were repeatedly published, and that he had detailed hearing rights to respond to any and all charges.

In recent years, there has been a tendency for respondents in ethical complaints to file lawsuits against members of the ethics committee. For this reason, many state associations no longer have adjudication procedures and take an exclusively educative approach, leaving adjudication up to the national association.

Complaints to Ethics Committees

APA's Ethics Committee periodically publishes an analysis of its actions in the *American Psychologist.* In 1995 there were approximately 420 inquiries received by the Ethics Committee, with 116 complaints ultimately filed. Complaints were filed against approximately .14% of the APA membership (APA, 1996a). Based on categorization of the underlying behavior (rather than the basis for processing the case), violation of dual relationships was the category with the largest number of complaints in 1995 (46% of the cases). About 60% of these dual relationship cases were of a sexual nature. Other categories with a significant number of complaints were: insurance and fee problems, test misuse issues, confidentiality violations, termination and supervision matters, and child custody evaluations (1996a). Beginning in 1997, NASP's Ethics Committee is required to maintain records regarding the number and nature of all written complaints filed against NASP members and individuals who hold the NCSP certificate (III).

Reasons for Unethical Conduct

According to Keith-Spiegel and Koocher (1985), there is no one profile that describes psychologists who become ethics violators. Code of ethics violations may occur because the psychologist is unaware of the parameters of appropriate conduct. This may occur because the psychologist is poorly trained, inexperienced, or fails to maintain up-to-date knowledge. These violations also may occur when a psychologist who usually works within the parameters of appropriate practice fails to think through a situation carefully. Some psychologists suffer from personal emotional problems or situational stressors that impair professional judgment and performance. Finally, a few psychologists (fortunately only a few) are self-serving and put their needs before those of their clients.

Peer Monitoring

Both APA and NASP require its members to monitor the ethical conduct of their professional colleagues (*EP* Principle C; NASP-PPE, III, A, #8). Both associations support attempts to resolve the issue informally before filing a complaint. NASP's code states that practitioners should "attempt to resolve suspected detrimental or unethical practices on an informal level" (NASP-PPE, III, A, #8). They "make every effort to discuss the ethical principles with other professionals who may be in violation" (NASP-PPE, III, A, #8). Psychologists document specific instances of suspected violations as well as attempts to resolve such violations (NASP-PPE, III, A, #8).

If, however, informal efforts are not productive, "the appropriate professional organization is contacted for assistance, and procedures established for questioning ethical practice are followed" (NASP-PPE, III, A, #8). Practitioners "enter this process thoughtfully and with the concern for the well-being of all parties involved" (NASP-PPE, III, A, #8).

Although most practitioners are aware of their obligation to report unethical conduct, many are reluctant to do so. In a survey of members of APA Division 29, 14% of the respondents reported that it was always or under most circumstances unethical to file an ethics complaint against a colleague (Pope, Tabachnick, & Keith-Spiegel, 1987). Keith-Spiegel and Koocher (1985) provide a helpful list of hints for engaging in informal peer monitoring.

UNLAWFUL CONDUCT

Civil Liability

Civil liability, simply stated, "means that one can be sued for acting wrongly toward another or for failing to act when there was a recognized duty to do so" (Hopkins & Anderson, 1985, p. 21). Civil liability rests within the basic framework of the law of tort. Hummel et al. (1985) describe the law of tort as follows:

> Common tort comes from the Latin *torquere* meaning "to twist." The basic concept of tort, which comes from old English law, is that each individual has a legal and social obligation to protect other individuals in society. If one person breaches or twists the relationship and someone is injured, then the injured party may sue and be compensated for the damages. (Hummel et al., 1985, p. 68)

There are two categories of torts of interest to school psychology practitioners, constitutional torts and common torts.

Constitutional Torts

As noted in Chapter 2, school personnel need to be familiar with Section 1983 of the Civil Rights Act of 1871. Under Section 1983, any person whose constitutional rights (or rights under federal law) have been violated by a government official may sue for damages in federal court, and the official may be held liable for the actual damages. A pupil whose civil rights have been violated under Section 1983 may sue in federal court the school board, principal, teacher, and/or school psychologist responsible.

A number of student lawsuits concerning school disciplinary actions (e.g., illegal search and seizure, unreasonable corporal punishment) have been filed under Section 1983. School officials may have qualified immunity from Section 1983 lawsuits. The standard for qualified immunity applicable to government (school) officials is as follows: "[G]overnment officials performing discretionary functions are shielded from liability for civil damages unless their conduct violated clearly established statutory or constitutional rights of which a reasonable person would have known" (*Harlow v. Fitzgerald,* 1982, p. 2738). Hummel et al. (1985) suggest that school personnel generally will not be held liable in Section 1983 lawsuits as long as they are "acting clearly within the scope of their authority for the betterment of those they serve" (p. 78; for example, see *Landstrom v. Illinois Department of Children and Family Services,* 1990). However, if they are acting outside of their authority and violate a pupil's civil rights (e.g., a school psychologist becomes involved in unreasonable student search and seizure), then the psychologist may be held personally liable (Hummel et al., 1985).

Common Torts

Common torts are applicable to psychologists in the schools and in private practice. Hummel et al. (1985) identify several different types of common torts. We will focus here on professional negligence or malpractice. Negligence occurs when an unintentional act results in injury, damage, or loss, and the court rules a reasonable person could have anticipated the harmful results. For negligence to exist, the court must find there was a duty on the part of the actor to protect others, a failure on the part of the actor to exercise appropriate care, and the act is the cause of injury (Hummel et al., 1985).

When acting in a professional capacity, one is expected to provide "due care," or a level of care that is "standard" in the profession. Malpractice occurs when there is harm to the client as a result of professional negligence, with negligence defined as the departure from acceptable professional standards (Hummel et al., 1985). To succeed in a malpractice claim, the plaintiff must prove: (a) a professional relationship was formed between the psychologist and plaintiff so that the psychologist owed a legal duty of care to the plaintiff, (b) the duty of care was breached, that is, there is a standard of care and the practitioner breached that standard, (c) the client suffered harm or injury, and (d) the practitioner's breach of duty to practice within the standard of care was the proximate cause of the client's injury; that is, the injury was a reasonably foreseeable consequence of the breach (Bennett, Bryant, VandenBos, & Greenwood, 1990). Malpractice is difficult to prove, as most often the client must establish that emotional harm occurred as a result of negligence on the part of the psychologist (Knapp, 1980).

Once it has been determined that a psychologist owed a legal duty to the plaintiff, how does the court determine the standard of care? As Bennett et al. (1990) note, in most cases, the courts look to the profession itself to identify the customary standard of care used by others in the same field. Expert testimony may be used to establish the customary standard of care. In addition, codes of ethics and professional standards may be presented as evidence of the parameters of accepted practice. Sometimes the client's condition is a key factor in determining the expected standard of care (e.g., acceptable and reasonable actions in handling a suicidal adolescent). If the psychologist is not qualified to work with a particular type of problem situation, he or she is obligated to refer the client to someone with appropriate training (Bennett et al., 1990).

According to Woody (1988), the key words related to defining the appropriate standard of care are ordinary, reasonable, and prudent. Ordinary pertains to what is accepted or customary practice. Reasonable relates to the appropriate and adequate use of professional knowledge and judgment. Prudent means the exercise of caution, not in the sense of being traditional or conservative, but rather maintaining adequate safeguards. As Knapp (1980) notes, the courts do not expect psychologists to be all-knowing and perform without error. They do not decide malpractice from the application of standard techniques.

Trends in Malpractice

Many APA members participate in a professional liability insurance program designed by the American Psychological Association Insurance Trust (APAIT). APAIT maintains statistics on the number and types of lawsuits against the 36,000 practitioners who carry its insurance. APAIT reported an average of 125 claims per year between 1976 and 1989. This suggests that the likelihood of a psychologist being sued is less than .5%. APAIT's data show the following issues (from most to least frequent) underlying liability lawsuits: sexual improprieties, other dual relationships, fee collection, undue influence, breach of contract, abandonment, failure to cure/poor results, failure to refer, and failure to treat (Bennett et al., 1990). It is difficult to identify trends in malpractice as they relate to school psychologists specifically. According to Remley (1985), school personnel and educators are rarely sued.

Risk Management

Although educators are rarely sued, it does not mean that they cannot be sued. Legal experts advise psychologists to minimize the risk of malpractice suits by engaging in risk management. Woody (1988) describes three aspects of risk management. The first is making professional decisions after an analysis of their ethical, regulatory, and legal risks. The other two are more proactive. The second aspect is the cultivation of favorable impressions of one's practice; in other words, an emphasis on public relations and public information so that people know who you are and the kind of services you provide. The third aspect is the development of a professional practice that is efficient and effective.

Risk management implies that we cannot eliminate risk. But when confronted by a malpractice suit, we may be able to point to a practice that reflects sound principles of professional behavior (third aspect), a reputation that is positive and based on knowledge of our activities (second aspect), and the specific principles that led to the professional decision in question (first aspect). The reader is encouraged to consult Bennett et al. (1990) for an extensive discussion of risk management and information about what to do if you are sued.

Professional Liability Insurance

To protect themselves, and perhaps ease some of their fear of litigation, some school psychologists purchase professional liability insurance. Prior to purchasing a policy, school psychologists should investigate what type of coverage, if any, is provided by their employers, and whether any professional liability insurance is provided by their membership in a professional union, such as the National Education Association or American Federation of Teachers. In choosing an insurance policy, there are several points to keep in mind. First, some professional liability policies cover school psychologists only when their services are performed as those of an educational institution employee. In other words, they do not cover private practice. Such policies are generally much less expensive than those that do cover private work.

Second, policies may be either claims made or occurrence based. Under the former, you are covered only if you were insured both when the alleged malpractice took place *and* when the claim was filed. Under the latter, an occurrence-based policy, you are covered as long as you were insured when the alleged malpractice took place, regardless of when the claim was filed.

Third, many policies will only pay when the defendant denies the allegation. Some policies put severe limitations on coverage for sexual misconduct. Be sure to study the policy carefully to know what is and is not covered.

Fourth, many policies reserve the right to select legal counsel and to settle the case. This may be discouraging to practitioners who want their day in court. The psychologist may still hire his or her own attorney to work with the one supplied by the insurance carrier, but that is an additional expense.

Policies offered by national organizations are probably the easiest to find, but may prove to have less than desirable features. Even national organizations may have difficulty finding suitable policies to offer their members, a problem experienced by NASP in past years. The difficulty is not that school psychologists are a great risk, but that there are not enough of them purchasing the insurance to make it worthwhile for the carrier to offer it, particularly since the statute of limitations on filing claims was eliminated several years ago, increasing the risk over time. See Bennett et al. (1990) for additional information on professional liability insurance.

EDUCATIONAL MALPRACTICE

Case 11–1

Daniel Hoffman entered kindergarten in the New York City school system in September 1956. Shortly thereafter he was seen by a psychologist in the school system, who determined he had an IQ of 74 and recommended he be placed in a class for children with retarded mental development. The psychologist, however, was not sure of his findings because Daniel suffered from a severe speech disability, and Daniel's inability to communicate verbally made it difficult to assess his intelligence. As a result, the psychologist recommended that Daniel "be reevaluated within a 2-year period so that a more accurate estimation of his abilities can be made."

Case 11–1 *(Continued)*

Daniel was placed in a special class, and his academic progress was monitored by his teachers by the use of achievement tests. However, the school failed to have his abilities reevaluated as recommended by the psychologist. Daniel remained in the classroom for retarded children for 12 years. In 1968, he was transferred to an occupational training center for retarded youth. His IQ was retested at that time and found to be normal (FSIQ of 94 on the WAIS). This score indicated he was not eligible for continued enrollment in the training program.

Daniel subsequently filed suit against the Board of Education of the City of New York, alleging that the board was negligent in its original assessment of his intellectual ability and that the board negligently failed to retest him pursuant to the psychologist's recommendation. He further claimed that these negligent acts and omissions caused him to be misclassified and inappropriately placed in a class for retarded children, which ultimately resulted in injury to his intellectual and emotional well-being and reduced his ability to obtain employment (adapted from Hoffman v. Board of Education of the City of New York, *1979).*

In the 1970s and early 1980s, a number of educational malpractice suits were filed against school districts. The courts have ruled on two kinds of educational negligence or malpractice suits. Instructional malpractice suits have been filed when a student did not achieve academically what his or her parents expected. Instructional malpractice claims have invariably failed for several reasons. First, the courts prefer not to intervene in the administration of the public schools except in unusual circumstances involving clear violations of constitutional rights or federal law. Second, the courts have held that award of monetary damages for instructional malpractice suits would be overly burdensome to the public education system in terms of both time and money (*Peter W. v. San Francisco Unified School District,* 1976). In addition, as noted in *Donohue v. Copiague Union Free School District* (1979), it would be difficult, if not impossible, to prove a causal link between teacher malpractice and student failure.

A second kind of educational malpractice is called assessment-placement malpractice. Assessment-placement malpractice suits have been filed when a student is placed inappropriately due to incorrect assessment (e.g., *B.M. v.*

State of Montana, 1982; *Hoffman,* 1979). *Hoffman* (Case 11–1) raised concerns that the courts might award monetary damages to misclassified students in assessment-malpractice cases. In this case, the lower court found in Daniel's favor and issued a $750,000.00 liability judgment against the school board. On appeal, however, the decision of the lower court was reversed. The court at the appeals level decided that there were "no gross violations of defined public policy" and reiterated the principle that courts ought not to interfere with the professional judgment of those charged with the responsibility for the administration of the schools (1979, p. 379).

To date, assessment-placement malpractice suits have generally been unsuccessful. Although the courts have typically refused to award monetary damages to misclassified/misplaced students, compensatory education has been awarded as a substitute for damages in some cases (Turnbull, 1990; see also *Brantley v. Independent School District No. 625,* 1996).

CONCLUDING COMMENTS

Professional associations such as APA and NASP engage in a number of activities to ensure that a high quality of service is provided by members. However, the responsibility for appropriate professional conduct ultimately rests with the individual practitioner.

As school psychologists, we are expected to provide services consistent with our codes of ethics, professional standards, and law. When we fail to do so, we may face charges of ethical misconduct or malpractice.

STUDY AND DISCUSSION

Questions for Chapter 11

1. Why do professional associations such as APA and NASP develop codes of ethics and sanction members who do not abide by them?
2. What are some of the reasons for unethical conduct?
3. What are your responsibilities with regard to peer monitoring?
4. What is civil liability? What are constitutional torts?
5. What is negligence? What is malpractice? What aspects of the situation do courts evaluate to determine whether malpractice

(Continued)

occurred? How is appropriate standard of care generally determined?

6. What is educational malpractice? Are educational malpractice suits typically successful?

Discussion

You and a fellow student (a friend) are placed at the same school for your first practicum experience. You are aware that he/she is a problem drinker but thus far he/she has been able to conceal his/her problem from the program faculty. You discover that your fellow student drinks before coming to practicum, and you have observed some erratic behavior and poor judgment at the practicum site. What should you do? What will you do? Why? (adapted from Bernard & Jara, 1986). See Bernard and Jara (1986) and Bersoff (1995).

Epilogue

ETHICS, PROFESSIONAL STANDARDS, AND ADVOCACY

According to NASP's code of ethics, school psychologists act as advocates for the rights and welfare of pupils (NASP-PPE, IV, A, #1, #2). Consistent with the general ethical principle of responsibility to community and society, practitioners also promote school policies to enhance the welfare of students, and they may work as advocates for change at the state and national level to better protect the interests and rights of children.

Throughout this book, we have advanced the view that the primary purpose of our codes of ethics is *to protect the public.* Codes of ethics were not created to protect the professional (Wonderly, 1989). However, in this epilogue we illustrate how our codes of ethics and professional standards can be a source of support for the practitioner when advocacy for the rights and educational needs of children brings the psychologist in conflict with the school. This is particularly likely to occur if, in the face of limited resources, the school is resistant to providing legally mandated services.

In the case of *Forrest v. Ambach* (1980, 1983), Forrest, a school psychologist, claimed that she was fired from her position for actions that were ethically and legally mandated. For example, she claimed to have been criticized for conducting full and comprehensive evaluations and writing comprehensive reports. Also, she was allegedly criticized for recommending services the child needed as opposed to services the schools offered. She also claimed to have been criticized for discussing her conclusions with parents and for dissenting from the views of other professionals during staffings. This is a case where ethics and law are clearly on the side of the school psychologist, serving to defend the nature of her practice. The *amici curiae* brief written by Bersoff (1981) for APA, and filed in support of her case, is an outstanding example of how law and ethics can serve to support a high quality of professional service by the practitioner.

The judge in her initial appeal (1980) wrote, "The ethical standards of any professional employed by a school board cannot be cavalierly dismissed as irrelevant to the employer-employee relationship" (p. 122). The judge went on, "If, in fact, petitioner was dismissed solely due to her attempt to adhere to statutory mandates and her own professional standards as a psychologist, then her dismissal by said school board would be arbitrary, capricious, and unconstitutional" (p. 123).

Despite the fact that the state commissioner of education ultimately found that her dismissal was not based on these actions, and her firing was upheld, school psychologists should be encouraged by the judge's ruling in the case. By adhering to professional standards in the delivery of services, school psychologists may increase their freedom to utilize best practices in the field, as well as provide themselves with protection when advocacy for children brings them in conflict with the school.

CONCLUDING COMMENTS

In attempting to write as current a book as we could, we have been impressed by the speed with which law and ethics can change. You, the school psychologist, must take it from here. This means maintaining your currency regarding new developments in ethics and law and also working proactively for school policies and law to better serve the interests and rights of children.

STUDY AND DISCUSSION

Questions for Epilogue

1. What does it mean to be a child advocate? (See McMahon, 1993). Should practitioners assume the role of client advocate within the school system or teach parents how to advocate on behalf of their own child? (See Alper, Schloss, & Schloss, 1994).
2. School psychologists at times face ethical dilemmas because of their dual functions as client advocate and employee (Helton, 1992; Jann, Hyman, & Reinhardt, 1992). In times of limited school resources, school psychologists may experience an increase in pressure to practice unethically. For example, when resources are limited, psychologists may be encouraged to recommend inexpensive, rather than appropriate, placements and interventions and limit information provided to parents, rather than fully inform them of their rights and choices.

   What strategies will you use to avoid conflicts between your ethical responsibilities to the client and administrative pressure to make decisions that are not in the best interests of the client? How will you successfully resist administrative pressures to practice unethically?

Appendix A

*NASP'S PRINCIPLES FOR PROFESSIONAL ETHICS**

I. INTRODUCTION

The formal principles that elucidate the proper conduct of a professional school psychologist are known as *Ethics*. By virtue of joining the Association, each NASP member agrees to abide by the *Ethics,* acting in a manner that shows respect for human dignity and assures a high quality of professional service. Although ethical behavior is an individual responsibility, it is in the interest of an association to adopt and enforce a code of ethics. If done properly, members will be guided towards appropriate behavior, and public confidence in the profession will be enhanced. Additionally, a code of ethics should provide due process procedures to protect members from potential abuse of the code. The *Ethics* have been written to accomplish these goals.

The principles in this manual are based on the assumptions that: 1) school psychologists will act as advocates for their students/clients, and 2) at the very least, school psychologists will do no harm. These necessitate that school psychologists "speak up" for the needs and rights of their students/clients even at times when it may be difficult to do so. School psychologists are also constrained to provide only those services for which they have acquired an acknowledged level of experience, training, and competency. Beyond these basic premises, judgment is required to apply the ethical principles to the fluid and expanding interactions between school and community.

There are many different sources of advice for the proper way to behave; local policies, state laws, federal laws, credentialing standards, professional association position statements, and books that recommend "Best Practices" are just a few. Given one's employment situation and the array of recommendations, events may develop in which the ethical course of action is unclear.

The Association will seek to enforce the Ethical Principles upon its members. The NASP Standards for the Provision of School Psychological Services are typically not enforced, although all members should work toward achieving the hallmarks of quality services delivery that are described therein. Similarly, "position statements" and "best practices" documents are not adjudicated. The guidance of the Ethical Principles is intentionally broad, to make it more enduring than other documents that reflect short-term opinions about specific actions shaped by local events, popular trends, or recent developments in the field. The practitioner must use judgment to infer the situation-specific rule from the general principle. The lack of a specific reference to a particular action does not indicate permission or provide a defense against a charge of unethical practice. (For example, the document frequently refers to a school psychologist's relationships with a hypothetical "student/client." Since school psychologists work in a wide variety of settings, there is no single term that neatly identifies the "other" individual in the professional relationship. Therefore, one should apply these *Principles* in all professional situations, realizing that one is not released from responsibility simple because another individual is not strictly a "student" or a "client.")

The principles in this manual are organized into several sections as a result of editorial judgment. Therefore, principles discussed in one section may also apply to other sections. Every school psychologist, regardless of position (e.g. practitioner, researcher, university trainer, supervisor, state or federal consultant, administrator of psychological services) or setting (e.g. public or private school, community agency, hospital, university, private practice) should reflect upon the theme represented in each ethical principle to determine its application to her/his individual situation. For example, although a given principle may specifically discuss responsibilities towards "clients," the intent is that the standard would also apply to supervisees, trainees, and research participants. At times, the *Ethics* may require a higher standard of behavior than the prevailing policies and pertinent laws. Under such conditions, members should adhere to the *Ethics.* Ethical behavior may occasionally be forbidden by policy or law, in which case members are expected to declare their dilemma and work to bring the discrepant regulations into compliance with the *Ethics.* To obtain additional assistance in applying these principles to your particular setting, consult with experienced school psychologists, and seek advice from the National Association of School Psychologists or your state school psychology association.

II. PROFESSIONAL COMPETENCY

A. General

1. School psychologists recognize the strengths and limitations of their training and experience, engaging only in practices for which they are qualified. They must continually seek additional training with the welfare of children, families, the school community, and their trainees or supervisees in mind.
2. Competence levels, education, training and experience are accurately represented to clients in a professional manner.
3. School psychologists do not use affiliations with persons, associations, or institutions to imply a level of professional competence which exceeds that which has actually been achieved.
4. School psychologists are aware of their limitations and enlist the assistance of other specialists in supervisory, consultative or referral roles as appropriate in providing services.
5. School psychologists engage in continuing professional development. They remain current regarding developments in research, training, and professional practices that benefit children, families, and schools.
6. School psychologists refrain from any activity in which their personal problems or conflicts may interfere with professional effectiveness. Competent assistance is

sought to alleviate conflicts in professional relationships.

7. School psychologists know the *Principles for Professional Ethics* and thoughtfully apply them to situations within their employment setting. Ignorance or misapplication of an ethical principle is not a reasonable defense against a charge of unethical behavior.

III. PROFESSIONAL RELATIONSHIPS AND RESPONSIBILITIES

A. General

1. School psychologists are committed to the application of their professional expertise for the purpose of promoting improvement in the quality of life for students, their families, and the school community. This objective is pursued in ways that protect the dignity and rights of those involved. School psychologists accept responsibility for the appropriateness of their treatments and professional practices.
2. School psychologists respect all persons and are sensitive to physical, mental, emotional, political, economic, social, cultural, ethnic, and racial characteristics, gender, and sexual orientation, and religion.
3. School psychologists are responsible for the direction and nature of their personal loyalties or objectives. When these commitments may influence a professional relationship, the school psychologist informs all concerned persons of relevant issues in advance.
4. School psychologist in all settings maintain professional relationships with students, parents, the school and community. Consequently, parents and students are to be fully informed about all relevant aspects of school psychological services in advance. The explanation should take into account language and cultural differences, cognitive capabilities, developmental level, and age so that the explanation may be understood by the student, parent, or guardian.
5. School psychologists shall attempt to resolve situations in which there are divided or conflicting interests in a manner which is mutually beneficial and protects the rights of all parties involved.
6. School psychologists do not exploit clients through professional relationships nor condone these actions in their colleagues. All individuals, including students, clients, employees, colleagues, and research participants, will not be exposed to deliberate comments, gestures, or physical contacts of a sexual nature. School psychologists do not harass or demean others based on personal characteristics. School psychologists do not engage in sexual relationships with their students, supervisees, trainees, or past or present clients.
7. Personal and business relations with students/clients or their parents may cloud one's judgment. School psychologists are aware of these situations and avoid them whenever possible.
8. School psychologists attempt to resolve suspected detrimental or unethical practices on an informal level. If informal efforts are not productive, the appropriate professional organization is contacted for assistance, and procedures

established for questioning ethical practice are followed:

a. The filing of an ethical complaint is a serious matter. It is intended to improve the behavior of a colleague that is harmful to the profession and/or the public. Therefore, school psychologists make every effort to discuss the ethical principles with other professionals who may be in violation.
b. School psychologists enter into this process thoughtfully and with concern for the well-being of all parties involved. They do not file or encourage the filing of an ethics complaint that is frivolous or motivated by revenge.
c. Some situations may be particularly difficult to analyze from an ethical perspective. School psychologists consult ethical standards from related fields and seek assistance from knowledgeable, experienced school psychologists, and relevant state/national associations to ascertain an appropriate course of action.
d. School psychologists document specific instances of suspected ethical violations (date, time, relevant details) as well as attempts to resolve these violations.

9. School psychologists respect the confidentiality of information obtained during their professional work. Information is revealed only with the informed consent of the client, or the client's parent or legal guardian, except in those situations in which failure to release information would result in clear danger to the client or others. Obsolete information will be shredded or otherwise destroyed before placement in recycling bins or trash receptacles.
10. School psychologists discuss confidential information only for professional purposes and only with persons who have a legitimate need to know. Confidential materials should be shredded before disposal.
11. School psychologists inform their clients of the limits of confidentiality.

B. Students

1. School psychologists understand the intimate nature of consultation, assessment, and direct service. They engage only in professional practices which maintain the dignity and integrity of students and other clients.
2. School psychologists explain important aspects of their professional relationships with students and clients in a clear, understandable manner. The explanation includes the reason why services were requested, who will receive information about the services provided, and the possible outcomes.
3. When a child initiates services, school psychologists understand their obligation to respect the rights of a student or client to initiate, participate in, or discontinue services voluntarily. When another party initiates services, the school psychologist will make every effort to secure voluntary participation of the child/student.
4. Recommendations for program changes or additional service will be discussed, including any alternatives which may be available.

C. Parents, Legal Guardians, and Appointed Surrogates

1. School psychologists explain all services to parents in a clear, understandable manner. They strive to propose a set of options which take into account the values and capabilities of each parent. Service provision by interns, practicum students, etc. should be explained and agreed to in advance.
2. School psychologists recognize the importance of parental support and seek to obtain this by assuring that there is direct parent contact prior to seeing the student/client on an on-going basis. (Emergencies and "drop-in" self-referrals will require parental notification as soon as possible. The age and circumstances under which students/clients may seek services without parental consent varies greatly; be certain to comply with III-E-5.) They secure continuing parental involvement by a frank and prompt reporting to the parent of findings and progress that conforms to the limits of previously determined confidentiality.
3. School psychologists encourage and promote parental participation in designing services provided to their children. When appropriate, this includes linking interventions between the school and the home, tailoring parental involvement to the skills of the family, and helping parents to gain the skills needed to help their children.
4. School psychologists respect the wishes of parents who object to school psychological services and attempt to guide parents to alternative community resources.
5. School psychologists discuss recommendations and plans for assisting the student/client with the parent. The discussion includes alternatives associated with each set of plans, showing respect for the ethnic/cultural values of the family. The parents are advised as to sources of help available at school and in the community.
6. School psychologists discuss the rights of parents and students regarding creation, modification, storage, and disposal of confidential materials that will result from the provision of school psychological services.

D. Service Delivery

1. School psychologists are knowledgeable of the organization, philosophy, goals, objectives, and methodologies of the setting in which they are employed.
2. School psychologists recognize that an understanding of the goals, processes and legal requirements of their particular workplace is essential for effective functioning within that setting.
3. School psychologists attempt to become integral members of the client systems to which they are assigned. They establish clear roles for themselves within that system and the local community.
4. School psychologists who provide services to several different groups may encounter situations when loyalties are conflicted. As much as possible, the stance of the school psychologist is made known in advance to all parties to prevent misunderstandings.
5. School psychologists promote changes in their employing agencies that will benefit their clients.

E. Community

1. School psychologists are also citizens, thereby accepting the same

responsibilities and duties as any member of society. They are free to pursue individual interests, except to the degree that these compromise professional responsibilities.

2. School psychologists may act as individual citizens to bring about social change in a lawful manner. Individual actions should not be presented as, nor suggestive of representing the field of school psychology or the Association.
3. As employees or employers, in public or private domains, school psychologists do not engage in or condone practices that discriminate against clients based on race, handicap, age, gender, sexual orientation, religion, national origin, economic status, or native language.
4. School psychologists avoid any action that could violate or diminish the civil and legal rights of clients.
5. School psychologists adhere to federal, state, and local laws and ordinances governing their practice. If regulations conflict with ethical guidelines, school psychologists seek to resolve such conflict through positive, respected, and legal channels.

F. Related Professions

1. To best meet the needs of students and clients, school psychologists cooperate with other professional disciplines in relationships based on mutual respect.
2. School psychologists recognize the competence of other professionals. They encourage and support the use of all resources to best serve the interests of students and clients.
3. School psychologists strive to explain their field and their professional competencies, including roles, assignments, and working relationships to other professionals.
4. School psychologists cooperate and coordinate with other professionals and agencies with the rights and needs of their client in mind. If a client is receiving similar services from another professional, school psychologists promote coordination of services.
5. The student or client is referred to another professional for services when a condition is identified which is outside the professional competencies or scope of the school psychologist.
6. When transferring the intervention responsibility for a student or client to another professional, school psychologist ensure that all relevant and appropriate individuals, including the student/client when appropriate, are notified of the change and reasons for the change.
7. When school psychologists suspect the existence of detrimental or unethical practices, the appropriate professional organization is contacted for assistance in determining the procedures established by that profession for examining the practice in question.

G. Other School Psychologists

1. School psychologists who employ, supervise, or train other professionals accept the obligation to provide continuing professional development. They also provide appropriate working conditions, fair and timely evaluation, and constructive consultation.
2. School psychologists who supervise interns are responsible for all professional practices of the supervisees. They assure the students/clients and the profession

that the intern is adequately supervised.

IV. PROFESSIONAL PRACTICES—PUBLIC AND PRIVATE SETTINGS

A. Advocacy

1. School psychologists consider the students or clients to be their primary responsibility, acting as advocates for their rights and welfare. When choosing a course of action, school psychologists take into account the rights of each individual involved and the duties of the school personnel.
2. School psychologists' concerns for protecting the rights and welfare of students are communicated to the school administration and staff, as the top priority in determining services.

B. Assessment and Intervention

1. School psychologists will maintain the highest standard for educational and psychological assessment.
   a. In conducting psychological, educational, or behavioral evaluations, or in providing therapy, counseling, or consultation services, due consideration will be given to individual integrity and individual differences.
   b. School psychologists respect differences in age, gender, sexual orientation, and socioeconomic,cultural, and ethnic backgrounds. They select and use appropriate assessment or treatment procedures, techniques, and strategies.
2. School psychologists are knowledgeable about the validity and reliability of their instruments and techniques, choosing those that have up-to-date standardization data and are applicable and appropriate for the benefit of the student/client.
3. School psychologists combine observations, background information, and information from other disciplines in order to reach comprehensive conclusions.
4. School psychologists use assessment techniques, counseling and therapy procedures, consultation techniques, and other direct service methods that the profession considers to be responsible, research-based practice.
5. School psychologists do not condone the use of psychological or educational assessment techniques, or the mis-use of the information these techniques provide, by unqualified persons in any way, including teaching, sponsorship, or supervision.
6. School psychologists develop interventions which are appropriate to the presenting problems and are consistent with data collected. They modify or terminate the treatment plan when the data indicate the plan is not achieving the desired goals.

C. Use of Materials and Technology

1. School psychologists maintain test security, preventing the release of underlying principles and specific content that would undermine the use of the device. School psychologists are responsible for the security requirements specific to each instrument they use.
2. School psychologists uphold copyright laws. Permission is obtained from authors to reproduce non-copyrighted published instruments.
3. School psychologists will obtain written prior consent or else remove identifying data presented in public lectures or publications.

4. When producing materials for consultation, intervention, teaching, public lectures, or publication, school psychologists acknowledge sources and assign credit to those whose ideas are reflected in the product. Recognition is given in proportion to the contribution. Plagiarism of ideas or product is a violation of professional ethics.
5. School psychologists do not promote or encourage inappropriate use of computer generated test analyses or reports. For example, a school psychologist would not offer an unedited computer report as one's own writing, nor use a computer scoring system for tests in which one has no training. They select scoring and interpretation services on the basis of accuracy and professional alignment with the underlying decision rules.
6. School psychologists maintain full responsibility for any technological services used. All ethical and legal principles regarding confidentiality, privacy, and responsibility for decisions apply to the school psychologist and cannot be transferred to equipment, software companies, or data processing departments.
7. Technological devices should be used to improve the quality of client services. School psychologists will resist applications of technology that ultimately reduce the quality of service.
8. To ensure confidentiality, student/client records are not transmitted electronically without a guarantee of privacy. (For example, a receiving FAX machine must be in a secure location and operated by employees cleared to work with confidential files; e-mail messages must be encrypted or else stripped of all information that identifies the student/client.)

D. Research, Publication and Presentation

1. When designing and implementing research in schools, school psychologists choose topics, and employ research methodology, subject selection techniques, data gathering methods, and analysis and reporting techniques which are grounded in sound research practice.
2. Prior to initiating research, school psychologists working in agencies without review committees should have at least one other colleague, preferably a school psychologist, review the proposal.
3. In publishing reports of their research, school psychologists provide discussion of limitations of their data and acknowledge existence of disconfirming data, as well as alternate hypotheses and explanations of their findings.
4. School psychologists take particular care with information presented through various impersonal media (e.g., radio, television, public lectures, articles in the popular press, promotional materials.) Recipients should be informed that the information does not result from or substitute for a professional consultation. The information should be based on research and experience within the school psychologist's recognizedl sphere of competence. The statements should be consistent with these ethical principles, and should not mistakenly represent the field of school psychology or the Association.

E. Reporting Data and Conference Results

1. School psychologists ascertain that student or client information reaches only authorized persons.

a. The information is adequately interpreted so that the recipient can better help the student or client.
b. The school psychologist assists agency recipients to establish procedures to properly safeguard the confidential material.
2. School psychologists communicate findings and recommendations in language readily understood by the intended recipient. These communications describe potential consequences associated with the proposals.
3. School psychologists prepare written reports in such form and style that the recipient of the report will be able to assist the student or client. Reports should emphasize recommendations and interpretations; unedited computer-generated reports, preprinted "check-off" or "fill-in-the-blank reports, and reports which present only test scores or brief narratives describing a test are seldom useful. Reports should include an appraisal of the degree of confidence which could be assigned to the information. Alterations of reports previously released should be done only by the original author.
4. School psychologists review all of their written documents for accuracy, signing them only when correct. Interns and practicum students are clearly identified as such, and their work is co-signed by the supervising school psychologist.
5. School psychologists comply with all laws, regulations and policies pertaining to the adequate storage and disposal of records to maintain appropriate confidentiality of information.

V. PROFESSIONAL PRACTICES—PRIVATE SETTINGS

A. Relationship with School Districts
1. Some school psychologists are employed in both the public and private sectors, and in so doing, may create a conflict of interest. School psychologist operating in both sectors recognize the importance of ethical standards, the separation of roles, and take full responsibility for protecting and completing informing the consumer of all potential concerns.
2. A school psychologist, while working in the private sector, may not accept any form of remuneration from clients who are entitled to the same service provided by the same school psychologist while working in the public sector. This includes students who attend the non-public schools within the school psychologist's public school assignment area.
3. School psychologists in private practice have an obligation to inform parents of any free school psychological services available from the public or private schools prior to delivering such services for remuneration.
4. School psychologists working in both public and private sectors will conduct all private practice outside of the hours of contracted public employment.
5. School psychologists engaged in private practice do not use tests, materials, equipment, facilities, secretarial assistance, or other services belonging to the public sector employer, unless approved in advance through a written agreement.

B. Service Delivery
   1. School psychologists conclude a financial agreement in advance of service delivery.
      a. School psychologists ensure to the best of their ability that the client clearly understands the agreement.
      b. School psychologists neither given nor receive any remuneration for referring clients for professional services.
   2. School psychologists in private practice adhere to the conditions of a contract until service thereunder has been performed, the contract has been terminated by mutual consent, or the contract has otherwise been legally terminated.
   3. School psychologists in private practice prevent misunderstandings resulting from their recommendations, advice, or information. Most often, direct consultation between the school psychologist in private practice and the school psychologist responsible for the student in the public sector will resolve minor differences of opinion without unnecessarily confusing the parents, yet keep the best interests of the student or client in mind.
   4. Personal diagnosis and therapy are not given by means of public lectures, newspaper columns, magazine articles, radio and television programs, or mail. Any information shared through mass media activities is general in nature and is openly declared to be so.

C. Announcements/Advertising
   1. Appropriate announcement of services, advertising and public media statements may be necessary for school psychologists in private practice. Accurate representations of training, experience, services provided and affiliation are done in a restrained manner. Public statements must be made on sound and accepted theory, research, and practice.
   2. Listings in telephone directories are limited to the following: name/names, highest relevant degree, state certification/licensure status, national certification status, address, telephone number, brief identification of major area of practice, office hours, appropriate fee information, foreign languages spoken, policy regarding third party payments, and license number.
   3. Announcements of services by school psychologists in private practice are made in a formal, professional manner, using the guidelines of section 2, above. Clear statements of purposes with unequivocal descriptions of the experiences to be provided are given. Education, training, and experience of all staff members are appropriately specified.
   4. School psychologists in private practice may use brochures in the announcement of services. The brochures may be sent to professional persons, schools, business firms, governmental agencies and other similar organizations.
   5. Announcements and advertisements of the availability of publications, products, and services for sale are professional and factual.
   6. School psychologists in private practice do not directly solicit clients for individual diagnosis or therapy.
   7. School psychologists do not compensate in any manner a representative of the press, radio or television in return for personal professional publicity in a news item.

Appendix B

*ETHICAL PRINCIPLES OF PSYCHOLOGISTS AND CODE OF CONDUCT**

INTRODUCTION

The American Psychological Association's (APA's) Ethical Principles of Psychologists and Code of Conduct (hereinafter referred to as the Ethics Code) consists of an Introduction, a Preamble, six General Principles (A–F), and specific Ethical Standards. The Introduction discusses the intent, organization, procedural considerations, and scope of application of the Ethics Code. The Preamble and General Principles are *aspirational* goals to guide psychologists toward the highest ideals of psychology. Although the Preamble and General Principles are not themselves enforceable rules, they should be considered by psychologists in arriving at an ethical course of action and may be considered by ethics bodies in interpreting the Ethical Standards. The Ethical Standards set forth *enforceable* rules for conduct as psychologists. Most of the Ethical Standards are written broadly, in order to apply to psychologists in varied roles, although the application of an Ethical Standard may vary depending on the context. The Ethical Standards are not exhaustive. The fact that a given conduct is not specifically addressed by the Ethics Code does not mean that it is necessarily either ethical or unethical.

Membership in the APA commits members to adhere to the APA Ethics Code and to the rules and procedures used to implement it. Psychologists and students, whether or not they are APA members, should be aware that the Ethics Code may be applied to them by state psychology boards, courts, or other public bodies.

This Ethics Code applies only to psychologists' work-related activities, that is, activities that are part of the psychologists' scientific and professional functions or that are psychological in nature. It includes the clinical or counseling practice of psychology, research, teaching, supervision of trainees, development of assessment instruments, conducting assessments, educational counseling, organizational consulting, social intervention, administration, and other activities as well. These work-related activities can be distinguished from the purely private conduct of a psychologist, which ordinarily is not within the purview of the Ethics Code.

The Ethics Code is intended to provide standards of professional conduct that can be applied by the APA and by other bodies that choose to adopt them. Whether or not a psychologist has violated the Ethics Code does not by itself determine whether he or she is legally liable in a court action, whether a contract is enforceable, or whether other legal consequences occur. These results are based on legal rather than ethical rules. However, compliance with or violation of the Ethics Code may be admissible as evidence in some legal proceedings, depending on the circumstances.

In the process of making decisions regarding their professional behavior, psychologists must consider this Ethics Code, in addition to applicable laws and psychology board regulations. If the Ethics Code establishes a higher standard of conduct than is required by law, psychologists must meet the higher ethical standard. If the Ethics Code standard appears to conflict with the requirements of law, then psychologists make known their commitment to the Ethics Code and take steps to resolve the conflict in a responsible manner. If neither law nor the Ethics Code resolves an issue, psychologists should consider other professional materials and the dictates of their own conscience, as well as seek consultation with others within the field when this is practical.

The procedures for filing, investigating, and resolving complaints of unethical conduct are described in the current Rules and Procedures of the APA Ethics Committee. The actions that APA may take for violations of the Ethics Code include actions such as reprimand, censure, termination of APA membership, and referral of the matter to other bodies. Complainants who seek remedies such as monetary damages in alleging ethical violations by a psychologist must resort to private negotiation, administrative bodies, or the courts. Actions that violate the Ethics Code may lead to the imposition of sanctions on a psychologist by bodies other than APA, including state psychological associations, other professional groups, psychology boards, other state or federal agencies, and payors for health services. In addition to actions for violation of the Ethics Code, the APA Bylaws provide that APA may take action against a member after his or her conviction of a felony, expulsion or suspension from an affiliated state psychological association, or suspension or loss of licensure.

PREAMBLE

Psychologists work to develop a valid and reliable body of scientific knowledge based on research. They may apply that knowledge to human behavior in a variety of contexts. In doing so, they perform many roles, such as researcher, educator, diagnostician, therapist, supervisor, consultant, administrator, social interventionist, and expert witness. Their goal is to broaden knowledge of behavior and, where appropriate, to apply it pragmatically to improve the condition of both the individual and society. Psychologists respect the central importance of freedom of inquiry and expression in research, teaching, and publication. They also strive to help the public in developing informed judgments and choices concerning human behavior. This Ethics Code provides a common set of values upon which psychologists build their professional and scientific work.

This Code is intended to provide both the general principles and the decision rules to cover most situations encountered by psychologists. It has as its primary goal the welfare and protection of the individuals and groups with whom psychologists work. It is the individual responsibility of each psychologist to aspire to the highest possible standards of conduct. Psychologists respect and protect human and civil rights, and do not knowingly participate in or condone unfair discriminatory practices.

The development of a dynamic set of ethical standards for a psychologist's work-related conduct requires a personal commitment to a lifelong effort to act ethically; to encourage ethical behavior by students, supervisees, employees, and colleagues, as appropriate; and to consult with others, as needed, concerning ethical problems. Each psychologist supplements, but does not violate, the Ethics Code's values and rules on the basis of guidance drawn from personal values, culture, and experience.

GENERAL PRINCIPLES

Principle A: Competence

Psychologists strive to maintain high standards of competence in their work. They recognize the boundaries of their particular competencies and the limitations of their expertise. They provide only those services and use only those techniques for which they are qualified by education, training, or experience. Psychologists are cognizant of the fact that the competencies required in serving, teaching, and/or studying groups of people vary with the distinctive characteristics of those groups. In those areas in which recognized professional standards do not yet exist, psychologists exercise careful judgment and take appropriate precautions to protect the welfare of those with whom they work. They maintain knowledge of relevant scientific and professional information related to the services they render, and they recognize the need for ongoing education. Psychologists make appropriate use of scientific, professional, technical, and administrative resources.

Principle B: Integrity

Psychologists seek to promote integrity in the science, teaching, and practice of psychology. In these activities psychologists are honest, fair, and respectful of others. In describing or reporting their qualifications, services, products, fees, research, or teaching, they do not make statements that are false, misleading, or deceptive. Psychologists strive to be aware of their own belief systems, values, needs, and limitations and the effect of these on their work. To the extent feasible, they attempt to clarify for relevant parties the roles they are performing and to function appropriately in accordance with those roles. Psychologists avoid improper and potentially harmful dual relationships.

Principle C: Professional and Scientific Responsibility

Psychologists uphold professional standards of conduct, clarify their professional roles and obligations, accept appropriate responsibility for their behavior, and adapt their methods to the needs of different populations. Psychologists consult with, refer to, or cooperate with other professionals and institutions to the extent needed to serve the best interests of their patients, clients, or other recipients of their services. Psychologists' moral standards and conduct are personal matters to the same degree as is true for any other person, except as psychologists' conduct may compromise their professional responsibilities or reduce the public's trust in psychology and psychologists. Psychologists are concerned about the ethical compliance of their colleagues' scientific and professional conduct. When appropriate, they consult with colleagues in order to prevent or avoid unethical conduct.

Principle D: Respect for People's Rights and Dignity

Psychologists accord appropriate respect to the fundamental rights, dignity, and worth of all people. They respect the rights of individuals to privacy, confidentiality, self-determination, and autonomy, mindful that legal and other obligations may lead to inconsistency and conflict with the exercise of these rights. Psychologists are aware of cultural, individual, and role differences, including those due to age, gender, race, ethnicity, national origin, religion, sexual orientation, disability, language, and socioeconomic status. Psychologists try to eliminate the effect on their work of biases on those factors, and they do not knowingly participate in or condone unfair discriminatory practices.

Principle E: Concern for Others' Welfare

Psychologists seek to contribute to the welfare of those with whom they interact professionally. In their professional actions, psychologists weigh the welfare and rights of their patients or clients, students, supervisees, human research participants, and other affected persons, and the welfare of animal subjects of research. When conflicts occur among psychologists' obligations or concerns, they attempt to resolve these conflicts and to perform their roles in a responsible fashion that avoids or minimizes harm. Psychologists are sensitive to real and ascribed differences in power between themselves and others, and they do not exploit or mislead other people during or after professional relationships.

Principle F: Social Responsibility

Psychologists are aware of their professional and scientific responsibilities to the community and the society in which they work and live. They apply and make public their knowledge of psychology in order to contribute to human welfare. Psychologists are concerned about and work to mitigate the causes of human suffering. When undertaking research, they strive to advance human welfare and the science of psychology. Psychologists try to avoid misuse of their work. Psychologists comply with the law and encourage the development of law and social policy that serve the interests of their patients and clients and the public. They are encouraged to contribute a portion of their professional time for little or no personal advantage.

ETHICAL STANDARDS

1. General Standards

These General Standards are potentially applicable to the professional and scientific activities of all psychologists.

1.01 Applicability of the Ethics Code

The activity of a psychologist subject to the Ethics Code may be reviewed under these Ethical Standards only if the activity is part of his or her work-related functions or the activity is psychological in nature. Personal activities having no connection to or effect on psychological roles are not subject to the Ethics Code.

1.02 Relationship of Ethics and Law

If psychologists' ethical responsibilities conflict with law, psychologists make known their commitment to the Ethics Code and take steps to resolve the conflict in a responsible manner.

1.03 Professional and Scientific Relationship

Psychologists provide diagnostic, therapeutic, teaching, research, supervisory, consultative, or other psychological services only in the context of a defined professional or scientific relationship or role. (See also Standards 2.01, Evaluation, Diagnosis, and Interventions in Professional Context, and 7.02, Forensic Assessments.)

1.04 Boundaries of Competence

(a) Psychologists provide services, teach, and conduct research only within the boundaries of their competence, based on their education, training, supervised experience, or appropriate professional experience.

(b) Psychologists provide services, teach, or conduct research in new areas or involving new techniques only after first undertaking appropriate study, training, supervision, and/or consultation from persons who are competent in those areas or techniques.

(c) In those emerging areas in which generally recognized standards for preparatory training do not yet exist, psychologists nevertheless take reasonable steps to ensure the competence of their work and to protect patients, clients, students, research participants, and others from harm.

1.05 Maintaining Expertise

Psychologists who engage in assessment, therapy, teaching, research, organizational consulting, or other professional activities maintain a reasonable level of awareness of current scientific and professional information in their fields of activity, and undertake ongoing efforts to maintain competence in the skills they use.

1.06 Basis for Scientific and Professional Judgments

Psychologists rely on scientifically and professionally derived knowledge when making scientific or professional judgments or when engaging in scholarly or professional endeavors.

1.07 Describing the Nature and Results of Psychological Services

(a) When psychologists provide assessment, evaluation, treatment, counseling, supervision, teaching, consultation, research, or other psychological services to an individual, a group, or an organization, they provide, using language that is reasonably understandable to the recipient of those services, appropriate information beforehand about the nature of such services and appropriate information later about results and conclusions. (See also Standard 2.09, Explaining Assessment Results.)

(b) If psychologists will be precluded by law or by organizational roles from providing such information to particular individuals or groups, they so inform those individuals or groups at the outset of the service.

1.08 Human Differences

Where differences of age, gender, race, ethnicity, national origin, religion, sexual orientation, disability, language, or socioeconomic status significantly affect psychologists' work concerning particular individuals or groups, psychologists obtain the training, experience, consultation, or supervision necessary to ensure the competence of their services, or they make appropriate referrals.

1.09 Respecting Others

In their work-related activities, psychologists respect the rights of others to hold values, attitudes, and opinions that differ from their own.

1.10 Nondiscrimination

In their work-related activities, psychologists do not engage in unfair discrimination based on age, gender, race, ethnicity, national origin, religion, sexual orientation, disability, socioeconomic status, or any basis proscribed by law.

1.11 Sexual Harassment

(a) Psychologists do not engage in sexual harassment. Sexual harassment is sexual solicitation, physical advances, or verbal or nonverbal conduct that is sexual in nature, that occurs in connection with the psychologist's activities or roles as a psychologist, and that either: (1) is unwelcome, is offensive, or creates a hostile workplace environment, and the psychologist knows or is told this; or (2) is sufficiently severe or intense to be abusive to a reasonable person in the context. Sexual harassment can consist of a single intense or severe act or of multiple persistent or pervasive acts.

(b) Psychologists accord sexual-harassment complainants and respondents dignity and respect. Psychologists do not participate in denying a person academic admittance or advancement, employment, tenure, or promotion, based solely upon their having made, or their being the subject of, sexual-harassment charges. This does not preclude taking action based upon the outcome of such proceedings or consideration of other appropriate information.

1.12 Other Harassment

Psychologists do not knowingly engage in behavior that is harassing or demeaning to persons with whom they interact in their work based on factors such as those persons' age, gender, race, ethnicity, national origin, religion, sexual orientation, disability, language, or socioeconomic status.

1.13 Personal Problems and Conflicts

(a) Psychologists recognize that their personal problems and conflicts may interfere with their effectiveness. Accordingly, they refrain from undertaking an activity when they know or should know that their personal problems are likely to lead to harm to a patient, client, colleague, student, research participant, or other person to whom they may owe a professional or scientific obligation.

(b) In addition, psychologists have an obligation to be alert to signs of, and to obtain assistance for, their personal problems at an early stage, in order to prevent significantly impaired performance.

(c) When psychologists become aware of personal problems that may interfere with their performing work-related duties adequately, they take appropriate measures, such as obtaining professional consultation or assistance, and determine whether they should limit, suspend, or terminate their work-related duties.

1.14 Avoiding Harm

Psychologists take reasonable steps to avoid harming their patients or clients, research participants, students, and others with whom they work, and to minimize harm where it is foreseeable and unavoidable.

1.15 Misuse of Psychologists' Influence

Because psychologists' scientific and professional judgments and actions may affect the lives of others, they are alert to and guard against personal, financial, social, organizational, or political factors that might lead to misuse of their influence.

1.16 Misuse of Psychologists' Work

(a) Psychologists do not participate in activities in which it appears likely that their skills or data will be misused by others, unless corrective mechanisms are available. (See also Standard 7.04, Truthfulness and Candor.)

(b) If psychologists learn of misuse or misrepresentation of their work, they take reasonable steps to correct or minimize the misuse or misrepresentation.

1.17 Multiple Relationships

(a) In many communities and situations, it may not be feasible or reasonable for psychologists to avoid social or other nonprofessional contacts with persons such as patients, clients, students, supervisees, or research participants. Psychologists must always be sensitive to the potential harmful effects of other contacts on their work and on those persons with whom they deal. A psychologist refrains from entering into or promising another personal, scientific, professional, financial, or other relationship with such persons if it appears likely that such a relationship reasonably might impair the psychologist's objectivity or otherwise interfere with the psychologist's effectively performing his or her functions as a psychologist, or might harm or exploit the other party.

(b) Likewise, whenever feasible, a psychologist refrains from taking on professional or scientific obligations when preexisting relationships would create a risk of such harm.

(c) If a psychologist finds that, due to unforeseen factors, a potentially harmful multiple relationship has arisen, the psychologist attempts to resolve it with due regard for the best interests of the affected person and maximal compliance with the Ethics Code.

1.18 Barter (With Patients or Clients)

Psychologists ordinarily refrain from accepting goods, services, or other nonmonetary remuneration from patients or clients in return for psychological services because such arrangements create inherent potential for conflicts, exploitation, and distortion of the professional relationship. A psychologist may participate in bartering *only* if (1) it is not clinically contraindicated, *and* (2) the relationship is not exploitative. (See also Standards 1.17, Multiple Relationships, and 1.25, Fees and Financial Arrangements.)

1.19 Exploitative Relationships

(a) Psychologists do not exploit persons over whom they have supervisory, evaluative, or other authority such as students, supervisees, employees, research participants, and clients or patients. (See also Standards 4.05–4.07 regarding sexual involvement with clients or patients.)

(b) Psychologists do not engage in sexual relationships with students or supervisees in training over whom the psychologist has evaluative or direct authority, because such relationships are so likely to impair judgment or be exploitative.

1.20 Consultations and Referrals

(a) Psychologists arrange for appropriate consultations and referrals based principally on the best interests of their patients or clients, with appropriate consent, and subject to other relevant considerations, including applicable law and contractual obligations. (See also Standards 5.01, Discussing the Limits of Confidentiality, and 5.06, Consultations.)

(b) When indicated and professionally appropriate, psychologists cooperate with other professionals in order to serve their patients or clients effectively and appropriately.

(c) Psychologists' referral practices are consistent with law.

1.21 Third-Party Requests for Services

(a) When a psychologist agrees to provide services to a person or entity at the request of a third party, the psychologist clarifies to the extent feasible, at the outset of the service, the nature of the relationship with each party. This clarification includes the role of the psychologist (such as therapist, organizational consultant, diagnostician, or expert witness), the probable uses of the services provided or the information obtained, and the fact that there may be limits to confidentiality.

(b) If there is a foreseeable risk of the psychologist's being called upon to perform conflicting roles because of the involvement of a third party, the psychologist clarifies the nature and direction of his or her responsibilities, keeps all parties appropriately informed as matters develop, and resolves the situation in accordance with this Ethics Code.

1.22 Delegation to and Supervision of Subordinates

(a) Psychologists delegate to their employees, supervisees, and research assistants only those responsibilities that such persons can reasonably be expected to perform competently, on the basis of their education, training, or experience, either independently or with the level of supervision being provided.

(b) Psychologists provide proper training and supervision to their employees or supervisees and take reasonable steps to see that such persons perform services responsibly, competently, and ethically.

(c) If institutional policies, procedures, or practices prevent fulfillment of this obligation, psychologists attempt to modify their role or to correct the situation to the extent feasible.

1.23 Documentation of Professional and Scientific Work

(a) Psychologists appropriately document their professional and scientific work in order to facilitate provision of services later by them or by other professionals, to ensure accountability, and to meet other requirements of institutions or the law.

(b) When psychologists have reason to believe that records of their professional services will be used in legal proceedings involving recipients of or participants in their work, they have a responsibility to create and maintain documentation in the kind of detail and quality that would be consistent with reasonable scrutiny in an adjudicative forum. (See also Standard 7.01, Professionalism, under Forensic Activities.)

1.24 Records and Data

Psychologists create, maintain, disseminate, store, retain, and dispose of records and data relating to their research, practice, and other work in accordance with law and in a manner that permits compliance with the requirements of this Ethics Code. (See also Standard 5.04, Maintenance of Records.)

1.25 Fees and Financial Arrangements

(a) As early as is feasible in a professional or scientific relationship, the psychologist and the patient, client, or other appropriate recipient of psychological services reach an agreement specifying the compensation and the billing arrangements.

(b) Psychologists do not exploit recipients of services or payors with respect to fees.

(c) Psychologists' fee practices are consistent with law.

(d) Psychologists do not misrepresent their fees.

(e) If limitations to services can be anticipated because of limitations in financing, this is discussed with the patient, client, or other appropriate recipient of services as early as is feasible. (See also Standard 4.08, Interruption of Services.)

(f) If the patient, client, or other recipient of services does not pay for services as agreed, and if the psychologist wishes to use collection agencies or legal measures to collect the fees, the psychologist first informs the person that such measures will be taken and provides that person an opportunity to make prompt payment. (See also Standard 5.11, Withholding Records for Nonpayment.)

1.26 Accuracy in Reports to Payors and Funding Sources

In their reports to payors for services or sources of research funding, psychologists accurately state the nature of the research or service provided, the fees or charges, and where applicable, the identity of the provider, the findings, and the diagnosis. (See also Standard 5.05, Disclosures.)

1.27 Referrals and Fees

When a psychologist pays, receives payment from, or divides fees with another professional other than in an employer-employee relationship, the payment to each is based on the services (clinical, consultative, administrative, or other) provided and is not based on the referral itself.

2. Evaluation, Assessment, or Intervention

2.01 Evaluation, Diagnosis, and Interventions in Professional Context

(a) Psychologists perform evaluations, diagnostic services, or interventions only within the context of a defined professional relationship. (See also Standard 1.03, Professional and Scientific Relationship.)

(b) Psychologists' assessments, recommendations, reports, and psychological diagnostic or evaluative statements are based on information and techniques (including personal interviews of the individual when appropriate) sufficient to provide appropriate substantiation for their findings. (See also Standard 7.02, Forensic Assessments.)

2.02 Competence and Appropriate Use of Assessments and Interventions

(a) Psychologists who develop, administer, score, interpret, or use psychological assessment techniques, interviews, tests, or instruments do so in a manner and for purposes that are appropriate in light of the research on or evidence of the usefulness and proper application of the techniques.

(b) Psychologists refrain from misuse of assessment techniques, interventions, results, and interpretations and take reasonable steps to prevent others from misusing the information these techniques provide. This includes refraining from releasing raw test results or raw data to persons, other than to patients or clients as appropriate, who are not qualified to use such information. (See also Standards 1.02, Relationship of Ethics and Law, and 1.04, Boundaries of Competence.)

2.03 Test Construction

Psychologists who develop and conduct research with tests and other assessment techniques use scientific procedures and current professional knowledge for test design, standardization, validation, reduction or elimination of bias, and recommendations for use.

2.04 Use of Assessment in General and With Special Populations

(a) Psychologists who perform interventions or administer, score, interpret, or use assessment techniques are familiar with the reliability, validation, and related standardization or outcome studies of, and proper applications and uses of, the techniques they use.

(b) Psychologists recognize limits to the certainty with which diagnoses, judgments, or predictions can be made about individuals.

(c) Psychologists attempt to identify situations in which particular interventions or assessment techniques or norms may not be applicable or may require adjustment in administration or interpretation because of factors such as individuals' gender, age, race, ethnicity, national origin, religion, sexual orientation, disability, language, or socioeconomic status.

2.05 Interpreting Assessment Results

When interpreting assessment results, including automated interpretations, psychologists take into account the various test factors and characteristics of the person being assessed that might affect psychologists' judgments or reduce the accuracy of their interpretations. They indicate any significant reservations they have about the accuracy or limitations of their interpretations.

2.06 Unqualified Persons

Psychologists do not promote the use of psychological assessment techniques by unqualified persons. (See also Standard 1.22, Delegation to and Supervision of Subordinates.)

2.07 Obsolete Tests and Outdated Test Results

(a) Psychologists do not base their assessment or intervention decisions or recommendations on data or test results that are outdated for the current purpose.

(b) Similarly, psychologists do not base such decisions or recommendations on tests and measures that are obsolete and not useful for the current purpose.

2.08 Test Scoring and Interpretation Services

(a) Psychologists who offer assessment or scoring procedures to other professionals accurately describe the purpose, norms, validity, reliability, and applications of the procedures and any special qualifications applicable to their use.

(b) Psychologists select scoring and interpretation services (including automated services) on the basis of evidence of the validity of the program and procedures as well as on other appropriate considerations.

(c) Psychologists retain appropriate responsibility for the appropriate application, interpretation, and use of assessment instruments, whether they score and interpret such tests themselves or use automated or other services.

2.09 Explaining Assessment Results

Unless the nature of the relationship is clearly explained to the person being assessed in advance and precludes provision of an explanation of results (such as in some organizational consulting, preemployment or security screenings, and forensic evaluations), psychologists ensure that an explanation of the results is provided using language that is reasonably understandable to the person assessed or to another legally authorized person on behalf of the client. Regardless of whether the scoring and interpretation are done by the psychologist, by assistants, or by automated or other outside services, psychologists take reasonable steps to ensure that appropriate explanations of results are given.

2.10 Maintaining Test Security

Psychologists make reasonable efforts to maintain the integrity and security of tests and other assessment techniques consistent with law, contractual obligations, and in a manner that permits compliance with the requirements of this Ethics Code. (See also Standard 1.02, Relationship of Ethics and Law.)

3. Advertising and Other Public Statements

3.01 Definition of Public Statements

Psychologists comply with this Ethics Code in public statements relating to their professional services, products, or publications or to the field of psychology. Public statements include but are not limited to paid or unpaid advertising, brochures, printed matter, directory listings, personal resumes or curricula vitae, interviews or comments for use in media, statements in legal proceedings, lectures and public oral presentations, and published materials.

3.02 Statements by Others

(a) Psychologists who engage others to create or place public statements that promote their professional practice, products, or activities retain professional responsibility for such statements.

(b) In addition, psychologists make reasonable efforts to prevent others whom they do not control (such as employers, publishers, sponsors, organizational clients, and representatives of the print or broadcast media) from making deceptive statements concerning psychologists' practice or professional or scientific activities.

(c) If psychologists learn of deceptive statements about their work made by others, psychologists make reasonable efforts to correct such statements.

(d) Psychologists do not compensate employees of press, radio, television, or other communication media in return for publicity in a news item.

(e) A paid advertisement relating to the psychologist's activities must be identified as such, unless it is already apparent from the context.

3.03 Avoidance of False or Deceptive Statements

(a) Psychologists do not make public statements that are false, deceptive, misleading, or fraudulent, either because of what they state, convey, or suggest or because of what they omit, concerning their research, practice, or other work activities or those of persons or organizations with which they are affiliated. As examples (and not in limitation) of this standard, psychologists do not make false or deceptive statements concerning (1) their training, experience, or competence; (2) their academic degrees; (3) their credentials (4) their institutional or association affiliations; (5) their services; (6) the scientific or clinical basis for, or results or degree of success of, their services; (7) their fees; or (8) their publications or research findings. (See also Standards 6.15, Deception in Research, and 6.18, Providing Participants With Information About the Study.)

(b) Psychologists claim as credentials for their psychological work, only degrees that (1) were earned from a regionally accredited educational institution or (2) were the basis for psychology licensure by the state in which they practice.

3.04 Media Presentations

When psychologists provide advice or comment by means of public lectures, demonstrations, radio or television programs, prerecorded tapes, printed articles, mailed material, or other media, they ake reasonable precautions to ensure that (1) the statements are based on appropriate psychological literature and practice, (2) the statements are otherwise consistent with this Ethics Code, and (3) the recipients of the information are not encouraged to infer that a relationship has been established with them personally.

3.05 Testimonials

Psychologists do not solicit testimonials from current psychotherapy clients or patients or other persons who because of their particular circumstances are vulnerable to undue influence.

3.06 In-Person Solicitation

Psychologists do not engage, directly or through agents, in uninvited in-person solicitation of business from actual or potential psychotherapy patients or clients or other persons who because of their particular circumstances are vulnerable to undue influence. However, this does not preclude attempting to implement appropriate collateral contacts with significant others for the purpose of benefiting an already engaged therapy patient.

4. Therapy

4.01 Structuring the Relationship

(a) Psychologists discuss with clients or patients as early as is feasible in the therapeutic relationship appropriate issues, such as the nature and anticipated course of therapy, fees, and confidentiality. (See also Standards 1.25, Fees and Financial Arrangements, and 5.01, Discussing the Limits of Confidentiality.)

(b) When the psychologist's work with clients or patients will be supervised, the above discussion includes that fact, and the name of the supervisor, when the supervisor has legal responsibility for the case.

(c) When the therapist is a student intern, the client or patient is informed of that fact.

(d) Psychologists make reasonable efforts to answer patients' questions and to avoid apparent misunderstandings about therapy. Whenever possible, psychologists provide oral and/or written information, using language that is reasonably understandable to the patient or client.

4.02 Informed Consent to Therapy

(a) Psychologists obtain appropriate informed consent to therapy or related procedures, using language that is reasonably understandable to participants. The content of informed consent will vary depending on many circumstances; however, informed consent generally implies that the person (1) has the capacity to consent, (2) has been informed of significant information concerning the procedure, (3) has freely and without undue influence expressed consent, and (4) consent has been appropriately documented.

(b) When persons are legally incapable of giving informed consent, psychologists obtain informed permission from a legally authorized person, if such substitute consent is permitted by law.

(c) In addition, psychologists (1) inform those persons who are legally incapable of giving informed consent about the proposed interventions in a manner commensurate with the persons' psychological capacities, (2) seek their assent to those interventions, and (3) consider such persons' preferences and best interests.

4.03 Couple and Family Relationships

(a) When a psychologist agrees to provide services to several persons who have a relationship (such as husband and wife or parents and children), the psychologist attempts to clarify at the outset (1) which of the individuals are patients or clients and (2) the relationship the psychologists will have with each person. This clarification includes the role of the psychologist and the probable uses of the services provided or the information obtained. (See also Standard 5.01, Discussing the Limits of Confidentiality.)

(b) As soon as it becomes apparent that the psychologist may be called on to perform potentially conflicting roles (such as marital counselor to husband and wife and then witness for one party in a divorce proceeding), the psychologist attempts to clarify and adjust, or withdraw from, roles appropriately. (See also Standard 7.03, Clarification of Role, under Forensic Activities.)

4.04 Providing Mental Health Services to Those Served by Others

In deciding whether to offer or provide services to those already receiving mental health services elsewhere, psychologists carefully consider the treatment issues and the potential patient's or client's welfare. The psychologist discusses these issues with the patient or client, or another legally authorized person on behalf of the client, in order to minimize the risk of confusion and conflict, consulting with the other service providers when appropriate, and proceeds with caution and sensitivity to the therapeutic issues.

4.05 Sexual Intimacies With Current Patients or Clients

Psychologists do not engage in sexual intimacy with current patients or clients.

4.06 Therapy With Former Sexual Partners

Psychologists do not accept as therapy patients or clients persons with whom they have engaged in sexual intimacies.

4.07 Sexual Intimacies With Former Therapy Patients

(a) Psychologists do not engage in sexual intimacies with a former therapy patient or client for at least two years after cessation or termination of professional services.

(b) Because sexual intimacies with a former therapy patient or client are so frequently harmful to the patient or client, and because such intimacies undermine public confidence in the psychology profession and thereby deters the public's use of needed services, psychologists do not engage in sexual intimacies with former therapy patients and clients even after a two-year interval except in the most unusual circumstances. The psychologist who engages in such activity after the two years following cessation or termination of treatment bears the burden of demonstrating that there has been no exploitation, in light of all relevant factors, including (1) the amount of time that has passed since therapy terminated, (2) the nature and duration of the therapy, (3) the circumstances of termination, (4) the patient's or client's personal history, (5) the patient's or client's current mental status, (6) the likelihood of adverse impact on the patient or client and others, and (7) any statements or actions made by the therapist during the course of therapy suggesting or inviting the possibility of a posttermination sexual or romantic relationship with the patient or client. (See also Standard 1.17, Multiple Relationships.)

4.08 Interruption of Services

(a) Psychologists make reasonable efforts to plan for facilitating care in the event that psychological services are interrupted by factors such as the psychologist's illness, death, unavailability, or relocation or by the client's relocation or financial limitations. (See also Standard 5.09, Preserving Records and Data.)

(b) When entering into employment or contractual relationships, psychologists provide for orderly and appropriate resolution of responsibility for patient or client care in the event that the employment or contractual relationship ends, with paramount consideration given to the welfare of the patient or client.

4.09 Terminating the Professional Relationship

(a) Psychologists do not abandon patients or clients. (See also Standard 1.25e, under Fees and Financial Arrangements.)

(b) Psychologists terminate a professional relationship when it becomes reasonably clear that the patient or client no longer needs the service, is not benefiting, or is being harmed by continued service.

(c) Prior to termination for whatever reason, except where precluded by the patient's or client's conduct, the psychologist discusses the patient's or client's views and needs, provides appropriate pretermination counseling, suggests alternative service providers as appropriate, and takes other reasonable steps to facilitate transfer of responsibility to another provider if the patient or client needs one immediately.

5. Privacy and Confidentiality

5.01 Discussing the Limits of Confidentiality

(a) Psychologists discuss with persons and organizations with whom they establish a scientific or professional relationship (including, to the extent feasible, minors and their legal representatives) (1) the relevant limitations on confidentiality, including limitations where applicable in group, marital, and family therapy or in organizational consulting, and (2) the foreseeable uses of the information generated through their services.

(b) Unless it is not feasible or is contraindicated, the discussion of confidentiality occurs at the outset of the relationship and thereafter as new circumstances may warrant.

(c) Permission for electronic recording of interviews is secured from clients and patients.

5.02 Maintaining Confidentiality

Psychologists have a primary obligation and take reasonable precaution to respect the confidentiality rights of those with whom they work or consult, recognizing that confidentiality may be established by law, institutional rules, or professional or scientific relationships. (See also Standard 6.26, Professional Reviewers.)

5.03 Minimizing Intrusions on Privacy

(a) In order to minimize intrusions on privacy, psychologists include in written and oral reports, consultations, and the like, only information germane to the purpose for which the communication is made.

(b) Psychologists discuss confidential information obtained in clinical or consulting relationships, or evaluative data concerning patients, individual or organizational clients, students, research participants, supervisees, and employees, only for appropriate scientific or professional purposes and only with persons clearly concerned with such matters.

5.04 Maintenance of Records

Psychologists maintain appropriate confidentiality in creating, storing, accessing, transferring, and disposing of records under their control, whether these are written, automated, or in any other medium. Psychologists maintain and dispose of records in accordance with law and in a manner that permits compliance with the requirements of this Ethics Code.

5.05 Disclosures

(a) Psychologists disclose confidential information without the consent of the individual only as mandated by law, or where permitted by law for a valid purpose, such as (1) to provide needed professional services to the patient or the individual or organizational client, (2) to obtain appropriate professional consultations, (3) to protect the patient or client or others from harm, or

(4) to obtain payment for services, in which instance disclosure is limited to the minimum that is necessary to achieve the purpose.

(b) Psychologists also may disclose confidential information with the appropriate consent of the patient or the individual or organizational client (or of another legally authorized person on behalf of the patient or client), unless prohibited by law.

5.06 Consultations

When consulting with colleagues, (1) psychologists do not share confidential information that reasonably could lead to the identification of a patient, client, research participant, or other person or organization with whom they have a confidential relationship unless they have obtained the prior consent of the person or organization or the disclosure cannot be avoided, and (2) they share information only to the extent necessary to achieve the purposes of the consultation. (See also Standard 5.02, Maintaining Confidentiality.)

5.07 Confidential Information in Databases

(a) If confidential information concerning recipients of psychological services is to be entered into databases or systems of records available to persons whose access has not been consented to by the recipient, then psychologists use coding or other techniques to avoid the inclusion of personal identifiers.

(b) If a research protocol approved by an institutional review board or similar body requires the inclusion of personal identifiers, such identifiers are deleted before the information is made accessible to persons other than those of whom the subject was advised.

(c) If such deletion is not feasible, then before psychologists transfer such data to others or review such data collected by others, they take reasonable steps to determine that appropriate consent of personally identifiable individuals has been obtained.

5.08 Use of Confidential Information for Didactic or Other Purposes

(a) Psychologists do not disclose in their writings, lectures, or other public media, confidential, personally identifiable information concerning their patients, individual or organizational clients, students, research participants, or other recipients of their services that they obtained during the course of their work, unless the person or organization has consented in writing or unless there is other ethical or legal authorization for doing so.

(b) Ordinarily, in such scientific and professional presentations, psychologists disguise confidential information concerning such persons or organizations so that they are not individually identifiable to others and so that discussions do not cause harm to subjects who might identify themselves.

5.09 Preserving Records and Data

A psychologist makes plans in advance so that confidentiality of records and data is protected in the event of the psychologist's death, incapacity, or withdrawal from the position or practice.

5.10 Ownership of Records and Data

Recognizing that ownership of records and data is governed by legal principles, psychologists take reasonable and lawful steps so that records and data remain available to the extent needed to serve the best interests of patients, individual or organizational clients, research participants, or appropriate others.

5.11 Withholding Records for Nonpayment

Psychologists may not withhold records under their control that are requested and imminently needed for a patient's or client's treatment solely because payment has not been received, except as otherwise provided by law.

6. Teaching, Training Supervision, Research, and Publishing

6.01 Design of Education and Training Programs

Psychologists who are responsible for education and training programs seek to ensure that the programs are competently designed, provide the proper experiences, and meet the requirements for licensure, certification, or other goals for which claims are made by the program.

6.02 Descriptions of Education and Training Programs

(a) Psychologists responsible for education and training programs seek to ensure that there is a current and accurate description of the program content, training goals and objectives, and requirements that must be met for satisfactory completion of the program. This information must be made readily available to all interested parties.

(b) Psychologists seek to ensure that statements concerning their course outlines are accurate and not misleading, particularly regarding the subject matter to be covered, bases for evaluating progress, and the nature of course experiences. (See also Standard 3.03, Avoidance of False or Deceptive Statements.)

(c) To the degree to which they exercise control, psychologists responsible for announcements, catalogs, brochures, or advertisements describing workshops, seminars, or other non-degree-granting educational programs ensure that they accurately describe the audience for which the program is intended, the educational objectives, the presenters, and the fees involved.

6.03 Accuracy and Objectivity in Teaching

(a) When engaged in teaching or training, psychologists present psychological information accurately and with a reasonable degree of objectivity.

(b) When engaged in teaching or training, psychologists recognize the power they hold over students or supervisees and therefore make reasonable efforts to avoid engaging in conduct that is personally demeaning to students or supervisees. (See also Standards 1.09, Respecting Others, and 1.12, Other Harassment.)

6.04 Limitation on Teaching

Psychologists do not teach the use of techniques or procedures that require specialized training, licensure, or expertise, including but not limited to hypnosis, biofeedback, and projective techniques, to individuals who lack the prerequisite training, legal scope of practice, or expertise.

6.05 Assessing Student and Supervisee Performance

(a) In academic and supervisory relationships, psychologists establish an appropriate process for providing feedback to students and supervisees.

(b) Psychologists evaluate students and supervisees on the basis of their actual performance on relevant and established requirements.

6.06 Planning Research

(a) Psychologists design, conduct, and report research in accordance with recognized standards of scientific competence and ethical research.

(b) Psychologists plan their research so as to minimize the possibility that results will be misleading.

(c) In planning research, psychologists consider its ethical acceptability under the Ethics Code. If an ethical issue is unclear, psychologists seek to resolve the issue through consultation with institutional review boards, animal care and use committees, peer consultations, or other proper mechanisms.

(d) Psychologists take reasonable steps to implement appropriate protections for the rights and welfare of human participants, other persons affected by the research, and the welfare of animal subjects.

6.07 Responsibility

(a) Psychologists conduct research competently and with due concern for the dignity and welfare of the participants.

(b) Psychologists are responsible for the ethical conduct of research conducted by them or by others under their supervision or control.

(c) Researchers and assistants are permitted to perform only those tasks for which they are appropriately trained and prepared.

(d) As part of the process of development and implementation of research projects, psychologists consult those with expertise concerning any special population under investigation or most likely to be affected.

6.08 Compliance With Law and Standards

Psychologists plan and conduct research in a manner consistent with federal and state law and regulations, as well as professional standards governing the conduct of research, and particularly those standards governing research with human participants and animal subjects.

6.09 Institutional Approval

Psychologists obtain from host institutions or organizations appropriate approval prior to conducting research, and they provide accurate information about their research proposals. They conduct the research in accordance with the approved research protocol.

6.10 Research Responsibilities

Prior to conducting research (except research involving only anonymous surveys, naturalistic observations, or similar research), psychologists enter into an agreement with participants that clarifies the nature of the research and the responsibilities of each party.

6.11 Informed Consent to Research

(a) Psychologists use language that is reasonably understandable to research participants in obtaining their appropriate informed consent (except as provided in Standard 6.12, Dispensing With Informed Consent). Such informed consent is appropriately documented.

(b) Using language that is reasonably understandable to participants, psychologists inform participants of the nature of the research; they inform participants that they are free to participate or to decline to participate or to withdraw from the research; they explain the foreseeable consequences of declining or withdrawing; they inform participants of significant factors that may be expected to influence their willingness to participate (such as risks, discomfort, adverse effects, or limitations on confidentiality, except as provided in Standard 6.15, Deception in Research); and they explain other aspects about which the prospective participants inquire.

(c) When psychologists conduct research with individuals such as students or subordinates, psychologists take special care to protect the prospective participants from adverse consequences of declining or withdrawing from participation.

(d) When research participation is a course requirement or opportunity for extra credit, the prospective participant is given the choice of equitable alternative activities.

(e) For persons who are legally incapable of giving informed consent, psychologists nevertheless (1) provide an appropriate explanation, (2) obtain the participant's assent, and (3) obtain appropriate permission from a legally authorized person, if such substitute consent is permitted by law.

6.12 Dispensing With Informed Consent

Before determining that planned research (such as research involving only anonymous questionnaires, naturalistic observations, or certain kinds of archival research) does not require the informed consent of research participants, psychologists consider applicable regulations and institutional review board requirements, and they consult with colleagues as appropriate.

6.13 Informed Consent in Research Filming or Recording

Psychologists obtain informed consent from research participants prior to filming or recording them in any form, unless the research involves simply naturalistic observations in public places and it is not anticipated that the recording will be used in a manner that could cause personal identification or harm.

6.14 Offering Inducements for Research Participants

(a) In offering professional services as an inducement to obtain research participants, psychologists make clear the nature of the services, as well as the risks, obligations, and limitations. (See also Standard 1.18, Barter [With Patients or Clients].)

(b) Psychologists do not offer excessive or inappropriate financial or other inducements to obtain research participants, particularly when it might tend to coerce participation.

6.15 Deception in Research

(a) Psychologists do not conduct a study involving deception unless they have determined that the use of deceptive techniques is justified by the study's prospective scientific, educational, or applied value and that equally effective alternative procedures that do not use deception are not feasible.

(b) Psychologists never deceive research participants about significant aspects that would affect their willingness to participate, such as physical risks, discomfort, or unpleasant emotional experiences.

(c) Any other deception that is an integral feature of the design and conduct of an experiment must be explained to participants as early as is feasible, preferably at the conclusion of their participation, but no later than at the conclusion of the research. (See also Standard 6.18, Providing Participants With Information About the Study.)

6.16 Sharing and Utilizing Data

Psychologists inform research participants of their anticipated sharing or further use of personally identifiable research data and of the possibility of unanticipated future uses.

6.17 Minimizing Invasiveness

In conducting research, psychologists interfere with the participants or milieu from which data are collected only in a manner that is warranted by an appropriate research design and that is consistent with psychologists' roles as scientific investigators.

6.18 Providing Participants With Information About the Study

(a) Psychologists provide a prompt opportunity for participants to obtain appropriate information about the nature, results, and conclusions of the research, and psychologists attempt to correct any misconceptions that participants may have.

(b) If scientific or humane values justify delaying or withholding this information, psychologists take reasonable measures to reduce the risk of harm.

6.19 Honoring Commitments

Psychologists take reasonable measures to honor all commitments they have made to research participants.

6.20 Care and Use of Animals in Research

(a) Psychologists who conduct research involving animals treats them humanely.

(b) Psychologists acquire, care for, use, and dispose of animals in compliance with current federal, state, and local laws and regulations, and with professional standards.

(c) Psychologists trained in research methods and experienced in the care of laboratory animals supervise all procedures involving animals and are responsible for ensuring appropriate consideration of their comfort, health, and humane treatment.

(d) Psychologists ensure that all individuals using animals under their supervision have received instruction in research methods and in the care, maintenance, and handling of the species being used, to the extent appropriate to their role.

(e) Responsibilities and activities of individuals assisting in a research project are consistent with their respective competencies.

(f) Psychologists make reasonable efforts to minimize the discomfort, infection, illness, and pain of animal subjects.

(g) A procedure subjecting animals to pain, stress, or privation is used only when an alternative procedure is unavailable and the goal is justified by its prospective scientific, educational, or applied value.

(h) Surgical procedures are performed under appropriate anesthesia; techniques to avoid infection and minimize pain are followed during and after surgery.

(i) When it is appropriate that the animal's life be terminated, it is done rapidly, with an effort to minimize pain, and in accordance with accepted procedures.

6.21 Reporting of Results

(a) Psychologists do not fabricate data or falsify results in their publications.

(b) If psychologists discover significant errors in their published data, they take reasonable steps to correct such errors in a correction, retraction, erratum, or other appropriate publication means.

6.22 Plagiarism

Psychologists do not present substantial portions or elements of another's work or data as their own, even if the other work or data source is cited occasionally.

6.23 Publication Credit

(a) Psychologists take responsibility and credit, including authorship credit, only for work they have actually performed or to which they have contributed.

(b) Principal authorship and other publication credits accurately reflect the relative scientific or professional contributions of the individuals involved, regardless of their relative status. Mere possession of an institutional position, such as Department Chair, does not justify authorship credit. Minor contributions to the research or to the writing for publications are appropriately acknowledged, such as in footnotes or in an introductory statement.

(c) A student is usually listed as principal author on any multiple- authored article that is substantially based on the student's dissertation or thesis.

6.24 Duplicate Publication of Data

Psychologists do not publish, as original data, data that have been previously published. This does not preclude republishing data when they are accompanied by proper acknowledgment.

6.25 Sharing Data

After research results are published, psychologists do not withhold the data on which their conclusions are based from other competent professionals who seek to verify the substantive claims through reanalysis and who intend to use such data only for that purpose, provided that the confidentiality of the participants can be protected and unless legal rights concerning proprietary data preclude their release.

6.26 Professional Reviewers

Psychologists who review material submitted for publication, grant, or other research proposal review respect the confidentiality of and the proprietary rights in such information of those who submitted it.

7. Forensic Activities

7.01 Professionalism

Psychologists who perform forensic functions, such as assessments, interviews, consultations, reports, or expert testimony, must comply with all other provisions of this Ethics Code to the extent that they apply to such activities. In addition, psychologists base their forensic work on appropriate knowledge of and competence in the areas underlying such work, including specialized knowledge concerning special populations. (See also Standards 1.06, Basis for Scientific and Professional Judgments; 1.08, Human Differences; 1.15, Misuse of Psychologists' Influence; and 1.23, Documentation of Professional and Scientific Work.)

7.02 Forensic Assessments

(a) Psychologists' forensic assessments, recommendations, and reports are based on information and techniques (including personal interviews of the individual, when appropriate) sufficient to provide appropriate substantiation for their findings. (See also Standards 1.03, Professional and Scientific Relationship; 1.23, Documentation of Professional and Scientific Work; 2.01, Evaluation, Diagnosis, and Interventions in Professional Context; and 2.05, Interpreting Assessment Results.)

(b) Except as noted in (c), below, psychologists provide written or oral forensic reports or testimony of the psychological characteristics of an individual only after they have conducted an examination of the individual adequate to support their statements or conclusions.

(c) When, despite reasonable efforts, such an examination is not feasible, psychologists clarify the impact of their limited information on the reliability and validity of their reports and testimony, and they appropriately limit the nature and extent of their conclusions or recommendations.

7.03 Clarification of Role

In most circumstances, psychologists avoid performing multiple and potentially conflicting roles in forensic matters. When psychologists may be called on to serve in more than one role in a legal proceeding—for example, as consultant or expert for one party or for the court and as a fact witness—they clarify role expectations and the extent of confidentiality in advance to the extent feasible, and thereafter as changes occur, in order to avoid compromising their professional judgment and objectivity and in order to avoid misleading others regarding their role.

7.04 Truthfulness and Candor

(a) In forensic testimony and reports, psychologists testify truthfully, honestly, and candidly and, consistent with applicable legal procedures, describe fairly the bases for their testimony and conclusions.

(b) Whenever necessary to avoid misleading, psychologists acknowledge the limits of their data or conclusions.

7.05 Prior Relationships

A prior professional relationship with a party does not preclude psychologists from testifying as fact witnesses or from testifying to their services to the extent permitted by applicable law. Psychologists appropriately take into account ways in which the prior relationship might affect their professional objectivity or opinions and disclose the potential conflict to the relevant parties.

7.06 Compliance With Law and Rules

In performing forensic roles, psychologists are reasonably familiar with the rules governing their roles. Psychologists are aware of the occasionally competing demands placed upon them by these principles and the requirements of the court system, and attempt to resolve these conflicts by making known their commitment to this Ethics Code and taking steps to resolve the conflict in a responsible manner. (See also Standard 1.02, Relationship of Ethics and Law.)

8. Resolving Ethical Issues

8.01 Familiarity With Ethics Code

Psychologists have an obligation to be familiar with this Ethics Code, other applicable ethics codes, and their application to psychologists' work. Lack of awareness or misunderstanding of an ethical standard is not itself a defense to a charge of unethical conduct.

8.02 Confronting Ethical Issues

When a psychologist is uncertain whether a particular situation or course of action would violate this Ethics Code, the psychologist ordinarily consults with other psychologists knowledgeable about ethical issues, with state or national psychology ethics committees, or with other appropriate authorities in order to choose a proper response.

8.03 Conflicts Between Ethics and Organizational Demands

If the demands of an organization with which psychologists are affiliated conflict with this Ethics Code, psychologists clarify the nature of the conflict, make known their commitment to the Ethics Code, and to the extent feasible, seek to resolve the conflict in a way that permits the fullest adherence to the Ethics Code.

8.04 Informal Resolution of Ethical Violations

When psychologists believe that there may have been an ethical violation by another psychologist, they attempt to resolve the issue by bringing it to the attention of that individual if an informal resolution appears appropriate and the intervention does not violate any confidentiality rights that may be involved.

8.05 Reporting Ethical Violations

If an apparent ethical violation is not appropriate for informal resolution under Standard 8.04 or is not resolved properly in that fashion, psychologists take further action appropriate to the situation, unless such action conflicts with confidentiality rights in ways that cannot be resolved. Such action might include referral to state or national committees on professional ethics or to state licensing boards.

8.06 Cooperating With Ethics Committees

Psychologists cooperate in ethics investigations, proceedings, and resulting requirements of the APA or any affiliated state psychological association to which they belong. In doing so, they make reasonable efforts to resolve any issues as to confidentiality. Failure to cooperate is itself an ethics violation.

8.07 Improper Complaints

Psychologists do not file or encourage the filing of ethics complaints that are frivolous and are intended to harm the respondent rather than to protect the public.

Appendix C

*STANDARDS FOR THE PROVISION OF SCHOOL PSYCHOLOGICAL SERVICES**

1.0 Definitions

1.1 A *School Psychologist* is a professional psychologist who has met all requirements for credentialing as stipulated in the appropriate NASP standards. The credential is based upon the completion of a school psychology training program which meets the criteria specified in the NASP *Standards for Training and Field Placement Programs in School Psychology.*

1.2 A *Supervising School Psychologist* is a professional psychologist who has met all NASP requirements for credentialing, and who has been designated by an employing agency as a supervisor responsible for school psychological services in the agency. Coursework or other training in the supervision of school personnel is desirable.

1.3 *Parent(s),* as used in these *Standards,* includes both biological parent(s) and legal guardian(s) or appointed surrogates.

2.0 Standards for Administrative Agencies

The purpose of this section of the standards is to provide guidance to federal and state administrative agencies in regard to administrative organization, laws, policies, and regulations as they pertain to the provision of school psychological services.

2.1 FEDERAL LEVEL ADMINISTRATIVE AGENCIES

2.1.1 ORGANIZATION

The federal education agency should employ a supervising school psychologist in order to accomplish the following objectives:

2.1.1.1 To provide professional leadership and assistance to the federal education agency, state education agencies, and the school psychology profession in regard to standards, policies, and procedures for program delivery, and for utilization, funding, education and training, and inservice education of school psychological services personnel.

2.1.1.2 To participate in the administration of federal programs providing funding for school psychological services in state, intermediate, and local education agencies, and for the education and training of school psychologists.

2.1.1.3 To encourage and assist in evaluation, research, and dissemination activities; to determine the effectiveness of school psychological education, training, and service programs; to determine needed changes; and to identify and communicate exemplary practices to training and service units.

2.1.1.4 To assure that consistent communication is established and maintained among professional organizations, federal, state, and local education agencies, and university training programs involved in providing and developing school psychological services.

2.1.2 LAWS

2.1.2.1 The Congress of the United States should ensure that the rights of all parents and children are protected by the creation and modification of laws which provide for the services of school psychologists. These services, as related to students' need, include, but are not limited to, consultation, assessment, research, program planning/evaluation, and direct service for individuals, groups, and systems. These services should be available to all children, their families, and school personnel.

2.1.2.2 The Congress should ensure that school psychological services, as related to students' needs, are provided in a free and appropriate manner to all children, their families, and school personnel in need of such services.

2.1.2.3 The Congress should ensure that federal laws recognize the appropriate involvement of school psychologists in educational programs and that adequate federal funding is made available for the education, training, services, and continuing professional development of school psychologists in order to guarantee appropriate and effective services.

2.1.2.4 The Congress should create no laws which effectively prohibit the credentialed school psychologist from the ethical and legal practice of his/her profession in the public or private sector, or which would be in violation of these standards.

2.1.3 REGULATIONS

2.1.3.1 All federal agencies should utilize the services of the federal educational agency school psychologist in developing and implementing regulations pursuant to all relevant federal laws.

2.1.3.2 All federal agencies should seek the advice and consultation of the National Association of School Psychologists prior to the adoption of regulations pursuant to any federal law which relates to the education or mental health of students and/or families, or which otherwise involves or should reasonably involve the profession of school psychology.

2.1.3.3 Federal agencies should promulgate regulations consistent with the principles set forth in these *Standards* and the NASP *Principles for Professional Ethics.*

2.2 STATE LEVEL ADMINISTRATION AGENCIES

2.2.1 ORGANIZATION

Each state educational agency (SEA) should employ at least one full-time supervising school psychologist, as defined in section 1, for each 500 (or fewer) school psychologists within the state. An equivalent ratio should be maintained if there are more than 500 school psychologists. It is recognized that this ratio may vary based upon administrative structures, available resources, and types of programs served, however the intention is to assign the individual(s) full-time (1.0 FTE) to the supervision of school psychology. Appropriate objectives to be accomplished by the SEA school psychologist(s) include the following:

2.2.1.1 To provide professional leadership assistance to the SEA, local educational agencies, and the profession with regard to standards, policies, and procedures for school psychology program delivery.

2.2.1.2 To support the utilization, funding, education, training, and in-service education of school psychologists.

2.2.1.3 To participate in the administration of state and federal programs providing funding for school psychological services in intermediate and local educational agencies, and for the education and training of school psychologists.

2.2.1.4 To encourage and assist in evaluation, research, and dissemination activities to determine the effectiveness of school psychological education, training, and service programs; to determine needed changes; and to identify and communicate exemplary practices to training and service units.

2.2.1.5 To maintain communication with and assure consultation with state school psychological associations and practicing school psychological personnel into the policy making of the SEA.

2.2.1.6 To communicate with the federal education agency school psychologist to ensure recognition of state issues and to facilitate consultation regarding federal policy.

2.2.2 LAWS

2.2.2.1 All state legislative bodies should ensure that the rights of all parents and children are protected by the creation and modification of laws which provide for the services of school psychologists. As related to students' needs, these services include, but are not limited to, consultation for individuals, groups, and systems, assessment, program planning/evaluation, research, and direct service. These services are available to all children, their families, and school personnel.

2.2.2.2 The state legislature should ensure that school psychological services, as related to students' needs, are provided in a free and appropriate way to all children, their families, and school personnel in need of such services.

2.2.2.3 The state legislature should ensure that state laws recognize the appropriate involvement of school psychologists in educational programs.

2.2.2.4 The state legislature should ensure that adequate funding is made available for the education, training, services, and continuing professional development of school psychologists in order to guarantee appropriate and effective services.

2.2.2.5 The state legislature should ensure that state laws provide for the credentialing of school psychologists consistent with NASP standards.

2.2.2.6 The state legislature should create no laws which

prohibit the school psychologists from the ethical and legal practice of his/her profession in the public or private sector, or that prevent the school psychologist from practicing in a manner consistent with these *Standards.*

2.2.2.7 The state legislature should ensure that there are sufficient numbers of adequately prepared and credentialed school psychologists to provide services consistent with these *Standards.* In most settings, this will require at least one full-time school psychologist for each 1,000 children served by the LEA, and a maximum of four schools served by one school psychologist. It is recognized that this ratio may vary based upon the needs of children served, the type of program served, available resources, distance between schools, and other unique characteristics.

2.2.3 REGULATIONS

2.2.3.1 All state agencies should utilize the services of the SEA school psychologist(s) in developing and implementing administrative rules pursuant to all relevant state laws, federal laws, and regulations.

2.2.3.2 All state agencies should seek the advice and consultation of the state school psychologists' professional association prior to the adoption of rules pursuant to any state law, federal law, or regulation which involves or should reasonably involve the profession of school psychology.

2.2.3.3 All state education agencies should utilize the services of the SEA school psychologist(s) and the school psychologists' professional association in the SEA review and approval of school psychology training programs.

2.2.3.4 All state education agencies should utilize the services of the SEA school psychologist(s) and the school psychologists' professional association in developing and implementing administrative rules for credentialing school psychologists. Such rules shall be consistent with NASP *Standards for the Credentialing of School Psychologists.*

2.2.3.5 State education agencies should promulgate regulations consistent with the principles set forth in these *Standards* and the NASP *Principles for Professional Ethics.*

3.0 STANDARDS FOR EMPLOYING AGENCIES

The purpose of these standards is to provide employing agencies with specific guidance regarding the organization, policies, and practices needed to assure the provision of adequate school psychological services.

3.1 COMPREHENSIVE CONTINUUM OF SERVICES

Employing agencies assure that school psychological services are provided in a coordinated, organized fashion, and are deployed in a manner which ensures the provision of a comprehensive continuum of services as outlined in Section 4.0 of these *Standards.* Such services are available to all students served by the agency and are available to an extent sufficient to meet the needs of the population served. Breadth or availability of services should not be dictated by the funding source. (For example, some Districts have been known to limit services to special education students only because the school psychology budget came from special education sources. Similarly, other Districts provided assessment services only because funds were taken from State or Federal assessment grants. Both cases are considered to be mistakes in the attempt to provide comprehensive school psychological services to all students.)

3.2 PROFESSIONAL EVALUATION, SUPERVISION, AND DEVELOPMENT

3.2.1 SUPERVISION

Employing agencies assure that an effective program of supervision and evaluation of school psychological services exists. School psychologists, in cooperation with their employing agencies, are responsible for the overall development, implementation, and professional supervision of school psychological service programs, and are responsible for articulating those programs to others in the employing agency and to the agency's constituent groups.

3.2.2 SUPERVISOR(S)

The school psychological services program is supervised by a designated school psychologist who meets the requirements for a supervising school psychologist (Section 1.2) and who demonstrates competencies needed for effective supervision.

3.2.3 AVAILABILITY OF SUPERVISION

Supervision is available to all school psychologists to an extent sufficient to ensure the provision of effective and accountable services (see Section 4.6 for specific requirements). In most cases, one supervising school psychologist should be employed for every ten school psychologists to be supervised (an equivalent ratio should be maintained for part-time supervisors). It is recognized that this ratio may vary based upon the type of program served, staff needs, and other unique characteristics.

3.2.4 INTERN SUPERVISION

A credentialed school psychologist meeting the requirements of a supervising school psychologist, with at least one year of experience at the employing agency, supervises no more than two school psychology interns at any given time (consistent with the NASP *Standards for Training and Field Placement Programs in School Psychology*), unless the supervising school psychologist has no other assigned duties. In such cases, a maximum of six school psychology interns may be supervised at any given time.

3.2.5 PEER REVIEW

After attaining independent practice status (see Section 4.5), school psychologists continue to receive appropriate supervision. The independent practitioner engages in peer review with other school psychologists. (Peer review involves mutual assistance with self-examination of services and the development of plans to continue professional growth and development). Employing agencies assure that school psychologists are given appropriate time and support for peer review activities.

3.2.6 ACCOUNTABILITY AND PROGRAM EVALUATION

Employing agencies assure that school psychologists develop a coordinated plan for accountability and evaluation of all services provided in order to maintain and improve the effectiveness of services. Such plans include specific, measurable objectives pertaining to the planned effects of services on all relevant elements of the system. Evaluation and revision of these plans occurs on a regular basis.

3.2.7 CONTINUING PROFESSIONAL DEVELOPMENT

Employing agencies recognize that all school psychologists, not just those holding national certification, are obligated to continue their professional training and development through participation in a recognized Continuing Professional Development (CPD) program (see Section 4.6). Employing agencies provide release time and financial support for such activities.

They recognize documented continuing professional development activities in the evaluation and advancement of school psychologists. Private practitioners who contract to provide services are responsible for their own CPD program, and these activities should also be encouraged by employing agencies.

3.3 CONDITIONS FOR EFFECTIVE SERVICE DELIVERY

In order to assure that employment conditions enable school psychologists to provide effective services, employing agencies adopt policies and practices ensuring that Section 3.3.1 through 3.3.4 are met.

3.3.1 School psychologists are not subjected to administrative constraints which prevent them from providing services in full accordance with these *Standards* and NASP *Principles for Professional Ethics.* When administrative policies conflict with these *Standards* or the NASP *Ethics,* the principles outlined in the *Standards* or *Ethics* take precedence in determining appropriate practices of the school psychologist.

3.3.2 School psychologists have appropriate involvement with the general policy making of the employing agency and the development of programs affecting the staff, students, and families they serve.

3.3.3 School psychologists have appropriate professional autonomy in determining the nature, extent, and duration of services they provide. Specific activities are defined within the profession, although school psychologists frequently collaborate and seek advice from others in determining appropriate service delivery. Legal, ethical, and professional standards and guidelines are considered by the practitioner in making decisions regarding practice (see Section 4.4).

3.3.4 School psychologists have access to adequate clerical assistance, appropriate professional work materials, sufficient office and work space, and general working conditions that enhance the delivery of effective services. Included are test materials, access to private telephone and office, secretarial services, therapeutic aids, professional literature (books, journals), computers and related technology, and so forth.

3.4 CONTRACTUAL SERVICES

It is recognized that employing agencies may obtain school psychological services on a contractual basis in order to ensure the provision of adequate services to all children. However, each student within the educational system must be assured the full range of school psychological services necessary to maximize his/her success and adjustment in school. When an employing agency utilizes contractual services, the following standards are observed:

3.4.1 Contractual school psychological services encompass the same comprehensive continuum of services as that provided by regularly employed school psychologists. Overall, psychological services are not limited to any specific type of service and include opportunities for follow-up and continuing consultation appropriate to the needs of the student. Individual contracts for services may be limited as long as comprehensive services are provided overall.

3.4.2 Psychologists providing contractual school psychological services provide those services in a manner consistent with these *Standards,* NASP *Principles for Professional Ethics,* and other relevant professional guidelines and standards.

3.4.3 Persons providing contractual psychological services are fully-credentialed school psychologists as defined by these *Standards*. In specific limited instances, however, services by psychologists in other specialty areas (e.g., clinical, industrial/organizational, neuropsychology, etc.) might be used to supplement school psychological services in a coordinated manner.

3.4.4 Contractual school psychological services are not to be utilized as a means to decrease the amount and quality of school psychological services provided by an employing agency. They may be used to augment programs but not to supplant them.

3.4.5 School psychologists providing contractual services are given appropriate access and information. They are familiar with the instructional resources of the employing agency to ensure that students they serve have the same opportunities as those served by regularly employed school psychologists.

3.4.6 Contractual school psychological services are provided in a manner which protects the due process rights of students and their parents as defined by state and federal laws and regulations.

3.4.7 Contracting for services is not to be used as a means to avoid legitimate employee rights, wages, or fringe benefits.

3.4.8 Psychologists providing contractual school psychological services will encourage regular evaluation of the continued need for the service as well as the quality of the service.

3.5 NON-BIASED ASSESSMENT AND PROGRAM PLANNING

Employing agencies should adopt policies and practices in accordance with the following standards:

3.5.1 GENERAL PRINCIPLES

3.5.1.1 School psychologists use assessment techniques to provide information which is helpful in maximizing student achievement, educational success, psychological adjustment, and behavioral adaptation.

3.5.1.2 School psychologists have autonomous decision-making responsibility (as defined in Section 4.4) to determine the type, nature, and extent of assessment techniques they use in student evaluation.

3.5.1.3 School psychologists have autonomy (as defined in Section 4.4) in determining the content and nature of reports.

3.5.1.4 Whenever possible, school psychologists use assessment techniques and instruments which have established validity and reliability for the purposes and populations for which the procedures are intended. In addition, certain clinical procedures and measures at the 'research' stage of development may be used by practitioners trained in their use provided the reliability and validity of the procedures are reported and clearly distinguished from those techniques which meet standards.

3.5.1.5 School psychologists use, develop, and encourage assessment practices which increase the likelihood of the development of effective educational interventions and follow-up.

3.5.2 PROFESSIONAL INVOLVEMENT

3.5.2.1 A multi-disciplinary team is involved in assessment, program decision making, and evaluation. The team conducts periodic evaluations of its performance to ensure continued effectiveness.

3.5.2.2 The multi-disciplinary team includes a fully trained and certified school psychologist.

3.5.2.3 The school psychologist communicates a written minority position to all involved when in disagreement with the multi-disciplinary team position.

3.5.3 NON-BIASED ASSESSMENT TECHNIQUES

3.5.3.1 Assessment procedures and program recommendations are chosen to maximize the student's opportunities to be successful in the general culture, while respecting the student's ethnic background.

3.5.3.2 Multifaceted assessment batteries are used which include a focus on the student's strengths.

3.5.3.3 Communications are held and assessments are conducted in the client's dominant spoken language or alternative communication system. All student information is interpreted in the context of the student's socio-cultural background and the setting in which she/he is functioning.

3.5.3.4 Assessment techniques (including computerized techniques) are used only by personnel professionally trained in their use and in a manner consistent with these *Standards*.

3.5.3.5 School psychologists promote the development of objective, valid, and reliable assessment techniques.

3.5.3.6 Interpretation of assessment results is based upon empirically validated research.

3.5.4 PARENT/STUDENT INVOLVEMENT

3.5.4.1 Informed written consent of parent(s) and/or student (if the student has reached the age of majority) is obtained in the native language (or form of communication) of the parents/guardians before assessment and special program implementation.

3.5.4.2 The parent(s) and/or student is fully informed of all essential information considered and its relevancy to decision-making.

3.5.4.3 The parent(s) and/or student is encouraged to participate in decision-making meetings.

3.5.4.4 The parent(s) and/or student is routinely notified that an advocate can participate in conferences focusing on assessment results and program recommendations.

3.5.4.5 A record of meetings regarding assessment results and program recommendations is available to all directly concerned.

3.5.5 EDUCATIONAL PROGRAMMING AND FOLLOW-THROUGH

3.5.5.1 School psychologists are involved in determining options and revisions of educational programs to ensure that they are adaptive to the needs of students.

3.5.5.2 The contributions of diverse cultural backgrounds should be emphasized in educational programs.

3.5.5.3 School psychologists follow-up on the efficacy of their recommendations.

3.5.5.4 Student needs are given priority in determining educational programs.

3.5.5.5 Specific educational prescriptions result from the assessment team's actions.

3.5.5.6 Where a clear determination of the student's needs does not result from initial assessment, a diagnostic intervention or teaching program is offered as part of additional assessment procedures.

3.5.5.7 Regular, systematic review of the student's program is conducted and includes program modifications as necessary.

3.6 SCHOOL PSYCHOLOGICAL RECORDS

3.6.1 The employing agency's policy on student records is consistent with state and federal rules and laws, and ensures the protection of the confidentiality of the student and his/her family. The policy specifies the types of data developed by the school psychologist which are classified as school or pupil records. The policy gives clear guidance regarding which documents belong to the school and which are the personal property of the school psychologist.

3.6.2 Parents may inspect and review any personally identifiable data relating to their child which were collected, maintained, or used in his/her evaluation. Although test protocols are part of the student's record, school psychologists protect test security and observe copyright restrictions.

3.6.3 Access to psychological records is restricted to those permitted by law who have legitimate educational interest in the records.

3.6.4 School psychologists interpret school psychological records to non- psychologists who qualify for access.

3.6.5 School psychological records are only created and maintained when the information is necessary and relevant to legitimate educational program needs and when parents (or student if age of majority has been attained) have given their informed consent for the creation of such a record. This consent is based upon full knowledge of purposes for which information is sought, and the personnel who will have access to it. The school psychologist assumes responsibility for assuring the accuracy and relevancy of the information recorded.

3.6.6 School psychological records are systematically reviewed, and when necessary purged, in keeping with relevant federal and state laws in order to protect children from decisions based on incorrect, misleading, or out-of-date information.

4.0 Standards for the Delivery of Comprehensive School Psychological Services

The purpose of these standards is to ensure the delivery of comprehensive services by school psychologists.

4.1 ORGANIZATION OF SCHOOL PSYCHOLOGICAL SERVICES

4.1.1 School psychological services are planned, organized, directed, and reviewed by school psychologists.

4.1.2 School psychologists participate in determining the recipients and the type of school psychological services offered.

4.1.3 The goals and objectives of school psychological services are consistent with these standards and available in written form.

4.1.4 A written set of procedural guidelines for the delivery of school psychological services is followed and made available upon request.

4.1.5 A clearly stated referral system is in writing and is communicated to parents, staff members, students, and other referral agents.

4.1.6 The organization of school psychological services is in written form and includes lines of responsibility, supervisory, and administrative relationships.

4.1.7 Where two or more school psychologists are employed, a coordinated system of school psychological services is in effect within that unit.

4.1.8 Units providing school psychological services include sufficient professional and support personnel to achieve their goals and objectives.

4.2 RELATIONSHIP TO OTHER UNITS AND PROFESSIONALS

4.2.1 The school psychological services unit is responsive to the needs of the population that it serves. Psychological services are periodically and systematically reviewed to ensure their conformity with the needs of the population served.

4.2.2 School psychologists establish and maintain relationships with other professionals (e.g., pediatricians, bilingual specialists, audiologists) who provide services to children and families. They collaborate with these professionals in prevention, assessment, and intervention efforts as necessary. They also cooperate with advocates representing children and their families.

4.2.3 Providers of school psychological services maintain a cooperative relationship with colleagues and co-workers in the best mutual interests of clients, in a manner consistent with the goals of the employing agency. Conflicts should be resolved in a professional manner.

4.2.4 School psychologists develop plans for the delivery of services in accordance with best professional practices.

4.2.5 School psychologists employed within a school setting help coordinate the services of mental health providers from other agencies (such as community mental health centers, child guidance clinics, or private practitioners) to ensure a continuum of services.

4.2.6 School psychologists are knowledgeable about community agencies and resources. They provide liaison and consulting services to the community and agencies regarding psychological, mental health, and educational issues.

4.2.6.1 School psychologists communicate as needed with state and community agencies and professionals (e.g., child guidance clinics, community mental health centers, private practitioners) regarding services for children, families, and school personnel. They refer clients to these agencies and professionals as appropriate.

4.2.6.2 School psychologists are informed of and have the opportunity to participate in community agency staffings of cases involving their clients.

4.2.6.3 Community agency personnel are invited to participate in school system conferences concerning their clients (with written parental permission).

4.3 COMPREHENSIVE SCHOOL PSYCHOLOGICAL SERVICES DELIVERY

School psychologists provide a range of services to their clients. These consist of direct and indirect services which require involvement with the entire educational system: (a) the students, teachers, administrators, and other school personnel; (b) the families, surrogate caretakers, and other community and regional agencies, and resources which support the educational process; (c) the organizational, physical, temporal, and curricular variables which play major roles within the system; and (d) a variety of other factors which may be important on an individual basis.

The intent of these services is to promote mental health and facilitate learning of students. Comprehensive school psychological services are comprised of diverse activities. These activities complement one another and therefore are most accurately viewed as being integrated and coordinated rather than discrete services. However, for descriptive purposes, they will be listed and described separately. The following are the services that comprise the delivery system:

4.3.1 CONSULTATION: the act of meeting to discuss, decide, or plan, typically regarding primary prevention or the reasons for an identified problem, and the resulting intervention(s). The school psychologist usually does not personally provide the intervention, but guides those who do. (See direct service for contrast.)

4.3.1.1 School psychologists consult and collaborate with parents, school, and outside personnel regarding mental health, behavioral, and educational concerns.

4.3.1.2 School psychologists design and develop procedures for preventing disorders, promoting mental health and learning, and improving educational systems.

4.3.1.3 School psychologists provide skill enhancement activities (such as inservice training, organizational development, parent counseling, program planning and evaluation, vocational development, and parent education programs) to school personnel, parents, and others in the community, regarding issues of human learning, development, and behavior.

4.3.1.4 School psychologists facilitate the delivery of services by assisting those who play major roles in the educational system (i.e., parents, school personnel, community agencies).

4.3.2 PSYCHOLOGICAL AND PSYCHOEDUCATIONAL ASSESSMENT: the process of obtaining data about human functioning according to the current practices of the fields of psychology and education for the purpose of identifying critical factors and evaluating their importance for answering referral questions.

4.3.2.1 School psychologists conduct multifactored psychological and psychoeducational assessments of children and youth as appropriate.

4.3.2.2 Psychological and psychoeducational assessments include evaluation, as appropriate, of the areas of: personality, emotional status, social skills and adjustment, intelligence and cognitive functioning, scholastic aptitude, adaptive behavior, language and communication skills, academic knowledge and achievement, sensory and perceptual-motor functioning, educational setting, family/environmental/cultural influences, career and vocational development, aptitude, and interests.

4.3.2.3 School psychologists utilize a variety of instruments, procedures, and techniques. Interviews, observations, and behavioral evaluations are included in these procedures.

4.3.2.4 When conducting psychological and psychoeducational assessments, school psychologists have explicit regard for the context and setting in which their assessments take place and will be used.

4.3.2.5 School psychologists adhere to the NASP resolutions regarding non-biased assessment and programming for all students (see Section 3.5.3). They also are familiar with and consider the *Standards for Educational and Psychological Tests* (developed by APA, AERA, and NCME) and other related publications in the use of assessment techniques.

4.3.3 DIRECT SERVICE: techniques applied in a face-to-face situation (e.g., individual/group counseling, classroom-based interventions, etc.) designed to enhance the mental health, behavior, personality, social competency, academic or educational status of the student/client, or prevent difficulties in these areas. (Contrast with **consultation.**)

4.3.3.1 School psychologists provide direct service to facilitate the functioning of individuals, groups, and/or organizations.

4.3.3.2 School psychologists design direct service programs to enhance cognitive, affective, social, and vocational development.

4.3.3.3 School psychologists develop collaborative relationships with their clients and involve them in the assessment, direct service, and program evaluation procedures.

4.3.4 SUPERVISION: the process of overseeing and managing the activities of a school psychologist for the purpose of quality assurance, assistance with difficult assignments, and the improvement of performance.

4.3.4.1 School psychologists provide and/or engage in supervision, peer review, and continuing professional development as specified in Section 3.2 and 4.6.

4.3.5 RESEARCH: the process of careful, systematic investigation to discover or establish facts.

4.3.5.1 School psychologists design, conduct, report, and utilize the results of research of a psychological and educational nature. All research conducted is in accordance with relevant ethical guidelines of the profession (e.g., APA *Ethical Principles in the Conduct of Research with Human Participants*), with particular concern for obtaining informed consent, notifying subjects of the expected length of participation, and protecting subjects from breach of confidentiality, coercion, harm, or danger. Applied and/or basic research should be pursued, focusing on:

(a) Psychological functioning of human beings;

(b) Psychoeducational assessment tools and procedures;

(c) Educational programs and techniques applied to individual cases and groups of various sizes;

(d) Educational processes;

(e) Social system interactions and organizational factors associated with school communities; and

(f) Psychological treatments and techniques applied to individual cases or groups.

4.3.5.2 School psychologists' involvement in research can range from support or advisory services to having direct responsibility for one or more major components of a research project. These components may include planning, data collecting, data analyzing, disseminating, and translating research into practical applications within the school community.

4.3.6 PROGRAM PLANNING AND EVALUATION: the process of designing and judging the effectiveness of educational structures at all levels.

4.3.6.1 School psychologists provide program planning and evaluation services to assist in decision-making activities.

4.3.6.2 School psychologists serve on committees responsible for developing and planning educational and educationally-related activities.

4.4 AUTONOMOUS FUNCTIONING

School psychologists have professional autonomy in determining the nature, scope, and extent of their specific services. These activities are defined within the profession, although school psychologists frequently collaborate with and seek advice from others in determining appropriate services delivery. Legal, ethical, and professional standards and guidelines are considered by the practitioner in making decisions regarding practice. All practice is restricted to those areas in which the school psychologist has received formal training and supervised experience.

4.4.1 PROFESSIONAL RESPONSIBILITY AND BEST PRACTICES

Professional autonomy is associated with professional responsibility. The ultimate responsibility for providing appropriate comprehensive school psychological services rests with the individual practitioner.

While being cognizant of the fact that there often are not explicit guidelines to follow in providing comprehensive school psychological services, the individual practitioner has a responsibility to adhere to the best available and most appropriate standards of practice. There is no substitute for sensitive, sound, professional judgment in the determination of what constitutes best practice. Active involvement in supervision and other continuing professional development activities will assist the practitioner in adhering to best professional practices.

4.5 INDEPENDENT PRACTICE

A credentialed school psychologist who has completed a school psychology training program which meets the criteria specified in the NASP *Standards for Training and Field Placement Programs in School Psychology* and three years of satisfactory, properly supervised experience is considered qualified for personally supervised, independent practice with peer review, regardless of working setting. (NOTE: "independent practice" as used in this paragraph refers to autonomous functioning within the employing agency. Contrast this with the licensure rules various states have for "private practice.")

4.6 CONTINUING PROFESSIONAL DEVELOPMENT

* dynamic + fluid nature of school psychology

The practice of school psychology has and will continue to undergo significant changes as new knowledge and technological advances are introduced. The development of new intervention techniques, assessment procedures, computerized assistance, and so forth, will require that practitioners keep abreast of these innovations as well as obtain appropriate professional education and training in these areas. All school psychologists will actively participate in activities designed to continue, enhance, and upgrade their professional training and skills and to help ensure quality service provision. These efforts are documented by participation in Continuing Professional Development (CPD) programs, as sponsored by NASP or other organizations, although they are not limited to such activities. Memberships in professional organizations, reading of professional journals and books, discussions of professional issues with colleagues, and so forth, are also an integral component of a school psychologist's overall CPD activity.

4.6.1 Participation in CPD activities and the maintenance of high professional standards and practice are continuing obligations of the school psychologist. These obligations are assumed when one initially engages in the practice of school psychology and should be required for continued credentialing.

4.6.2 School psychologists receive supervision by a supervising school psychologist for the first three years of full-time employment (or the equivalent) as a school psychologist. The supervisor shares professional responsibility and accountability for the services provided. While the level and extent of supervision may vary, the supervisor maintains a sufficiently close relationship to meet this standard. Individual face-to-face supervision is engaged in for a minimum of one hour per week or the equivalent (e.g., two hours bi-weekly). Standards for intern supervision are contained in the NASP *Standards for Training and Field Placement Programs in School Psychology.*

4.6.3 After completion of the first three years of supervision, all school psychologists continue to engage in supervision and/or peer review on a regular basis, and further their professional development by actively participating in CPD activities. The level and extent of these activities may vary depending on the needs, interests, and goals of the school psychologist, with more comprehensive service delivery requiring more extensive related professional exchanges. At a minimum, however, these activities are at the level required for successful participation in an appropriate CPD program.

4.6.4 School psychologists, who after three years no longer have required supervision, engage in peer review activities. These may include discussion of cases and professional issues designed to assist with problem solving, decision-making, and appropriate practice.

4.6.5 School psychologists readily seek additional assistance from supervisors, peers, or colleagues with particularly complex or difficult cases, and/or when expanding their services into new areas or those in which they infrequently practice (e.g., low incidence assessment).

4.6.6 Nationally Certified School Psychologists engage in continuing professional development as a requirement of certificate renewal.

4.7 ACCOUNTABILITY

4.7.1 School psychologists perform their duties in an accountable manner by keeping records of these efforts, evaluating their effectiveness, and modifying their practices and/or expanding their services as needed.

4.7.2 School psychologists devise systems of accountability and outcome evaluation which aid in documenting the effectiveness of intervention efforts and other services they provide.

4.7.3 Within their service delivery plan, school psychologists include a regular evaluation of their progress in achieving goals. This evaluation should include consideration of the cost effectiveness of school psychological services in terms of time, money, and resources, as well as the availability of professional and support personnel. Evaluation of the school psychological delivery system is conducted internally, and when possible, externally as well (e.g., through state educational agency review, peer review). This evaluation includes an assessment of effectiveness, efficiency, continuity, availability, and adequacy of services.

4.7.4 School psychologists are accountable for their services. They should make information available about their services, and provide consumers with the opportunity to participate in decision-making concerning such issues as initiation, termination, continuation, modification, and evaluation of their services. Rights of the consumer should be taken into account when performing these activities.

4.8 PRIVATE PRACTICE

4.8.1 School psychologists practicing in the private sector provide comprehensive services and adhere to the same standards and guidelines as those providing services in the public sector.

4.8.2 School psychologists document that they have formal training, supervised experience, licensure and/or certification, and demonstrated competence, in any areas of service they intend to deliver to clients within the private sector. They also have a responsibility to actively engage in CPD activities.

4.8.3 School psychologists in private practice adhere to the NASP *Principles for Professional Ethics,* and practice only within their area of competence. If the services needed by clients fall outside the school psychologist's area of competence, they are referred elsewhere for assistance.

4.8.4 It is the responsibility of the school psychologist engaging in private practice to inform the client that school psychological services are available without charge from the client's local school district.

4.8.5 School psychologists do not provide services on a private basis to students who attend the school(s) to which the school psychologist is assigned, or would normally be expected to serve. This includes students who attend nonpublic schools served by the school psychologist.

no private service

4.8.6 School psychologists offering school psychological services in the private sector ensure that, prior to the commencement of treatment/services, the client fully understands any and all fees associated with the services, and any potential financial assistance that may be available (i.e., third-party reimbursement).

fees in private service

4.8.7 Parents must be informed by the school psychologist that if a private school psychological evaluation is to be completed, this evaluation constitutes only one portion of a multi-disciplinary team evaluation. Private services must be equally comprehensive to those described in Section 4.3.

4.8.8 School psychologists in private practice provide and maintain written records in a manner consistent with Section 3.6.

4.9 PROFESSIONAL ETHICS AND GUIDELINES

Each school psychologist practices in full accordance with the NASP *Principles for Professional Ethics,* and these *Standards.*

5.0 Standards for School Psychology Training Programs

Each school psychology training program should meet the criteria specified in the NASP *Standards for Training and Field Placement Programs in School Psychology.*

References

Adler, T. (1993, September). APA, two other groups to revise test standards. *APA Monitor,* pp. 24–25.

Aiken, L. R. (1987). *Assessment of intellectual functioning.* Boston: Allyn & Bacon.

Alberto, P. A., & Troutman, A. C. (1982). *Applied behavior analysis for teachers.* Columbus, OH: Merrill.

Alexander, L. (1992/1993). U.S. Department of Education notice of policy guidance. *Individuals with Disabilities Education Law Report, 19,* 463–466.

Allington, R. L., & McGill-Frazen, A. (1992). Unintended effects of educational reform in New York. *Educational Policy, 6,* 397–414.

Alper, S. K., Schloss, P. J., & Schloss, C. N. (1994). *Families of students with disabilities: Consultation and advocacy.* Boston: Allyn & Bacon.

American Counseling Association. (1988). *Ethical standards.* Alexandria, VA: Author.

American Educational Research Association, American Psychological Association, & National Council on Measurement in Education. (1985). *Standards for educational and psychological testing.* Washington, DC: American Psychological Association.

American Psychiatric Association. (1994). *Diagnostic and statistical manual of mental disorders* (4th ed., Rev.). Washington, DC: Author.

American Psychological Association. (1981). Specialty guidelines for the delivery of services by school psychologists. *American Psychologist, 36,* 670–681.

American Psychological Association. (1982). *Ethical principles in the conduct of research with human participants.* Washington, DC: Author.

American Psychological Association. (1986). *Guidelines for computer-based tests and interpretations.* Washington, DC: Author.

American Psychological Association. (1989). *Ethical principles of psychologists.* Washington, DC: Author.

American Psychological Association. (1992). Ethical principles of psychologists and code of conduct. *American Psychologist, 47,* 1597–1611.

American Psychological Association. (1993a). Guidelines for providers of psychological services to ethnic, linguistic, and culturally diverse populations. *American Psychologist, 48,* 45–48.

American Psychological Association. (1993b). Record keeping guidelines. *American Psychologist, 48,* 45–48.

American Psychological Association. (1995). *Reforming America's schools: Psychology's role.* (Available from the APA Center for Psychology in Schools and Education, American Psychological Association, 750 First Street, NE, Washington, DC 20002-4242)

American Psychological Association. (1996a). Report of the Ethics Committee, 1995. *American Psychologist, 51,* 1279–1286.

American Psychological Association. (1996b). Rules and procedures. *American Psychologist, 51,* 529–548.

American Psychological Association. (1996c). Statement on the disclosure of test data. *American Psychologist, 51,* 644–648.

American Psychological Association Committee on Legal Issues. (1996). Strategies for private practitioners coping with subpoenas or compelled testimony for client records or test data. *Professional Psychology: Research and Practice, 27,* 245–251.

Bailey, J. A. (1980, March). School counselors: Test your ethics. *The School Counselor,* 285–293.

Baker, E. L., O'Neil, H. F., & Linn, R. L. (1993). Policy and validity prospects for performance-based assessment. *American Psychologist, 48,* 1210–1218.

Baldick, T. L. (1980). Ethical discrimination ability of intern psychologists: A function of training in ethics. *Professional Psychology, 11,* 276–282.

Bardon, J. I. (1987). The translation of research into practice in school psychology. *School Psychology Review, 16,* 317–328.

Barkley, R. A. (1989). Attention deficit–hyperactivity disorder. In E. J. Mash & R. A. Barkley (Eds.), *Treatment of childhood disorders* (pp. 39–72). New York: Guilford Press.

Batsche, G. M., & Peterson, D. W. (1983). School psychology and projective assessment: A growing incompatibility. *School Psychology Review, 12,* 440–445.

Bauder, D. (1989, February 6). Misdiagnosed as mentally retarded, deaf man spent years in institutions. *Midland Daily News,* p. B-1.

Beauchamp, T. L., & Childress, J. F. (1983). *Principles of biomedical ethics* (2nd ed.). New York: Oxford University Press.

Bell-Dolan, D., & Wessler, A. E. (1994). Ethical administration of sociometric measures: Procedures in use and suggestions for improvement. *Professional Psychology: Research and Practice, 25,* 23–32.

Bennett, B. E., Bryant, B. K., VandenBos, G., & Greenwood, A. (1990). *Professional liability and risk management.* Washington, DC: American Psychological Association.

Bergin, A. E. (1991). Values and religious issues in psychotherapy and mental health. *American Psychologist, 46,* 393–403.

Berman, A. L., & Jobes, D. A. (1991). *Adolescent suicide assessment and intervention.* Washington, DC: American Psychological Association.

Bernard, J., & Jara, C. (1986). The failure of clinical psychology graduate students to apply understood ethical principles. *Professional Psychology: Research and Practice, 17,* 313–315.

Bersoff, D. N. (1979). Regarding psychologists testily: The legal regulation of psychological assessment in the public schools. *Maryland Law Review, 39,* 27–120.

Bersoff, D. N. (1981). The brief for *amici curiae* in the matter of Forrest versus Ambach. *Academic Psychology Bulletin, 3,* 133–162.

Bersoff, D. N. (1982). Larry P. and PASE: Judicial report cards on the validity of individual intelligence tests. In T. Kratochwill (Ed.), *Advances in school psychology* (Vol. 2, pp. 61–95). Hillsdale, NJ: Erlbaum.

Bersoff, D. N. (1983). Children as participants in psychoeducational assessment. In G. B. Melton, G. P. Koocher, & M. J. Saks (Eds.), *Children's competence to consent* (pp. 149–177). New York: Plenum Press.

Bersoff, D. N. (1994). Explicit ambiguity: The 1992 ethics code as an oxymoron. *Professional Psychology: Research and Practice, 25,* 382–387.

Bersoff, D. N. (1995). *Ethical conflicts in psychology.* Washington, DC: American Psychological Association.

Bersoff, D. N. (1996). The virtue of principle ethics. *Counseling Psychologist, 24,* 86–91.

Bersoff, D. N., & Hofer, P. T. (1990). The legal regulation of school psychology. In C. R. Reynolds & T. B. Gutkin (Eds.), *The handbook of school psychology* (2nd ed., pp. 937–961). New York: Wiley.

Bersoff, D. N., & Koeppl, P. M. (1993). The relation between ethical codes and moral principles. *Ethics and Behavior, 3,* 345–357.

Bersoff, D. N., & Prasse, D. (1978). Applied psychology and judicial decision making: Corporal punishment as a case in point. *Professional Psychology, 9,* 400–411.

Bersoff, D. N., & Ysseldyke, J. E. (1977). Non-discriminatory assessment: The law, litigation, and implications for the assessment of learning disabled children. In S. Jacob (Ed.), *The law: Assessment and placement of special education students* (pp. 65–92). Lansing: Michigan Department of Education.

Blanck, P. D., Bellack, A. S., Rosnow, R. L., Rotheram-Borus, M. J., & Schooler, N. R. (1992). Scientific rewards and conflicts in human subjects research. *American Psychologist, 47,* 959–965.

Boatman, T. A., Davis, K. G., & Benbow, C. P. (1995). Best practices in gifted education. In A. Thomas & J. Grimes (Eds.), *Best practices in school psychology: III* (pp. 1083–1095). Washington, DC: National Association of School Psychologists.

Borum, R. (1996). Improving the clinical practice of violence risk assessment. *American Psychologist, 51,* 945–956.

Bower, E. M. (1982). Defining emotional disturbance: Public policy and research. *Psychology in the Schools, 19,* 55–60.

Bradley, K. L., & DuPaul, G. J. (1997). Attention-deficit/hyperactivity disorder. In G. G. Baer, K. M. Minke, & A. Thomas (Eds.), *Children's needs: II* (pp. 109–117). Bethesda, MD: National Association of School Psychologists.

Bradley-Johnson, S., Johnson, M. C., & Jacob-Timm, S. (1995). Where will—and where should—changes in education leave school psychology? *Journal of School Psychology, 33,* 187–200.

Brassard, M. R. (1997). Psychological and physical abuse. In G. G. Baer, K. M. Minke, & A. Thomas (Eds.), *Children's needs: II* (pp. 707–718). Bethesda, MD: National Association of School Psychologists.

Brock, S. E., & Sandoval, J. (1997). Suicidal ideation and behaviors. In G. G. Baer, K. M. Minke, & A. Thomas (Eds.), *Children's needs: II* (pp. 361–374). Bethesda, MD: National Association of School Psychologists.

Brooks-Gunn, J., & Furstenburg, F. F. (1989). Adolescent sexual behavior. *American Psychologist, 44,* 249–257.

Brophy, J. E., & Good, T. L. (1974). *Teacher-student relationships.* New York: Holt, Rinehart and Winston.

Brown, D., Pryzwansky, W. B., & Schulte, A. C. (1987). *Psychological consultation: Introduction to theory and practice.* Boston: Allyn & Bacon.

Brown, D. T. (1979). Issues in accreditation certification, and licensure. In G. D. Phye & D. J. Reschly (Eds.), *School psychology: Perspectives and issues* (pp. 49–82). New York: Academic Press.

Brown, W. E., & Payne, T. (1988). Policies, practices in public school discipline. *Academic Therapy, 23,* 297–301.

Burgdorf, R. L. (1991). The *Americans with Disabilities Act:* Analysis and implications of a second-generation civil rights statute. *Harvard Civil Rights-Civil Liberties Law Review, 26,* 413–522.

Burn, D. (1992). Ethical implications in cross-cultural counseling and training. *Journal of Counseling and Development, 70,* 578–583.

Callahan, C. M. (1997). Giftedness. In G. G. Baer, K. M. Minke, & A. Thomas (Eds.), *Children's needs: II* (pp. 431–448). Bethesda, MD: National Association of School Psychologists.

Campbell, D. T., & Fiske, D. W. (1959). Convergent and discriminate validation by the multitrait-multimethod matrix. *Psychological Bulletin, 56,* 81–105.

Canadian Psychological Association. (1991). *Canadian code of ethics for psychologists, revised 1991.* (Available from Canadian Psychological Association, 151 rue Slater St., Suite 205, Ottawa K1P 5H3)

Canter, A. (1989, November). Is parent permission always necessary? *Communique,* p. 9.

Canter, M. B., Bennett, B. E., Jones, S. E., & Nagy, T. F. (1994). *Ethics for psychologists.* Washington, DC: American Psychological Association.

Chalfant, J. C. (1989). Learning disabilities: Policy issues and promising approaches. *American Psychologist, 44,* 392–398.

Chalk, R., Frankel, M. S., & Chafer, S. B. (1980). *AAAS professional ethics project.* Washington, DC: American Association for the Advancement of Science.

Clarizio, H. F. (1987). Differentiating emotionally impaired from socially maladjusted students. *Psychology in the Schools, 24,* 237–242.

Cobb, C. T. (1995). Best practices in defining, implementing, and evaluation educational outcomes. In A. Thomas & J. Grimes (Ed.), *Best practices in school psychology: III* (pp. 325–336). Washington, DC: National Association of School Psychologists.

Cobb County (GA) School District. (1992). OCR complaint investigation letter of findings. *Individuals with Disabilities Education Law Report, 19,* 29–32.

Coles, N. S. (1981). Bias in testing. *American Psychologist, 36,* 1067–1077.

Cone, T. E., & Wilson, L. R. (1981). Quantifying a severe discrepancy: A critical analysis. *Learning Disability Quarterly, 3,* 76–87.

Conoley, J. C., & Bahns, T. (1995). Best practices in supervision of interns. In A. Thomas & J. Grimes (Eds.), *Best practices in school psychology: III* (pp. 111–112). Washington, DC: National Association of School Psychologists.

Conoley, J. C., & Conoley, C. W. (1982). *School consultation: A guide to practice and training.* New York: Pergamon Press.

Cooper, S. (1984). Minors' participation in therapy decisions: A written therapist-child agreement. *Journal of Child Adolescent Psychotherapy, 1,* 93–96.

Corey, G., Corey, M. S., & Callanan, P. (1993). *Issues and ethics in the helping professions* (4th ed.). Belmont, CA: Brooks/Cole.

Corrao, J., & Melton, G. B. (1988). Legal issues in school-based behavior therapy. In J. C. Witt, S. N. Elliot, & F. M. Gresham (Eds.), *Handbook of behavior therapy in education* (pp. 377–399). New York: Plenum Press.

Coughlin, E. K. (1988, November 30). Psychologist sentenced for giving false data to federal government. *Chronicle of Higher Education,* p. A5.

Council of Administrators of Special Education (CASE). (nd). *Student access, a resource guide for educators: Section 504 of the Rehabilitation Act of 1973.* (Available from

Council of Administrators of Special Education, 615 16th Street N.W., Albuquerque, NM 87104)

Council for Children with Behavior Disorders Executive Committee. (1987). Position paper on definition and identification of students with behavior disorders. *Behavioral Disorders, 13,* 9–19.

Curtis, M. J., Hunley, S., & Prus, J. (1995). *Handbook of certification and licensure requirements for school psychologists* (5th ed.). Silver Spring, MD: National Association of School Psychologists.

Curtis, M. J., & Meyers, J. (1985). Best practices in school-based consultation: Guidelines for effective practice. In A. Thomas & J. Grimes (Eds.), *Best practices in school psychology* (pp. 79–84). Kent, OH: National Association of School Psychologists.

Curtis, M. J., & Stollar, S. A. (1996). Applying principles and practices of organizational change to school reform. *School Psychology Review, 25,* 409–417.

Dalton, J. H. (1984). Discussing ethical issues in practicum courses. *Teaching of Psychology, 11,* 186–188.

Dana, R. H. (1994). Testing and assessment ethics for all persons: Beginning and agenda. *Professional Psychology: Research and Practice, 25,* 349–354.

Davila, R. R. (1991/1992). Response to letter of inquiry from D. J. Rose. *Individuals with Disabilities Education Law Report, 18,* 531–532.

Davis, J. L., & Mickelson, D. J. (1994). School counselors: Are you aware of ethical and legal aspects of counseling? *The School Counselor, 42,* 5–13.

Davis, J. M., & Sandoval, J. (1982). Applied ethics for school-based consultants. *Professional Psychology, 13,* 543–551.

Davis, J. M., Sandoval, J., & Wilson, M. P. (1988). Strategies for the primary prevention of adolescent suicide. *School Psychology Review, 17,* 559–569.

Dawson, M. M. (1987). Beyond ability grouping: A review of the effectiveness of ability grouping and its alternatives. *School Psychology Review, 17,* 559–569.

Dawson, M. M. (1995). Best practices in promoting alternatives to ability grouping. In A. Thomas & J. Grimes (Eds.), *Best practices in school psychology: III* (pp. 347–357). Washington, DC: National Association of School Psychologists.

DeMers, S. T. (1994). Legal and ethical issues in school psychologists' participation in psychopharmacological interventions with children. *School Psychology Quarterly, 9,* 41–52.

DeMers, S. T., & Bersoff, D. (1985). Legal issues in school psychological practice. In J. R. Bergan (Ed.), *School psychology in contemporary society: An introduction* (pp. 319–339). Columbus, OH: Merrill.

DeMers, S. T., & Bricklin, P. (1995). Legal, professional, and financial constraints on psychologists' delivery of health care services in school settings. *School Psychology Quarterly, 10,* 217–235.

Diener, E., & Crandall, R. (1978). *Ethics in social and behavioral research.* Chicago: University of Chicago Press.

Discipline under Section 504. (1996, November 22). *The Special Educator, 12*(1), 6–8.

Eades, R. W. (1986). The school counselor or psychologist and problems of defamation. *Journal of School Law, 15,* 117–120.

East Lansing (MI) Public Schools. (1992). OCR complaint investigation letter of findings. *Individuals with Disabilities Education Law Report, 19,* 40–43.

Eberlein, L. (1987). Introducing ethics to beginning psychologists: A problem-solving approach. *Professional Psychology: Research and Practice, 18,* 353–359.

Elliott, S. N. (1991). Authentic assessment: An introduction to a neobehavioral approach to classroom assessment. *School Psychology Quarterly, 6,* 273–278.

Engin, A. W. (1983). National organizations. In G. W. Hynd (Ed.), *The school psychologist* (pp. 27–44). Syracuse, New York: Syracuse University Press.

Eversole, T. (1993, September). Lesbian, gay and bisexual youth in school. *Communique,* 9–10.

Eyde, L. D., Robertson, G. J., Krug, S. E., Moreland, K. L., Robertson, A. G., Shewan, C. M., Harrison, P. L., Porch, B. E., Hammer, A. L., & Primoff, E. S. (1993). *Responsible test use: Case studies for assessing human behavior.* Washington, DC: American Psychological Association.

Fagan, T. K., & Wise, P. S. (1994). *School psychology: Past, present, and future.* New York: Longman.

Fairfield-Suisun Unified School District. (1989). OCR complaint investigation letter of findings. *Education for the Handicapped Law Report, 353*(Suppl. 242), 205–208.

Fanibanda, D. K. (1976). Ethical issues of mental health consultation. *Professional Psychology, 7,* 547–552.

Federal genesis of comprehensive protection of student educational record rights: *The Family Educational Rights and Privacy Act of 1974.* (1975). *Iowa Law Review, 61,* 74–95.

Ferguson, L. R. (1978). The competence and freedom of children to make choices regarding participation in research: A statement. *Journal of Social Issues, 34,* 114–121.

FERPA Office. (1986, December 2). Response to letter of inquiry from R. E. Thomas. *Education for the Handicapped Law Report, 211,* 420–424.

Fine, M. A., & Kurdek, L. A. (1993). Reflections on determining authorship credit and authorship order on faculty-student collaborations. *American Psychologist, 48,* 1141–1147.

Fine, M. A., & Ulrich, L. P. (1988). Integrating psychology and philosophy in teaching a graduate course in ethics. *Professional Psychology: Research and Practice, 19,* 542–546.

Fischer, L., & Sorenson, G. P. (1996). *School law for counselors, psychologists, and social workers* (3rd ed.). White Plains, New York: Longman.

Fisher, C. B., & Fryberg, D. (1994). Participant partners: College students weigh the costs and benefits of deceptive research. *American Psychologist, 49,* 417–427.

Flanagan, D. P., Andrews, T. J., & Genshaft, J. L. (1997). The functional utility of intelligence tests with special education populations. In D. P. Flanagan, J. L. Genshaft, & P. L. Harrison (Eds.), *Contemporary intellectual assessment* (pp. 457–483). New York: Guilford Press.

Flaugher, R. L. (1978). The many definitions of test bias. *American Psychologist, 33,* 671–679.

Fleming, E. R., & Fleming, D. C. (1987). Involvement of minors in special educational decision-making. *Journal of Law & Education, 16,* 389–402.

Forman, S. G., & Pfeiffer, A. (1997). Substance use and abuse. In G. G. Baer, K. M. Minke, & A. Thomas (Eds.), *Children's needs: II* (pp. 917–924). Bethesda, MD: National Association of School Psychologists.

Forman, S. G., & Randolph, M. K. (1987). Children and drug abuse. In A. Thomas & J. Grimes (Eds.), *Children's needs: Psychological perspectives* (pp. 182–189). Washington, DC: National Association of School Psychologists.

Fuchs, D., & Fuchs, L. S. (1988). Mainstream assistance teams to accommodate difficult-to-teach students in general education. In J. L. Graden, J. E. Zins, & M. J. Curtis (Eds.), *Alternative educational delivery systems* (pp. 49–70). Washington, DC: National Association of School Psychologists.

Furlong, M., Morrison, G. M., Chung, A., Bates, M., & Morrison, R. L. (1997). School violence. In G. G. Bear, K. M. Minke, & A. Thomas (Eds.), *Childrens needs: II* (pp. 245–256). Bethesda, MD: National Association of School Psychologists.

Furstenberg, F. F., Brooks-Gunn, J., & Chase-Lansdale, L. (1989). Teenaged pregnancy and childbearing. *American Psychologist, 44,* 313–320.

Gallagher, J. J. (1989). A new policy initiative: Infants and toddlers with handicapping conditions. *American Psychologist, 44,* 387–391.

Gallessich, J. (1982). *The profession and practice of consultation.* San Francisco: Jossey-Bass.

Gawthrop, J. C., & Uhlemann, M. R. (1992). Effects of the problem-solving approach in ethics training. *Professional Psychology: Research and Practice, 23,* 38–42.

Goh, D. (1997, June). New standards for testing released for public comment. *Communique,* p. 33.

Graden, J., Casey, A., & Bonstrom, O. (1985). Implementing a prereferral intervention system: Part II. The data. *Exceptional Children, 51,* 487–496.

Gredler, G. R. (1997). Issues in school readiness. In G. G. Baer, K. M. Minke, & A. Thomas (Eds.), *Children's needs: II* (pp. 489–499). Bethesda, MD: National Association of School Psychologists.

Greenbaum, S., & Turner, B. (Eds.). (1989). *Safe schools overview: NSSC resource paper.* Malibu, CA: U.S. Department of Justice, U.S. Department of Education, and Pepperdine University.

Gresham, F. M. (1991). Alternative psychometrics for authentic assessment. *School Psychology Quarterly, 6,* 305–309.

Grisso, T., & Vierling, L. (1978). Minor's consent to treatment: A developmental perspective. *Professional Psychology, 9,* 412–427.

Grunder, T. M. (1978). Two formulas for determining the readability of subject consent forms. *American Psychologist, 33,* 773–774.

Gutkin, T. B. & Curtis, M. J. (1990). School-based consultation: Theory, techniques, and research. In T. B. Gutkin & C. R. Reynolds (Eds.), *The handbook of school psychology* (2nd ed., pp. 577–611). New York: Wiley.

Haas, L. J., & Malouf, J. L. (1989). *Keeping up the good work: A practitioner's guide to mental health ethics.* Sarasota, FL: Professional Resource Exchange.

Haas, L. J., Malouf, J. L., & Mayerson, N. H. (1986). Ethical dilemmas in psychological practice: Results of a national survey. *Professional Psychology: Research and Practice, 17,* 316–321.

Haefli, K., Pryor, J. B., & Landau, S. (1995). Best practices in addressing HIV/AIDS issues in the school. In A. Thomas & J. Grimes (Eds.), *Best practices in school psychology: III* (pp. 383–395). Washinton, DC: National Association of School Psychologists.

Hakola, S. R. (1992). Legal rights of students with attention deficit disorder. *School Psychology Quarterly, 7,* 285–297.

Hammill, D. D., Brown, L., & Bryant, B. R. (1989). *A consumer's guide to tests in print.* Austin, TX: Pro-Ed.

Handelsman, M. M. (1986a). Problems with ethics training by "osmosis." *Professional Psychology: Research and Practice, 17,* 371–372.

Handelsman, M. M. (1986b). Ethics training at the master's level: A national survey. *Professional Psychology: Research and Practice, 17,* 24–26.

Hansen, J. C., Green, S., & Kutner, K. B. (1989). Ethical issues facing school psychologists working with families. *Professional School Psychology, 4,* 245–255.

Hansen, J. C., Himes, B. S., & Meier, S. (1990). *Consultation: Concepts and practices.* Englewood Cliffs, NJ: Prentice-Hall.

Hare, R. (1981). The philosophical basis of psychiatric ethics. In S. Bloch & P. Chodoff (Eds.), *Psychiatric ethics* (pp. 31–45). Oxford, England: Oxford University Press.

Harrar, W. R., VandeCreek, L., & Knapp, S. (1990). Ethical and legal aspects of clinical supervision. *Professional Psychology: Research and Practice, 21,* 37–41.

Harris, A., & Kapche, R. (1978). Behavior modification in schools: Ethical issues and suggested guidelines. *Journal of School Psychology, 16,* 25–33.

Harvey, V. S. (1997). Improving readability of psychological reports. *Professional Psychology: Research and Practice, 28,* 271–274.

Hehir, T. (1993, October 25). Response to letter of inquiry from McDonald. *Individuals with Disabilities Education Law Report, 20,* 1159–1160.

Heller, K. A., Holtzman, W. H., & Messick, S. (1982). *Placing children in special education: A strategy for equity.* Washington, DC: U.S. Department of Commerce, National Technical Information Service.

Helton, G. (1992, March). *School psychologist's response to administrative pressure to act unethically.* Paper presented at the National Association of School Psychologists Convention, Nashville, TN.

Henderson, D. H. (1986). Constitutional implications involving the use of corporal punishment in the public schools. *Journal of Law & Education, 15,* 255–269.

Henker, B., & Whalen, C. K. (1989). Hyperactivity and attention deficits. *American Psychologist, 44,* 216–223.

Herlihy, B., & Sheeley, V. L. (1987). Privileged communication in selected helping professions: A comparison among statutes. *Journal of Counseling and Development, 65,* 479–483.

Heumann, J. E. (1993). Response to letter of inquiry from G. Warrington. *Individuals with Disablities Education Law Report, 20,* 539–540.

Hindman, S. E. (1986). The law, the courts, and the education of behaviorally disordered students. *Behavior Disorders, 11,* 280–289.

Hobbs, N. (1975). *The futures of children.* San Francisco: Jossey-Bass.

Holmes, D. S. (1976). Debriefing after psychological experiments: II. Effectiveness of postexperimental desensitizing. *American Psychologist, 31,* 868–875.

Holmes, D. S., & Urie, R. C. (1975). Effects of preparing children for psychotherapy. *Journal of Consulting and Clinical Psychology, 43,* 311–318.

Hopkins, B. R., & Anderson, B. S. (1985). *The counselor and the law* (2nd ed.). Alexandria, VA: American Association for Counseling and Development.

Horton, C. B. (1995). Best practices in response to child maltreatment. In A. Thomas & J. Grimes (Eds.), *Best practices in school psychology: III* (pp. 963–976). Washington, DC: National Association of School Psychologists.

Horton, C. B., & Cruise, T. K. (1997). Child sexual abuse. In G. G. Baer, K. M. Minke, & A. Thomas (Eds.), *Children's needs: II* (pp. 719–727). Bethesda, MD: National Association of School Psychologists.

Hostetler, A. J. (1988, June). Indictment: Congress send message on fraud. *APA Monitor,* p. 5.

Hubsch, A. W. (1989). Education and self-government: The right to education under state constitutional law. *Journal of Law & Education, 18,* 93–133.

Hughes, J. N. (1986). Ethical issues in school consultation. *School Psychology Review, 15,* 489–499.

Hummel, D. L., Talbutt, L. C., & Alexander, M. D. (1985). *Law and ethics in counseling.* New York: Van Nostrand-Reinhold.

Hyman, I. A. (1990). *Reading, writing, and the hickory stick.* Lexington, MA: Lexington Books.

Hyman, I. A., Barrish, B. M., & Kaplan, J. (1997). Corporal punishment. In G. G. Baer, K. M. Minke, & A. Thomas (Eds.), *Children's needs: II* (pp. 235–243). Bethesda, MD: National Association of School Psychologists.

In the Matter of a Child with Disabilities. (1992). Ruling of a Connecticut hearing officer. *Individuals with Disabilities Education Law Report, 19,* 198–203.

Irvin, T. B. (1979, January 9). Response to letter of inquiry from W. A. Hafner. *Education for the Handicapped Law Report, 23*(Suppl.), 181–182.

Jacob, S., & Brantley, J. C. (1987a). Ethical and legal considerations for microcomputer use in special education. In D. L. Johnson, C. D. Maddux, & A. C. Candler (Eds.), *Computers in the special education classroom* (pp. 185–194). New York: Haworth Press.

Jacob, S., & Brantley, J. C. (1987b). Ethical-legal problems with computer use and suggestions for best practices: A national survey. *School Psychology Review, 16,* 69–77.

Jacob, S., & Brantley, J. C. (1989). Ethics and computer-assisted assessment: Three case studies. *Psychology in the Schools, 26,* 163–167.

Jacob-Timm, S. (1996). Ethical and legal issues associated with the use of aversives in the public schools: The SIBIS controversy. *School Psychology Review, 2,* 184–198.

Jacob-Timm, S., & Hartshorne, T. S. (1994). Section 504 and school psychology. *Psychology in the Schools, 31,* 26–39.

Jann, R. J., Hyman, I. A., & Reinhardt, J. A. (1992, March). *The consequences of supervisory pressure to act unethically: A national survey.* Paper presented at the Nation Association of School Psychologists Convention, Nashville, TN.

Jitendra, A. K., & Rohena-Diaz, E. (1996). Language assessment of students who are linguistically diverse: Why a discrete approach is not the answer. *School Psychology Review, 25,* 40–56.

Jobes, D. A., & Berman, A. L. (1993). Suicide and malpractice liability: Assessing and revising policies, procedures, and practice in outpatient settings. *Professional Psychology: Research and Practice, 24,* 91–99.

Johnson, T. P. (1993). Managing student records. *West's Education Law Quarterly, 2,* 260–276.

Joint Committee on Testing Practices. (1988/1989). Code of fair testing practices. *American Psychologist, 44,* 1065–1067.

Kagle, J. D., & Kopels, S. (1994). Confidentiality after Tarasoff. *Health & Social Work, 19,* 217–222.

Kalichman, S. C. (1993). *Mandated reporting of suspected child abuse.* Washington, DC: American Psychological Association.

Kaser-Boyd, N., Adelman, H. S., & Taylor, L. (1985). Minors' ability to identify risks and benefits of therapy. *Professional Psychology: Research and Practice, 16,* 411–417.

Kaufman, A. S. (1994). *Intelligent testing with the WISC-III.* New York: Wiley.

Kavale, K. (1990). Effectiveness of special education. In T. B. Gutkin & C. R. Reynolds (Eds.), *The handbook of school psychology* (2nd ed., pp. 868–898). New York: Wiley.

Keith-Spiegel, P. (1983). Children and consent to participate in research. In G. B. Melton, G. P. Koocher, & M. J. Saks (Eds.), *Children's competence to consent* (pp. 179–211). New York: Plenum Press.

Keith-Spiegel, P., & Koocher, G. P. (1985). *Ethics in psychology.* Hillsdale, NJ: Erlbaum.

Kenowa Hills (MI) Public Schools. (1992/1993). OCR complaint investigation letter of findings. *Individuals with Disabilities Education Law Report, 19,* 525–526.

Kirkland, M., & Ginther, D. (1988). Acquired immune deficiency syndrome in children: Medical, legal, and school-related issues. *School Psychology Review, 17,* 304–310.

Kirp, D. (1973). Schools as sorters. *University of Pennsylvania Law Review, 121,* 705–797.

Kitchener, K. S. (1986). Teaching applied ethics in counselor education: An integration of psychological processes and philosophical analysis. *Journal of Counseling and Development, 64,* 306–310.

Knapp, S. (1980). A primer on malpractice for psychologists. *Professional Psychology, 11,* 606–612.

Knapp, S., & VandeCreek, L. (1982). Tarasoff: Five years later. *Professional Psychology, 13,* 511–516.

Knapp, S., & VandeCreek, L. (1985). Psychotherapy and privileged communications in child custody cases. *Professional Psychology: Research and Practice, 16,* 398–407.

Knoff, H. M. (1983). Personality assessment in the schools: Issues and procedures for school psychologists. *School Psychology Review, 12,* 391–398.

Kubiszyn, T., Brown, R. T., & DeMers, S. T. (1997). Pediatric psychopharmacology. In G. G. Baer, K. M. Minke, & A. Thomas (Eds.), *Children's needs: II* (pp. 925–934). Bethesda, MD: National Association of School Psychologists.

Lake Washington (WA) School District No. 414. (1985, June 28). OCR complaint investigation letter of findings. *Individuals with Disabilities Education Law Report, 257*(Suppl. 150), 611–615.

Lakin, M. (1994). Morality in group and family therapies: Multiperson therapies and the 1992 ethics code. *Professional Psychology: Research and Practice, 25,* 344–348.

Landau, S., Pryor, J. B., & Haefli, K. (1995). Pediatric HIV: School-based sequelae and curricular interventions for infection prevention and social acceptance. *School Psychology Review, 24,* 213–229.

Lasser, J., & Tharinger, D. (1997). Sexual minority youth. In G. G. Bear, K. M. Minke, & A. Thomas (Eds.), *Children's needs: II* (pp. 769–780). Bethesda, MD: National Association of School Psychologists.

Lichtenstein, R. (1981). Comparative validity of two preschool screening tests: Correlational and classificational approaches. *Journal of Learning Disabilities, 14,* 68–72.

Lim, J. (1993, May 19). OCR policy letter to regional offices. *Special Education Report,* p. 5.

Lohrmann, S., & Zirkel, P. A. (1995, November 10). Helping you make the call. *The Special Educator, 11,* 1, 6.

Lopez, E. C. (1995). Best practices in working with bilingual children. In A. Thomas & J. Grimes (Eds.), *Best practices in school psychology: III* (pp. 1111–1121). Washington, DC: National Association of School Psychologists.

Lopez, E. C. (1997). The cognitive assessment of limited English proficient and bilingual children. In D. P. Flanagan, J. L. Genshaft, & P. L. Harrison (Eds.), *Contemporary intellectual assessment* (pp. 503–516). New York: Guilford Press.

Lopez, E. C., & Gopaul-McNicol, S. (1997). English as a second language. In G. G. Baer, K. M. Minke, & A. Thomas (Eds.), *Children's needs: II* (pp. 523–531). Bethesda, MD: National Association of School Psychologists.

Martens, B. K., & Keller, H. R. (1987). Training school psychologists in the scientific tradition. *School Psychology Review, 16,* 32–37.

Martin, R. (1979). *Educating handicapped children: The legal mandate.* Champaign, IL: Research Press.

Martin, R. (1992). *Continuing challenges in special education law* (looseleaf notebook). Urbana, IL: Carle Media.

Martin, R. P. (1985, April). Ethics column—Parents' rights to copies of test protocols: A draft position statement of the Division 16 Ethics Committee. T*he School Psychologist,* p. 9.

Matarazzo, J. D. (1986). Computerized psychological test interpretations. *American Psychologist, 41,* 14–24.

McConaughy, S. H., & Skiba, R. J. (1993). Comorbidity of externalizing and internalizing problems. *School Psychology Review, 22,* 421–436.

McDermott, P. A., & Watkins, M. W. (1985). *M-MAC Microcomputer systems manual.* San Antonio, TX: The Psychological Corporation.

McKee, P. W. (1996). Q & A with Patrick McKee. *The Special Educator, 11*(13), 3.

McMahon, T. J. (1993). On the concept of child advocacy: A review of theory and methodology. *School Psychology Review, 22,* 744–755.

McNamera, K. M. (1995). Best practices in substance abuse prevention programs. In A. Thomas & J. Grimes (Eds.), *Best practices in school psychology: III* (pp. 369–382). Washington, DC: National Association of School Psychologists.

Meara, N. M., Schmidt, L. D., & Day, J. D. (1996). Principles and virtues: A foundation for ethical decisions, policies, and character. *Counseling Psychology, 24,* 4–77.

Meddin, B. J., & Rosen, A. L. (1986). Child abuse and neglect: Prevention and reporting. *Young Children, 41,* 26–30.

Medway, F. J., & Rose, J. S. (1986). Grade retention. In T. R. Kratochwill (Ed.), *Advances in school psychology* (Vol. 5, pp. 141–175). Hillsdale, NJ: Erlbaum.

Mehrens, W. A., & Lehmann, I. J. (1978). *Measurement and evaluation in education and psychology* (2nd ed.). New York: Holt, Rinehart and Winston.

Melton, G. B., & Gray, J. W. (1988). Ethical dilemmas in AIDS research. *American Psychologist, 43,* 60–64.

Melton, G. B., Koocher, G. P., & Saks, M. J. (Eds.). (1983). *Children's competence to consent.* New York: Plenum Press.

Messick, S. (1965). Personality measurement and the ethics of assessment. A*merican Psychologist, 20,* 136–142.

Messick, S. (1980). Test validity and the ethics of assessment. *American Psychologist, 35,* 1012–1027.

Messick, S. (1984). Assessment in context: Appraising student performance in relation to instructional quality. *Educational Researcher, 13,* 3–8.

Messick, S. (1995). Validity of psychological assessment. *American Psychologist, 50,* 741–749.

Messina, D. J. (1988). Corporal punishment v. classroom discipline: A case of mistaken identity. *Loyola Law Review, 34,* 35–110.

Meyers, J., Parsons, R. D., & Martin, R. (1979). *Mental health consultation in the schools.* San Francisco: Jossey-Bass.

Mini-series on authentic assessment. (1991). *School Psychology Quarterly, 6*(4).

Mowder, B. (1983). Assessment and intervention in school psychological services. In G. W. Hynd (Ed.), *The school psychologist* (pp. 145–167). Syracuse, NY: Syracuse University Press.

Muehleman, T., Pickens, B. K., & Robinson, F. (1985). Informing clients about the limits to confidentiality, risks, and their rights: Is self-disclosure inhibited? *Professional Psychology: Research and Practice, 16,* 385–397.

Nagle, R. J. (1987). Ethics training in school psychology. *Professional School Psychology, 2,* 163–171.

National Association of School Psychologists. (1984). *Professional conduct manual.* Stratford, CT: Author.

National Association of School Psychologists. (1986). *Standards.* Stratford, CT: Author.

National Association of School Psychologists. (1992). *Professional conduct manual.* Silver Spring, MD: Author.

National Association of School Psychologists. (1997). *Professional conduct manual* (3rd ed.). Bethesda, MD: Author.

National Association of State Boards of Education. (1992). *Winners all: A call for inclusive schools.* Alexandria, VA: Author.

National Center for Education Statistics. (1993). *Digest of education statistics.* Washington, DC: U.S. Department of Education.

National Commission for the Protection of Human Subjects of Biomedical and Behavioral Science Research. (1979). The Belmont report: Ethical principles and guidelines for the protection of human subjects of biomedical and behavioral research. *The Federal Register,* pp. 12065–12073.

National Commission on Testing and Public Policy. (1990). *From gatekeeper to gateway: Transforming testing in America.* Chestnut Hill, MA: National Computer Systems, Boston College.

National Institutes of Health. (1991). National Institutes of Health consensus development conference statement. *In NIH consensus development conference on the treatment of destructive behaviors in persons with developmental disabilities* (NIH Publication No. 91-2410, pp. 1–29). Washington, DC: U.S. Government Printing Office.

Newman, J. L. (1993). Ethical issues in consultation. *Journal of Counseling and Development, 72,* 148–156.

Overcast, T. D., & Sales, B. D. (1982). The legal rights of students in the elementary and secondary public schools. In C. R. Reynolds & T. B. Gutkin (Eds.), *The handbook of school psychology* (pp. 1075–1100). New York: Wiley

Page, E. B. (1980). Tests and decisions for the handicapped: A guide to evaluation under the new laws. *The Journal of Special Education, 14,* 423–483.

Pelham, W. E. (1993). Psychopharmacology for children with attention-deficit hyperactivity disorder. *School Psychology Review, 22,* 199–227.

Peterson, S. A., & Brofcak, A. M. (1997). Street-level bureaucrats and AIDS policy: The case of the school psychologist. *Professional Psychology: Research and Practice, 28,* 81–86.

Physicians' desk reference (51st ed.). (1997). Montvale, NJ: Medical Economics.

Plante, T. G. (1995). Training child clinical predoctoral interns and postdoctoral fellows in ethics and professional issues: An experiential model. *Professional Psychology: Research and Practice, 26,* 616–619.

Poland, S. (1995). Best practices in suicide intervention. In A. Thomas & J. Grimes (Eds.), *Best practices in school psychology: III* (pp. 459–468). Washington, DC: National Association of School Psychologists.

Poland, S., Pitcher, G., & Lazarus, P. J. (1995). Best practices in crisis intervention. In A. Thomas & J. Grimes (Eds.), *Best practices in school psychology: III* (pp. 445–458). Washington, DC: National Association of School Psychologists.

Ponterotto, J. G., Casas, J. M., Suzuki, L. A., & Alexander, C. M. (Eds.). (1995). *Handbook of multicultural counseling.* Thousand Oaks, CA: Sage.

Pope, K. S., Tabachnick, B. G., & Keith-Spiegel, O. (1987). The beliefs and behaviors of psychologists as therapists. *American Psychologist, 42,* 993–1006.

Prilleltensky, I. (1991). The social ethics of school psychology: A priority for the 1990's. *School Psychology Quarterly, 6,* 200–222.

Prilleltensky, I. (1997). Values, assumptions, and practices: Assessing the moral implications of psychological discourse and action. *American Psychologist, 52,* 517–535.

Prus, J., Draper, A., Curtis, M. J., & Hunley, S. (1995). Appendix VII: Summary of credentialing requirements for school psychologists in public school settings. In A. Thomas & J. Grimes (Eds.), *Best practices in school psychology: III* (pp. 1237–1239). Washington, DC: National Association of School Psychologists.

Prus, J., & Mittelmeier, K. (1995). Appendix VIII: Summary of licensure requirements for independent practice in psychology and school psychology. In A. Thomas & J. Grimes (Eds.), *Best practices in school psychology: III* (pp. 1249–1256). Washington, DC: National Association of School Psychologists.

Prus, J., White, G. W., & Pendleton, A. (1987). *Handbook of certification and licensure requirements for school psychologists* (4th ed.). Washington, DC: National Association of School Psychologists.

Pryzwansky, W. B. (1993). The regulation of school psychology: A historical perspective on certification, licensure, and accreditation. *Journal of School Psychology, 31,* 219–235.

Purcell, C. W. (1984). Limiting the use of corporal punishment in American schools: A call for more specific legal guidelines. *Journal of Law & Education, 13,* 183–195.

Rafoth, M. A., & Carey, K. (1995). Best practices in assisting with promotion and retention decisions. In A. Thomas & J. Grimes (Eds.), *Best practices in school psychology: III* (pp. 413–420). Washington, DC: National Association of School Psychologists.

Remley, T. P. (1985). The law and ethical practices in elementary and middle schools. *Elementary School Guidance and Counseling, 19,* 181–189.

Remley, T. P., Herlihy, B., & Herlihy, S. (1997). The U.S. Supreme Court decision in Jaffee v. Remond: Implications for counselors. Jour*nal of Counseling and Development, 75,* 213–218.

Repp, A. C., & Singh, N. N. (Eds.). (1990). *Perspectives on the use of nonaversive and aversive interventions with persons with developmental disabilities.* Pacific Grove, CA: Brooks/Cole.

Reschly, D. J. (1979). Nonbiased assessment. In G. D. Phye & D. J. Reschly (Eds.), *School psychology: Perspectives and issues* (pp. 215–253). New York: Academic Press.

Reschly, D. J. (1988). Special education reform: School psychology revolution. *School Psychology Review, 17,* 459–475.

Reschly, D. J. (1997). Diagnostic and treatment utility of intelligence tests. In D. P. Flanagan, J. L. Genshaft, & P. L. Harrison (Eds.), *Contemporary intellectual assessment* (pp. 437–456). New York: Guilford Press.

Reschly, D. J., & Wilson, M. S. (1995). School psychology practitioners and faculty: 1986 to 1991–92 trends in demographics, roles, satisfaction, and system reform. *School Psychology Review, 24,* 2–80.

Rest, J. R. (1984). Research on moral development: Implications for training counseling psychologists. *Counseling Psychologist, 12,* 19–29.

Reutter, E. E. (1994). *The law of public education* (4th ed.). Westbury, New York: Foundation Press.

Reynolds, C. R., & Kaiser, S. M. (1990). Test bias in psychological assessment. In C. R. Reynolds & T. B. Gutkin (Eds.), *The handbook of school psychology* (2nd ed., pp. 487–525). New York: Wiley.

Rialto (CA) Unified School District. (1989). OCR complaint investigation letter of findings. *Education for the Handicapped Law Report,* 353(Suppl. 241), 201–204.

Rosenberg, S. L. (1995). Best practices in maintaining an independent practice. In A. Thomas & J. Grimes (Eds.), *Best practices in school psychology: III* (pp. 145–152). Washington, DC: National Association of School Psychologists.

Ross, R. P. (1995). Best practices in implementing intervention assistance teams. In A. Thomas & J. Grimes (Eds.), *Best practices in school psychology: III* (pp. 227–237). Washington, DC: National Association of School Psychologists.

Ross, R. P., & Harrison, P. L. (1997). Ability grouping. In G. G. Baer, K. M. Minke, & A. Thomas (Eds.), *Children's needs: II* (pp. 457–465). Bethesda, MD: National Association of School Psychologists.

Ross, W. D. (1930). *The right and the good.* Oxford, England: Claredon Press.

Ross-Reynolds, G., & Hardy, B. S. (1985). Crisis counseling for disparate adolescent sexual dilemmas: Pregnancy and homosexuality. *School Psychology Review, 14,* 300–312.

Rushton, C. H., Will, J. C., & Murray, M. G. (1994). To honor and obey-DNR orders and the school. *Pediatric Nursing, 10,* 581–585.

Russell-Sage Foundation. (1970). *Guidelines for the collection, maintenance, and dissemination of pupil records.* Hartford: Connecticut Printers.

Sainker, E. (1984, May). Letters [Letters to the editor]. *NASP Committee on Computer and Technological Applications in School Psychology Newsletter,* 10.

Salvia, J., & Ysseldyke, J. E. (1988). *Assessment in special and remedial education* (4th ed.). Boston: Houghton Mifflin.

Sanchez, J. M. (1992). Expelling the Fourth Amendment from American schools: Students' rights six years after T.L.O. *Journal of Law & Education, 21,* 381–413.

Sandoval, J., & Brock, S. E. (1996). The school psychologist's role in suicide prevention. *School Psychology Quarterly, 11,* 169–185.

Sattler, J. M. (1988). *Assessment of children* (3rd ed.). San Diego, CA: Sattler.

Schill, K. (1993, Fall). Violence among students: Schools' liability under Section 1983. *School Law Bulletin,* 1–11.

Schimmel, D., & Fischer, L. (1977). *The rights of parents in the education of their children.* Columbia, MD: National Committee for Citizens in Education.

Shah, S. A. (1969). Privileged communications, confidentiality, and privacy: Privileged communications. *Professional Psychology, 1,* 159–164.

Sherry, P. (1991). Ethical issues in the conduct of supervision. *Counseling Psychologist, 19,* 566–584.

Shinn, M. R. (1995). Best practices in curriculum-based measurement and its use in a problem-solving model. In A. Thomas & J. Grimes (Eds.), *Best practices in school psychology: III* (pp. 547–567). Washington, DC: National Association of School Psychologists.

Short, R. J., & Shapiro, S. K. (1993). Conduct disorders: A framework for understanding and intervention in schools and communities. *School Psychology Review, 22,* 362–375.

Shrag, J. A. (1991/1992). Response to letter of inquiry from J. V. Osowaski. *Individuals with Disabilities Education Law Report, 18,* 532–534.

Shrag, J. A. (1992). Response to letter of inquiry from H. C. Parker. *Individuals with Disabilities Education Law Report, 18,* 963–965.

Siegel, M. (1979). Privacy, ethics, and confidentiality. *Professional Psychology, 10,* 249–258.

Slenkovich, J. E. (1986, June). School districts can be sued for inadequate suicide prevention programs. *The Schools' Advocate,* pp. 1–3.

Slenkovich, J. E. (1986, November). The specific learning disability—A review of the legal requirements. *The Schools' Advocate,* pp. 41–42, 44–47.

Slenkovich, J. E. (1987, June). Chemical dependency doesn't fit within "other health impaired." *The Schools' Advocate,* p. 103.

Slenkovich, J. E. (1987, December). Counseling not same as psychological services. *The Schools' Advocate,* p. 143.

Slenkovich, J. E. (1988, February). The seriously emotionally disturbed definition. *The Schools' Advocate,* pp. 153–164.

Slenkovich, J. E. (1988a, March). Student records act revisited. *The Schools' Advocate,* pp. 165–170.

Slenkovich, J. E. (1988b, March). Students succeeding in regular education do not qualify as learning disabled. *The Schools' Advocate,* p. 166.

Slenkovich, J. E. (1988c, March). When is a service a related service? *The Schools' Advocate,* p. 168.

Slenkovich, J. E. (1992, May). School counselors have mandatory duty to prevent off-campus suicides. *The Schools' Advocate,* pp. 570–572.

Smith, T. S., McGuire, J. M., Abbott, D. W., & Blau, B. I. (1991). Clinical ethical decision making: An investigation of the rationales used to justify doing less than one believes one should. *Professional Psychology: Research and Practice, 22,* 235–239.

Society for Research in Child Development. (1990, Winter). SRCD ethical standards for research with children. *SRCD Newsletter,* pp. 5–7.

Society for Research in Child Development. (1991, Fall). Report from the Committee for Ethical Conduct in Child Development Research. *SRCD Newsletter,* p. 6.

Solomon, R. S. (1984). *Ethics: A brief introduction.* New York: McGraw-Hill.

Special section on authentic assessment. (1993). *Phi Delta Kappan, 74*(6).

Stewart, K. J. (1984). School psychologists as researchers: An approach for initiating training and practice. *Psychology in the Schools, 21,* 211–214.

Stoiber, K. C. (1997). Adolescent pregnancy and parenting. In G. G. Baer, K. M. Minke, & A. Thomas (Eds.), *Children's needs: II* (pp. 653–665). Bethesda, MD: National Association of School Psychologists.

Swoboda, J. S., Elwork, A., Sales, B. D., & Levine, D. (1978). Knowledge of and compliance with privileged communication and child-abuse-reporting laws. *Professional Psychology, 9,* 448–457.

Taft, R. (1965). Comments of Senator Robert Taft. *U.S. Code Congressional and Administrative News,* p. 1450.

Taube, D. O., & Elwork, A. (1990). Researching the effects of confidentiality law on patients' self-disclosures. *Professional Psychology: Research and Practice, 21,* 72–75.

Taylor, L., & Adelman, H. S. (1989). Reframing the confidentiality dilemma to work in children's best interests. *Professional Psychology: Research and Practice, 20,* 79–83.

Taylor, L., Adelman, H. S., & Kaser-Boyd, N. (1985). Minors' attitude and competence toward participation in psychoeducational decisions. *Professional Psychology: Research and Practice, 16,* 226–235.

Tharinger, D., & Stafford, M. (1995). Best pactices in individual counseling of elementary-age students. In A. Thomas & J. Grimes (Eds.), *Best practices in school psychology: III* (pp. 893–907). Washington, DC: National Association of School Psychologists.

Thomas, A., & Grimes, J. (Eds.). (1995). *Best practices in school psychology: III.* Washington, DC: National Association of School Psychologists.

Thompson, R. A. (1990). Vulnerability in research: A developmental perspective on research risk. *Child Development, 61,* 1–16.

Tindall, R. (1979). School psychology: The development of a profession. In G. D. Phye & D. J. Reschly (Eds.), *School psychology: Perspectives and issues* (pp. 3–24). New York: Academic Press.

Tokunaga, H. T. (1984). Ethical issues in consultation: An evaluative review. *Professional Psychology, 15,* 811–821.

Turnbull, H. R. (1990). *Free appropriate public education* (3rd ed.). Denver, CO: Love.

Tymchuk, A. J. (1981). Ethical decision-making and psychological treatment. *Journal of Psychiatric Treatment and Evaluation, 3,* 507–513.

Tymchuk, A. J. (1985). Ethical decision-making and psychology students' attitudes toward training in ethics. *Professional Practice of Psychology, 6,* 219–232.

Tymchuk, A. J. (1986). Guidelines for ethical decision making. *Canadian Psychology, 27,* 36–43.

Tymchuk, A. J., Drapkin, R., Major-Kingsley, S., Ackerman, A. B., Coffman, E. W., & Baum, M. S. (1982). Ethical decision making and psychologists' attitudes toward training in ethics. *Professional Psychology, 13,* 412–421.

U.S. Census Bureau. (1992). *Statistical abstracts of the United States* (112th ed.). Washington, DC: U.S. Department of Commerce.

U.S. Department of Education. (1991). Joint policy memorandum. *Individuals with Disabilities Education Law Report, 18,* 116–119.

U.S. Department of Education. (1997, September 19). Memorandum on "Initial Disciplinary Guidance Related to Removal of Children with Disabilities from Their Current Educational Placement for Ten School Days or Less" [On-line]. Available from the U.S. Department of Education website: http://www.ed.gov/offices/OSERS/IDEA/memo.html

U.S. Department of Health and Human Services. (1991, 1992). HHS policy clarification. *Individuals with Disabilities Education Law Report, 18,* 558–565.

Van Houten, R., Axelrod, S., Bailey, J. S., Favell, J. E., Foxx, R. N., Iwata, B. A., & Lovaas, O. I. (1988). The right to effective behavioral treatment. *The Behavior Analyst, 11,* 111–114.

Viadero, D. (1987, December). Debate grows on use of Ritalin in schools. *Communique,* pp. 1, 12.

Walding, J. K. (1990). Whatever happened to *Parham* and *Institutionalized Juveniles:* Do minors have procedural rights in the civil commitment area? *Law & Psychology Review, 14,* 281–302.

Waldo, S. L., & Malley, P. (1992). *Tarasoff* and its progeny: Implications for the school counselor. *The School Counselor, 40,* 46–54.

Watson, H., & Levine, M. (1989). Psychotherapy and mandated reporting of child abuse. *American Journal of Orthopsychiatry, 59,* 246–256.

Weirda, B. (1987, November). Related services—The medical exclusion. *The Schools' Advocate,* pp. 137–139.

Weithorn, L. A. (1983). Involving children in decisions affecting their own welfare: Guidelines for professionals. In G. B. Melton, G. P. Koocher, & M. J. Saks (Eds.), *Children's competence to consent* (pp. 235–260). New York: Plenum Press.

Welfel, E. R. (1992). Psychologist as ethics educator: Successes, failures, and unanswered questions. *Professional Psychology: Research and Practice, 23,* 182–189.

Welfel, E. R., & Kitchener, K. S. (1992). Introduction to the special section: Ethics education—An agenda for the '90s. *Professional Psychology: Research and Practice, 23,* 179–181.

Welfel, E. R., & Lipsitz, N. E. (1984). Ethical behavior of professional psychologists: A critical analysis of the research. *The Counseling Psychologist, 12,* 31–41.

Wigmore, J. H. (1961). *Evidence* (Vol. 3, Sec. 2285). Boston: Little, Brown.

Wolters, O. L., Brouwers, P., & Moss, H. A. (1995). Pediatric HIV disease: Effect on cognition, learning, and behavior. *School Psychology Quarterly, 10,* 305–328.

Wonderly, D. (April, 1989). Introductory comments. *Ethical behavior: Is there adequate training and support?* Symposia presented at the National Association of School Psychologists Convention, Boston, MA.

Woodcock, R. W., & Johnson, M. B. (1989). *Woodcock-Johnson Psycho-Educational Battery-Revised.* Allen, TX: DLM Teaching Resources.

Woody, R. H. (1988). *Protecting your mental health practice.* San Francisco: Jossey-Bass.

WtL Publishing. (1995). *Standard Score Regression Comparison 3.1* [Computer software]. Little Rock, AK: Author.

Ysseldyke, J. E., & Christenson, S. L. (1988). Linking assessment to intervention. In J. L. Graden, J. E. Zins, & M. J. Curtis (Eds.), *Alternative educational delivery systems* (pp. 91–109). Washington, DC: National Association of School Psychologists.

Ysseldyke, J. E., & Geenen, K. (1996). Integrating the special education and compensatory education systems into the school reform process: A national perspective. *School Psychology Review, 25,* 418–430.

Zachary, R. A., & Pope, S. K. (1984). Legal and ethical issues in the clinical use of computerized testing. In M. D. Schwartz (Ed.), *Using computers in clinical practice* (pp. 151–164). New York: Haworth Press.

Zingaro, J. C. (1983). Confidentiality: To tell or not to tell. *Elementary School Guidance and Counseling, 17,* 261–267.

Zins, J. E., & Forman, S. G. (1988). Primary prevention in the schools: What are we waiting for? *School Psychology Review, 17,* 539–541.

Zirkel, P. A., & Kincaid, J. M. (1993). *Section 504, the ADA, and the schools* (looseleaf). Horsham, PA: LRP.

Zirkel, P. A., & Reichner, H. F. (1986). Is the *In Loco Parentis* doctrine dead? *Journal of Law & Education, 15,* 271–283.

Table of Cases

"A" Family, In the Matter of the, 602 P.2d 157 (Mont. 1979).

Aguilar v. Felton, 473 U.S. 402, 105 S.Ct. 3232, 87 L.Ed.2d 290 (1985), *rev'd sub nom.* Agostini v. Felton, No. 96–552 (U.S. June 23, 1997).

Alamo Heights Independent School District v. State Board of Education, 790 F.2d 1153 (5th Cir. 1986).

A.W. v. Northwest R-1 School District, 813 F.2d 158 (8th Cir. 1987), *cert. den.*, 108 S.Ct. 144.

Baker v. Owen, 395 F.Supp 294 (D.C. M.D. N.C., 1975), *aff'd,* 423 U.S. 908.

Battle v. Commonwealth of Pennsylvania, 629 F.2d 269 (3rd Cir. 1980).

Bellotti v. Baird, 443 U.S. 622 (1979).

Benskin v. Taft City School District, 14 Clearinghouse Review 529 (1980).

B.M. v. State of Montana, 649 P.2d 425 (Mont. 1982).

Board of Education of the Hendrick Hudson Central School District v. Rowley, 458 U.S. 176, 102 S.Ct. 3034 (1982).

Board of Education, Sacramento City Unified School District v. Holland, 786 F.Supp. 874 (E.D. Cal. 1992), *aff'd sub nom.* Sacramento City Unified School District, Board of Education v. Rachel H., 14 F.3d 1398 (9th Cir. 1994), *cert. denied sub nom.* Sacramento City Unified School District Board of Education v. Holland, 114 S.Ct. 2697 (1994).

Brantley v. Independent School District No. 625, 24 IDELR 696 (D.Minn. 1996).

Brown v. Board of Education, 347 U.S. 483 (1954).

California Association of School Psychologists v. Superintendent of Public Instruction, 21 IDELR 130 (N.D. Cal. 1994).

Cedar Rapids Community Sch. Dist. v. Garret F. by Charlene F., 24 IDELR 648 (N.D. Iowa 1996).

Christopher M. v. Corpus Christi Independent School District, 17 IDELR 990, 992 (5th Cir. 1991).

Clevenger v. Oak Ridge School Board, 744 F.2d 514 (6th Cir. 1984).

Cordrey v. Euckert, 917 F.2d 1460 (6th Cir. 1990).

Crawford v. Honig, 37 F.3d 485 (9th Cir. 1994).

Cronin v. Board of Education of East Ramapo Central School District, 689 F.Supp. 197 (S.D.N.Y. 1988).

Daniel R.R. v. Texas Board of Education, El Paso Independent School District, 874 F.2d 1036 (5th Cir. 1989).

Darlene L. v. Illinois State Board of Education, 563 F.Supp. 1340 (N.D. Ill. 1983).

Debra P. v. Turlington, 730 F.2d 1405 (11th. Cir. 1984).

Department of Education, State of Hawaii v. Katherine Dorr, 531 F.Supp. 517 (D. Haw. 1982), *aff'd,* 727 F.2d 809 (9th Cir. 1984).

Detsel v. Board of Education of the Auburn Enlarged City School District, 637 F.Supp. 1022 (N.D.N.Y. 1986), *aff'd,* 820 F.2d 587 (2d Cir. 1987), *cert. den.,* 108 S.Ct. 495 (1987).

Detsel by Detsel v. Sullivan, 895 F.2d 58 (2nd Cir. 1990).

Devries v. Fairfax County School Board, 882 F.2d 876 (4th Cir. 1989).

Diana v. State Board of Education, Civ. Act. No. C-70–37 (N.D. Cal., 1970, *further order,* 1973).

Dickens by Dickens v. Johnson County Board of Education, 661 F.Supp. 155 (E.D.Tenn. 1987).

District 27 Community School Board v. Board of Education of the City of New York, 502 N.Y.S.2d 325 (Sup. 1986).

Doe v. Belleville Public School District No. 118, 672 F.Supp. 342 (S.D.Ill. 1987).

Donohue v. Copiague Union Free School District, 391 N.E.2d 1352 (N.Y. 1979).

Eisel v. Board of Education of Montgomery County, 597 A.2d 447 (Md. 1991).

Elizabeth S. v. Thomas K. Gilhool, 558 Educ. of the Handicapped L. Rep. 461 (D.C. M.D. Pa. 1987).

Epperson v. State of Arkansas, 393 U.S. 97, 89 S.Ct. 266 (1968).

Fay v. South Colonie Central School District, 802 F.2d 21 (2nd Cir. 1986).

Flour Bluff Independent School District v. Katherine M., 24 IDELR 673 (5th Cir. 1996).

Forrest v. Ambach, Supp., 436 N.Y.S.2d 119 (1980); 463 N.Y.S.2d 84 (1983).

Fulginiti v. Roxbury Township Public School, 24 IDELR 218 (D.N.J. 1996).

Garcia by Garcia v. Miera, 817 F.2d 650 (10th Cir. 1987).

Garland Independent School District v. Wilks, 657 F.Supp. 1163 (N.D. Tex. 1987).

Georgia Association of Retarded Citizens v. McDaniel, 716 F.2d 1565 (11th Cir. 1983).

Georgia State Conference of Branches of NAACP v. State of Georgia, 775 F.2d 1403 (11th Cir. 1985).

Goss v. Lopez, 419 U.S. 565, 95 S.Ct. 729 (1975).

Greer v. Rome City School District, 950 F.2d 688 (11th Cir. 1991).

Guadalupe Organization, Inc. v. Tempe Elementary School District No. 3, Civ. No. 71–435 (D. Ariz., 1972).

Hall v. Tawney, 621 F.2d 607 (4th Cir. 1980).

Harlow v. Fitzgerald, 457 U.S. 800, 102 S.Ct. 2727 (1982).

Hayes v. Unified School District No. 377, 669 F.Supp. 1519 (D.Kan. 1987).

H.L. Etc., Appellant v. Scott M. Matheson, 101 S.Ct. 1164 (1981).

Hobson v. Hansen, 269 F.Supp. 401, 514 (D.D.C. 1967), *aff'd. sub nom,* Smuck v. Hobson, 408 F.2d 175 (D.C. Cir. 1969).

Hodgson v. Minnesota, 648 F. Supp. 756, 853 F.2d 1452, 42 U.S. 917, 106 L.Ed.2d 587 (1989).

Hoffman v. Board of Education of the City of New York, 49 N.Y.2d 121, 424 N.Y.S.2d 376 (1979).

Honig v. Doe, 108 S.Ct. 592 (1988).

Ingraham v. Wright, 430 U.S. 651, 97 S.Ct. 1401 (1977).

Irving Independent School District v. Tatro, 468 U.S. 883, 104 S.Ct. 3371 (1984).

Jaffee v. Redmond, 51 F.3d 1346, 1358, 116 S.Ct. 334 (1996).

John K. and Mary K. v. Board of Education for School District #65, Cook County, 504 N.E.2d 797 (Ill.App. 1 Dist. 1987).

Johnson v. Independent School District No. 4 of Bixby, Tulsa County, Oklahoma, 921 F.2d 1022 (10th Cir. 1990).

Kelson v. The City of Springfield, 767 F.2d 651 (9th Cir. 1985).

Kerkam v. McKenzie, 931 F.2d 84 (D.C. Cir. 1991).

Landstrom v. Illinois Department of Children and Family Services, 892 F.2d 670 (7th Cir. 1990).

Larry P. v. Riles, 343 F.Supp. 1306 (D.C. N.D. Cal., 1972), *aff'd.,* 502 F.2d 963 (9th Cir. 1974), *further proceedings,* 495 F.Supp. 926 (D.C. N.D. Cal., 1979), *aff'd.,* 502 F.2d 693 (9th Cir. 1984).

Lau v. Nichols, 414 U.S. 563 (1974).

Lyons by Alexander v. Smith, 829 F.Supp. 414 (D.D.C. 1993).

Marshall v. American Psychological Association, No. 87–1316 (D.D.C., December 7, 1987).

Martinez v. The School Board of Hillsborough County, Florida, 675 F.Supp. 1574 (M.D.Fla. 1987).

Max M. v. Thompson, 566 F.Supp. 1330, 1388 (N.D. Ill. (1983) *(Max I),* 592 F.Supp. 1437, 1450 (N.D. Ill. 1984) *(Max II).*

McKenzie v. Jefferson, 566 F.Supp. 404 (D.D.C. 1983).

McNeal v. Tate County School District, 508 F.2d 1017 (5th Cir. 1975)

Merriken v. Cressman, 364 F.Supp. 913 (D.C. E.D. Pa. 1973).

Mills v. Board of Education of District of Columbia, 348 F.Supp. 866 (1972); *contempt proceedings,* 551 Educ. of the Handicapped L. Rep. 643 (D.D.C. 1980).

Morales v. Turman, 383 F.Supp. 53 (D.C. E.D. Tex. 1974).

New Jersey v. T.L.O., 469 U.S. 325 (1985).

New York State Association for Retarded Children v. Carey, 393 F.Supp. 715 (D.C. E.D. N.Y. 1975).

Ohio v. Akron Center for Reproductive Health, 493 U.S. 802, L.Ed.2d 9 (1989).

Parents Against Abuse in Schools v. Williamsport Area School District, 594 A.2d 796 (Pa. Commw. Ct. 1991).

Parham v. J.R., 422 U.S. 584 (1979).

P.A.S.E. (Parents in Action in Special Education) v. Hannon, 506 F.Supp. 831 (N.D. Ill. 1980).

Penna v. New York State Division for Youth, 419 F.Supp. 203 (D.C. S.D. N.Y. 1976).

Pennsylvania Association for Retarded Citizens (P.A.R.C.) v. Commonwealth of Pennsylvania, 334 F.Supp. 1257 (D.C. E.D. Pa. 1971), 343 F.Supp. 279 (D.C. E.D. Pa. 1972).

Pesce v. J. Sterling Morton High School, 830 F.2d 789 (7th Cir. 1987).

Peter W. v. San Francisco Unified School District, 60 Cal.App.3d 814 (1976).

Phillis P. v. Claremont Unified School District, 183 Cal.App.3d 1193 (1986).

Planned Parenthood of Central Missouri v. Danforth, 428 U.S. 52 (1976).

Planned Parenthood of Southeastern Pennsylvania v. Casey, 112 S.Ct. 2791 (1992).

Rettig v. Kent City School District, 788 F.2d 328 (6th Cir. 1986).

Riley v. Ambach, 551 Educ. of the Handicapped L. Rep. 668 (E.D.N.Y. 1980), *rev'd* 668 F.2d 635 (2nd Cir. 1981), *further proceedings,* 508 F.Supp. 1222 (E.D. N.Y. 1982).

Roland M. v. Concord School Committee, 910 F.2d 983 (1st Cir. 1990).

San Antonio Independent School District v. Rodriguez, 411 U.S. 1, 93 S.Ct. 1278 (1973).

Sandlin v. Johnson, 643 F.2d 1027 (4th Cir. 1981).

School Board of Nassau County, Florida v. Arline, 107 S.Ct. 1123 (1987).

School Committee of the Town of Burlington, Massachusetts v. Department of Education of Massachusetts, 471 U.S. 359 (1985).

Simmons v. Hooks, 843 F.Supp. 1296 (E.D.Ark. 1994).

Spielberg v. Henrico County Public Schools, 853 F.2d 256 (4th Cir. 1988).

State v. Grover, 437 N.W.2d. 60 (Minn. 1989).

Tarasoff v. Regents of California, 118 Cal.Rptr. 129, 529 P.2d 553 (Cal. 1974). (Tarasoff I) Tarasoff v. Regents of California, 131 Cal.Rptr. 14, 551 P.2d 334 (Cal. 1976). (Tarasoff II)

Thomas v. Atascadero Unified School District, 662 F.Supp. 376 (C.D.Cal. 1987).

Timothy W. v. Rochester, New Hampshire School District, 875 F.2d 954 (1st Cir. 1989).

Tinker v. Des Moines Independent Community School District, 393 U.S. 503, 89 S.Ct. 733 (1969).

T.S. v. Ridgefield Board of Education, 808 F.Supp. 926 (D. Conn. 1992).

Valerie J. v. Derry CO-OP School District, 771 F.Supp. 492 (D.N.H. 1991).

Wolman v. Walter, 433 U.S. 229, 97 S.Ct. 2593 (1977).

Wyatt v. Stickney, 325 F.Supp. 781 (M.D. Ala. N.D. 1971), 334 F.Supp. 1341 (1971), 344 F.Supp. 373, 387 (M.D. Ala. N.D. 1972).

*Table of Federal Legislation**

Americans with Disabilities Act of 1990 or *ADA* (Pub. L. No. 101-336), 42 U.S.C. § 12101. Regulations regarding nondiscrimination in state and local government services appear at 28 C.F.R. Part 35 (1996).

Bilingual Education Act of 1968 was added as an amendment to the *Elementary and Secondary Education Act of 1965. Improving America's Schools Act of 1994* includes continued funding for bilingual education, 20 U.S.C.A. § 7401 (West Supp. Pamphlet 1997).

Child Abuse Prevention, Adoption, and Family Services Act of 1988 (Pub. L. No. 100-294), 42 U.S.C. § 1501.

Civil Rights Act of 1871 or "Section 1983," 42 U.S.C. § 1983.

Civil Rights Act of 1964 (Pub. L. No. 88-352), 42 U.S.C. § 2000d.

Education Amendments of 1972 (Pub. L. No. 92-318), 20 U.S.C. § 1681.

Education for All Handicapped Children Act of 1975 (Pub. L. No. 94-142), renamed the *Individuals with Disabilities Education Act* in 1990, 20 U.S.C. Chapter 33.

Education for the Handicapped Act Amendments of 1986 (Pub. L. No. 99-457). Now Part C of the *Individuals with Disabilities Education Act.*

Elementary and Secondary Education Act of 1965 or *ESEA* (Pub. L. No. 89-750). The *Improving America's Schools Act of 1994* includes the most recent amendments to *ESEA,* 20 U.S.C.A. § 1621 (West Supp. Pamphlet 1997).

Family Educational Rights and Privacy Act of 1974 (a part of Pub. L. No. 93-380) is commonly called "FERPA" or "The Buckley Amendment," 20 U.S.C. § 1232g. Regulations implementing FERPA appear at 34 C.F.R. § Part 99 (1996).

Goals 2000: Educate America Act (Pub. L. No. 103-227), 20 U.S.C.A. 5801 (West Supp. Pamphlet 1997).

Handicapped Children's Protection Act of 1986 (Pub. L. No. 99-372). Now part of the *Individuals with Disabilities Education Act.*

"Hatch Amendment" See *Protection of Pupil Rights Amendment.*

* U.S.C. refers to the *United States Code* (published by the U.S. government); U.S.C.A. refers to the *United States Code Annotated* (published by West Publishing Company); C.F.R. refers to the *Code of Federal Regulations* (published by the U.S. government).

Improving America's Schools Act of 1994 or *IASA* (Pub. L. No. 103-382), 20 U.S.C.A. § 6301 (West Supp. Pamphlet 1997). Includes the most recent amendments to *ESEA*.

Individuals with Disabilities Education Act (Pub. L. No. 101-476), 20 U.S.C. Chapter 33. Amended by Pub. L. No. 105-17 in June, 1997. Regulations appear at 34 C.F.R. Part 300. New regulations are expected by June, 1998.

Jacob K. Javits Gifted and Talented Students Education Act of 1988 (Pub. L. No. 100-297). Now part of *Improving America's Schools Act of 1994*.

National Research Act of 1974 (Pub. L. No. 93-348), 42 U.S.C. § 289. Regulations appear at 45 C.F.R. Part 46.

The Protection of Pupil Rights Amendment (previously Hatch Amendment). A 1978 amendment to *ESEA*. Amended in 1994 by Pub. L. No. 103-227. Regulations appear at 34 C.F.R. Part A § 98 (1996). New regulations are due late 1997.

The Rehabilitation Act of 1973 (Pub. L. No. 93-112), 29 U.S.C. § 794. Regulations implementing Section 504 appear at 34 C.F.R. Part 104 (1996).

School-to-Work Opportunity Act of 1994 (Pub. L. No. 103-239), 20 U.S.C.A. § 6101 (West Supp. Pamphlet 1997).

Index